**PEARSON
BACCALAUREATE**

History

A Comprehensive Guide to

Paper 1

D1397863

BRIAN MIMMACK • EUNICE PRICE • DANIELA SENÉS

PEARSON

Heinemann is an imprint of Pearson Education Limited, a company incorporated in England and Wales, having its registered office at Edinburgh Gate, Harlow, Essex, CM20 2JE. Registered company number: 872828

www.pearsonbaccalaureate.com

Heinemann is a registered trademark of Pearson Education Limited

Text © Pearson Education Limited 2009

First published 2009

13 12 11 10
10 9 8 7 6 5 4 3 2

ISBN 978 0 435994 49 5

Copyright notice

All rights reserved. No part of this publication may be reproduced in any form or by any means (including photocopying or storing it in any medium by electronic means and whether or not transiently or incidentally to some other use of this publication) without the written permission of the copyright owner, except in accordance with the provisions of the Copyright, Designs and Patents Act 1988 or under the terms of a licence issued by the Copyright Licensing Agency, Saffron House, 6–10 Kirby Street, London EC1N 8TS (www.cla.co.uk). Applications for the copyright owner's written permission should be addressed to the publisher.

Copyright © 2009 Pearson Education, Inc. or its affiliates. All Rights Reserved. This publication is protected by copyright, and permission should be obtained from the publisher prior to any prohibited reproduction, storage in a retrieval system, or transmission in any form or by any means, electronic, mechanical, photocopying, recording, or likewise. For information regarding permissions, write to Pearson Curriculum Group Rights & Permissions, One Lake Street, Upper Saddle River, New Jersey 07458.

Edited by Chris McNab
Designed by Tony Richardson
Typeset by Oxford Designers & Illustrators
Original illustrations © Pearson Education Limited 2009
Illustrated by Oxford Designers & Illustrators
Cover design by Tony Richardson
Picture research by Joanne Forrest Smith
Cover photo © Birgit Kinder/East Side Gallery, Berlin
Printed in China (GCC/02)

Acknowledgements

The authors and publisher would like to thank the following individuals and organisations for permission to reproduce photographs:

Alamy Images/Russ Bishop 262cl; Peter Greenhalgh (UKpix.com) 262c; INTERFOTO 252tr; Stock Connection Distribution/Guy Cali 4c; The Print Collector 263tl; Victor Watts 114cl; Whitehead Images 114bl; www.archelaus-cards.com/William Kemp Starrett Life Magazine 27 Dec 1929 256t; Baha Boukhari/Cartooning for Peace 151b; Bayerische Staatsbibliothek 41t; The Herb Block Foundation 181c; British Cartoon Archive/www.cartoons.ac.uk/ Express Syndication/Michael Cummings published in the Sunday Express on 20 May 1990 195b; Nicholas Garland published in the *Independent* on 16 Jun 1989 245b; Kevin Kallaugher published in the *Observer* 22 Sep 1985 239b; News Group Newspapers Ltd/Stanley Franklin 246c; Solo Syndication/Associated Newspapers published in the *Daily Express*, London, 10 May 1919 36t; David Low published in the *Evening Standard* newspaper, 19 Jan 1933 12c; published in *The Star* on 24 Jan 1921 31t; published in *The Star* newspaper, Jul 1920 34c; published in *The Star* on 30 Dec 1921 52c; first published by *The Star* newspaper on 1 Dec 1925 76t; first published by the *Evening Standard* in Nov 1931 80b; first published by the *Evening Standard* on 24 Jul 1935 88c; Telegraph Media Group, Nicholas Garland 248b; Chambers Art Gallery 170t; Corbis 115c; Bettmann 3t, 20bl, 20br, 20cr, 124b, 147b, 157b, 177cr, 216cl, 223cl, 252br, 261cl, 261cr, 263tc; Christel Gerstenberg 263bl; Hulton Deutsch Collection 70tl, 255b; Reuters 245c; Kevin Lamarque 260t; Wally McNamee 218tl; Heinrich Sanden 83br; Swim Link 216tl; Sygma 197c, 201c; Sygma/Henri Bureau 177br, 213c, 218cl; Ted Spiegel 257t; Peter Turnley 204c; Getty Images 83cr, 258–259t, 261c; AFP 132b, 223cr; AFP/Rene Jarland 113c; Hulton Archive 72tl, 75bc, 138b; Robert Nickelsberg 182b; Tom Stoddart Collection 207c; Juergen Stumpe 262cr; Roger Viollet 75cr; Hoover Institution Archives/ Poster Collection RU/SU1968 63bc; David Horsey, *Seattle Post-Intelligencer* 5b, 118b; Israel Images/Kalman Givon 116b; Dan Porges 141t; iStockphoto/Kristoffer Hamilton 4t; Yaakov Kirschen/DryBonesBlog.com 150b; Jeff Koterba/Omaha World-Herald 195t; Kanstantsin Khatsyanouski 190c; David King Collection 3cl and cr; Stefan R Landsberger Collection/http://chineseposters.net 5br, 216r, 235c, 240b, 240t; Carlos Latuff 164c; Library of Congress/Edmund Valtman 5t, 196t; Nebelspalter, 28 November 1956, 129b; Nicholson from *The Australian* www.nicholsoncartoons.com.au 252cr; *Punch* Cartoon Library 30b, 62t, 90b; Rex Features 263br, Assaf Shilo 160c; UN Photolibrary: UN Cartographic Section Palestine Land Ownership by Sub-Districts, no.94 (b) August 1950 107t; University of San Diego 20cl, 22c, 58t, 258br; Wikipedia/GNU Free Documentation license 177 (cra); Yonas Media/The Plastic People of the Universe 202c; Zapiro/Mail and Guardian 163b.

The publisher and authors would also like to thank Birgit Kinder and the East Side Gallery in Berlin for their permission to reproduce the Trabant graffiti on the cover. For more information, please visit www.eastsidegallery-berlin.com.

The publisher and authors would also like to thank the following for permission to use © material:

From a telegram of the Chinese Soviet Government (6 October 1932), translated by Stuart R. Schram (1969) in his *The Political Thought of Mao Tse-tung*, Praeger Publishers. From *The League of Nations – Its Life and Times 1920–1946* by F. S. Northedge (1986) © Continuum. From *Paris Peace Conference 1919: Proceedings of the Council of Four March 24–April 18* by Paul Mantoux and translated by John Boardman Whitton (1964). From *The Economic Consequences of the Peace* (1919) by John M. Keynes, used with permission of Palgrave Macmillan. From *The Weimar Republic 1919–33* (page 30) by Ruth Henig (1988), used with permission of Routledge. From *Europe between the Wars* by Martin Kitchen (1988), used with permission of Pearson Education Ltd. From *Peacemakers, Six Months that Changed the World* by Margaret MacMillan (2001), reproduced by permission of the publisher John Murray (Publishers). From *The First World War Peace Settlements 1919–25* by Erik Goldstein (2002), used with permission of Pearson Education Ltd. From a speech by Winston Churchill (13 July 1934), used with permission of Curtis Brown Ltd. From *Soviet Russia and the West, 1920–1927: A Documentary Survey* by Xenia Joukoff Eudin (1957), used with permission of Stanford University Press. From *On the Origins of War and the Preservation of Peace* by Donald Kagan (1996), used with permission of Random House. From *The Lights that Failed* by Zara Steiner (2005), used by permission of the Oxford University Press. From *French Foreign and Defence Policy, 1918–1940: The Decline and Fall of a Great Power* (page 60) by Robert Boyce (1998), used with permission of Routledge. From *The Struggle for Germany, 1914–1945* by Lionel Kochan (1963), used with permission of Miriam Kochan. From *The Lost Peace. International Relations in Europe 1918–39* by Anthony Adamthwaite (1977), used with permission of Adam Adamthwaite. From *Europe Between the Wars* by Martin Kitchen (1998), used with permission of Pearson Education Ltd. From *Gustav Stresemann: His Diaries, Letters, and Papers Volume II* translated by Eric Sutton (1937), used with permission of Palgrave Macmillan. From *The Gathering Storm* by Winston Churchill (1948), used with permission of Curtis Brown Ltd. From *The Great Dictators: International Relations 1918–1939* by E.G. Rayner (1992), reproduced by permission of Hodder & Stoughton Ltd. From *Japan over Asia* by W. H. Chamberlin (1937), used with permission of Carl E. Krumpe. From a memorandum of Sir John Simon, Foreign Secretary, to the British Cabinet (23 November 1931). Crown copyright material is reproduced with the permission of the Controller of HMSO and the Queen's Printer for Scotland. From a memorandum by Sir Anthony Eden (c. December 1935) © Continuum. From a speech by Benito Mussolini (2 October 1935), translated by Shepard Bancroft Clough and Salvatore Maximilian Saladino (1968) in their *A History of Modern Italy: Documents, Readings, and Commentary*, Columbia University Press, and used with permission of Shepard A. Clough. From *The Making of the Second World War* by Anthony Adamthwaite (1977), used with permission of Anthony Adamthwaite. From the *Deutsche Zeitung*, 28 June 1919, translated by Louis Leo Snyder (1966) in his *The Weimar Republic: A History of Germany from Ebert to Hitler*, © Wiley. From *A Shattered Peace. Versailles 1919 and the Price We Pay Today* by David A. Andelman (2007), © Wiley. From *The Palestine Israel Conflict* by Gregory Harms (2005), used with permission of Pluto Press. From *Palestine and the Arab-Israeli Conflict* by Charles D. Smith (2006), used with permission of Bedford/St. Martin's. From "Plan Dalet" (10 March 1948), translated by Walid Khalidi (1988) in the *Journal of Palestine Studies*, used with permission of the University of California Press. From *The Origins of the Arab-Israeli Wars* by Ritchie Ovendale (1984), used with permission of Pearson Education Ltd. From *The Palestine-Israeli Conflict* by Dan Cohn-Sherbok and Dawoud el-Alami (2002), used with permission of Oneworld Publications. From a statement by the Soviet Ministry of Foreign Affairs (16 April 1955), translated by RSA Novosti. From a speech by Gamal Abdel Nasser (28 July 1956), used with permission of BBC Monitoring. From "The Sèvres Protocol", translated by Keith Kyle in his *Suez* (2003), used with permission of IB Tauris. From *Full Circle. The Memoirs of the Rt. Hon. Sir Anthony Eden* by Anthony Eden (1960), © Continuum. From "New Crisis, Old Lessons – The Suez Crisis of 1956" by Robert Fisk (2003), © Independent. From "Identity Card" by Mahmoud Darwish (1964), © Riad el-Rayyes Books. From "General's Words Shed a New Light on the Golan" by Serge Schmemann (1997), used with permission of *The New York Times*. From *A Concise History of the Arab-Israeli Conflict* by Ian Bickerton and Carla Klausner (2004), © Prentice Hall. From "Try to Remember Some Details" by Yehuda Amichai (1983), translated by Chana Bloch (1996) in *The Selected Poetry of Yehuda Amichai*, University of California Press, used with permission of the University of California Press. From *The Arab Israeli Conflict* by T. G. Fraser (1980, 2004), used with permission of Palgrave Macmillan. From "The Munich Massacre" by Mitchell Bard (2009), copyright American-Israeli Cooperative Enterprise and reprinted with permission. From "Where Does History Come From?" by Alun Munslow (2002), used with permission of *History Today*. From a telegram from Valeriu Georgescu to Petru Burlacu (20 June 1967), translated by the Cold War International History Project (CWIHP), www.CWIHP.org, and used by permission of the Woodrow Wilson International Center for Scholars (Copyright 1991–2005). From "New Lessons from the Six-Day War" by Sandy Tolan (2006), and adapted from his *The Lemon Tree: An Arab, A Jew, and the Heart of the Middle East* (Bloomsbury, 2006), used with permission of Sandy Tolan. From "Why Diplomacy Failed to Avert the Six Day War" by Moshe Raviv, Copyright 2007 The Washington Institute for Near East Policy. Reprinted with permission. From *Armageddon Averted* by Stephen Kotkin (2003), used by permission of Oxford University Press, Inc. From *The Soviet Union 1917–1991* by Martin McCauley (1993), used with permission of Pearson Education Ltd. From *A History of Modern Russia* by Robert Service (2003), used with permission of Penguin UK and Harvard. From *The Soviet Union Under Brezhnev* by William Tompson (2003), used with permission of Pearson Education Ltd. Article 6 of the Soviet Constitution of 1977, translated by Novosti Press Agency Publishing House. From a speech by Leonid Brezhnev (24 February 1976), translated by Novosti Press Agency Publishing House. From *The Rise and Fall of the Soviet Empire: Political Leaders from Lenin to Gorbachev* © by Dmitri Volkogonov and translated by Harold Shukman (1999), reprinted with permission of HarperCollins Publishers Limited (Also published as *Autopsy of an Empire: The Seven Leaders*

Who Built the Soviet Regime). From minutes of the meeting of the Plenum of the Central Committee of the Communist Party of the Soviet Union on 23 June 1980, translated by the Cold War International History Project (CWIHP), www.CWIHP.org, and used by permission of the Woodrow Wilson International Center for Scholars (Copyright 1991–2005). From *Hammer & Tickbale* by Ben Lewis (2008), used with permission of George Weidenfeld and Nicholson, Ltd, an imprint of The Orion Publishing Group, London. From *The Gorbachev Factor* by Archie Brown (1997), used by permission of Oxford University Press, Inc. From "Gorbachev in Minority at Politburo Meeting on Chernobyl, Medvedev Says" by Kevin Devlin (1986), used with permission of the Open Society Archives. From "Turning Point at Chernobyl" by Mikhail Gorbachev (2006), © Project Syndicate, 2009. Used with permission. From *The Dark Continent* by Mark Mazower (1998), used with permission of Random House and of AM Heath & Co. From "Exhbition 'Images of "Solidarity"'. Solid Art", by Wladyslaw Serwatowski (2005), © Adam Mickiewicz Institute. From "Europe Remembering the Velvet Revolution" by Misha Glenny (interviewer) and Klara Pospisilova (interviewee) (1999), used with permission of BBC News. From "What Happened in Eastern Europe in 1989?" by Daniel Chirot (1991), in his (ed.) *The Crisis of Leninism and the Decline of the Left*, used with permission of the University of Washington Press. From *The Berlin Wall* by Frederick Taylor (2007), © HarperPerennial. From *The Rise of Modern China* by Immanuel C.Y. Hsu (2000), used by permission of Oxford University Press, Inc. From *A Great Trial in Chinese History*, untraced. From *Modern China* by Edwin E. Moise (1994), used with permission of Pearson Education Ltd. From *Mao's China and After: A History of the People's Republic* by Maurice Meisner, Reprinted with the permission of the Free Press, a Division of Simon & Schuster, Inc, Third Edition. Copyright © 1977, 1986 by The Free Press. Copyright © 1999 by Maurice Meisner. All rights reserved. From *China under Communism* (pages 99, 110, 120) by Alan Lawrance (1998), used with permission of Routledge. From Deng Xiaoping's speech "Emancipate the Mind, Seek Truth from Facts and Unite as One in Looking to the Future" (13 December 1978), translated by the Foreign Languages Press and published in their *Deng Xiaoping, Speeches and Writings* (1984). From "A Pivotal Moment for China", used with the permission of Radio Free Asia, written by Bao Tong for broadcast on the RFA Mandarin service of Radio Free Asia and translated by Luisetta Mudie (copyright RFA 2008). From "Building Socialism with a Specifically Chinese Character" by Deng Xiaoping (30 June 1984) and translated by the Foreign Languages Press. From a speech by Hu Yaobang (1980), translated by the United States Foreign Broadcast Information Service. From a poster by Wei Jingsheng (5 December 1978), in Wei Jingsheng, "Appendix I", from THE COURAGE TO STAND ALONE by Wei Jingsheng, translated by Kristina M. Torgeson, copyright © 1997 by Wei Jingsheng, used by permission of Viking Penguin, a division of Penguin Group (USA) Inc. and Penguin UK. From *The People's Republic of China since 1949* by Michael Lynch (1998), reproduced by Permission of Hodder & Stoughton Ltd. From "Democracy, Reform, and Modernization" by Lizhi Fang (18 November 1986) and translated by James H. Williams, published in their *Bringing Down the Great Wall: Writings on Science, Culture, and Democracy in China* (1992), and used with permission of Random House. From a speech of Deng Xiaoping (9 June 1989), translated by Xinhua. From the minutes of a meeting of the Politburo in March 1979, translated by the Cold War International History Project (CWIHP), www.CWIHP.org, and used by permission of the Woodrow Wilson International Center for Scholars (Copyright 1991–2005). From *The Soviet Experience in Afghanistan: Russian Documents and Memoir* by Svetlana Savranskaya, copyright 1995–2008 National Security Archive. All rights reserved. From *The Fifty Year War* by Norman Friedman (2000), used with permission of the Naval Institute Press. Excerpted from THE GREAT CRASH OF 1929 by John Kenneth Galbraith. Copyright © 1954, 1955, 1961, 1972, 1979, 1988, 1997 by John Kenneth Galbraith. Used by permission of Houghton Mifflin Harcourt Publishing Company. All rights reserved. From "Crash Memories" by Reuben L. Cain (interviewee for *American Experience*), ©1996–2009 WGBH Educational Foundation, used by permission of PBS. From *The Uses and Abuses of History* by Margaret Macmillan (2009), © Random House. Also published as *Dangerous Games*. From *The Idea of History* by R.G. Collingwood (1939, 1956), used by permission of the Oxford University Press, Inc. From a speech by Tony Blair (17 Feb 2003), © Labour Party. From *Hope and Memory* by Tzvetan Todorov (2003), © Princeton University Press. From "What is History Now?" by Richard Evans (2002), in David Cannadine (ed.) *What is History Now?* Used with permission of Palgrave Macmillan.

Every effort has been made to contact copyright holders of material reproduced in this book. Any omissions will be rectified in subsequent printings if notice is given to the publishers.

The assessment statements and various examination questions have been reproduced from IBO documents and past examination papers. Our thanks go to the International Baccalaureate Organization for permission to reproduce its intellectual copyright.

This material has been developed independently by the publisher and the content is in no way connected with nor endorsed by the International Baccalaureate Organization.

Websites
There are links to relevant websites in this book. In order to ensure that the links are up to date, that the links work, and that the sites are not inadvertently linked to sites that could be considered offensive, we have made the links available on the Heinemann website at www.heinemann.co.uk/hotlinks. When you access the site, the express code is 4495P.

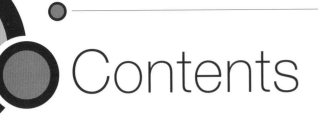

Contents

General Introduction vii

Chapter 1:   The Source Paper: Outline and Guidelines
             for Students 1

Chapter 2:   Prescribed Subject 1: Peacemaking,
             Peacekeeping – International Relations
             1918–36

             Treaties and Mandates 1918–32 18

Chapter 3:   Prescribed Subject 1: Peacemaking,
             Peacekeeping – International Relations
             1918–36

             International Crises 1923–36 56

Chapter 4:   Prescribed Subject 2: The Arab-Israeli
             Conflict 1945–79

             Palestine and Israel 1945–56 92

Chapter 5:   Prescribed Subject 2: The Arab-Israeli
             Conflict 1945–79

             Wars and Peace 1963–79 131

Chapter 6:   Prescribed Subject 3: Communism in
             Crisis 1976–89

             The Fall of Communism: The USSR and
             Eastern Europe 1976–89 165

Chapter 7:   Prescribed Subject 3: Communism in
             Crisis 1976–89

             China After Mao 1976–89 211

Chapter 8:   Theory of Knowledge 250

Further Reading   265

Index   270

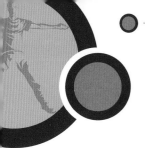

General Introduction

This book will help you to prepare for Paper 1 (Route 2) in the International Baccalaureate (IB) History exam. The book starts by setting out the kinds of sources used in the exam, along with advice on how to evaluate them. Following this chapter, you will find two chapters on each of the Prescribed Subjects, and finally a chapter on Theory of Knowledge (ToK).

By using this book, you will develop an understanding of the more general aims of the IB History course, as well as the skills and understanding of the past that are reflected in the structure and the assessment objectives of Paper 1.

What are the aims of the IB History course?

This book focuses specifically on Route 2, so you are probably studying the 19th and/ or 20th century. Whether you are studying this subject at Higher or Standard Level, you will need to take a broad view of how past events have brought us to where we are today. These events took place not only on one continent or during one time period, but were inter-connected. To understand fully the impact of the Cold War, for instance, as well as the relationship between the USA and the USSR, you need to consider the emergence of **communist** China and how this affected events in Africa and the Americas. Similarly, the results of World War I affected not only Europe, but were also instrumental in the emergence of independence movements in Asia and Africa. Awareness of how events that are separated by both time and space are nevertheless linked together in cause and effect is one of the most important lessons to be learned during the IB History course.

Communist
A social and economic system in which no participant owns significantly more than any other, either because property is commonly held or because private property does not exist.

When you read historical material, whether it is a speech by Hitler or a text book (like this one), you need to be critically aware and to ask yourself questions about where the information you are reading comes from. This perspective should become second nature to you once you have become used to evaluating sources. Paper 1 focuses on encouraging you to consider the origins of historical information. For instance, questions you might ask include:

- How do historians carry out their research?
- Are all historical sources useful?
- Are all historical sources reliable?
- Are secondary sources more useful than primary sources?

Questioning sources is a really important skill and you will use it not only when you read about history, but also when watching the news or reading an Internet site. There is nothing like studying history to make you more discerning about the origins of information.

IB History also helps you to consider the importance of the past in relation to your own identity. History plays a strong role in any society's 'collective memory' and this helps us to feel we belong to a particular ethnic or national group. (Is this a good thing or a bad thing?)

IB Learner Profile

When the IB sets out a course curriculum, they have in mind certain qualities that they want a student to develop. These are not abstract ideas; everything you learn and do as part of the IB programme aims to contribute to the development of these qualities. This objective applies to your study of history.

Throughout the study of the Prescribed Subjects in Paper 1, you will become more knowledgeable about the world around you; learn to handle historical sources confidently; and critically digest and summarize accurately what they actually say – developing your communication skills.

You will also become a critical inquirer as you develop skills to challenge the sources. Be prepared to change your mind. History is full of interpretations and is made up not only of factual accounts of events in the past, but also judgements that we make about the past. Historians ask questions about past events and the answers they come up with vary according to the kinds of sources they use and also the opinions they have. When you research a topic or an aspect of a topic, try to see if you can find more than one interpretation. For example, the establishment of the State of Israel in 1948 is still a source of controversy. If you hold a particular opinion about this, see if you can read about a different point of view. Then, gather your evidence and analyze it to come up with a logical, well-argued answer.

A student guide to using this book

This book covers the Prescribed Subjects for History Paper 1 at Higher and Standard Levels. These are:
- Prescribed Subject 1: Peacemaking, Peacekeeping – International Relations 1918–36
- Prescribed Subject 2: The Arab-Israeli Conflict 1945–79
- Prescribed Subject 3: Communism in Crisis 1976–89

You are required to study one Prescribed Subject in depth for your IB exam. The book provides detailed information on all the areas on which the source-based questions focus, and gives you additional background information for a better understanding of each area.

The book includes within each chapter:
- Timelines of events to help you put each Prescribed Subject into context.
- Analysis, interpretation and evaluation of key events.
- Primary and secondary sources relevant to each area of the Prescribed Subjects, helping you to recognize and work with different types of sources, including documents, photographs, cartoons and tables of statistics.
- Source-based exercises to familiarize you with the type and structure of the questions in Paper 1.
- Examples of students' responses to questions, to let you see different approaches and reflect on their content and technique.
- Examiner's Comments to show the strengths and weaknesses of each student response and make recommendations on possible improvements.
- Examiner's Hints: these boxes provide insight into how to answer questions in order to achieve the highest marks in examinations. Also, they present strategies to make an effective use of your time in the exam and explain how to avoid making some of the typical mistakes for each type of question on Paper 1.
- Review and research activities to help you summarize the main points from each chapter and expand your knowledge.

- ToK Time boxes: these boxes will enable you to think about and discuss some ToK issues related to the context in which they are placed. They will prompt you to consider ToK-type issues such as how language is used in single-party states or whether international peace is a universal principle.
- Information boxes: these boxes appear alongside the text and explain or give you additional information about some relevant topics and words that may be unfamiliar.

Also included in this book are:
- A chapter on how to analyze and evaluate different types of historical sources.
- A chapter on ToK to help you think about the links between the study and writing of history and ways of knowing.
- A sample Paper 1 for each Prescribed Subject to give you some exam practice.

IB History assessment objectives

This book covers the IB assessment objectives relevant to Paper 1. Exercises are based on the structure of Paper 1 questions, and Examiner's Hints and Examiner's Comments show how to reach the highest levels of performance for each assessment objective.

Assessment objective 1: Knowledge and understanding

You will learn how to recall and select relevant historical knowledge, and demonstrate an understanding of the meaning and significance of historical sources and their context.

Assessment objective 2: Application and interpretation

You will learn how to compare and contrast historical sources as evidence and to explain whether they support, complement or contradict each other.

Assessment objective 3: Synthesis and evaluation

You will learn how to evaluate different types of historical sources and explain their value and limitations; to synthesize evidence from both historical sources and your background knowledge; and appreciate why and how opinions and interpretations differ.

How this book works
Information boxes

As well as the main text, there are a number of coloured boxes in every chapter, each with its own distinctive icon. These boxes provide different information and stimulus:

Theory of Knowledge

There are ToK boxes throughout the book. These boxes will enable you to consider ToK issues as they arise and in context. Often they will just contain a question to stimulate your thoughts and discussion.

ToK Time
Think about how important humour can be in helping people deal with living in a single party state.

Interesting facts

These boxes contain information which will deepen and widen your knowledge, but which do not fit within the main body of the text.

Diktat
A harsh unilateral settlement imposed by the victors on the defeated.

Examiner's hints

These boxes can be found alongside questions and exercises. They provide insight into how to answer a question in order to achieve the highest marks in an examination. They also identify common pitfalls when answering such questions and suggest approaches that examiners like to see.

● **Examiner's hint**
When you are asked to look for an answer in a source, underline the relevant points and then focus on the information that you need to answer the question. Don't list everything, only what is relevant.

Examiner's comments

These boxes can be found after student answers. They include an assessment of how well a question has been answered along with suggestions of how an answer may be improved.

> **Examiner's comments**
> This is a good answer that gets straight to the point. Tom could have avoided repeating himself though, and also given some explanation for *novostroika*, or left this sentence out as it is not really necessary.

Review boxes

These boxes are found at the end of a section and give a brief overview of the content. A short list of questions can act as prompts for you to identify and organize the main points of the section.

REVIEW SECTION

This section has looked at the political protest that emerged in China during the 1980s. In the West, it is assumed that economic change leads, inevitably, to political change. During the Industrial Revolution of the 18th and 19th centuries, as people moved into the cities and as entrepreneurs became wealthy, demand grew for a fairer distribution of political power. People wanted laws that reflected a new economic reality and to have influence on policy making. Over time, more people were given the right to vote for different political parties that sprang up to represent different economic interests. Would this also happen in China or was it possible for people to accept prosperity without the kind of democracy familiar in multi-party states?

By 1979, the democracy movement had taken hold in China, but this ebbed and flowed throughout the 1980s ending with the events of Tiananmen Square.

Consider the following questions and see if you can come up with answers using the sources and the text in this section:

Review questions

1 Why was Deng Xiaoping concerned about the growth of the democracy movement?

2 Compare and contrast the events of 1979, 1986 and 1989 – in what ways were these protests by the supporters of democratic reform similar and different?

3 Why, do you think, did the leadership of the CCP respond so harshly to the Tiananmen Square protests in 1989?

THE SOURCE PAPER: OUTLINE AND GUIDELINES FOR STUDENTS

This purpose of this chapter is to introduce you to the Source Paper, which is Paper 1 of the International Baccalaureate History Examination. Whether you are taking Standard Level or a Higher Level examination makes no difference as, rather unusually, the sources and questions are the same for both examinations.

The first part of this chapter will discuss how historians use sources. The second part will look carefully at the types of sources you can expect to see on an IB History paper. The third section will then analyze the types of questions that you can expect to get in the examination and the different levels of knowledge you will need to be able to answer them properly. Finally, this chapter will look at some student sample answers and analyze what was answered well and how the answers could have been improved to score higher marks.

Outline of Paper 1

There are three Prescribed Subjects assessed in Paper 1:
- Peacemaking, Peacekeeping – International Relations 1918–36
- The Arab-Israeli Conflict 1945–79
- Communism in Crisis 1976–89

The themes for each Prescribed Subject are taken from the IB History Guide, focusing specifically on the bullet points (found on pages 24–25). The wording for the title of the set of questions is the same as in the Guide, to indicate the theme of the sources used – e.g. 'These sources relate to the principle of collective security and early attempts at peacekeeping (1920–25).'

For each Prescribed Subject there will usually be four written sources and one visual- or table-based source. The length of the written sources does not have to be equal, but they will be approximately 750 words in total (including **attribution**). A variety of sources will probably be used, taken from a selection of contemporary and more recent material. There should be some background information about the writer (e.g. Professor of United States History at Yale; A Russian journalist). In some cases the sources might have been edited and ellipses (usually seen as three dots – …) will be used when three or more lines of text are deleted. In some sources, alternative words will be placed in brackets, if a word is seen as particularly difficult, e.g. 'belligerent' [warlike]. Remember that you can use a simple translating dictionary in many IB examinations and you should ask your IB coordinator if you are entitled to have one. Electronic dictionaries are, however, not allowed.

 Attribution
This is the information accompanying each source telling you where it comes from.

There will be four questions on each Prescribed Subject. You will be given five minutes' reading time, during which you are not allowed to write anything, and you will then have one hour to answer the four questions. The first question is usually divided into two parts: 1a) and 1b). An analysis of the different types of questions you can expect to see is given below.

Sources and the historian

If you were to ask someone in the street what the study of history is about, the answer would probably be something to do with historical facts – dates, important people etc. What most people do not realize is that a fact by itself is of little value to an historian. The fact that Hitler became Chancellor of Germany on 30 January 1933 is of as much use to an historian as a scientist saying that oxygen is a gas. The task of an historian is to find out as much as possible about the meaning of a particular historical event, i.e. why did it occur and what were its consequences? In order to answer these two questions the historian has to accumulate as much information about the event as possible. In an ideal world this should amount to everything known about the event, but this is simply impossible. An historian can never have access to all knowledge about any event for many reasons – censorship, the huge amount of material which has to be sifted, the impossibility of accessing all the information available and so on. The historian must therefore select the appropriate sources that relate to any event.

Here is the fundamental problem of being an historian. By making this selection, the historian can lose his or her objectivity, because the reasons why a particular source is chosen are dependent upon the historian's interests, cultural background, training, language ability and any other factors that affect the selection of a source. An historian must consider the reliability of a source and how accurate it is in relation to the events it is describing. Can the account given by a particular source be authenticated by other sources? Historians must carefully check information from sources against each other to arrive at a conclusion that could be considered valid. An historian must be sceptical when using sources that appear to give only one side of the event.

When answering a source paper in IB History, you are essentially comparing and contrasting sources against each other to arrive at a conclusion, which you can justify. In simple terms, you are being an historian.

The types of sources

When analyzing sources, the simplest means are often the best. Try using the 'five question' approach, also known as the 'five Ws':
- Who wrote or produced it? (Origin)
- When? (Origin)
- Where? (Origin)
- Why? (Purpose)
- For whom? i.e. who was the intended audience of the source? (Purpose)

Ask these five simple questions of any source and your answers will help you to understand any type of source: non-textual or textual.

Non-textual

Non-textual means any source that is not written as you would see it in a book or letter. In many cases they are visual rather than written, although you might also see a chart or a table of statistics. In IB History examinations the most common non-textual sources that have been used include photographs, cartoons, posters, statistics or tabular sources, graphs, maps and paintings (or photographs of paintings).

Photographs

Over time the reasons why photographs have been taken have changed. In the 19th century they were used to record an event, or document how someone looked, almost as if the photograph was a portrait painted by an artist. In many of these photographs the subjects have been posed and, whether we realize it or not, when we know that we are being photographed we change our behaviour or our posture. If, in a photograph, everyone is looking at the camera you can be almost certain that this has been staged. Look at the photograph at the top of page 3. Spontaneous or not? How can you tell?

● **Examiner's hint**
You should be very careful when using the terms 'primary' and 'secondary' when analyzing sources. Experience shows us that too many students cannot tell the difference between them. Avoid saying that a source is valuable because it is primary. It may be the case, it may not; it will largely depend on valuable 'for what'? Students also use the terms 'reliable', 'useful', 'utility' and 'valuable' interchangeably, but there are differences between these four words. In the IB examination it is better to talk about a source's values and limitations. You should keep your approach to analyzing the sources as simple as possible.

The original caption read as follows. 'Here the latest consignment of Japanese troops are shown leaving the Japanese capital for Manchuria, the scene of the present Sino-Japanese conflict.'

You must remember that the person taking the photograph is not neutral and has a particular reason for taking it. Why is the particular photograph above being taken? What is the photographer trying to convey to the intended audience? What is surprising to IB examiners is the number of times in IB source examinations students write that what a photograph depicts is an accurate representation of the events it is recording. The context of where and when a photograph is taken must also be taken into account when analyzing it. There have always been, and always will be, countries that censor what is published in newspapers or books to rewrite history.

STUDENT STUDY SECTION

QUESTION

Here is a famous example of photo doctoring involving Trotsky and Lenin. What differences can you see in the two photographs? Why was this change made?

The change was made because after Trotsky was exiled from the Soviet Union he became a non-person to the Soviet government and his images were removed from all records.

However, despite their obvious limitations, photographs do have tremendous value for historians in that they can document particular events better than many other sources. A picture of, for example, Hiroshima in August 1945 after the dropping of the atomic bomb on the city powerfully communicates to the world the devastation and destruction of the city.

Cartoons

One of the most common non-textual sources in IB source examinations is the cartoon. This type of source can be challenging to understand. Cartoons refer to something that was current at the time, and if you do not know the context of the cartoon and the events or people to which it refers, then you may not be able to understand its message. Cartoons tend to oversimplify the events they are describing, so may not explain the full reality of events.

Finally, of course, cartoonists use symbols to represent the characters or countries they have drawn. For example, what does this image represent?

Most of you should immediately say – the Soviet Union. And this?

Again, most of you should recognize this as a symbol for death. It is the grim reaper carrying a scythe, although this symbol may not be readily recognizable to all students, depending on their cultural backgrounds.

Remember that a cartoon is someone's personal view of events and therefore has a subjective element to it. A cartoon must be direct because any meaning that is implied or indirect may cause you to misunderstand its meaning. For this reason, cartoons will also often have captions that will help you to identify their message.

● **Examiner's hint**
You are not expected to be able to identify people in cartoons. Normally the source booklet will give you this sort of information and include the names of those who appear in a cartoon.

Cartoon by David Horsey in the *Seattle Post-Intelligencer*, 2001.

● **Examiner's hint**
Look at the text in the top-left hand side. Who do you think is saying it? Who are the countries in 'the neighborhood'? Which one is the odd one out?

STUDENT STUDY SECTION

QUESTION
What do you think is the message in the following cartoon?

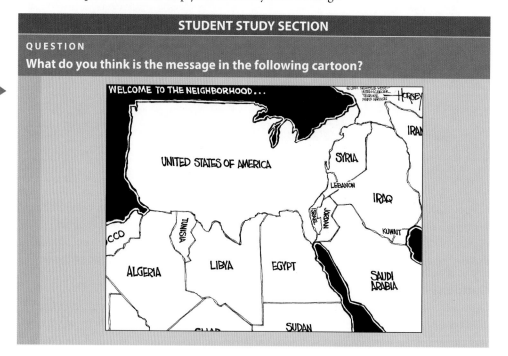

Here is another cartoon with a student's answer. Try to work out the meaning yourself before reading Gustav's answer.

A cartoon by Edmund Valtman, an American cartoonist (1991). The man in the cartoon is Mikhail Gorbachev.

● **Examiner's hint**
Did you count the pieces? There are 15 of them. Why do you think Valtman included this number? What do the cracks signify?

Student Answer – *Gustav*

The cartoon shows the effects of Gorbachev's policies of *glasnost* and *perestroika* on the Soviet Union. The broken sickle is meant to show the break-up of the Soviet Union into 15 pieces. Each piece represents one of the new countries such as Latvia or Uzbekistan, which were created out of the former territory that was the Soviet Union. Valtman shows that these countries themselves are unstable as they are full of cracks. Gorbachev looks a little shocked by the results of his policies.

Examiner's comments

Gustav's answer is excellent and would receive full marks, as it sets the cartoon in context and clearly identifies the ideas the cartoonist had in his mind when he drew the cartoon. As with photographs, cartoons are a very powerful way of conveying a message, but in an IB History examination please remember that you can allow yourself between five and eight minutes to find out what that message is and write your answer.

Posters, graphs and paintings

The most important details about these sources are who made them and for what purpose – although the 'five question' approach can also be used. There are many different types of poster: election campaign posters, announcements of concerts or events, propaganda posters, military recruitment posters and so on. Look at the poster to the right. Without any background research, what do you think the poster is about?

The fact that it is a Chinese government-produced poster issued after 1979 helps you to understand its significance. In 1979 China introduced the 'one-child' policy. The message is that in an already over-populated country having only one child will ensure

Wall poster distributed in China after 1979.

that the child is happy and well fed. This message implies that China, as a country, will grow better and stronger as a result of the new birth policy.

Students are sometimes surprised to see statistics and graphs in a history source examination, but it is perfectly appropriate to include this type of source, particularly when dealing with any economic theme. The graph below could be included in any question on the effects of the Treaty of Versailles on Germany in the early 1920s (although there is some debate about this cause and effect relationship), and it is a simple task to explain the decline in value of the German Reichsmark in that time period.

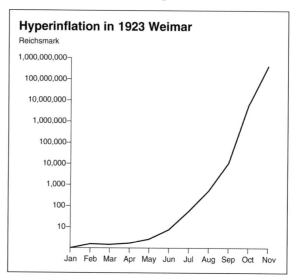

Maps and paintings occur very rarely in the Source Paper, but there is no reason why they could not appear. Maps, in particular, can be used to make a political point rather than simply express a geographical reality. Ask the 'five questions' and be careful when analyzing a map. Look at this example.

Map 1
British mandate for Palestine, 1920–48. Source: The Pedagogic Centre, The Department for Jewish Zionist Education, The Jewish Agency for Israel.

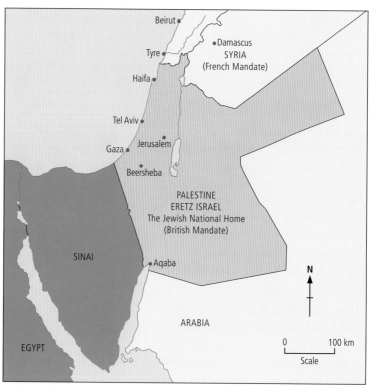

While the map is one that shows the British mandates after World War I, it is certainly debatable whether the Palestine section should be subtitled 'The Jewish National Home' during the dates included in the caption, as it includes the territory in the British mandate east of the River Jordan.

Textual sources

Textual sources are simply too numerous to list, but the most common ones used in IB History source examinations are books, letters, treaties, diaries, newspapers, magazine articles, diplomatic documents, telegrams, written records of interviews, poetry and speeches. In all cases, the introductory lines at the beginning of the source will give you all the information you need to analyze it. Use the 'five question' approach.

STUDENT STUDY SECTION

Here are a few examples for you to think about. The theme of the Prescribed Subject is the Tiananmen Square Massacre known by the Chinese as the 'June 4th Incident'.

QUESTIONS

What limitations might the following sources have?

Source A: an extract from the memoirs of an eyewitness of the 1989 Tiananmen Square incident, published in Beijing in 2009. The witness was born in 1929.

Source B: an extract from the *People's Daily*, a Chinese government newspaper, 6 June 1989.

Source C: an extract from John Smith, *China in the Twentieth Century*, 2001. John Smith is a well-known writer of history textbooks for schools. (This source is fictional.)

Source D: an extract from the diary of a Chinese woman killed on 4 June in Tiananmen Square as she was taking part in a protest demonstration, published in New York in 2008.

Source A: the examiner would be looking for comments about the age of the eyewitness, the time lapse between the event and the publication of the memoir and the fact that it was published in China. **Source B:** the extract is published two days after the incident in a newspaper run by the Communist Party. Think of what limitations may be present because of this time lag. **Source C:** this book covers the whole of the 20th century so only a tiny part of the book would deal with the incident. The author, who is used to writing school textbooks rather than academic works, may not be an expert on China. Also, it is unlikely that he was present during the incident. **Source D:** the woman was taking part in the protest so she was probably opposed to the policies of Deng Xiaoping. A question should be raised about how the diary ended up in New York and was published there in 2008.

The following type of source has caused students difficulty in the past. What is its origin?

Source E: an extract from a speech by Nasser to the Egyptian National Assembly on 29 May 1967 taken from Walter Laqueur and Barry Rubin (eds), *The Arab-Israel Reader*, 2001.

The examiners are interested in Nasser's speech, not the book source. Always evaluate the extract itself. Do not theorize that the editors might have changed the content of the speech.

Interestingly, while it would seem that diaries are very valuable sources to an historian, they are not as reliable as you might think. The Soviet expert Orlando Figes in *The Whisperers* has commented that no diary in Stalinist time should be relied upon. It would simply have been too incriminating for the writer to tell the truth in a diary – the writer would have been mortally afraid that it would be discovered by the secret police. You should also ask why anyone would keep a diary in the first place? Diaries are simply someone's personal recollection of events.

● **Examiner's hint**
Do not make comments saying that a source has been translated and therefore we do not know if the translation is accurate. Rarely is this a useful comment to make. Nor should you write that, as it is an extract from a source, we do not have access to the entire source and this is a limitation. Neither of these comments is likely to receive credit.

● **Examiner's hint**
To judge the value and limitations of sources, look at the purpose behind them.

ToK Time

The historian Marc Bloc has written: 'A document is like a witness, and like most witnesses it rarely speaks until one begins to question it.'
Explain what you think Bloc means by this statement. What evidence could you come up with to either agree or disagree with this **assertion**?

Assertion

An assertion is an unsubstantiated statement.

Types of exam question

The IB History Guide clearly identifies the objectives that the source paper is assessing. Paper 1 assesses the following objectives of the history course:

Question	Objective
The first question will test understanding of a source in part (a) and part (b).	1. Knowledge and understanding Understand historical sources
The second question will test analysis of sources through the comparison and contrast of two sources.	2. Application and interpretation Compare and contrast historical sources as evidence
The third question will ask students to discuss two sources in relation to their origins, purpose, values and limitations.	3. Synthesis and evaluation Evaluate historical sources as evidence
The fourth question will test evaluation of sources and contextual knowledge.	1. Knowledge and understanding Demonstrate an understanding of historical context 3. Synthesis and evaluation Evaluate and synthesize evidence from both historical sources and background knowledge

Source: www.ibo.org

In practice, what does this mean the questions will look like in the Higher Level and Standard Level examination paper?

Questions 1a and 1b

These two parts will be worth a maximum of 5 marks together. Remember that there are 25 marks for this paper and 60 minutes to answer the questions. This means that somewhere between 10 and 12 minutes should be spent on these two parts of Question 1.

The wording of 1a) and 1b) will be something like this:

'According to Source A, why did…?'

'What does Source B suggest about…?'

'What message is portrayed by Source E?'

'What is the significance of Source C…?' ('Significance' asks you to explain the source's importance, not just give its meaning.)

These questions are intended for you to show your knowledge and understanding of the sources.

Question 2

● Examiner's hint

Remember that examiners are not allowed to include half marks or + and – when they are marking your exam, so make sure that you have made your points clearly enough so that you can receive full marks.

This question is worth 6 marks, so how much time do you think that you will have to answer it in the exam?

The wording of Question 2 will be something like this:

'Compare and contrast the views expressed about… in Sources A and C.'

In other words, what are the similarities and differences in the way that the sources refer to a particular event? Please note that **ONLY TWO SOURCES** will be used.

● Examiner's hint

You should try to link your Question 2 answers in a running analysis like the following example: 'Source A mentions this…, but on the other hand Source C says…'

The following might help you by seeing what examiners are told to do when marking your Question 2.

> *If only one source is discussed award a maximum of (2 marks). If the two sources are discussed separately award (3 marks) or with excellent linkage (4–5 marks). For*

maximum (6 marks) expect a detailed running comparison/contrast. Award up to (5 marks) if two sources are linked/integrated in either a running comparison or contrast.

Another way that Question 2 might be phrased is the following: 'In what ways do the views expressed in Source B support the conclusions in Source D?'

Again, here is what examiners are told to do when marking this type of Question 2:

End-on description of the sources would probably be worth (3 marks) if the comparative element is only implicit, and (4 marks) with explicit linkage. If the linkage is excellent or detailed material is presented in a comparative framework (5 or 6 marks) could be scored.

The wording of Question 2 may focus on issues of consistency. For example: 'How consistent are the accounts in Sources A and C in their description of Israel's reaction to the 1972 Munich massacre?'

The examiners' advice for this type of Question 2 is as follows:

If only one source is addressed award a maximum of (2 marks). If the two sources are discussed separately award (3 marks) or with excellent linkage (4–5 marks). For maximum (6 marks) expect a detailed running comparison.

This question is intended for you to show your application and interpretation of the sources.

Question 3

This question is worth 6 marks, so how much time do you think that you will have to answer it in the exam? The wording of Question 3 will be something like this: 'With reference to their origin and purpose, what are the value and limitations of Source A and Source C for historians studying the policies of Deng Xiaoping.'

Here is what the examiners are told to do when marking Question 3:

Ideally there will be a balance between the two sources, and each one can be marked out of (3 marks), but allow a 4/2 split. If only one source is assessed, mark out of (4 marks). For a maximum of (6 marks) candidates must refer to both origin and purpose, and value and limitations, in their assessment.

This question is intended for you to show your synthesis and evaluation of the sources.

Question 4

This question is worth 8 marks, so how much time do you think that you will have to answer it in the exam? Do your time estimates for all four questions add up to 60 minutes? If not, recalculate your time allocation for each question, based on how many marks they are worth, so that you are under 60 minutes.

The wording of Question 4 will be something like this: 'Using these sources and your own knowledge analyze the importance of the Italian invasion of Abyssinia for international relations between 1934 and 1936.'

Here is the examiners' advice for marking Question 4.

... credit other relevant material. If only source material or only own knowledge is used, the maximum mark that can be obtained is (5 marks). For maximum (8 marks), expect argument, synthesis of source material and own knowledge, as well as references to the sources used.

This question is intended for you to show your knowledge, understanding, synthesis and evaluation of the sources.

● **Examiner's hint**
Make sure you start off analyzing the second source mentioned in the question and then see how far these opinions are supported by the first source.

● **Examiner's hint**
For this type of Question 2, make sure you start with the first source mentioned in the question and then see how far these opinions are supported by the second source.

● **Examiner's hint**
Always do the two sources separately and analyze the sources in the order given in the question – origin, purpose, value and limitations. Remember that without understanding the purpose of a source it is impossible to judge accurately its values and limitations. A source may also have more than one purpose. Too many students outline in great detail the content of the two sources, i.e. what they are actually saying. This wastes time and is not responding to the **rubric** of the question.

 Rubric
What you are expected to do. In this case deal with the origin, purpose, value and limitations of the two sources.

● Examiner's hint

Question 4 requires use of all the sources and your own knowledge to write a mini-essay. This is a very challenging type of question and needs to be practised. Try to steer yourself away from a very mechanical approach in your answer. You need to make sure your answer explains how everything you use – whether source material or own knowledge – contributes to answering the question.

ToK Time

'The truth of anything at all doesn't lie in someone's account of it. It lies in all the small facts of the time.' – Josephine Tey, *The Daughter of Time*

How can you apply this idea to historical 'truth'? Think of an event you have studied and see whether or not the gathering of 'small facts of the time' makes it 'true.'

Command term

The words in the question that tell the student what the examiner is looking for in a good answer.

STUDENT STUDY SECTION

Below are three student answers to the last question on a source paper. In Paper 1 these are questions 4, 8 and 12. Ignore the content of the answers and look at the approaches the three students have taken to the **command term**.

Question 4

Using the sources and your own knowledge, to what extent do you agree that 'Israel carried out the war [1967 Six Day War] to defend the very existence of the state'? (8 marks)

You will see three different approaches. Which do you think will receive the highest marks and why? What are the weaknesses of the other two answers? Look at the way that the students have responded to the **command term**.

Student Answer A – *Jack*

Source A indicates that the Six-Day War was the outcome of Arab countries instigating violence towards Israel as a direct result of fearing the Soviet's Union role to be in the war, when the USSR could have adopted a more peaceful, constructive position.

Source B, however, shows a more obscure cycle of events. It depicts both countries displaying false pretences: Nasser asserting threats in public against Israel, but in reality attempting to arrange more peaceful negotiations through American dignitaries, wary of the possibility of all-out war. At the same time, Israel contacted America warning of an imminent Arab attack, either falling for Nasser's public threats or, and what appears to be more likely, attempting to solidify America's alliance to them by using a ploy of imminent attack as means to dominate Nasser and deter his forces.

Source C furthers this theory, depicting the Israeli ambassador asking US Secretary of State Rusk for a solid alliance between the two, so if Nasser were to attack, America would publicly declare themselves to fight Nasser. Rusk showed reluctance, citing constitutional decisions. The only new US support Israel received was the State Department giving the Egyptian ambassador a good talking to.

Source D shows Nasser on 26 May 1967 requesting that the US take no military action against the Arabs, assuring President Johnson that his current actions were only to prove the weakness of the alliances between the United States and Israel and Jordan and Saudi Arabia. Nasser states that should Johnson grant his request, he shall ally himself to the whim of President Johnson.

Source E sums up what is implied above, that America and Israel effectively stole the land from the Arabs by crushing them with the scare of far superior forces.

Student Answer B – *Miriam*

The statement is true to some extent, as Israel feared a new invasion from the surrounding Arab states, as an increasingly hostile rhetoric had been developing between Israel and Egypt. Nasser had made a request, that 'the US undertake no direct military action in the form of landings, shifting of naval fleet, or otherwise' (Source D). Nasser wanted to retake the buffer zone that had been created after the 1956 Suez-Sinai Crisis, and reclaim the land so that Egypt's and Israel's borders would be connected again, thereby making Israel feel threatened by Egypt. Moreover, Nasser initiated the 'closing of the Tiran Straits' (Source A), which Israel saw as a hostile move, and making them fear that Nasser intended to annex Israel once more. Egypt and Syria had also signed a mutual defence pact, making Israel unsure of their intentions. On the other hand, at that time 'Nasser was reiterating to Westerners his reluctance to engage Israel' (Source B), and he announced to a friend, that he 'had no intention of fighting' (Source D). Moreover, the Soviets 'continued to urge Nasser away from war' (Source B). The Soviet Union was providing Egypt with weapons, but did not want the conflict to accelerate to a world war, as the Cold War was taking place at the time and the United States was backing Israel.

Student Answer C – *Philip*

After the first two wars between Arabs and Israel, in 1948 and 1956, the situation in the whole Middle East had not yet settled, because of the lack of reciprocal recognition between the various states and Israel. The Six Day War of 1967 was another example of the diverging opinions and policies between the Arab states, mainly Egypt in this case, and Israel. As Source A assesses: 'Israel carried out the war to defend the very existence of the state', as well as 'actions undertaken by Nasser for the evacuation of UN troops [...] and war-like declarations by Egyptian leaders.' On the other hand, the Israeli government is discharged of every accusation and is also considered acting in the best interest to make the state of Israel survive, nothing more. Moreover the Soviet Union is also blamed to have brought the conflict to a new escalation, because it militarily supported the Arab states. This might seem a very fair and straightforward conclusion considering the events and the Israeli point of view. However it must be clear that these are only a portion of the causes of the conflict. Israel's position and well-being had been assured in the previous two conflicts by their victories, the conquering of new land and the acquired alliance with the United States, the world's Superpower, whose only threat was the Soviet Union. This thesis is clearly portrayed by Source E: the comic compared what is a 'myth' of this war to what is most probable truth about the cause of the war. The 'myth' is the Israeli struggle to survive, while on the other hand the Six Day War was just another plan to extend Israel's borders, and the success was achieved only through the US military help. It is a clear representation of how Egypt could not be a real threat for the Israeli State, and how, therefore, historians are brought to disagree with the initial statement. Source D reports a message from Nasser himself, who assures the US he 'had no intention of fighting', and how he expected the United States to take an impartial position on the matter, so as not to unbalance the conflict. This is another proof that the war was not caused only by the aggressive nature of Nasser and his policies, but also in the fact that the cooperation with other nations, such as the US, helped the conflict to break out. Source C supports the quote from Source A, following the argument that it was an inevitable conflict if Israel wanted to survive. However Source B is the one that is probably closest to reality because of its lack of extremism, while asserting that each side has proclaimed itself not inclined to fighting, but at the same time the war had broken out.

 ToK Time
How do political leaders attempt to maintain their 'credibility'? Which is more important for this objective when addressing the public – reason, morality or emotion?

Examiner's comments

Jack's approach is very mechanical. The question is not set up well and there is no individual knowledge displayed. Many teachers tell their students that by using each of the five sources they will be guaranteed to get 5 marks. This is not so. There needs to be a clear attempt to focus the sources on the question explicitly.

Miriam's approach is better in style as there is a linkage between the sources and her own knowledge. There is also a clear attempt at answering the question. Her weaknesses are that there is very little outside knowledge and Sources C and E are not used.

Philip's is the best of the three answers. It is a mini-essay that sets the question up at the beginning and directly answers it. A criticism would be that it needs a little more specific own knowledge to add to the source, but this essay would certainly be at the top end of the mark scheme.

Sources, questions and answers

Here is a sample source exam based on Prescribed Subject 1: Peacemaking, Peacekeeping – International Relations 1918–36. These sources refer to the Japanese invasion of Manchuria and its consequences.

SOURCE A

From a statement by Lord Ponsonby to the House of Lords, 2 November 1932. Lord Ponsonby was Labour leader of the House of Lords from 1931 to 1935.

Considering the delicacy of the situation, and the grave character of the international issues involved, considering the arduous [strenuous] nature of any investigation on the spot in so large a territory, and the need for unanimity [agreement], the noble Earl, Lord Lytton, who was chosen as Chairman of that Commission, and who was subjected for a period to very severe illness, should, I think, be warmly congratulated on the Report that he has issued. It is comprehensive in the way in which it has marshalled all the relevant facts. It is admirably lucid [clear] in style, which is not very usual in reports of this kind, and it is simple and direct in its conclusions. Perhaps I may be allowed to say that I consider that the noble Earl, Lord Lytton, and his colleagues on the Commission have rendered a great public service in the way they have discharged this difficult international duty, which, had it been accomplished with less decision and with less discretion, might have added further confusion to the already vexed [difficult] question of the Far East.

SOURCE B

Cartoon by David Low, a British Cartoonist, published in the *Evening Standard* newspaper, 19 January 1933.

THE DOORMAT.

STUDENT STUDY SECTION

QUESTION 1a

What does Source A suggest about the Lytton Report? (3 marks)

Student Answer A – *Briony*

Source A praises the Lytton Commission for carrying out a hard job under difficult circumstances especially as Lord Lytton was ill for part of the time.

Student Answer B – *Angelo*

In Source A Lord Ponsonby congratulates Lord Lytton for the report he has written. Ponsonby considers that the Commission's Report is 'clear', 'simple and direct' and 'comprehensive'. He considers that, regarding the difficulty of the task, Lytton has managed to produce an excellent document which achieved consensus among the Committee. Ponsonby also believes that the Report was completed quickly in order to resolve the difficult situation in Manchuria.

Examiner's comments

Briony has only understood part of the source's message. This answer would receive 1 mark. Briony needs to go into more detail, explaining her answer. Angelo has quoted directly from Source A and has paraphrased the other parts of the answer. He has certainly done enough to reach maximum marks. Although examiners recommend paraphrasing, rather than direct quoting, in this case it is quite difficult to find good alternatives for the quoted words. Angelo has demonstrated a good understanding of the source

QUESTION 1b
What is the message conveyed by the cartoon? (2 marks)

Student Answer A – *John*

The message conveyed in the cartoon is that the League of Nations' reaction to Japan's occupation of Manchuria in 1931 showed the weakness of the League. A Japanese soldier (implying military force) is walking all over the League, showing Japan's rejection of the principles upon which the League of Nations was based and ignoring the 'honour of nations'. The League in return has been unable to do anything about Japan's action and is desperately trying to show the world that it is a body that still has an important role to play in world affairs.

Examiner's comments

Would you give John 2 marks for his answer? How many sentences did he write? Are there too many, or just right or too few?

● **Examiner's hint**

What symbols are there in the cartoon? A militaristic Japan; dirty boots trampling the League of Nations; the League's headquarters in Geneva; John Simon, the British Foreign Minister with a 'face-saving' kit; Japan being greeted with flowers; a piece of paper with the words 'Honour of Nations' written on it; a welcoming carpet; the League as a doormat. By listing all of these you have gained no marks, as you have not answered the question! The date of January 1933 is important. The cartoon refers to the Japanese invasion of Manchuria in September 1931. The League of Nations sent the Lytton commission to investigate and it produced its report in October 1932, condemning Japan. In February 1933, Japan left the League, formally announcing this decision the following March.

SOURCE C

From a telegram of the Chinese Soviet Government, 6 October 1932

Now the Commission of Enquiry of the league of imperialist robbers– the Lytton Commission – has already published its report regarding the dismemberment [carving up] of China. This report is an admirable document shown to the Chinese popular masses by the imperialists regarding the dismemberment they propose to inflict on China, and yet the Kuomintang, which is selling out and dishonouring the country, as well as the government which is the emanation [creation] of the Kuomintang, have accepted it completely! ... The Lytton Report is the bill of sale by which imperialism reduced the Chinese people to slavery! The Soviet Government calls on the popular masses of the whole country to participate in an armed uprising under the direction of the Soviet Government, to wage a national revolutionary war in order to tear to shreds the Lytton Report, and to oppose all the new projects of the imperialists for dismembering China, repressing the Chinese revolution, and attacking the Soviet regions and the Soviet Union. Let us hurl out of China, Japanese imperialism and all other imperialisms in order to obtain the complete liberation and independence of the Chinese people!

SOURCE D

From F. S. Northedge, *The League of Nations – its life and times 1920–1946*, 1986. Northedge was Professor of International Relations at the London School of Economics.

Nevertheless, the Report was clear that without a declaration of war, a large area of what was indisputably Chinese territory has been forcibly seized and occupied by the armed forces of Japan and has, in consequence of this operation, been separated from and declared independent of the rest of China… As events were to show, the Japanese had no intention of isolating Manchuria from their relations with China; on the contrary, they meant to master both Manchuria and China and the two together under their own control. Lacking this insight into the Japanese frame of mind (and the fact that such an outcome hardly seems to have been thought of by the Lytton commission shows how readily Japanese professions of innocence were taken at their face value), the Report's proposals for a settlement now seem little more than well-intentioned daydreaming.

SOURCE E

From US Department of State, *Peace and War: United States Foreign Policy, 1931–1941,* **1943**

The United States Ambassador to Japan, Joseph C. Grew, reported to Secretary Stimson on August 13, 1932 … that the Japanese military machine had been 'built for war', felt prepared for war, and would 'welcome war'; that it had never yet been beaten and possessed unlimited self-confidence. After consolidating their position in Manchuria the Japanese military forces proceeded, early in January 1933, to extend the boundaries of the new puppet state by the occupation of the province of Jehol in North China. The Japanese Ambassador, in a conversation of January 5 with Secretary Stimson, stated that Japan had no territorial ambition south of the Great Wall. The Secretary reminded the Ambassador that a year previously the latter had said that Japan had no territorial ambitions in Manchuria. The Ambassador replied that no Japanese Cabinet which advocated a compromise on the Manchuria question could survive in Japan and that the Manchuria incident must be regarded as closed.

Complete answer to source exam – Jerome

STUDENT STUDY SECTION

QUESTION 1a

What does Source A suggest about the Lytton Report? (3 marks)

Source A suggests that the Lytton Report was very effective in its structure. According to Lord Ponsonby, it was drafted by Lord Lytton, who chaired the commission responsible for handling the Manchurian situation for the League of Nations. The account praises the Report for being very 'lucid' and comprehensive in that it addressed 'all the relevant facts.' Source A is very approving of the report and states that it is a 'great public service' because its clear 'decision and […] discretion' are the only way to calm the situation in the Far East that might else have escalated.

Examiner's comments

Three clear points are made here – full marks.

QUESTION 1b

What is the message conveyed by the cartoon? (2 marks)

The cartoon portrays the message that Japan disregarded the League of Nations in the Manchurian crisis. It is by a British cartoonist who is criticizing the League for letting Japan walk all over it. A League official seems to be bowing down to the Japanese soldier and welcoming him into the building. Thus, it is suggesting that the League allowed Japan to take advantage of it and simply invade Manchuria without stopping it. Additionally, the man on his knees is powdering the League with a 'face-saving kit', implying that although the League is taking no action it is taking care to polish its image.

Examiner's comments

Although Jerome does not include all of the references in the cartoon, his answer is clearly worth full marks. It has put the cartoon in context and successfully explained enough of the images in it to show that he clearly understands the message behind the cartoon.

Compare and contrast the views expressed about Japan's actions in the 1930s in Sources D and E. (6 marks)

Sources D and E convey information about Japan's actions regarding China in the 1930s. They agree in general on Japan's actions, but have some discrepancies in their portrayal of her ambitions.

Both sources recognize that Japan was keen to expand into China and that Manchuria was only the first step in this process. Japan's aims were clearly expansionist. This can be seen by Source D's statement that she had 'no intention of isolating Manchuria' and by Source E's claim that she wished to further 'extend the boundaries' of the new state. They both also agree that one of Japan's main aims was to exert 'control' (Source D) over her 'new puppet state' (Source E), meaning that the issue involved political manipulation of Manchuria and any other territory that would be gained.

However, there are also discrepancies between the two sources. While Source E continually underscores that fact that Japan would 'welcome war', and makes a consistent effort to mention war as a continued part of her strategy because 'no Japanese Cabinet which advocated a compromise on the Manchurian question could survive in Japan', Source D maintains that the Manchurian crisis occurred 'without a declaration of war.' Source D also only claims that the League accepted Japan's claims that she did not wish to expand further, and Source E explains Japan's goals to extend to Jehol, but that she wished to stop at the Great Wall. Source E also expressed that the United States did not trust Japan's declaration of her ambitions, while Source D claims that nobody had any 'insight into the Japanese frame of mind' and that everyone trusted her 'professions of innocence.'

Examiner's comments

Jerome has two comparisons and three contrasts with development and linkage. Full marks.

With reference to their origin and purpose, discuss the value and limitations of Source A and Source C for historians studying the Manchurian crisis. (6 marks)

Source A is an extract from a statement made to the House of Lords by Lord Ponsonby on November 2, 1932. Because Lord Ponsonby was the Labour leader of the House, the purpose of the speech was to convince the members of the House that the Lytton Report would be successful. Thus, Ponsonby's aim was to convince the British aristocracy that 'the international issues' were being handled appropriately and that no danger existed.

The document has several values and limitations for historians studying the Manchurian crisis. First, it offers a British opinion on the document and thus can be helpful to an historian in that he or she can discover different viewpoints about the document and that the British believed it would be successful, as opposed to an opinion that they knew the Lytton report would fail. It also presents several strengths of the report, such as the fact that it was 'direct.' It also shows in what way information about the report was presented to the public.

However, the source has many limitations. Firstly, of course it does not state that the report was unsuccessful and that the Japanese did not respond. It is also clearly very opinionated – Ponsonby calls Lord Lytton 'noble,' clearly showing that the opinion in the report is not the general international opinion.

Source C is from a telegram of the Chinese Soviet government, written on 6 October 1932. It is intended to sway the Russian government in favour of the Chinese and her people and to convince them to help China to keep not only Japan, but also the other 'imperialists' out.

With this, the source has several strengths. One is that the Chinese opinion of the Lytton Report is very clearly stated. China considered the west 'imperialist robbers' and did not approve of their intervention. Hence, another reason for the League's failure in the Manchurian crisis can be found by historians. Additionally, international repercussions can be studied because a clear split not only between China and Japan, but also between communism and capitalism is represented.

However, the purpose of the document is to convince, and so it has several limitations. Historians cannot trust the fact that the Japanese were set on 'dismembering China,' because strong language has obviously been chosen to convince the Soviets that action was necessary. It is exaggerated in that it claims that the Lytton report aims to reduce 'the Chinese people to slavery' and thus should not be studied for its historical accuracy on the aims of the Lytton report, but rather for Chinese rejection of League intervention and their motivations for this. A further limitation present is that it does not show how the Soviets reacted or how the Chinese responded to the League itself.

Examiner's comments

The purpose is weak for Source C, and value and limitations for Source A could be more incisive – 5 marks.

QUESTION 4

Using these sources and your own knowledge analyze the importance of the Japanese invasion of Manchuria for international relations between 1931 and 1936. (8 marks)

Manchuria was important for international relations between 1931 and 1936 because it not only led to the breakdown of the League of Nations, but also because it shaped future alliances.

Source B shows that Japan set an example for other aggressor nations by taking advantage of the League of Nations and disregarding her orders. It showed that the League would bow to powerful nations that used aggression as a means of achieving their goals. This meant that in 1935, when Mussolini sent troops to Abyssinia and the League was asked to intervene, Italy knew she faced no serious threat. The League did not take any action against Japan because she had no military and no power to employ an economic weapon. Although it attempted to set an embargo on Italy after Abyssinia as it had attempted to be 'simple and direct in its conclusions' (Source A) with Japan, Mussolini followed Japan's example of ignoring League mandates. Hence, the Manchurian crisis set the scene for future international relations because war became a viable form of diplomacy and the League could not interfere – it led to the breakdown of the League of Nations as a whole.

The Manchurian crisis also shaped international relations because it 'added further confusion' (Source A) to the situation in the Far East by destroying Sino-Japanese relations. It was clear that Japan 'had no intention of isolating Manchuria' (Source D) and that expansion into China was their main goal. Japan in general was isolated from the West because nobody had any insight into 'the Japanese frame of mind' and her actions made her known as an aggressor to the League of Nations. East-West relations suffered enormously, and even China distanced herself from the 'imperialist robbers' (Source C) of the West. Thus, while the League had initially been intended by Wilson to ensure peace between countries, it separated the rift between East and West. This is confirmed by Source E, which states that the United States began to distrust Japan due to her inconsistency and lies about her 'territorial ambitions in Manchuria.'

The Manchurian crisis played a large role in international relations after 1931 because it began the breakdown of the League of Nations. Even though the League was finally gaining more members, Manchuria showed countries that they would not be punished for any aggressive action they took. Thus, Italy and Russia followed suit. This led to the League losing prominent members such as Japan after the Manchuria Crisis, Italy after Abyssinia, and Russia after the Winter War. She was no longer capable of stopping war. Furthermore, the crisis also led to East-West and communist-capitalist strains. Britain and France were no longer trusted by the East and by Italy for their indecision and inability to take action, and the United States no longer trusted Japan. China began seeking relations with Russia to strengthen her alliances. Manchuria was the beginning of a breakdown of order that would lead to World War II.

Examiner's comments

Jerome has used all the sources and some of his own knowledge, even when he has gone outside the dates identified in the question and part of his answer is irrelevant. This would give him 7 marks. Jerome's answer scored 23/25 and is a clear Grade 7 response.

REVIEW SECTION

This chapter has introduced you to the Source Paper and has discussed how historians use sources. You have also been shown the various types of sources and questions you can expect to see in an IB History Paper 1 examination. Finally, this chapter has analyzed some student sample answers to see what was answered well and what could have been improved to score higher marks. In the following chapters, you will be introduced to the three Prescribed Subjects for your examination. As you read through them, try to use the 'five questions' wherever possible to help you analyze any source.

TREATIES AND MANDATES 1918–32

Introduction

World War I (1914–18) was the first war of its kind. Billions were spent on fighting a war that no one had anticipated in its scale and length, as countries from all continents became involved in the conflict. It produced unparalleled levels of casualties and displaced people, both among the military forces and the civilian populations. The post-war world was faced with many crises. European economies were confronted with having to pay the cost of war and of reconstruction. National economies, which had been organized around wartime production, had to return to peacetime production; international trade needed to be re-established. Roads and railway lines needed relaying, hospitals and houses had to be rebuilt and vast amounts of arable land returned to their former condition by the removal of unexploded shells. During the war, birth rates had dropped dramatically and agricultural productivity fallen. Famine, poverty and the consequent spread of diseases – aggravated by the devastating influenza epidemic of 1918–19 – led to many more casualties.

Russian Revolution

The Russian Revolution of October/November 1917 led to the establishment of a Bolshevik government led by Vladimir Lenin (1870–1924), which meant the rise of the first government ruled by Marxist ideas.

But it was not only World War I that had shaken the world. The **Russian Revolution** of October 1917 had brought the first communist government to power. The inter-war period (1918–39) was heavily influenced by events in Bolshevik Russia, as decision-making countries were torn between punishing those nations they considered responsible for the outbreak of war and, at the same time, keeping the world safe from communism.

This chapter analyzes the aims of the peacemakers attending the Paris Peace Conference as they drafted the treaties to end World War I, the extent to which such aims were reflected in the different peace treaties produced, and the impact of the treaties on Europe. It also explores different events that both contributed to and conspired against the enforcement of the treaties in the next 20 years.

Timeline – 1918–32	
1918	World War I Armistice
1919	Paris Peace Conference
	Treaty of Versailles with Germany
	Treaty of St Germain with Austria
	Treaty of Neuilly with Bulgaria
1920	Treaty of Trianon with Hungary
	Treaty of Sèvres with Turkey
1921–22	Washington Naval Conference
1923	Treaty of Lausanne
1930	London Conference
1932	Geneva Disarmament Conference

Section I:
Aims of the participants and peacemakers: Wilson and the Fourteen Points

Background information

World War I ended on 11 November 1918. The German agreement to an armistice was based on a proposal drafted by US President Woodrow Wilson known as the Fourteen Points. The end of confrontations, however, did not mean the end of conflict. The war had brought about many changes on both the defeated and victorious sides. New systems of government were installed, replacing traditional monarchic, autocratic rule. The 1917 Russian Revolution had transformed the political map of Europe; Germany was no longer an empire ruled by the Kaiser, but had adopted a Republican system; this was also the case with Austria and with – now separated – Hungary. The Turkish government concluded an armistice, which acknowledged the loss of much of its territory to British and French administrations. In time, this loss would also contribute to the collapse of the Turkish Sultanate (rule by a Sultan). There was fear that revolutions might spread across the European continent as a result of the collapse of traditional empires, unrest in Russia and the resurgence of demands for **self-determination**.

The end of World War I had brought new hope to different ethnic groups which, by the time the Paris Peace Conference started, had already begun to make moves towards forming nations. Such was the case – among others – of Serbia, Croatia and Slovenia, who separated from the collapsing Austro-Hungarian Empire between October and December 1918 to form a South Slav state.

An additional factor that made the work of the peacemakers difficult was related to the expectations of the citizens in the victorious nations. The unparalleled scale of World War I had led many European governments to apply policies to encourage commitment to the war. Four years of nationalist propaganda in the participating nations had established firm roots. By the end of the war, the United Kingdom, France and the United States needed to respond to electorates demanding security, stability and compensation for the war efforts.

The political transformations, combined with the economic and social cost of war, all created a difficult context in which to draft a peace initially aimed at ending all wars and shaping a 'New Europe'. To this end, representatives of 32 nations met in Paris in January 1919, but there had been little time for anyone to become fully aware of the complexity of this new order.

The following section analyzes the aims of the main participants of the Paris Peace Conference and the extent to which they became a source of conflict during the negotiations leading to the Peace Treaties.

Self-determination
The aspiration of racial groups sharing territory, language or religion to form their own national state.

STUDENT STUDY SECTION

RESEARCH ACTIVITY

Individually or in pairs, find additional information on the background against which the Paris Peace Conference took place. Include economic factors, the demands of minority groups, the relationship among the most influential participants, the reasons behind the decision to hold the Conference in Paris, etc. Discuss the ways in which these factors may have influenced the development and the agenda of the Conference.

In your view, why was the Conference held so soon after the end of the war?

Wilson and the Fourteen Points

The Paris Peace Conference started on 18 January 1919. It was closely watched by millions of citizens around the world, who hoped it would resolve their issues and who demanded that those responsible for the outbreak of war be made to pay.

● **Examiner's hint**
Paper 1 exams include at least one visual source, which may be a photograph, cartoon, map or statistics table. It is therefore useful for you to familiarize yourself with some of the most important characters of the period so that you can recognize them in exams.

STUDENT STUDY SECTION

QUESTION
What do you think about the choice of location and opening date of the Paris Peace Conference? Discuss with your class the implications of such choices.

The leading statesmen attending the Versailles Conference were US President Woodrow Wilson, British Prime Minister David Lloyd George and French Premier Georges Clemenceau. Together they were known as the 'Big Three'. With Vittorio Orlando, the Italian Prime Minister, the group was known as the 'Big Four'.

US President Woodrow Wilson

French Premier Georges Clemenceau

British Prime Minister David Lloyd George

'The Big Three', Paris 1919

President Wilson's Fourteen Points aimed at eliminating the causes which, in his view, had led to the outbreak of war in 1914. They represented a proposal for a new political and international world order (New Diplomacy) in which open diplomacy, world disarmament, economic integration and – above all – a League of Nations were to guarantee that a tragedy such as World War I would not be repeated. They were based on territorial adjustments meant to solve the problems created by the collapse of the traditional empires of Germany, Austria-Hungary and Turkey and on the recognition of the desire for self-determination. Although they had played a fundamental role in bringing about the end of the war in 1918, the treaty concluded in 1919 differed from the Fourteen Points in many aspects.

The following is a summary of Wilson's Fourteen Points:

SOURCE A

I.   Open covenants of peace, openly arrived at, after which there shall be no private international understandings of any kind.

II.   Absolute freedom of navigation upon the seas, in peace and in war.

III. The removal, so far as possible, of all economic barriers and the establishment of an equality of trade conditions among all the nations.

IV.   Adequate guarantees given and taken that national armaments will be reduced to the lowest point consistent with domestic safety.

V.   A free, open-minded, and absolutely impartial adjustment of all colonial claims, based upon a strict observance of the principle that in determining all such questions of sovereignty the interests of the populations concerned must have equal weight with the equitable claims of the government whose title is to be determined.

VI.   The evacuation of all Russian territory for the independent determination of her own political development and national policy and for a sincere welcome into the society of free nations under institutions of her own choosing.

VII. Belgium must be evacuated and restored.

VIII. All French territory should be freed and the invaded portions restored, and the wrong done to France by Prussia in 1871 in the matter of Alsace-Lorraine should be righted.

IX.   A readjustment of the frontiers of Italy effected along clearly recognizable lines of nationality.

X.   The peoples of Austria-Hungary should be accorded the freest opportunity to autonomous development.

XI.   Rumania, Serbia, and Montenegro should be evacuated; occupied territories restored; Serbia accorded free and secure access to the sea; international guarantees of the political and economic independence and territorial integrity of the several Balkan states should be entered into.

XII. The Turkish portion of the present Ottoman Empire should be assured a secure sovereignty, but the other nationalities which are now under Turkish rule should be assured an undoubted security of life and an absolutely unmolested opportunity of autonomous development, and the Dardanelles should be permanently opened as a free passage to the ships and commerce of all nations under international guarantees.

XIII. An independent Polish state should be erected which should include the territories inhabited by indisputably Polish populations, which should be assured a free and secure access to the sea.

XIV. A general association of nations must be formed under specific covenants for the purpose of affording mutual guarantees of political independence and territorial integrity to great and small states alike.

STUDENT STUDY SECTION

QUESTION

How was President Wilson hoping to ensure the causes of World War I would not cause a major international conflict?

Revise your knowledge of the causes of the outbreak of World War I and make a list of them. Then, analyze the Fourteen Points and explain how you think these addressed the different causes of the war. Note which of the Fourteen Points you think relate to each cause identified on your list. This way you should clearly see how Wilson was hoping his points would contribute to preventing another major war.

SOURCE B

Cartoon published in *Literary Digest*, September 1920.

BLOWING BUBBLES.

SOURCE C

It must be a peace without victory...Victory would mean peace forced upon the loser, a victor's terms imposed upon the vanquished. It would be accepted in humiliation, under duress, at an intolerable sacrifice, and would leave a sting, resentment, a bitter memory upon which terms of peace would rest, not permanently, but only as upon quicksand. Only a peace between equals can last.

From a speech by President Wilson, January 1917

STUDENT STUDY SECTION

QUESTIONS

a) **What is the message conveyed by Source B?**

b) **Compare and contrast the messages expressed by Sources B and C.**

● **Examiner's hint**

(Question a) Cartoons often include political figures of the time. It is very helpful to start your interpretation by identifying them. This information is often, but not always, given to you. Therefore, throughout your study of the Prescribed Subject of your choice, you should become familiar with photographs and images of the main players. Question (b): here is a comparison/contrast question. Consider starting by explaining the message in Source B. Then discuss whether Source C supports or refutes the message in B. This type of question requires two important things: a) that you identify the points of comparison and contrast between the two sources, and b) that you include material from each source to illustrate your points.

Student Answer (Question b) – *Tom*

Source B shows President Wilson blowing bubbles from a pot labelled 'Idealism'. The bubble before him is the 'League of Nations', which is therefore viewed by the cartoonist as an idealistic thought – bubbles do not last long. Source C agrees with the idea of idealism because it says that World War I must end without victory. It is hard to think that victorious countries would accept this proposal and treat defeated nations as 'equals'. Both sources relate to how Wilson viewed the world. B shows him as the maker of the League of Nations and C is an address in which he explains his views himself. Both sources focus on the idea of an integrated world by the reference to the League of Nations in B and the idea of a world of equals in C.

However, C focuses on how to ensure peace in the future whereas B focuses on the League of Nations as an element to preserve peace. Another difference, linked to the above statement is that Source C was produced at a time when the war was being fought and before the USA formally entered the conflict but Source B was published at the end of the war, after the Treaty of Versailles had been signed by the Germans.

Examiner's comments

The candidate shows understanding of both sources and presents both comparisons and contrasts. The answer refers to specific elements in each source, although some direct quotation of C would have been more effective. A very perceptive comment is that which says that Source B was published at the end of the war, whereas Source C was produced while World War I was still being fought. Make sure you look at the caption of the sources and pay attention to the context in which each of the sources was produced. Candidates very often do not consider this type of information and many would have missed the point. This information will help you understand the sources more fully.

Reactions to the Fourteen Points

The proposals for free trade, the end of imperialism, the adoption of open diplomacy and the creation of a League of Nations clashed with the realist approach of those who wanted to ensure their countries were well prepared for the possibility of another war. Putting the resolution of conflicts in the hands of the League of Nations, for example, was viewed as a mechanism that would not always be compatible with the protection of national interests. As a result, the Fourteen Points were met with reservations by the British and French.

SOURCE D

The Allied Governments have given careful consideration to the correspondence which has passed between the President of the United States and the German Government. Subject to the qualifications which follow they declare their willingness to make peace with the Government of Germany on the terms of peace laid down in the President's address to Congress of January, 1918, and the principles of settlement enunciated in his subsequent addresses. In the conditions of peace laid down in his address to Congress of January 8, 1918, the President declared that invaded territories must be restored as well as evacuated and freed, the Allies feel that no doubt ought to be allowed to exist as to what this provision implies. By it they understand that compensation will be made by Germany for all damage done to the civilian population of the Allies and their property by the aggression of Germany by land, by sea and from the air.

→ point 8
france reinterpreted
"restored"

A statement issued by the Allied governments after the German government had indicated its willingness to consider signing an Armistice based on President Wilson's Fourteen Points, 1918.

STUDENT STUDY SECTION
QUESTION
What, according to Source D, was the Allies' attitude to Germany in 1918?

French aims

Clemenceau, the French Premier, saw it as essential that the peace treaties protected France from any future German aggression. French territory had been one of the major battlefields of World War I and in 1919 France did not believe it could defend its frontiers against Germany again. France aimed at preventing German recovery by the use of reparations, redrawing frontiers in continental Europe, limiting the size of the German armed forces and excluding Germany from the League of Nations.

Among the territorial claims France presented in Paris were the immediate return of Alsace and Lorraine and the annexations of the region of the Saar (to provide coal for the French industries) and of the left bank of the Rhine. Regarding its relationship to the Rhineland, 'France had historically aspired to control this region, which it felt would complete its natural border. France saw control of the Rhineland as a necessary part of its security against Germany and therefore one of its fundamental objectives. The Rhineland, though, was thoroughly German and to annex it would violate Wilsonian principles. The solution ultimately arrived at was to leave the Rhineland as a part of Germany, but to make it a demilitarized zone in which Germany could not maintain or deploy its forces' (Erik Goldstein, *The First World War Peace Settlements 1919–1925*, 2002). In other words, annexation of the Rhineland was a separate French demand that was not granted, but the demilitarization of the Rhineland was offered instead.

To guarantee further protection against a possible German invasion, Clemenceau supported the restoration of an independent Belgium, which would not be tied to neutrality treaties. The French support for the independence of Poland and Czechoslovakia revealed the desire to set up strong nations to the east of Germany as additional protection, since Russia could no longer be relied on for that task.

● **Examiner's hint**

A good starting point to answering the last question is to show the examiner you have understood MacMillan's quotation by explaining it briefly in your own words. Next, you can structure your answer by looking at how the sources and your own knowledge show that France aimed at punishing Germany for having caused World War I, how France was expecting to make Germany pay and how it hoped to prevent further German aggression. Provide evidence from the sources and your knowledge for each of the three points, i.e. punishment, payment, prevention.

SOURCE E

America is very far from Germany, but France is very near and I have preoccupations which do not affect President Wilson as they do a man who has seen the Germans for four years in his country. There are wrongs to be righted.

Georges Clemenceau comments on Franco-German relations, January 1919

STUDENT STUDY SECTION
QUESTIONS
a) **What is the message conveyed by the following?:**   'America is very far from Germany, but France is very near.'   'There are wrongs to be righted.'
b) **Explain the motivations behind the following French demands:**   The return of Alsace and Lorraine   The occupation of the Rhineland
c) **Historian Margaret MacMillan describes the French aims at Versailles as 'punishment, payment, prevention'. Using the sources and your own knowledge, explain how France was hoping to achieve these aims.**

British aims

It is debatable how much of the philosophy of the Fourteen Points was shared by the British representatives. Britain desired peace and understood it as a return to a balance of power in Europe, which would ensure that neither Germany nor France dominated the continent. It was in British economic interests to see a relatively rapid German economic recovery. Germany was an important market for British goods and, in the need to reactivate its own economy, one that Britain did not want to lose. Prime Minister Lloyd George also had to deal with the fact that expressions such as 'Hang the Kaiser' and 'we propose to demand the whole cost of the war from Germany' – which had been used in the last stages of the war – had contributed to his coming to power. Consequently, many sectors of British society expected their government to support hard punishment of Germany and considered that to be more important than fast European economic recovery.

Lloyd George's main concern was to avoid German feelings of revenge for an excessively hard treaty, thinking that could cause another war in the near future. He was also worried about events in Russia, where civil war against the Bolsheviks was being fought, and about how the expansion of **Bolshevism** could benefit from an unstable Germany. In March 1919, he produced the Fontainebleau Memorandum calling for reconciliation in Europe. The importance of this document is that it exposes the view that, unless the Germans perceived the treaty as fair, there was little hope it would succeed in preserving peace.

 Bolshevism
The Bolshevik Party, formed in 1903 and led by Vladimir Lenin, was responsible for the revolution of October 1917. The Bolsheviks promoted a form of communism based on the writings of Karl Marx aiming at a violent revolution to overthrow capitalism.

SOURCE F

To achieve redress our terms may be severe, they may be stern and even ruthless, but at the same time they can be so just that the country on which they are imposed will feel in its heart that it has no right to complain. But injustice, arrogance, displayed in the hour of triumph, will never be forgotten or forgiven.

From the Fontainebleau Memorandum by David Lloyd George, 25 March 1919

SOURCE G

M. Clemenceau: 'I said yesterday that I entirely agree with Mr. Lloyd George and President Wilson on how Germany should be treated; we cannot take unfair advantage of our victory; we must deal tolerantly with peoples for fear of provoking a surge of national feeling. But permit me to make a fundamental objection… Every effort must be made to be just toward the Germans; but when it comes to persuading them that we are just to them, that is another matter… Do not believe that these principles of justice that satisfy us will also satisfy the Germans.'

From a conversation between Wilson, Clemenceau and Lloyd George on the content of the Fontainebleau Memorandum, 27 March 1919

STUDENT STUDY SECTION

QUESTIONS

a) **On what grounds do you think Clemenceau made his objection?**

b) **Compare and contrast Sources F and G on the treatment to be given to Germany.**

c) **With reference to their origin and purpose, discuss the value and limitations of Source F and Source G for historians studying the aims of the participants of the Paris Peace Conference.**

● **Examiner's hint**
For Question C, consider the context in which these two sources were produced. Do you think the fact that F is a written document and that G is an extract of a conversation has any influence on the value and limitations of the sources?

ToK Time

'When you want to believe in something you also have to believe in everything that's necessary for believing in it.'

Explain how this quotation relates to the ways Clemenceau and Lloyd George believed Germany would react to the treaty.

It soon became clear that it would be difficult to reach a balance between the desire to achieve lasting peace while also punishing those held responsible for the outbreak of war. Finally, Clemenceau decided not to push all of the French views harder. The lack of support from the United States and Great Britain for France's extreme measures explains why the Versailles Treaty was not drafted on French terms; France needed both its allies in the aftermath of war. However, as will be discussed later, the French also became more flexible in their demands, as they were promised British and American support to guarantee French security.

SOURCE H

The whole existing order in its political, social, and economic aspects is questioned by the masses of the population from one end of Europe to the other… The greatest danger that I see in the present situation is that Germany may throw in her lot with Bolshevism and place her resources, her brains, her vast organizing power at the disposal of the revolutionary fanatics whose dream is to conquer the world for Bolshevism by force of arms. This danger is no mere chimera.

From the Fontainebleau Memorandum by David Lloyd George, 25 March 1919

● Examiner's hint

For Question C, when evaluating the value and limitations of Source H, you should consider the historical context in which it was produced: how does the fact that Source H was written at the time of the Paris Peace Conference influence its value and limitations?

STUDENT STUDY SECTION

QUESTIONS

a) **What reasons does Source H give for a fair treatment of Germany at the Paris Peace Conference?**

b) **What other reasons do you think Lloyd George may have had in mind to write the Fontainebleau Memorandum?**

c) **With reference to its origin and purpose, discuss the value and limitations of Source H for an historian studying the course of negotiations at the Paris Peace Conference.**

Italian aims

During the war, the Allies had made promises to different countries in order to obtain cooperation against the **Central Powers**. Italy, Romania and Greece, among other countries, had received territorial promises during the war that were now impossible to honour while, at the same time, respecting the Fourteen Points. The Italian demands for territory promised by the **Treaty of London** in 1915 – which included the northern part of the Dalmatian coast on the Adriatic Sea, Trieste and South Tyrol as well as a protectorate over Albania – clearly opposed the spirit of self-determination of the Fourteen Points. This situation was made more serious by the fact that in April 1919 the Italian representatives presented before the Council of Four additional demands, which included territory that had not been promised by the Treaty of London, such as the port of Fiume.

The Italian representatives were under intense pressure from home to produce a satisfactory treaty. The economic effort to fight the war had seriously affected the Italian economy. The country was suffering political problems and social unrest. Obtaining territory was considered essential to the recovery of the economy and to help strengthen the shaky political system.

The problem with the Italian demands was also that there was little sympathy for the nation – partly due to its association with Germany at the start of the war as well as too little consideration for their contribution to World War I. Italy was dissatisfied not only about the fact that the terms of the Treaty of London would not be honoured, but also with the treatment the Italian delegation received during the Conference as a 'lesser power'.

Central Powers

Germany, Austria-Hungary, Bulgaria and Turkey, who fought World War I against the Entente Powers of Great Britain, France, Russia and the allies that joined them during the course of the war.

Treaty of London (1915)

Secret pact signed in April 1915 between Italy and the Triple Entente which brought Italy into World War I in exchange for the promise of extensive territorial gains.

REVIEW SECTION

Review questions

1 Draw a chart comparing and contrasting the aims of the Big Three.

2 Start by listing the issues in one column (e.g. headed 'territorial changes'). Then name the other columns after each of the Big Four and explain what the aims of each were in relation to each listed issue.

3 Find points of conflict among the different issues.

STUDENT STUDY SECTION

QUESTIONS

a) **How does creating this chart help you anticipate the problems in the making of the Treaty of Versailles?**

b) **'Talking to Wilson is something like talking to Jesus Christ.' What are the implications of Clemenceau's opinion of US President Woodrow Wilson? Which of Wilson's ideas do you think were more likely to produce this statement?**

Section II:
The terms of the Paris Peace Treaties 1919–20: Versailles, St Germain, Trianon, Neuilly, Sèvres/ Lausanne 1923

Background information

Fundamental decisions at the Conference were taken mainly by US President Woodrow Wilson, French Premier Georges Clemenceau and British Prime Minister David Lloyd George. The defeated nations of Germany, Austria, Bulgaria, Hungary and Turkey were not allowed to take part in the negotiations leading to the drafting of the treaty. Russia did not attend the conference and Italy, which had fought alongside the Allies, soon felt it had been relegated to a secondary role.

Most discussions did not take place in sessions with the full attendance of the 32 participating countries. Instead, special commissions on different matters were established to speed up the decision-making process. France, Britain, the USA, Japan and Italy formed a Supreme Council represented by the leaders and foreign ministers of these nations. This was later replaced by a smaller version, the Council of Four (France, Britain, the USA and Italy). When the conference officially ended with the signing of the Treaty of Versailles with Germany, a Conference of Ambassadors was left to supervise the peace treaties with the other defeated nations.

Four separate treaties were signed:
- Treaty of St Germain with Austria (1919)
- Treaty of Trianon with Hungary (1920)
- Treaty of Neuilly with Bulgaria (1919)
- Treaty of Sèvres with Turkey (1920), later revised by the Treaty of Lausanne (1923)

These treaties were produced using the Treaty of Versailles with Germany as a template: all four defeated countries were to disarm, pay reparations and lose territory. Following the principle of self-determination, new nation states were set up.

This section analyzes the terms of the different peace treaties, the redistribution of territories in Europe and the problems that emerged as a result.

Treaty of Versailles

Wilson's Fourteen Points had been approved in 1918 as the basis for the peace treaty. However, as seen in the previous section, the conflicting aims of the three nations soon proved an obstacle to both the application of the Fourteen Points, as well as to the establishment of peace treaties that would ensure long-lasting peace.

The main areas of discussion at Paris were:
- Responsibility for the outbreak of war
- Reparations for the cost of and damage caused by the war
- The redistribution of territories in Europe and the colonies
- Disarmament
- The formation of an international organization with the aim of preventing conflicts such as World War I occurring again (the League of Nations will be treated separately in Chapter 3).

Responsibility for the outbreak of war

In 1918 few nations – apart from the Germans and their allies – believed that anyone other than Germany was responsible for starting the war. Not only was this the position of the leaders of the victorious nations at Versailles, but also the view of public opinion in many of these countries. Consequently, any representative of the victorious nations who might have even considered other views on responsibility for the outbreak of World War I would not have dared suggest them openly.

Establishing war responsibility was directly linked to determining who was to pay for the cost of war. The Commission on the Responsibility of the Authors of the War and on Enforcement of Penalties was given the task of establishing and assigning responsibilities for the outbreak of war. The Commission was formed by representatives from Britain, France, Italy, Japan, Belgium, Greece, Poland, Romania and Serbia.

SOURCE A

Responsibility [for the outbreak of World War I] rests first on Germany and Austria, secondly on Turkey and Bulgaria. The responsibility is made all the graver by reason of the violation by Germany and Austria of the neutrality of Belgium and Luxemburg, which they themselves had guaranteed. It is increased, with regard to both France and Serbia, by the violation of their frontiers before the declaration of war.

From Commission on the Responsibility of the Authors of the War and on Enforcement of Penalties report, 1919

STUDENT STUDY SECTION

QUESTION

According to Source A, why did the Commission consider Germany and Austria to bear more responsibility than Turkey and Bulgaria? To what extent do you agree with this view?

Reparations for the cost and damage of the war

SOURCE B

The Allied and Associated Governments affirm and Germany accepts the responsibility of Germany and her allies for causing all the loss and damage to which the Allied and Associated Governments and their nationals have been subjected as a consequence of the war imposed upon them by the aggression of Germany and her allies.

Article 231 of the Treaty of Versailles (later to be known as 'War Guilt Clause')

The significance of this article at the time was that it provided the legal arguments to make Germany pay for World War I. Three important questions to be discussed at Versailles included:

- What type of damage and cost would compose reparations? This refers to what would be included in the final sum for reparations: what type of damage would Germany be accountable for? Would indemnities be included? Or just property damage?
- What final figure would Germany have to pay?
- In what ways was Germany to pay? In gold, goods, etc.?

Article 232 of the peace treaty demanded that Germany compensated the Allies for 'all damage done to the civilian population of the Allied and Associated Powers'. This extended responsibility and implied Germany was accountable for the war pensions the Allied governments would have to pay, causing the total figure of reparations, still to be determined, to rise significantly. Compensation for the violation of the **Treaty of London (1839)**, leading to destruction in Belgium, was also included in the Treaty of Versailles.

It was still too early in 1919 to have an estimate of how much damage had been caused and how much reconstruction would cost. The issue led to heated debates in the Reparations Committee, mostly between France, Britain and the USA. Such disagreements were based on the fact that each country looked at reparations as instruments for different purposes:

- France prioritized security and worried about a quick German recovery and remilitarization. With that in mind, reparations were an economic burden to prevent Germany from threatening France in the future.
- Lloyd George hoped for a balance of power in continental Europe between the French and the Germans together with an economic recovery of Europe that would benefit the British **balance of trade**. Such recovery depended partly on the revival of Germany as a market for British goods. The challenge was to achieve this while satisfying the many in Britain who hoped reparations would reduce the financial burden on the country, which also owed money to the USA. This was not exclusive to Britain, but was also true of many countries that needed to find the means for reconstruction.
- US views on German reparations were more in line with those of the British and helped moderate French demands.

When trying to establish the figure for reparations, the dilemma arose about how much Germany theoretically owed and how much it could effectively pay. The disagreements over this explain why the final figure was not established until 1921. British economist **John Maynard Keynes** explained why this was so in *The Economic Consequences of the Peace*.

SOURCE C

If this round sum [reparations] had been named in the Treaty, the settlement would have been placed on a more business-like basis. But this was impossible for two reasons. Two different kinds of false statements had been widely promulgated, one as to Germany's capacity to pay,

 Treaty of London (1839)
Treaty signed by European nations which, in Article 7, recognized the independence and neutrality of Belgium. In 1914, the Germans referred to it as a 'scrap of paper' and asked Britain to ignore it, which Britain refused to do. When Germany invaded Belgium, Britain considered itself at war with the aggressor.

Balance of trade
The difference in value between the total exports and total imports of a country during a specific period of time.

John M. Keynes
Keynes was the representative of the British Treasury at the Paris Peace Conference until 7 June 1919. He opposed reparations as discussed at Versailles on the grounds that they would bankrupt Germany and thereby compromise international stability and security.

the other as to the amount of the Allies' claims in respect of the devastated areas. The fixing of either of these figures presented a dilemma. A figure for Germany's prospective capacity to pay … would have fallen hopelessly short of popular expectations both in England and in France. On the other hand, a definitive figure for damage done which would not disastrously disappoint the expectations which had been raised in France and Belgium might have been … open to damaging criticism on the part of the Germans.

From John M. Keynes, *The Economic Consequences of the Peace,* 1919

Not establishing a definite figure for German reparations during the Peace Conference created problems about the legitimacy of reparations in the future. The fact that the Reparations Commission reached a final figure of 6,600 million British pounds only in 1921 implied that when Germany signed the Treaty of Versailles in June 1919, it signed a **'blank cheque'** for reparations.

Blank cheque
A cheque bearing a signature but no stated amount.

In what ways was Germany to pay?

The third issue related to reparations was to determine how Germany was going to pay. The gold reserves in the Reichsbank (German Central Bank) were insufficient and it was determined that Germany would also pay in kind, with goods that included coal, cattle and even fishing boats.

● **Examiner's hint**
Paper 1 asks that you evaluate two sources. You are expected to comment on their origins and purpose and explain how these contribute to their value and limitations for historians studying the issues to which the sources refer. An effective structure to this answer is to treat the sources separately, as opposed to what you are required to do for questions when sources are compared and contrasted. This way you can check that you have approached all four aspects of the evaluation for each source more easily.

STUDENT STUDY SECTION

QUESTION
With reference to their origins and purpose, assess the value and limitations of Source B and Source C for an historian studying the discussions on reparations held at Versailles.

SOURCE D

The Reckoning – German: 'Monstrous, I call it. Why it's fully a quarter of what we should have made them pay, if we'd won.' Cartoon by Bernard Partridge, *Punch,* 1919.

SOURCE E

UNLIMITED INDEMNITY

LOW

'Perhaps it would gee-up better if we let it touch earth.' Cartoon by David Low, drawn for a British newspaper, 1921.

STUDENT STUDY SECTION

QUESTIONS

a) **What message is conveyed by Source D?**

b) **What is the message conveyed by Source E? In what ways is the message different to that in Source D? Why do you think this is the case?**

The redistribution of territories in Europe

Negotiations of the peace terms to be presented to Germany included territorial changes affecting most of continental Europe. The collapse of empires was seen as an opportunity to create, out of such multi-racial political units, a map of Europe that would allow each nationality to live within its own borders. Wilson's Fourteen Points proposed respect for the principle of self-determination. This became – as many other ideals of the Fourteen Points – desirable but not always possible. The desire to respect self-determination was limited in several ways. For example, it was necessary to ensure that the new nations emerging had the economic resources (arable land, minerals, outlet to the sea) to make their independence sustainable. The consideration of such factors led to some nationals being left in countries where they constituted (large or small) minorities, such as Germans and Magyars in Czechoslovakia.

The Treaty of Versailles imposed several changes on German territory. Map 2 shows Europe at the outbreak of World War I. Map 3 details the territorial changes affecting Europe as a consequence of the Treaty of Versailles.

● **Examiner's hint**

For Question (a), read the caption carefully. Make sure you consider the date and place where the source was originally published. Whose point of view is the cartoon representing?

For Question (b), ask yourself what situation the cartoon is representing. Look for elements to support your answer. Starting your answer by stating 'The message in this cartoon is…' will help you keep focused on the demands of the question. Then, you can proceed to explain how the elements in the cartoon help express the message; in other words, you will be supporting your explanation of the message with evidence from the source.

Map 2
Europe in 1914

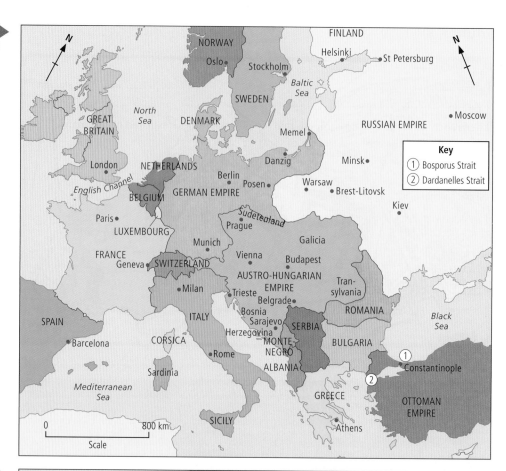

Map 3
Europe 1919 – New States

① **Alsace and Lorraine**
   ▶ *handed back to France*
② **Rhineland**
   ▶ *demilitarized zone*
③ **Saar**
   ▶ *under League of Nations*
   for 15 years
④ **Polish Corridor**
   ▶ *gave Poland an outlet to*
   the sea
⑤ **Danzig**
   ▶ *free city under League of*
   Nations
⑥ **East Prussia**
   ▶ *separated from the rest of*
   Germany
⑦ **Bosporus Strait**
⑧ **Dardanelles Strait**
⑨ **Eupen-Malmedy**
   ▶ *to Belgium*
⑩ **Memel**
   ▶ *to Lithuania*
⑪ **Upper Silesia**
   ▶ *to Poland*
⑫ **Northern Schleswig**
   ▶ *to Denmark*
⑬ **Macedonia**

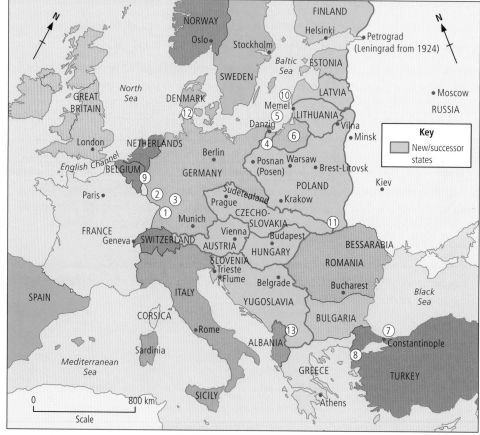

Alsace and Lorraine, which had been seized by Germany from France after the Franco-Prussian War (1871), were returned to France. Although France wanted the Rhineland, the treaty limited the French claim to making the area a demilitarized zone in which Germany would not be allowed to deploy military forces. An army of occupation was to be stationed west of the Rhine and in the bridgeheads at Cologne, Coblenz and Mainz.

The French demanded to be compensated for the coal mines destroyed by Germany in the war and claimed the coal-rich region of the Saarland as compensation. Rather than being given to France, the Saar was put under the administration of the League of Nations for 15 years, after which a **plebiscite** was to allow the inhabitants to decide whether they wished to return to Germany. In the meantime, the coal extracted was to go to France.

The creation of **Poland** to the east of Germany was a matter that Wilson had contemplated in his Fourteen Points, based on the principle of self-determination and which France related to its national security. The policy required providing Poland with the means to be economically independent to consolidate its position between Germany and the USSR. As a result, parts of Upper Silesia, Poznan and West Prussia formed part of the new Poland, which gained an outlet to the Baltic Sea. The major German port of Danzig (Gdansk) became a free city under the mandate of the League of Nations. The German province of East Prussia was separated from the rest of the country by a strip of land given to Poland to guarantee her access to the sea, creating what was known as the 'Polish Corridor'.

Other effects of the treaty included:

- The territories of Eupen and Malmedy were claimed by and given to Belgium.
- The German territory of North Schleswig, won by Germany from Denmark in 1864, became Danish.
- Memel was put under Allied control and later became Lithuanian.
- All territory received by Germany from Russia under the **Treaty of Brest-Litovsk** was to be returned; Estonia, Latvia and Lithuania were made independent states in line with the principle of self-determination.
- As another measure to limit her capacity for economic recovery, Germany was forbidden to unite with Austria (a move called *Anschluss* in German), now a separate nation from Hungary.
- Germany lost all her overseas colonies, which became mandates of the League of Nations, as well as trading rights in countries such as China and Egypt.

STUDENT STUDY SECTION

QUESTIONS

a) **With your class, discuss how significant you consider the territorial changes were for Germany.**

b) **If you were then told Germany lost 13 per cent of its territory in Europe and 7 million inhabitants but retained a population of 60 million (against, for example, 40 million inhabitants in France), would your answer to the question above be any different? If so, on what grounds?**

Disarmament

It was believed that one of the causes leading to World War I had been the arms race prevailing in Europe from the 1870s. Consequently, the Treaty of Versailles addressed disarmament in an attempt to eradicate another of the causes of World War I. The treaty obliged Germany to disarm to the lowest point compatible with internal security, while making reference to the promotion of international disarmament in the future.

Plebiscite
A vote by which the people of an entire country or district express an opinion for or against a proposal.

Poland
The Congress of Vienna (1815) partitioned Poland between Russia, Austria, and Prussia and created the Kingdom of Poland with the Russian Tsar as King. Although Poles were forced to assimilate into the new countries, Polish nationalism continued to exist and encouraged revolts throughout the 19th century up to the eve of World War I. Drafted into the armies of Russia and the Central Powers, Poles fought against Poles during the war. The withdrawal of Russia and the defeat of Austria-Hungary and Germany contributed to the resurgence of the idea that a free, independent Poland was possible at the end of World War I.

Treaty of Brest-Litovsk (1918)
Treaty signed in March 1918 between Germany and Bolshevik Russia, ending the latter's participation in the war and leading to its loss of the Baltic States, Poland, the Ukraine, Finland and territory in the Caucasus. The terms of the treaty have often been used to show how harshly Germany would have treated its enemies if it had won the war.

ToK Time
'The map is not the territory.' To what extent can maps help us understand the reasons for and results of conflict? Study the maps opposite and assess to what extent they can contribute to understand the problems arising from the need to redraw the map of Europe.

The following measures were taken to disarm Germany:

- German wartime weapons were to be destroyed.
- Germany was forbidden to have submarines, an air force, armoured cars or tanks. It was allowed to keep six battleships and an army of 100,000 men to provide internal security. An Allied army of occupation on the west bank of the Rhine was to be stationed in the area for 15 years.
- In the east of the Rhine, Germany had to respect a 50km exclusion zone (in which Germany was not allowed to send troops or keep military installations) and armies of occupation were stationed in bridgeheads (Cologne, Coblenz and Mainz).
- German **conscription** was banned.

Conscription
Compulsory enlistment in the armed forces.

Cartoon by David Low, published in *The Star* newspaper, July 1920.

SOURCE F

DAVID THE SPOKESMAN : "Off with the spiked hat ! What d'you think we fought for if not to abolish militarism ? "

STUDENT STUDY SECTION

QUESTION
What is the message conveyed by Source F?

Student Answer – *Katrina*

The cartoon, published in 1920, refers to the disarmament of Germany. David Lloyd George is demanding that Germany disarms to the maximum level. This is shown by the fact that the man representing Germany, who is not carrying any weapons and is on his knees, is asked to remove his spiked hat, a symbol of the Army. The fact that there is a cannon beside Lloyd George and that he is escorted by armed soldiers shows that the Allies had not disarmed, and did not seem to be ready even to consider this. Therefore, the tone of the cartoon is critical of their policy towards Germany.

Examiner's comments

This answer shows a clear understanding of the message of the cartoon in several ways. In the first place, it identifies the topic of the cartoon – German disarmament – in the opening line. Then, it identifies Lloyd George as the central character in the cartoon and it discusses his role in the scene. The bag next to the man on his knees helps identify that he represents the German nation. All elements: the standing soldiers, their weapons, the cannon are commented on and explanations are linked to the message of the question, German disarmament. This answer would receive full marks.

German reaction to Versailles

A draft of the treaty was handed to the German delegation at Versailles on 7 May 1919. Having been unable to participate in the negotiations, the Germans were shocked by the terms and denounced the treaty as a betrayal of the Fourteen Points and as a **diktat** to the German nation. The main objections, as we have already seen, were that they were being asked to sign a 'blank cheque' for reparations on the grounds of Article 231 – which they soon named the 'war guilt clause'. They also opposed the new frontiers to the east of Germany, especially the territory lost to Poland, which divided Germany into two. German disarmament and the exclusion of the country from the new League of Nations were also matters of resentment.

The Germans demanded a revision of the treaty but, although some minor issues were taken up, the treaty remained in essence much the same. Finally, on 16 June, they were again presented with the treaty and given five days to sign it while the Allies revised military plans to attack Germany should it refuse to sign.

The problem for Germany was not restricted to the terms of the treaty, but also to the fact that no one in the country wanted to pay the political price of signing it. Many politicians associated with the regime, among them those responsible for signing the Armistice in November 1918, were soon renamed the 'November criminals'. Political turmoil ruled Germany. Finally, on 28 June 1919, under a new government that President Ebert had been able to form, the German delegation signed the Treaty of Versailles, which in the words of Marshal Ferdinand Foch (a leading French Army commander) was to be 'an armistice for twenty years'. The German newspaper *Deutsche Zeitung* wrote: 'THE TREATY IS ONLY A SCRAP OF PAPER! We will seek vengeance for the shame of 1919.'

But the Germans were not the only ones dissatisfied with the treaty. Many French argued that Germany had not been crippled to the extent of providing France with long-term security and Clemenceau was the object of bitter criticism for what was viewed as a compromise to French security. He lost the election in January 1920 and retired from political life.

The treaty was also met with opposition in the USA. The US Congress refused to ratify it and join the League of Nations for fear of being dragged into European conflicts in the future. In Britain, the view that the treaty had been too hard on Germany was shared by many, such as John M. Keynes (see above, pages 29–30). The Italians, for their part, argued that the nation had been betrayed as 'they had won the war but lost the peace.'

Diktat
A harsh unilateral settlement imposed by the victors on the defeated.

STUDENT STUDY SECTION

QUESTION
How different were the terms of the Treaty of Versailles to Wilson's Fourteen Points and how significant, if at all, was the difference?

Cartoon first published in the *Daily Express*, London, 10 May 1919.

SOURCE G

THEIR TURN NEXT.

STUDENT STUDY SECTION

QUESTION
What is the message conveyed by Source G?

Student's Answer – Alex

The cartoon shows Germany coming out of a dental treatment room, after having lost teeth (territory). The man representing Germany seems to be in pain. The dentists were the Big Four: USA, France, Britain and Italy who are imposing painful terms on Germany. The other defeated nations are waiting for their turn and look very scared at the sight of how Germany was treated.

Examiner's comments

The answer above identifies several elements of the cartoon. The student could have also commented on the gag over the mouth of the character representing Germany, which could be interpreted as a sign of the fact that it was not allowed to complain about the terms of the Treaty. Also, some of the men waiting for their turn are in military uniform; Germany is not. This can be taken an indication of German disarmament. During an examination, there may not be time to comment on all of these elements, but it is good practice to try to explain as many of them as you can when revising.

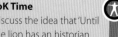

ToK Time
Discuss the idea that 'Until the lion has an historian of his own, the tale of the hunt will always glorify the hunter' (African proverb). What do you understand by this view? Does this view help you understand the conflicts between victorious and defeated nations in World War I any better? Are there other historical events which you have studied to which this view could be applied?

The Treaty of St Germain (1919)

Following World War I, the Austro-Hungarian Empire was split and Austria and Hungary became separate republics. This division led to the signing of separate treaties with Austria (St Germain, 1919) and Hungary (Trianon, 1920). The treaties aimed at the recognition of this new situation by the Austrian and Hungarian governments.

- The Treaty of St Germain implied formal Austrian recognition of the establishment of Czechoslovakia as an independent republic and of its annexation of Bohemia and Moravia. These territories included nearly three million German citizens, but they made Czechoslovakia a stronger country, a situation that France promoted.
- The creation of an independent state of Serbs, Croats and Slovenes (which would become known as Yugoslavia) was also contemplated by the Treaty of St Germain. This led to Austria's loss of Slovenia, Bosnia and Herzegovina.

- Poland gained Galicia from former Austria-Hungary while Italy received the South Tyrol, Trentino and Istria. Romania obtained Transylvania.
- Austria was forbidden to unite with any other country without the approval of the League of Nations.
- As with Germany, Austria was made to accept certain responsibility for war damage and, consequently, was subjected to arms limitations. The Treaty of St Germain also ordered the payment of reparations in kind (payment with goods or services).

The Austrians had many complaints about how the treaty overruled the principle of self-determination. Not only did they make reference to the fact that the terms of the treaty forbade union with Germany – which was the strongest of the complaints – but also that Austrian nationals were put under Italian (South Tyrol) and Czech (Sudetenland) rule, ignoring the principle of self-determination. The loss of industrially rich regions to Czechoslovakia and Poland and of more than 15 million citizens weakened Austria, which soon came to face severe economic problems.

The Treaty of Neuilly (1919)

Bulgaria joined World War I in 1915 in support of the Central Powers. This choice led to its being treated as a defeated nation and to the loss of territory. The toughest clause in the Treaty of Neuilly in 1919 was the loss of Bulgarian access to the Aegean Sea. Greece benefited by the weakening of Bulgaria in the region.

- Macedonia was returned to Greece, which also received West Thrace, causing Bulgaria to lose its access to the Aegean Sea.
- Bulgaria recognized the independence of Yugoslavia and their boundaries were adjusted.
- The treaty included clauses on reparations and limitations on the armed forces of Bulgaria.

STUDENT STUDY SECTION

QUESTION

Refer back to Maps 2 and 3. How significant do you consider the territorial losses for Austria to have been? Identify the countries that emerged in the former Austro-Hungarian territory as a result of the Treaty of St Germain.

Identify the territory lost by Bulgaria and gained by Greece.

The Treaty of Trianon (1920)

The Treaty of Trianon signed with Hungary formally accepted the disintegration of the Austro-Hungarian Empire, as Austria had done in 1919 through the Treaty of St Germain. The treaty was signed only in 1920 because of political unrest in Hungary and the establishment of a communist state under the leader of the Hungarian Communist Party, Bela Kun, which collapsed in August 1919.

Bitter complaints by the Hungarians were based on the fact that the newly formed Hungary had lost much territory in comparison to the Kingdom of Hungary, which had been part of the Austro-Hungarian Empire. More than three million Magyars (an ethnic group associated with Hungary) had been put under foreign rule, halving the size of the Hungarian population.

Other effects of the treaty were:
- Newly formed Czechoslovakia received Ruthenia and Slovakia.

- Croatia and Slovenia joined what would become known as Yugoslavia.
- Romania received Transylvania.

As in the Austrian case, the Treaty of Trianon contemplated the issue of relative Hungarian responsibility for the outbreak of the war and imposed reparations and limitations on its armed forces.

One of the beneficiaries of the treaty was Romania, who had joined the war on the Allied side in 1916. However, it could be said that the reason why Romania received territory was the Allied interest in its becoming a buffer state between Russia and the Dardanelles Straits, to prevent Russian access to the Mediterranean Sea.

STUDENT STUDY SECTION

QUESTION

Before the outbreak of World War I, the Kingdom of Hungary was part of the Austro-Hungarian Empire. Refer back to Maps 2 and 3 to understand the reasons why Hungary, now a separate country, objected to the territorial changes. Consider how other countries benefited at the expense of Hungary.

RESEARCH ACTIVITY

Individually or in pairs, find additional information on Bela Kun. How did he come to power in Hungary and why was he overthrown? How do you think these events impacted on the fear of expansion of Bolshevism in Europe?

The Treaty of Sèvres (1920)

The disintegration of the Ottoman Empire had long been expected and the fact that the empire had fought World War I on the side of the Central Powers accelerated events. The aims of the peacemakers were to set up new borders for Turkey in line with the principle of self-determination and to make certain that Turkey would be unable to cause fresh confrontations in the Balkans.

The decision to apply the principle of self-determination meant a serious revision of the territorial composition of Turkey. It was time to decide the fate of all the territories that did not have a Turkish ethnic majority. The weakening of Turkey meant the strengthening of other nations in the region such as Greece, which benefited from Sèvres.

The terms of the Treaty of Sèvres:

- The treaty ended Turkish control over North Africa and the Arab territories. Britain gained influence in the region by controlling **mandates** in Palestine and Iraq, with large oil resources (Mosul), while France received the Lebanon and Syria as mandates.
- Greece gained East Thrace, Smyrna and many Aegean islands. The treaty contemplated a plebiscite to take place in five years for Smyrna. The Turks were outraged at this clause, which ignored the principle of self-determination.
- Cyprus, under British occupation since 1878, became officially British.
- Germany's shares of the Turkish Petroleum Company were given to France.
- Italy acquired Adalia, Rhodes and the Dodecanese islands.
- Armenia and Kurdistan were to become independent states.
- Land was also lost to Bulgaria, leaving only the region around Constantinople (Istanbul) as Turkish territory in Europe.
- Under the terms of the Treaty of Sèvres, Britain, France and Italy kept troops in Turkey.
- Both the Dardanelles and the Bosporus Straits were open to shipping and put under the supervision of an international commission formed by Britain, France, Italy and Japan.
- Turkey was forced to pay reparations and its army was limited to 50,000 men.

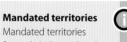

Mandated territories

Mandated territories formerly belonged to the German and Ottoman Empires and were placed under the administration of another country. The aim of this system was to help them reach the conditions that could guarantee they could operate as independent countries. The mandate system will be studied in detail in Chapter 4.

The Treaty of Sèvres soon proved to be difficult to implement. Nationalist opposition aimed to repudiate Sèvres and prevent the disintegration of the Turkish-speaking regions of the empire, led by Mustafa Kemal (Ataturk). War broke out between Greece and Turkey, and Greece was defeated. The political impact of the Greco-Turkish War brought the abdication of Greek King Constantine and the abolition of the Sultanate in Turkey, with Mustafa Kemal as the new leader of Turkey. By imposing such harsh terms on Turkey, the Allies had weakened the position of the Sultan, whose regime guaranteed observance of the treaty. The terms of Sèvres were revised and in 1923 the Treaty of Lausanne was drafted.

The Treaty of Lausanne (1923)

The Treaty of Sèvres had been too harsh on Turkey and had contributed to much of what had happened in the country since 1920. However, there was doubt among the Great Powers as to whether it was sensible to revise a treaty mostly as a result of its having been challenged by force.

The most significant changes in relation to Sèvres were:

- The return to Turkey of East Thrace (including Constantinople, Smyrna, some territory along the Syrian border and several Aegean islands).
- Turkish sovereignty over the Bosporus and Dardanelles **Straits** was recognized, although the area was to remain demilitarized and subject to international conventions.
- The withdrawal of foreign troops from Turkish territory.
- Reparation and demilitarization clauses were removed.

In return, Turkey renounced all claims on territories outside its new boundaries and undertook to guarantee the rights of its minorities. A separate agreement between Greece and Turkey provided for the compulsory exchange of minorities.

Lausanne contributed little to reducing the tension between Greece and Turkey, as future clashes in Cyprus would prove, and was heavily criticized in Britain, France and the USA. The Arabs, who had hoped for support for their independence after their participation against Turkey in World War I, were disappointed and preoccupied by the proposal of establishing a Jewish state in Palestine.

STUDENT STUDY SECTION

QUESTION
Using the sources in this section (including the maps) and your own knowledge, examine the view that none of the peace treaties laid the basis for a stable peace in Europe.

The Straits
The Bosporus and Dardanelles Straits connect the Mediterranean and the Black Sea. Sèvres demilitarized them and put the area under the control of the International Straits Commission of the League of Nations. Lausanne returned the zone to Turkey, but kept it demilitarized and open to free navigation. In 1936 the Montreux Convention abolished the International Straits Commission and gave Turkey control of the Bosporus and the Dardanelles Straits, allowing Turkey to remilitarize them. Fear of the aggressive policies of Germany and Italy led to the convention that authorized Turkey to close the Straits to warships of all countries when at war or threatened by aggression.

● Examiner's hint
The multiple sources type of question is the final one on the exam paper and it is good practice to do it last. It requires that you carefully analyze all five sources included, and that you relate them to the specific question asked. Answering Questions 1, 2 and 3 first should have helped you gain insight into the meaning and significance of each source in relation to Question 4. Remember it is important that you include knowledge of your own, which can either be new arguments in response to the question or additional material that may help you expand points offered by the sources. No matter how good your answer is, if it is only based on the sources or on your own knowledge you will only be able to obtain a maximum of 5 out of the 8 available marks.

Section III:
The geopolitical and economic impact of the Treaty of Versailles on Europe; the establishment and impact of the mandate system

The new frontiers drawn by the treaties impacted on the social, political and economic structures of both new and existing countries. They transformed the composition of the populations, redistributed natural resources and changed diplomatic relations among nations. This section aims at explaining how these **geopolitical factors** – combined with economic ones – affected Europe and played a part in the need to revise decisions taken in 1919.

Geopolitical factors
The combination of geographic, demographic and political factors in any society or state.

The Treaty of Versailles and Germany
Background information

World War I brought about the collapse of the German Empire in November 1918, when the Kaiser fled the country. In February 1919, the **Weimar Republic** was proclaimed, with Friedrich Ebert as its first President. One of the most challenging responsibilities ahead was the signing of the treaty to end the war. Despite having thought that negotiations would result in a treaty based on the Fourteen Points, the Germans had been presented with what they considered to be a dictated peace. This peace laid full responsibility for the war on Germany and her allies and demanded the handing over of German territory in Europe and overseas, as well as demilitarization and the payment of reparations. As we have seen, those responsible for signing the Armistice in November 1918 soon became known as the 'November criminals', and the association of the Weimar Republic with the Treaty of Versailles contributed to many of the political and economic problems faced by the new government.

Weimar Republic (1919–33)
The first federal parliamentary democratic government proclaimed in Germany, in November 1918. The Weimar Constitution made all men and women from the age of 20 eligible to vote. Faced with many internal and international crises, it came to an end in 1933 with the appointment of Hitler as Chancellor and the subsequent passing of the Enabling Act.

What was the impact of the Treaty of Versailles on Germany?

Germany lost approximately 12 per cent of its population and 13 per cent of its territory. This penalty included the loss of 48 per cent of its iron ore, 15 per cent of its agricultural production and 16 per cent of its coal. As shown in Map 3, Alsace and Lorraine were returned to France, the borders with Denmark and Belgium were adjusted, the Saarland was put under Allied military occupation and the Polish Corridor was carved out of German territory with one and a half million Germans living then under Poland. The *Anschluss* conditions prohibited the union with Austria and territory was lost to the formation of Czechoslovakia. These measures, combined with the war guilt clause, the loss of colonial territory overseas, reparations and demilitarization all created deep resentment of Versailles among the Germans. It also impacted negatively on the new Weimar Republic, which was held responsible for accepting such terms and played a part in the origin of the idea that the German Army had been 'stabbed in the back' by politicians.

The Weimar Republic inherited a heavy financial burden from World War I increased by the imposition of reparations by the Treaty of Versailles. Defeat forced Germany to pay rather than collect reparations. It was not long before Germany met financial difficulties in making the payments.

Although the Treaty of Versailles was harder on Germany than the Germans had expected, it could be argued that Germany was not totally weakened as a result of it. The collapse of the Austro-Hungarian, Russian and Ottoman Empires led to the establishment of new, smaller and weaker nations to the east of Germany. Geopolitically, Germany could be said to have gained from this.

SOURCE A

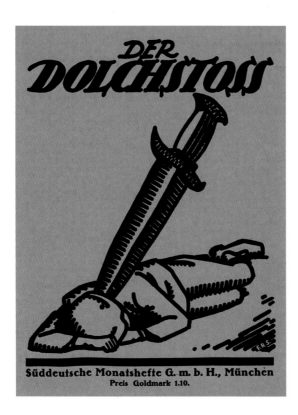

◀ 'The generic dagger', published on the cover of the magazine *Süddeutsche Monatshefte*, Munich, May 1924.

SOURCE B

The chaotic conditions in Germany over the winter of 1918–19, and the demobilisation of the army left hundreds of thousands of young men disorientated and thirsting for some sort of action. They found it in fighting on the streets against political opponents, joining in national fraternities or enlisting in irregular units which continued to fight after 1919 in the Baltic area and onto the Polish borders. Successive governments faced great difficulties in trying to retract German military force to 100,000, and in giving assurance to the allies that Germany was disarming to the limits stipulated by the Versailles Treaty. Large sections of the population resented the military restrictions and needed little encouragement to flout [disobey] them.

From Ruth Henig, *The Weimar Republic 1919–33*, 1998

STUDENT STUDY SECTION

QUESTION
What is the message conveyed by Source A?

Student Answer – *Raj*

This cartoon represents the idea that Germany was betrayed during World War I. We can see a German person stabbed with a knife in the back. It represents the German myth that the country had been betrayed and lost World War I not due to military defeat but to sabotage by sectors of the German society. The size of the knife, in relation to that of the person, can be taken as an indicator of how big the betrayal was thought to be.

● **Examiner's hint**
Some sources can offer many relevant points to the question being asked. However, because you are working within a time limit, it is useful to look at the marks awarded for a particular question to decide how many points you will make. If a source does not appear to offer a number of points equivalent to the marks awarded to the question, then consider the possibility that the examiner may be expecting you to develop the points offered for full marks.

ToK Time
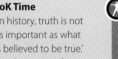
'In history, truth is not as important as what is believed to be true.' To what extent does this quotation apply to the German situation in 1918–20?

QUESTION
According to Source B, what was the impact of the Treaty of Versailles on Germany?

QUESTION
With reference to their origins and purpose, assess the value and limitations of Source A and Source B for an historian studying the impact of the Treaty of Versailles on Germany.

Student Answer – *Angela*

Source A is a cartoon published in Germany in 1924 showing a German citizen who has been stabbed in the back. Its value is that it shows the opinion of the German media at the time, one of disapproval of Versailles. The fact that the cartoon featured on the cover of the publication shows this was an important issue in Germany still in 1924. The limitation of Source A is that we do not know the political orientation of the publication.

Source B is an extract from a book written by a contemporary historian. Its value lies in the hindsight which the author has benefited from. Because it only seems to focus on the military, Source B may have limited usefulness to a historian who is researching the impact of Versailles in all aspects of German life.

Examiner's comments

This answer comments on the origins, purpose, value and limitations of both sources. However, most of the points made could be developed further. For example, the limitations of Source A can be expanded. We may not know the political orientation, but the fact that the cartoon featured on the cover of the magazine may be suggesting a high degree of approval of its message. Consequently, it may be viewed as propaganda against the Weimar government and, as such, it should not be taken at face value by an historian.

QUESTION
Compare and contrast Maps 2 and 3 (page 32). How did Germany's eastern frontiers change after World War I? Explain why it could be argued that Germany benefited from these new frontiers in 1919.

The readjustments of frontiers in Europe following the defeat of the Austro-Hungarian and Ottoman Empires

Background information

The post-war settlements created or restored states such as Yugoslavia, Czechoslovakia, Poland, Hungary, Austria, Finland, Latvia, Estonia and Lithuania. Albania, Romania, Bulgaria and Greece emerged from World War I with changed borders. It could be argued that with the post-war treaties Eastern Europe did not gain political stability, as new sources of conflict emerged. These were based on ethnic and cultural differences within these countries and on the consequent rivalries between them. The treaties imposed an additional challenge on the European countries. The new geopolitical situation was not only about learning to live as new or different national units, but also about re-establishing diplomatic relations among them.

The following section will analyze:
- Minorities and the impact of the principle of self-determination
- The political challenges for successor states

- The economic impact of the treaties
- The impact of the treaties on the diplomatic relations of the nations in the region.

The impact of the principle of self-determination and the issue of minorities

Many factors came into play in the design of post-war Europe. In the first place, there was the question of minorities. It had not always been possible to draw territorial boundaries that fully respected the principle of self-determination and – as a result of this – the peace treaties left millions of people as ethnic minorities under foreign rule. The cases of the South Tyrol becoming part of Italy, the establishment of the Polish Corridor (former German territory), which divided Germany into two, and that of the Sudetenland becoming part of the new state of Czechoslovakia are some of the examples of this point.

One of the reasons for what some saw as a disregard for the principle of self-determination was the fact that nations needed to be provided with the economic means to guarantee their stability and independence. The Polish Corridor, for example, was created to provide Poland with an outlet to the sea, both to strengthen its economy as well as for defence purposes. A landlocked Poland, trapped between Germany and Russia – who both resented their new neighbour – would have had limited chances of survival. In the meantime, the Polish Corridor separated East Prussia from the rest of Germany and put more than two million Germans under Polish rule, which created its own problems.

In many cases, minorities resented their new condition and conflicts emerged. Some of these conflicts were handled by plebiscites after 1919, while others remained unresolved and led to crises in the inter-war years. The new states signed minority treaties by which they committed themselves to a fair treatment of the minorities in their territories. The minority treaties were in turn supervised by the League of Nations.

STUDENT STUDY SECTION

RESEARCH ACTIVITY

Find out about one other region or territory in which the principle of self-determination was difficult to implement. Explain the nature and significance of that potential conflict.

Look for information about a plebiscite held after Versailles. What issues of self-determination did it address and how satisfactory was its outcome to the parties involved?

The political challenges for successor states

President Wilson had hoped the new successor states would adopt democratic forms of government, in the belief that democracy helped the preservation of peace. Although successor states often adopted democratic constitutions, the political systems emerging in many of these states could not really be considered democracies.

Why was it difficult for democracy to be enforced after World War I? As previous members of empires, the citizenship and their leaders lacked democratic tradition and experience. The racial tensions between ethnic groups were reflected in different political parties, contributing to political dissent and the destabilization of parliamentary governments. Underdeveloped industries, inefficient agricultural systems and trade barriers limited the development of the national economies, affecting standards of living and the expectations of the people.

STUDENT STUDY SECTION

RESEARCH ACTIVITY

Individually or in pairs, choose one European country formed after World War I and research its political system in the inter-war years. Was the country of your choice able to adopt a truly democratic system? If not, explain the reason and results of the failure to establish democracy. Share your findings with the rest of the class and take notes of the information you receive about other countries from your peers.

The economic impact of the treaties

World War I left a heavy burden on the European economies: low levels of production, shortages of food and of raw materials, debt, inflation. With the enforcement of treaties, new economic problems emerged. In the same way as it had been difficult to find a way to respect the principle of self-determination for all national groups, it had become equally difficult to distribute natural resources in a way acceptable to all.

The differences in economic resources between regions within the same country were a source of conflict, as the case of Poland shows. Prussian Poland (territory gained from Germany) was economically more advanced than Russian Poland, whose economy was based on agriculture. Some countries, like Austria, found they had lost significant industrial resources and needed to transform their economies to the production of agricultural goods.

Rather than forming part of a larger economic unit – such as an empire – each successor state now had its own currency and set up economic tariffs and barriers, all of which impacted negatively on their economic relations by making imported goods more expensive and trade slower. Also, trade with Bolshevik Russia was largely discontinued. Eastern European countries started looking for trading partners outside their region and became more dependent on the world economy.

The impact of the treaties on diplomatic relations

The changes imposed by the treaties on Europe affected relations between the nations. Either due to fear of losing the gains made through the treaties or to resentment of what were believed to be unfair terms, the treaties forced many countries to review their alliances. In order to understand how the peace treaties impacted on the diplomatic relations in Europe, here we will focus on the formation of the 'Little Entente' and the relations between some Eastern European nations and France. In the next chapter, you will find out about relations between two countries that had been diplomatically isolated after Versailles: Germany and Russia.

The Little Entente and France

Some successor states were fearful of losing their newly acquired status. Between 1920 and 1921 Czechoslovakia, Romania and Yugoslavia formed alliances with the aim of protecting one another from any Hungarian or Italian attempt to regain control over their territories, and to secure the terms of the Treaty of Trianon. France supported these alliances, as it viewed them as useful for providing a check on Germany from the east, now that Russia could not be relied on for that purpose. The French government began to seek agreements with the Little Entente nations, as well as with Poland. France promised assistance against any attempt to alter the 1919 boundaries.

However, it was clear that none of these alliances would give France the security from Germany it had before World War I with Russia as an ally. Moreover, French commitment to Poland particularly worried some diplomats in Paris, who feared that potential clashes between Poland, on one side, and either Russia or Germany on the other could end up dragging France into war. The balance to be achieved in the name of French security was certainly a very delicate one, and one that in the long term would be difficult to sustain.

SOURCE C

Fear of Hungarian revisionism resulted in the formation of the Little Entente between Czechoslovakia, Romania and Yugoslavia in a series of alliances in 1920 and 1921. This alliance system was extended with the conclusion of the Romanian-Polish pact in March 1921, which was specifically aimed against the Soviet Union, and the Polish-Czechoslovakian Neutrality Pact in November. From the outset the Little Entente was closely linked to France… France sent weapons and military missions to the Little Entente and there was a clear understanding that all four states would work together to uphold the treaties. France was now committed to defend Poland against both Germany and Russia, to thwart Hungary's revisionist ambition and support Yugoslavia against Italy. France thus undertook not only to be the principal guarantor of the Treaty of Versailles but also of the entire peace settlement.

From Martin Kitchen, *Europe between the Wars*, 1988

STUDENT STUDY SECTION

QUESTION
According to Source C, how were European relations transformed by the Little Entente?

● **Examiner's hint**
Do not comment on everything the source says, but only on what is relevant to the question. You can help yourself by underlining in the source points that relate to the question.

The mandate system
Background information

Wilson's Point Five demanded 'a free, open-minded, and absolutely impartial adjustment of all colonial claims, based upon a strict observance of the principle that in determining all such questions of sovereignty the interests of the populations concerned must have equal weight with the equitable claims of the government whose title is to be determined.' This point acknowledged that colonialism had been a major cause in the outbreak of World War I and, as such, it needed to be addressed. Given that distributing the colonies of the defeated nations among the victors would have gone against Point Five, it was decided that the territories were to be put under a mandate system of international administration supervised by the League of Nations. The mandatory nations had a responsibility for the wellbeing of those living in the mandated territories and were accountable to the League's Mandate Commission.

SOURCE D

To those colonies and territories which as a consequence of the late war have ceased to be under the sovereignty of the States which formerly governed them and which are inhabited by peoples not yet able to stand by themselves under the strenuous conditions of the modern world, there should be applied the principle that the well-being and development of such peoples form a sacred trust of civilisation and that securities for the performance of this trust should be embodied in this Covenant… The best method of giving practical effect to this principle is that the tutelage [guarding or supervising] of such peoples should be entrusted to advanced nations who by reason of their resources, their experience or their geographical position can best undertake this responsibility.

From Article 22 of the Covenant of the League of Nations

Mandates were classified into A, B or C categories according to their level of development. Territories of the former Ottoman Empire in the Middle East were considered to be among the most developed, and were therefore to be supervised by France and Britain for a limited period of time only. These territories were Mandates A. Most of former German African and some of Germany's Pacific colonies were Mandates B, and were considered to need more time before they could become independent. Finally, Mandates C, comprising other former German possessions in the Pacific, were regarded as needing closer supervision and were administered by the mandatory states as an integral part of their territories.

Though in principle the nature and establishment of the mandate system was discussed at Versailles, in practice the allocation of the colonies of the defeated nations had been agreed earlier. The beneficiaries were Britain, France, South Africa, New Zealand, Australia, Japan and Belgium. Italy received no colonies, increasing its frustration about the treaty.

Case study: The mandate system in Africa

In the years before World War I, there was a race among European nations to obtain colonies in Africa. The 'scramble for Africa', as it became known, was about imperialism and power for the European nations who wished to extend their dominions. A vastly unexplored continent at the time, Africa also offered valuable raw materials for the growing European industries. In 1884 the Berlin Colonial Conference divided the continent into spheres of influence among the major European powers, but in spite of this friction became inevitable. Conflict in Africa contributed to the tension leading up to the outbreak of war in 1914.

Following the spirit of the Fourteen Points, it was decided that African colonies would become mandates. The former German colonies, of which Germany had been stripped, needed to be put under the mandate of a European nation. Britain took control of former German East Africa and split Togoland and Cameroons with France. German South-West Africa was put under South African supervision.

In spite of the efforts of the League of Nations to ensure fair conditions in the mandates, the question is whether the mandate system was a continuation of imperialism under a different name. One of the arguments to support this view was the fact that although the League of Nations was given responsibility to supervise the administration of mandates, it had no legal power to transfer such administration if a country failed to fulfil its responsibilities as mandatory. Also, the term 'mandate' did not erase the gap between the 'advanced' and 'backward' people and equality between the races was not achieved. However limited, the mandate system became a system for accountability, a definite improvement from the colonial system.

STUDENT STUDY SECTION

RESEARCH ACTIVITY

'The mandate system was imperialism in disguise.'

Individually or in pairs, research the history of one of the mandated territories chosen from the map below during the inter-war years. Assess the extent to which the mandate system contributed to the development of the territory of your choice. You can help yourself by drawing a timeline of the most significant events.

Map 4

Africa 1920–32

Study the map below and analyze the territorial distribution of the continent.

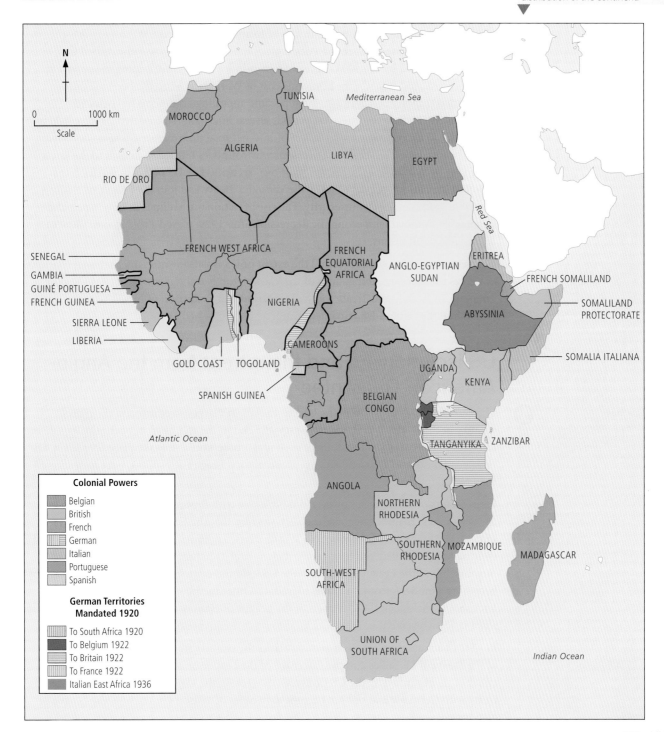

Colonial Powers

- Belgian
- British
- French
- German
- Italian
- Portuguese
- Spanish

German Territories Mandated 1920

- To South Africa 1920
- To Belgium 1922
- To Britain 1922
- To France 1922
- Italian East Africa 1936

Section IV:

Enforcement of the provisions of the treaties: US isolationism – the retreat from the Anglo-American Guarantee; disarmament – Washington, London, Geneva Conferences

Background information

The Paris Peace Settlement imposed severe disarmament clauses on Germany and restrictions on the armaments and troops of former German allies. Wilson's Fourteen Points saw world disarmament as a desirable aim. Public opinion worldwide had the destruction caused by World War I fresh in its mind, a factor contributing to support for disarmament. Additionally, the economic cost of World War I and the need to address the financial problems inherited from it became appealing arguments in favour of disarmament. During the inter-war period, several international conferences were held in an attempt to make progress on the aim of international disarmament. These ended with mixed results, however. Among the reasons why countries refused to disarm to the levels hoped for by Wilson was the fear for their own security. The US policy of isolation that followed the nation's refusal to ratify the Versailles Treaty and join the League of Nations contributed to the sense of insecurity. The rise of nationalist regimes in Italy, Japan and Germany, combined with economic depression after 1929, played a role in the failure of disarmament ambitions.

This section analyzes the causes and the extent of US isolationism in international relations as well as the successes and failures of the Washington Naval Agreements (1921–22), the London Conference and Treaty for the Limitation and Reduction of Naval Armament (1930) and the Geneva Disarmament Conference (1932–34).

US isolationism and the retreat from the Anglo-American Guarantee

Creditor
Entity or organization to whom money is owed by a debtor.

The end of World War I found the USA as the world's largest **creditor** and the richest country in the world. President Wilson saw the end of the war as an opportunity to redefine international relations so that wars of such magnitude would not take place ever again. His Fourteen Points and, in particular, his proposal for a League of Nations, were instruments for a New Diplomacy.

Large sectors of US society, however, did not agree with President Wilson's views. Many Congress members who agreed with the idea that the USA had a role to play in international relations did not believe Wilson's New Diplomacy was in the best interests of their nation. Some believed that, rather than having its national sovereignty affected by the membership of the League of Nations, the USA should contribute to international peace by becoming a model for other nations to imitate. Other members of Congress believed the USA should include in the Covenant of the League of Nations some reservations to prevent automatic involvement in European affairs as a consequence of US membership.

In spite of a massive effort campaigning across the country in support of the ratification of the Treaty of Versailles and the Covenant of the League of Nations, Wilson did not see either of them ratified by the US Congress. As a result, the USA signed a separate peace treaty with Germany and did not become a member of Wilson's brainchild, the League of Nations.

SOURCE A

The Americans had a complicated attitude towards the Europeans: a mixture of admiration for their past accomplishments, a conviction that the Allies would have been lost without the United States and a suspicion that, if the Americans were not careful, the wily Europeans would pull them into their toils again.

From Margaret MacMillan, *Peacemakers – Six Months that Changed the World*, 2001

SOURCE B

The United States is the world's best hope, but if you fetter [tie, bind] her in the interests and quarrels of other nations, if you tangle her in the intrigues of Europe, you will destroy her power for good and endanger her very existence. Leave her to march freely through the centuries to come as in the years that have gone… We would not have our politics distracted and embittered by the dissensions of other lands. We would not have our country's vigour exhausted or her moral force abated, by everlasting meddling and muddling in every quarrel, great and small, which afflicts the world.

From a speech by US Senator Henry Cabot Lodge in Washington D.C., 12 August 1919

STUDENT STUDY SECTION

QUESTION

Compare and contrast the views expressed by Sources A and B about the role of the USA in the world after World War I.

Student Answer – *Ingrid*

Both Source A and Source B refer to the relations between the USA and Europe after World War I. Source A explains how the USA views Europe at this point in time and Source B explains the aims of US foreign policy towards the European nations.

Both sources reflect the fear USA had of becoming involved in European confrontations in the future. Source A refers to 'a suspicion' that the USA had to be careful not to be 'pulled into' European 'toils again'. Source B conveys a similar idea by expressing that if 'you tangle her in the intrigues of Europe, you will… endanger her very existence'.

Both sources identify the USA as an important partner for Europe. Source B says that 'the United States is the world's best hope' while Source A mentions that the Americans have 'a conviction that the Allies would have been lost without the United States'.

However, while Source A mentions that the USA admires Europe, Source B is highly critical of the European nations and views them as intriguing, dissenting and quarrelling.

Examiner's comments

The answer clearly identifies similarities and differences between the sources. Each of these is dealt with in a separate paragraph and evidence is drawn from the sources to support each point offered. This is one of the strongest aspects of the answer.

● **Examiner's hint**
Source questions test not only whether you have understood the sources, but they go one step further to assess whether you can apply your understanding of the sources to a specific task – that of comparing and contrasting what they say about a specific issue. Therefore it is important that you are able to show not only what the similarities and differences between the sources are, but also where in each source you can identify the point of comparison and contrast.

Often during the Versailles Conference, the French delegation had expressed its preoccupation with the fate of the Rhineland, which was considered vital to the security of their country against German aggression. Having refused French proposals to incorporate the region to its territory or to occupy the Rhineland indefinitely, the Big Three finally compromised on the German demilitarization of the Rhineland for a period of 15 years. This option meant the territory remained under the sovereignty of Germany, but no troops could be stationed in it, a condition that was to be monitored by Allied forces. The agreement was partly reached because the USA and Britain offered France a military guarantee to come to her aid if Germany attacked. This guarantee became known as the Anglo-American Guarantee and was signed, with the Versailles Treaty, on 28 June 1919.

Wilson hoped that if it ever became necessary to honour the guarantee – after the end of the demilitarization period – the League of Nations would be able to take care of the aggression. The British, on the other hand, counted on the USA. The fact that neither the Treaty of Versailles nor any of the associated documents (which included the Anglo-American Guarantee) was ratified by the US Congress meant the guarantee never became binding for the USA and, consequently, not mandatory for Britain.

The impact of the retreat of the Anglo-American Guarantee

The retreat from the Anglo-American Guarantee needs to be understood not only in the light of the American policy of isolationism, but also in relation to the political atmosphere in Britain in the 1920s. There was little evidence that public opinion would support commitment to military alliances to maintain peace. The British feared being dragged into a conflict in the continent because of France. In an attempt to strengthen the containment of Germany, France had strengthened its ties with the Little Entente nations and with Poland (see pages 44–45). There was fear among British diplomats that these French commitments might lead to a confrontation with Germany which would force Britain to enter in defence of France.

Disarmament: Washington, London, Geneva conferences

The peace treaties had imposed disarmament on the defeated nations and it was hoped that the League of Nations would encourage disarmament at an international level. Several disarmament conferences took place in the inter-war period, with mixed results.

Washington Naval Agreements (1921–22)

Despite the policy of isolationism, in 1921 US President Warren Harding called for a conference to take place in Washington to discuss two issues: naval disarmament and the developments in the Far East. The Conference was attended by delegations of the USA, Britain, France, Japan and Italy and, for matters related to the Far East, Belgium, the Netherlands, Portugal and China joined the meeting.

The desire to discuss naval disarmament emerged from a need to avoid an expensive naval arms race among the powers. Even if the USA held the position of the strongest naval power in the world, there was little support in Congress to pass the Navy's proposal for further naval expansion. Britain hoped that a one-to-one ratio agreement (equality) with the USA would allow it to focus on other important matters, which depended on government investment and expenditure, without the risk of falling behind in naval terms. As for Japan, the nation had made significant progress in developing its navy, but it was clear to the government that further investment in the field would harm other sectors of the economy.

In relation to disarmament, the Washington Naval Conference produced several agreements:

The Four Power Agreement signed between the USA, Britain, France and Japan guaranteed the territorial rights of the signatories in their respective possessions in the Pacific. They also agreed to defend one another if such rights were threatened by third parties.

The Five Power Agreement (USA, Great Britain, France, Japan and Italy) asked signatories to limit their naval forces by the establishment of a ratio for the size of the fleets. The ratio was of 5:5:3 for the USA, Britain and Japan respectively, while France and Italy were allowed to have fleets half the size of the Japanese navy. In addition, the signatory nations promised not to build battleships and cruisers for a period of 10 years and to destroy ships (should they be above the ratio) until the ratio was reached.

The second issue on the agenda at Washington was the Far East and, in particular, China. The political instability in the country led to common fears that China might become the new international 'sick man' – as the Ottoman Empire had been in the past – and contribute to rivalries among nations with interests in the Pacific region. The result of these negotiations was the Nine Power Agreement.

The Nine Power Agreement (USA, Japan, China, France, Great Britain, Italy, Belgium, Netherlands and Portugal) reaffirmed the **Open Door Policy** and guaranteed the territorial integrity of China. Measures were also taken to assist China financially by giving her greater control over customs income. Japan also agreed to give back the Chinese territory of **Shantung Peninsula** to China.

To what extent were the Washington Naval Agreements successful?

- The Washington Naval Conference was the first step towards the application of a disarmament policy at an international level.
- The agreements included limitations on the use of submarines in war and a ban on the use of poison gas in warfare.
- At a national level, all countries involved avoided the economic costs of a naval race.
- France, though dissatisfied with her ratio, was allowed to build light ships and submarines for protection. In spite of this, the French considered they had been relegated to a second-class naval power and that, given the threat Germany posed, they were entitled to a special treatment that they did not receive.
- Italy, for its part, was satisfied with having gained parity with France.
- Members agreed not to build new fortifications in the Pacific.
- Although some progress was made on issues related to the Far East, critics of the Nine Power Agreement claim that it made no provisions for enforcement and failed to prevent crises like the Japanese invasion of Manchuria in 1931.
- An evaluation of the Washington Conference should acknowledge that the relative success of disarmament discussions may also be attributed to the fact that the number of nations involved was very small. Also, naval armaments can hardly be produced secretively and the assembling of vessels is a much slower process than the production of most other types of armaments. In other words, the successes in Washington did not necessarily point to success for disarmament conferences involving other technical areas or a greater number of countries.

Open Door Policy
A policy giving opportunity for commercial relations with a country to all nations on equal terms.

Shantung Peninsula
German-leased territory (1898) which Japan seized in 1914. At Versailles, Japan was granted the right to station troops in Shantung if it signed the treaty and joined the League.

SOURCE C

At the time the Washington Conference was widely hailed as a significant step towards international stability. The prospect of a financially crippling naval arms race had been prevented, the first substantive arms control treaty had been agreed, the navies of the great powers were to be limited, a clash between the major powers for dominance in east Asia and the Pacific had been avoided, and the Anglo-Japanese Alliance that had filled other states with such unease had been replaced by a broader agreement. It would prove to be only a short term solution. Within ten years, the Washington system had collapsed, largely due to the renewed Japanese bid for regional hegemony.

From Erik Goldstein, *The First World War Peace Settlements 1919–25*, 2002

SOURCE D

Together, the treaties signed at the Washington Conference served to uphold the status quo in the Pacific: they recognized existing interests and did not make fundamental changes to them. At the same time, the United States secured agreements that reinforced its existing policy in the Pacific, including the Open Door in China and the protection of the Philippines, while limiting the scope of Japanese imperial expansion as much as possible.

From the US Department of State, Office of the Historian, http://history.state.gov/milestones/1921–1936/NavalConference

SOURCE E

Cartoon published by British newspaper *The Star*, December 1921

● **Examiner's hint**
One of the most frequent problems with the first type of question here is that students answer on issues related to reliability rather than focusing on usefulness (value and limitations). Usefulness is assessed in terms of how much a particular source can help us understand the topic better. You could consider reading the sources with the following question in mind: 'What could an historian learn from this source about the significance of the Washington Conference?' This approach should help you focus on the value of the source regardless of whether it is reliable.

STUDENT STUDY SECTION

QUESTION

With reference to their origin and purpose, discuss the value and limitations of Source C and Source D for an historian assessing the significance of the Washington Naval Conference.

QUESTION

Using these sources and your own knowledge, assess the successes and failures of the Washington Naval Conference.

Student Answer – *Chang*

The Washington Naval Conference was called by the United States and attended by the USA, Britain, France, Japan and Italy among others. It aimed at reducing the pressure to continue investing in enlarging navies by reaching an agreement on the sizes of national navies based on a ratio system to be established among the countries. It also hoped to address some of the problems in the Far East.

One could argue that an important success of the Conference was the conference itself. After the withdrawal of the USA from European politics, this renewed will to discuss matters collectively and with the presence of the USA was welcome, so was American commitment to the Conference shown by its readiness to destroy ships in order to achieve the agreed ratio. This can be supported by Source D, which describes America's role in securing agreements in the Pacific that contributed to the Open Door Policy, as well as limiting Japanese expansion.

Washington did reduce the pressure to expand navies and therefore achieved its aim of allowing countries to focus their efforts on other areas of more urgent need. As stated in Source C: 'The prospect of a financially crippling naval arms race had been prevented'.

Washington helped to ease relations by enlarging the limited Anglo-Japanese Alliance – obsolete now after the collapse of the Russian and German Empires – to include France and Italy. This view is supported by Source C which mentions 'the Anglo-Japanese Alliance that had filled other states with such unease had been replaced by a broader agreement.'

The Nine Power Treaty to protect the integrity of China was not very successful and would soon collapse 'largely due to the renewed Japanese bid for regional hegemony', as stated in Source C. This can be explained as a failure of the Washington Conference to organize the means to enforce its terms.

Source E illustrates the failure to reach further agreements as a French responsibility and depicts the country as a very threatening force to naval peace. The country was unhappy with the ratio established at Washington and claimed it had rights to a larger navy than Italy because France had more overseas territories to look after.

The Washington Conference was a combination of successes and failures. It paved the way for future negotiations on disarmament; it was able to produce a policy on naval forces which was accepted by all participants. Although a step forward, Washington also demonstrated how difficult reaching an agreement on disarmament at an international level would become.

Examiner's comments

This answer has a solid structure and the candidate has made clear and relevant use of the sources, identifying successes and failures of the Washington Conference. However, there is no clear evidence of the use of supporting knowledge from outside the sources (own knowledge). This is a serious weakness in the answer. It is important to remember that own knowledge does not necessarily need to come in as additional arguments. Any of the arguments expressed above, which are supported by evidence from the sources, could have been further discussed with reference to outside knowledge.

London Conference and Treaty for the Limitation and Reduction of Naval Armament (1930)

The conference held in London in 1930 aimed at taking some further steps in naval disarmament by including submarines and smaller warships, which had not been contemplated by the Washington Agreements. At an international level, the world was undergoing one of the most severe economic crises and living under the period known as the 'Great Depression'.

One of the explanations given for the agreements reached in London is that all nations involved were suffering the effects of the economic depression and did not wish to divert resources into a naval race. The Treaty for the Limitation and Reduction of Naval Armament modified the naval ratio between the USA, Britain and Japan, benefiting the latter (who obtained parity in submarines). However, the treaty did not reduce the likelihood of war, as it allowed naval escalation in the event of an act of aggression by a non-signatory country.

Geneva Disarmament Conference (1932–34)

The League of Nations' Disarmament Commission began preparations for the Conference for the Reduction and Limitation of Armaments in 1926, with the Conference finally opening in Geneva in February 1932. The conference aimed at addressing not only naval disarmament, but arms reduction as a whole. It opened against a complex background of economic and political crises. Against this background, the aim of disarming to the lowest point compatible with internal security was viewed as idealistic – if not dangerous – by many statesmen and diplomats. Several issues related to how disarmament was to be agreed upon and put into practice were raised at Geneva, but overall results were disappointing.

One of the first difficulties diplomats faced at Geneva was that of how to reach an agreement on the meaning of the word 'disarmament'. The challenge involved distinguishing between offensive and defensive weapons to help decide which armaments were to be included in the disarmament and which would be allowed for defensive purposes. Negotiations on this issue led to friction and little was accomplished.

Yet the issue of disarmament was not limited to theoretical discussions. It was also extremely difficult to decide how it would be implemented and controlled. Who was to verify whether nations disarmed? Even German disarmament had been hard to control – negotiations carried out between Moscow and Berlin in the 1920s had allowed German military development in spite of the restrictions imposed by Versailles. Even if an international organization was appointed to enforce disarmament, how was it to operate without affecting the principle of sovereignty? What would be the limits to the rights of this organization? Finally, if a disarmed nation became victim of an act of aggression, who would come to its defence?

The conference failed to produce disarmament largely because the views of the participant nations on most of these issues were incompatible. Such incompatibility is best illustrated by analyzing the clashes between France and Germany. The former placed security ahead of disarmament and expressed its reluctance to disarm until it was offered more specific guarantees against German aggression. Germany (a member of the League of Nations since 1926), whose disarmament had been imposed by the Treaty of Versailles, demanded 'equality of rights'. Germany argued that either the other countries disarmed or Germany was allowed to rearm to their level, which was nothing less than a request for rearmament in the eyes of the French. Disarmament became a more idealistic objective after Adolf Hitler rose to power in January 1933 – he withdrew Germany from both the conference and from the League of Nations.

SOURCE F

For years Germany has been waiting in vain for the fulfilment of the promise of disarmament made to her by the others. It is the sincere desire of the national Government to be able to refrain from increasing our army and our weapons, insofar as the rest of the world is now also ready to fulfil its obligations in the matter of radical disarmament. For Germany desires nothing except an equal right to live and equal freedom… We are unfortunately faced by the fact that the Geneva Conference, in spite of lengthy negotiations, has so far reached no practical result. The decision regarding the securing of a real measure of disarmament has been constantly delayed by the raising of questions of technical detail and by the introduction of problems that have nothing to do with disarmament. This procedure is useless. The illegal state of one-sided disarmament and the resulting national insecurity of Germany cannot continue any longer. For fourteen years we have been disarmed, and for fourteen months we have been waiting for the results of the Disarmament Conference.

From a speech by Adolf Hitler to the German Reichstag, March 1933

SOURCE G

I am very glad that the Disarmament Conference is passing out of life into history. It is the greatest mistake to mix up disarmament with peace. When you have peace you will have disarmament. But there has been during these recent years a steady deterioration in the relations between different countries, a steady growth of ill-will, and a steady, indeed a rapid increase in armaments that has gone on through all these years in spite of the endless flow of oratory, of perorations, of well-meaning sentiments, of banquets, which have marked this epoch. Europe will be secure when the nations no longer feel themselves in great danger, as many of them do now.

From a speech by Winston Churchill, July 1934. Source: *The Gathering Storm*, 1948

STUDENT STUDY SECTION

QUESTIONS

a) Assess the value and limitations of Source F and Source G for an historian studying the reasons for the failure of the Geneva Disarmament Conference.

b) Using your own knowledge and the sources, explain to what extent you agree with the view that 'disarmament was a political and not a technical process'.

REVIEW SECTION

This chapter has explained the context in which the Paris Peace Conference developed by looking at the aims and roles of the peacemakers in their efforts to solve the problems faced in the aftermath of World War I. It has analyzed the Paris Peace Treaties and their impact on Europe, the problems solved and those created when enforcing the terms of the treaties. It has considered the reasons for the establishment of the mandate system. It has explored the effect of US isolationism on European affairs and examined the successes and failures of the attempts to disarm in the Washington, London and Geneva Conferences.

STUDENT STUDY SECTION

QUESTIONS

Write answers to the following questions, supporting your arguments with information both from the text and the sources.

a) 'The peace settlements after World War I were an unhappy compromise between fear and revenge.' How far do you agree with the statement?

b) Explain the attempts made to achieve disarmament in the inter-war period and analyze why results were limited.

c) To what extent did the peace treaties bring about a 'New Europe'?

3

Prescribed Subject 1: Peacemaking,
Peacekeeping – International Relations 1918–36

INTERNATIONAL CRISES 1923–36

Introduction

Chapter 2 analyzed the terms of the peace treaties that ended the war, their international impact and the limited results of several of the disarmament conferences that took place after World War I.

The following chapter looks at some of the different international events and crises between 1923 and 1936, and attempted solutions. While many countries expressed their disagreement with the treaties by appealing to the League of Nations, others decided to take matters into their own hands. The period 1924–29 saw an improvement of the terms of international relations in Europe, but the effects of the economic crisis that broke out in 1929 led to the rise of nationalism and challenges to the system of collective security. In this context, the weaknesses of the League of Nations became more apparent, as the Japanese invasion of Manchuria and the Italian invasion of Abyssinia were to demonstrate.

Timeline – 1920–36

1920 First meeting of the League of Nations
1922 Mussolini becomes Prime Minister in Italy
Treaty of Rapallo
1923 French occupation of the Ruhr
1924 Dawes Plan
1925 Locarno Treaties
1926 Germany is admitted to the League of Nations
1928 Briand–Kellogg Pact
1929 Young Plan
Wall Street Crash
1931 Japanese invasion of Manchuria
1932 World Disarmament Conference
1933 Hitler is appointed Chancellor in Germany
Japan withdraws from the League of Nations
Germany withdraws from the Disarmament Conference and the League of Nations
1934 The USSR is admitted to the League of Nations
1935 Stresa Conference
Anglo-German Naval Agreement
Mussolini's invasion of Abyssinia
1936 German remilitarization of the Rhineland

Section I:
The League of Nations: effects of the absence of the major powers; the principle of collective security and early attempts at peacekeeping (1920–25)

Background information

The formation of the League of Nations was discussed extensively at the Paris Peace Conference. President Wilson chaired the committee that gave life to the organization and produced its **Covenant** in April 1919. This document, considered the Constitution of the League of Nations, was incorporated into all the peace treaties of the Paris Settlement. Sir Eric Drummond was appointed first Secretary-General and the League's headquarters were established in Geneva.

This section analyzes the circumstances in which the League of Nations was created, its aims and methods, together with the effects of the absence of the USA, the **USSR** and Germany. It explores the successes and failures of the League in some of its early attempts at peacekeeping (1920–25).

The creation of the League of Nations

The League was created in extremely difficult circumstances. The world was just emerging from World War I and the treaties that ended the war were drafted in an atmosphere of tension and distrust. The tasks ahead for the League were complex. Border disputes, minority problems, disarmament, the supervision of mandates and the promotion of international cooperation in social and economic matters were some of the responsibilities of the organization. Although there had been attempts at the establishment of international bodies in the past, nothing like the League of Nations had been attempted and, therefore, there was no prior experience to rely on.

SOURCE A

The covenant makers in Paris in 1919 were forced to depend on their own judgments and their estimates of the probabilities of their work was done under the shadow of the peacemaking of Europe. Absorbed in that more immediate task, the Paris Conference as a whole gave little thought to the terms of the Covenant: perhaps the majority of its members did not think it worth while to bother with them. One group thought the League would prove a futility; another was so anxious to get any kind of League that they would not quibble over details. It thus happened that the Covenant was prepared in an academic way and adopted by the Conference without serious debate. In no stage of the process did it have the benefit of criticisms by a clear-headed opposition.

From John Spencer Bassett, *The League of Nations – A Chapter in World Politics,* **1930**

Covenant of the League of Nations

The Covenant of the League of Nations established the rules and regulations for the organization such as what issues the League was to discuss and rule on, the voting system to take decisions, and the organization and function of the different bodies which made up the League, among other issues.

USSR

In 1922 the Union of Soviet Socialist Republics, a federation of Soviet republics, was formally established. It is also referred to as the USSR. Russia was the largest republic of the Union.

SOURCE B

'The Rainbow', cartoon depicting the world on Noah's Ark, published in the *Literary Digest*, September 1919.

STUDENT STUDY SECTION

QUESTIONS

a) **What, according to Source A, were the problems facing the creation of the League of Nations?**

b) **'One group thought the League would prove a futility; another was so anxious to get any kind of League that they would not quibble over details' (Source A). To which countries do you think the author was referring? Explain your answer fully.**

c) **What message is conveyed by Source B?**

d) **Compare and contrast the views expressed about the League of Nations in Sources A and B.**

What were the aims of the League?

The main aims of the League of Nations were to promote international cooperation and to achieve international peace and security. The League aimed at promoting what became known as 'collective security', the idea that an organization of sovereign states would guarantee to take joint action in defence of one another against acts of aggression. The hope behind collective security was that its principle would help deter acts of aggression and, in that way, contribute to international peace. The principle of collective security promoted by the League of Nations was to be reaffirmed by specific international treaties.

The League of Nations was faced with several obstacles to achieving peace. Some countries were dissatisfied with the terms of the peace treaties and wanted changes to the terms. Others, who had made gains after the war, wanted to preserve the status quo. A challenge to the League of Nations arose in this context: were all members of the League prepared to commit themselves to maintain the order achieved after World War I? And a further question: was this a desirable situation for all?

STUDENT STUDY SECTION

QUESTION

Refer back to the information in Chapter 2 and explain which countries were dissatisfied with the peace settlement and, consequently, more interested in challenging the existing order. Which were more interested in preserving it? Explain your answers fully.

What were the instruments of the League of Nations for the fulfilment of its aims?

The Covenant of the League of Nations stated what situations were of concern to the organization, and how decisions on those issues were to be reached and implemented. In order to understand the strengths and weaknesses of the League, you should analyze both the Covenant and the structure of the organization.

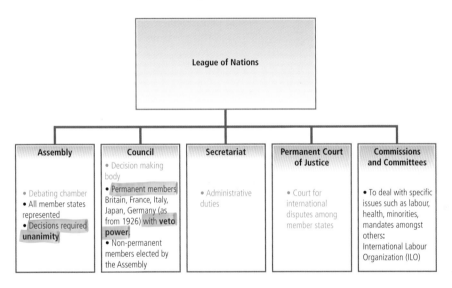

STUDENT STUDY SECTION

RESEARCH ACTIVITY

In class, discuss the strengths and weaknesses of the structure of the League. Refer to the requirement of unanimity in the Assembly and to the veto power of the permanent members in the Council. Why do you think they were incorporated into the League's procedures?

Look at the list of countries that became permanent members of the Council. To what extent do you consider they were representatives of a new international order?

Many of the successes of the League of Nations are related to the work of its Commissions and Committees. Find information about any two of them and discuss their aims and achievements.

Unanimity
Decision that requires the consensus / support of all members.

Veto power
Power of the permanent members of the Council to refuse to allow something to be done.

The Covenant of the League of Nations

The Covenant of the League of Nations detailed how the organization was to act in order to achieve and secure its aims. To understand the League's interventions in conflicts throughout the 1920s and 1930s, it's important that you become familiar with the instruments of the League as peacekeeper.

STUDENT STUDY SECTION

The following exercise aims at familiarizing you with some of the most relevant articles of the League of Nations. Read the extracts and discuss the questions below. You may find it useful to look up the full version of the Covenant for future reference.

Article 5: Except where otherwise expressly provided in this Covenant or by the terms of the present Treaty, decisions at any meeting of the Assembly or of the Council shall require the agreement of all the Members of the League represented at the meeting.

Article 8: The Members of the League recognise that the maintenance of peace requires the reduction of national armaments to the lowest point consistent with national safety and the enforcement by common action of international obligations.

Article 10: The Members of the League undertake to respect and preserve as against external aggression the territorial integrity and existing political independence of all Members of the League. In case of any such aggression or in case of any threat or danger of such aggression the Council shall advise upon the means by which this obligation shall be fulfilled.

Article 11: Any war or threat of war, whether immediately affecting any of the members of the League or not, is hereby declared a matter of concern to the whole League, and the League shall take any action that may be deemed wise and effectual to safeguard the peace of nations.

Article 16: Should any Member of the League resort to war … it shall ipso facto be deemed to have committed an act of war against all other Members of the League, which hereby undertake immediately to subject it to the severance of all trade or financial relations … and the prevention of all financial, commercial or personal intercourse between the nationals of the covenant-breaking State and the nationals of any other State, whether a Member of the League or not. It shall be the duty of the Council in such case to recommend to the several Governments concerned what effective military, naval or air force the Members of the League shall severally contribute to the armed forces to be used to protect the covenants of the League.

QUESTIONS

a) **Explain how the Covenant reflected the aims of the League of Nations.**

b) **President Wilson said that Article 10 was the 'heart of the matter and strikes at the taproot of war'. What do you think he meant and to what extent do you support his view?**

c) **Discuss the significance of Article 16: What did it aim to do? What methods were proposed to achieve this? Explain your answer fully.**

d) **Source A above claimed that 'the Paris Peace Conference gave little thought to the terms of the Covenant'. Discuss to what extent an analysis of the articles here supports this statement. Explain your answer fully.**

Three major instruments of the policy of the League were moral persuasion, economic sanctions and the use of military force. These three instruments were very important and you should analyze how effectively the League used them when learning about the League's interventions during the 1920s and 1930s.

- Moral persuasion implied the identification of a country's behaviour as aggressive and led to a diplomatic appeal for a change.
- If that failed, then economic sanctions were imposed on the aggressor.
- The last resort was the use of military force, for which the League had to rely on its members as it had no army of its own.

The absence of major powers – reasons and effects

Forty-two countries had joined the League of Nations by July 1920. For different reasons, the USA, Germany and Russia were not original members of the League. The USA never joined, although it did cooperate with several of the League's agencies and sent observers to some discussions. Germany became a member in 1926, but withdrew when Hitler came to power in 1933. Soviet Russia, which had been isolated from international affairs since the Bolshevik Revolution of 1917, only joined the League in 1934. Other original members of the League left, having a significant impact on the organization. Japan left in 1933 over disagreement with the League's treatment of the Manchurian Crisis. Italy left the League in 1937 after Mussolini's invasion of Abyssinia.

The absence of the USA

Despite President Wilson's efforts, the US Congress refused to ratify the Treaty of Versailles and also rejected membership of the League of Nations and turned to isolationism. Fear of being drawn into further European conflicts was an important reason for the American decision.

The League's opportunity to succeed was significantly reduced by the absence of the USA:

- The USA emerged from the war with its territory and economy unharmed and could therefore have assisted the League economically as well as militarily in the event of crises.
- Economic sanctions with US participation would have acted as an effective deterrent for any nation wishing to break the Covenant. Sanctions imposed by a League with US membership would have been more effective, as the sanctioned country would have been deprived of the US market.
- The US absence also contributed to the view that the League was a European club dominated by Britain and France.

Without the USA, Britain and France were indeed the strongest countries in the League. However, they had different views on what the role of the League of Nations should be. France wanted the League to be an instrument to enforce the treaties and prevent any revision that could affect her security. Britain, on the other hand, considered that some revision of the treaty might be both possible and beneficial and feared the application of sanctions that could affect her economic interests directly.

In spite of the decision to keep its distance from world politics by not joining the League of Nations, the USA continued to play a significant role in international relations after World War I. Chapter 2 focused on the disarmament conferences of which the USA was a part. Also, in the next sections, you will study the ways in which the USA became involved in European financial affairs.

SOURCE C

British cartoon 'The Gap in the Bridge', first published in *Punch*, December 1919.

SOURCE D

In all the League had to do during this first year of its existence it was profoundly affected by the refusal of the United States of America to become a member. It had been assumed that a project so American in origin and in its originality would, of course, be accepted in Washington. The news of its rejection in the United States created feelings of discouragement and even disgust in Europe… For a time men doubted if the League would go on without support from a great nation who was rich enough to salve [soothe] Europe's wounds and enough of a neutral to assuage [relieve] her jealousies. And then came second thought: the men of the Old World were forced to go on even though the New World's support was lessened by the absence of the most important New World nation.

From John Spencer Bassett, *The League of Nations – A Chapter in World Politics,* 1930

STUDENT STUDY SECTION

QUESTION

What, according to Source C was the significance of the absence of the USA in the League of Nations?

Student Answer – *Miguel*

The cartoon shows that the bridge has been designed by the USA, but is incomplete without it. The figure of Uncle Sam smoking shows that the USA is not affected by the decision.

Examiner's comments

The candidate has clearly identified three elements in the cartoon: 1) that the bridge has been designed by the USA; 2) that it is unfinished; 3) that the USA seems at ease with the situation. However, the question asks about the 'significance of the absence of USA' and this has not been the focus of the answer. Some elements that the candidate has omitted are very relevant to the significance:

- Look at the stone on which Uncle Sam is leaning and which is labelled 'Keystone'. Why do you think the author of the cartoon called it so? How does it reflect the significance of the absence of the USA?

- What, if any, is the significance of the fact that the gap is between the stones labelled France and England?

QUESTIONS

a) **Compare and contrast the views expressed about the absence of the USA in the League of Nations in Sources C and D.**

b) **In Chapter 2, you have studied the aims of Britain and France in relation to post-war Europe. To what extent were these ambitions consistent with the views they held about what the role of the League of Nations should be?**

● **Examiner's hint**
Source D mentions the effect in Europe of the US refusal to join the League. Does Source C refer to this point? When considering the contrasts between two sources, it is useful to look for any argument which is offered by one source and either omitted, or an opposing argument given by the other, but you will need to explain how the inclusions and omissions make the sources similar/different.

The absence of Russia

The year 1917 was one of turmoil in Russia. In February the Tsar was overthrown and a Provisional Government took control. In October that year, the Bolsheviks, led by Vladimir Lenin and Leon Trotsky, seized power. One of the reasons for continued unrest was Russia's participation in World War I, which ended under the Bolsheviks. Unrest in Russia soon turned to civil war as national opposition together with foreign intervention confronted the Bolshevik Red Army.

At the time of the Paris Peace Conference, Western nations were still fighting on Russian soil to prevent the consolidation of Bolshevism. The exclusion of Russia from the League of Nations in 1919 was based on the idea that Britain and France held that it would be better to isolate the new Bolshevik state, which was instigating communist uprisings in other parts of Europe. The Bolsheviks, for their part, saw the League as a capitalist club designed to contain the expansion of communism and shared with the Germans the idea that the League was an instrument to give moral authority to an unfair treaty.

SOURCE E

In its drive for security and de jure [legal] recognition, Soviet diplomacy again and again came up against the League of Nations. Here, as in other areas of diplomacy, the Soviets followed a dual policy: On the one hand they denounced the League as a coalition of predatory imperialist powers; on the other, they demanded to take part in such conferences of the League as affected Russian interests. The Soviet attitude towards the League had been influenced by the fact that Soviet Russia had not been invited to become a member, by the communist idea of capitalist encirclement, by the fear of any coalition or alliance of which Russia was not a member...

From Xenia Joukoff Eudin, *Soviet Russia and the West, 1920–1927: A Documentary Survey*, 1957

SOURCE F

Cartoon which reads in Russian *'League of Nations – Capitalists from all countries, unite!'* Artist unknown, c. 1917–20.

● **Examiner's hint**
(Question a) It is useful to start by explaining the meaning of the cartoon. What is the tone of Source F towards the League of Nations?

STUDENT STUDY SECTION

QUESTIONS

a) **Compare and contrast the views expressed about Russia's attitude to the League of Nations in Sources E and F.**

b) **How useful do you find Source F to be in explaining the reasons why the USSR rejected the League of Nations?**

The absence of Germany

Germany, like other defeated nations, was not invited to take part in the League. This decision overlooked the fact that, despite Versailles, the German capacity to recover had not been destroyed and Germany was still a strong European nation. As discussed in Chapter 2, Germany's eastern frontiers were a source of bitterness over the territories lost, but also a source of opportunity given the relative weakness of some of the new states east of Germany. Therefore, it can be said that the League would have benefited more by making Germany part of the new international order than by making it feel an outcast. Additionally, Germany's exclusion contributed to the image of the League as an organization of victorious countries. One only had to look at the membership of the Council to agree with that view.

German and Soviet isolation; the Treaty of Rapallo

Background information

The diplomatic isolation suffered by Germany and Russia brought the two former enemies closer together. They both resented post-war agreements and wished to see them revised. Germany's military pride had been shattered by the terms of Versailles and the country wanted to find a way to escape the control of the Allies and to strengthen its forces. The Russians wished to focus on their domestic problems rather than on the idea of exporting the revolution, a factor that contributed to the cooperation between the two states.

The Treaty of Rapallo (1922)

> *'Beware of throwing a hungry Russia and an angry Germany into each other's arms.'*
> Lloyd George, 1922

Disguised as a trade agreement between the two countries, the Treaty of Rapallo secretly addressed military cooperation and, as such, became a way to breach the Treaty of Versailles. The treaty was met with a mixture of surprise and indignation in Britain and France. The French government never believed the Russian reassurance that the treaty contained no secret industrial and military clauses and took a much harder line on its relations with Germany, an attitude that culminated in the French invasion of the Ruhr the following year. The alarm over Rapallo also reached Poland, who now saw her two greatest enemies united.

SOURCE G

In 1921 the Germans had begun a secret military collaboration with the Russians in whose land they could produce the tanks, airplanes and poison gas forbidden by Versailles and where they could train both Russians and Germans in their use. In April of the next year they signed the Treaty of Rapallo whereby Germany granted formal recognition to the Soviet Union and

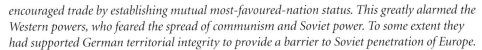

encouraged trade by establishing mutual most-favoured-nation status. This greatly alarmed the Western powers, who feared the spread of communism and Soviet power. To some extent they had supported German territorial integrity to provide a barrier to Soviet penetration of Europe.

From Donald Kagan, On the Origins of War and the Preservation of Peace, 1996

SOURCE H

The partnership between Berlin and Moscow confirmed the worst nightmares; the two great powers were in a position to stifle the successor states should they so wish. The challenge to the French security system was palpable; the threat to both Versailles and France's eastern alliances could hardly have been clearer.

Both the Soviet Union and Germany gained strength from their relations. Germany had an ally to the East and the USSR broke its isolation. During 1925–29 the Soviet Union and Germany signed treaties of both economic and strategic importance. Germany became the largest exporter to the USSR and produced weapons on Soviet territory.

From Zara Steiner, The Lights that Failed, 2005

STUDENT STUDY SECTION

QUESTIONS

a) **According to Source G, what were the aims of cooperation between Germany and the Soviet Union?**

b) **Using these sources and your own knowledge, assess the view that the diplomatic isolation of Germany and the Soviet Union brought more harm than good.**

● **Examiner's hint**

The answer to Question (b) should be presented as a mini-essay that requires some initial planning on your part. You need to remember that this is not an opportunity for you to write about everything you know on the topic, but rather one to show you can integrate the sources with your own knowledge and answer a specific question. When using sources, avoid general comments such as '… as seen in Source D' and quote or paraphrase the part of the source you refer to instead.

After 1923, relations between Germany and the West improved significantly as Europe lived a period know as the 'Locarno Honeymoon' (see pages 71–75 below). A significant event in that period was Germany's admittance into the League of Nations in 1926, to which it belonged until 1933. In 1934 the USSR joined the League of Nations. The reasons why the USSR seemed to have changed its negative view of the League of Nations and why the League accepted the incorporation are related to the changes in the international scenario of the 1930s, of which you will learn in the following sections.

Early attempts at peacekeeping (1920–25)

Background information

The early years of the League of Nations were ones of enthusiasm and hope. Membership grew steadily and the League's agencies were successful in several areas. Many countries set up their own League of Nations unions to support the League by spreading its spirit and raising funds.

But the work ahead was by no means easy. Many issues of border disputes presented before the League were either unresolved matters prior to the peace treaties or were created by the treaties. The League had to settle issues related to the enforcement of the peace treaties. Territories that had been put under the League had to be administered; the territories also needed to hold plebiscites to decide issues of self-determination.

The League had to co-exist with the Conference of Ambassadors, formed by Britain, France, Italy and Japan. This body was meant to act only between the signing of the Treaty of Versailles and the completion of the other peace treaties and until the League of Nations was fully ready to operate. However, the Conference not only continued to exist beyond then, but, in some conflicts, it overruled the League.

Timeline: Peacekeeping under the League of Nations

This timeline will help you identify some of the early attempts at peacekeeping by the League of Nations. It is not, however, a comprehensive catalogue of the League's work in international relations, as there were other conflicts in which the League also intervened.

1919	League of Nations founded
	Conflict over Teschen
1920	US Congress votes against membership of the League
	First session of the Council
	Conflict over Vilna
1920–21	Aaland Islands conflict
1921	Upper Silesia plebiscite
1923	Conflict over Memel
1924	Italian occupation of Corfu
	Conflict over Mosul
1925	Conflict between Greece and Bulgaria
1926	Germany becomes a member of the League
1931	Japanese invasion of Manchuria
1932	World Disarmament Conference starts
	War between Bolivia and Paraguay
1933	Japan withdraws from the League
	Germany withdraws from the League
1934	USSR becomes a member of the League
1935	Italian invasion of Abyssinia
1937	Italy withdraws from the League

It is important to study the League's early attempts at peacekeeping. Here are some examples.

The Aaland Islands (1920–21)

Although the Aaland Islands belonged to Finland, most Aalanders, ethnically Swedish, wanted to be ruled by Sweden. In 1921 Sweden and Finland took the issue before the League of Nations. The League decided not to make changes in the situation and recognized Finnish sovereignty, but promised it would protect the rights of the minorities. The decision, though not very popular, was accepted by all parties involved.

Vilna (1920)

The city of Vilna had been the capital of **Lithuania** when the state was first established many centuries ago. When Lithuania was restored as an independent country, Vilna was again to become the capital of the new Lithuanian state. Poland opposed this, arguing that Vilna should go to her as more than 30 per cent of the population of Vilna was Polish. Poland invaded Vilna and although Lithuania appealed to the League, the Poles did not evacuate the city. Finally, the Conference of Ambassadors awarded Vilna to Poland.

Upper Silesia (1921)

The rich coal area of Upper Silesia, inhabited by both Germans and Poles, was a bone of contention to both countries. The League of Nations carried out a plebiscite in March 1921 to decide to which country Upper Silesia should belong. The results favoured Germany, but were very close, leading to riots and confrontations between Poles and Germans. The

Lithuania

Poland and Lithuania were formally united in 1569. Russia, Prussia and Austria partitioned Poland in 1772, 1792 and 1795. With the 1795 partition, Lithuania was annexed by Russia, except for a small section in the south-west that was awarded to Prussia. This area was also incorporated into Russia in 1815. The Russians carried out a policy of Russification in Lithuania, enforcing Russian as the official language and repressing Lithuanian culture. Like the Poles, the Lithuanians rebelled against Russian control throughout the 19th century. Lithuania was occupied by Germany during World War I. In February 1918, Lithuanian nationalists declared Lithuania's independence, but the country soon faced the invasion of Bolshevik forces. The Lithuanian National Army forced the Bolsheviks out and in 1920 Moscow recognized Lithuanian independence. That same year conflict with Poland over Vilna broke out.

differences between Britain and France over the future of Upper Silesia also contributed to the conflict. While France refused to allow German troops to restore order and wanted Upper Silesia to go to Poland to strengthen her economy, Britain considered the result of the plebiscite should be respected and Upper Silesia incorporated into Germany. The matter was referred to the League of Nations, which split Upper Silesia between Poland and Germany, with more territory given to the former. The League's ruling was accepted by all nations involved.

Corfu (1923)

Italian members of a delegation working on an international boundary commission to settle disputes between Greece and Albania were murdered near the Greek town of Janina. Although this act could have been carried out either by Albanians or Greeks, Mussolini, the new Italian Prime Minister, blamed Greece. He demanded that the Greek government find those responsible and execute them and claimed that Greece should pay Italy compensation. When Greece refused, he bombarded and invaded the Greek island of Corfu. Greece appealed to the League of Nations, which determined that Mussolini should leave Corfu and that, after appropriate investigations, it would be determined whether Greece had to pay Italy compensation for the incident. Mussolini rejected the proposal and threatened to abandon the League. The matter was transferred to the Conference of Ambassadors who ruled in favour of the Italians. Italy received immediate compensation from Greece and abandoned Corfu.

Bulgaria (1925)

A clash between troops patrolling the border between Greece and Bulgaria broke out, resulting in the death of a Greek soldier. Greece invaded Bulgaria, who turned to the League for assistance. The League ordered a ceasefire and the Greek withdrawal from Bulgaria. Bulgaria was made to pay compensation for the act of aggression. The decision was accepted by both parties.

STUDENT STUDY SECTION

QUESTIONS

Study the examples above and, with your class, discuss the following questions:

a) **Which of the above would you consider successes for the League and which would you classify as failures? Explain your answer fully.**

b) **Which weaknesses of the League of Nations became apparent during these crises?**

RESEARCH ACTIVITY

From the timeline above, choose and research one conflict taking place before 1930 which has not been covered in this section. Assess the effectiveness of the League in dealing with it.

Section II:

The Ruhr Crisis (1923); Locarno and the 'Locarno Spring' (1925)

Background information

The enforcement of the peace treaties in the 1920s brought about confrontation in Europe, some of which was referred to the League of Nations for solution. In 1923, however, a crisis between France and Germany over the question of payment of reparations broke out, and France and Belgium invaded the German industrial area of the Ruhr in 1923.

After the Ruhr Crisis was resolved, international relations underwent a deep change. Several international treaties were signed with the aim of solving conflicts related to German reparations and some of the frontiers established by Versailles, as well as promoting collective security and rejecting the resort to war as an instrument to resolve conflicts.

We will now analyze the causes and results of the Ruhr Crisis and of the main diplomatic events of the period 1923–29: the Dawes Plan (1924); the Locarno Treaty (1925); Germany's admission to the League of Nations (1926), the Kellogg–Briand Pact (1928) and the Young Plan (1929).

The Ruhr Crisis (1923)

The end of World War I did not mean the end of the economic problems brought about by the war. During the early 1920s, global economic activity deteriorated as unemployment rose and productivity fell. Both victorious and defeated nations faced the effects of war and of the peace treaties. Countries that had economically benefited from the war, such as the USA and Japan, now encountered a world very much in debt and offering limited trading opportunities. New countries like Poland, Czechoslovakia and Yugoslavia had to confront the challenge of surviving as economic units. In this context, defeated nations began to experience difficulties in meeting the payment of war reparations.

Germany and reparations payments

In April 1921, the Reparations Committee announced the final figure of German reparations, 132 billion gold marks (equivalent to £6.6 billion). Germany was to pay 2 billion gold marks each year. It was not long, however, before Germany announced it found it impossible to pay such sums. Britain was prepared to accept the **moratorium** of reparations requested on several occasions by Germany. France, however, led by the former President and now Prime Minister Raymond Poincaré, rejected the proposal and began to explore ways in which they could ensure that reparation payments in kind were made.

In December 1922, Germany failed to pay and the following month French and Belgian troops invaded the industrial area of the Ruhr, adjacent to the Rhineland. The aim of the occupation was to force Germany to restart payment of reparations and to seize coal and timber as payment in kind.

The French occupation of the Ruhr

The occupation of the Ruhr was met with intense nationalism among the Germans. The government adopted a policy of **passive resistance** in the area that halted industrial production. Civil servants and industrialists were instructed not to follow orders from the French and a general strike was declared. The German government decided to support the strike by paying workers' salaries and compensating the industrialists financially for the loss. The French responded by imposing a blockade in the area and imprisoning workers who refused to cooperate.

Passive resistance and shortage of coal and exports put the German economy under extreme pressure. The government financed the crisis by printing money, a measure that soon led to **hyperinflation**. The value of the German mark plummeted, prices went up by the hour and family savings disappeared. The impact of hyperinflation on the German population was not only economic, but also social and political. Middle-class families

---

Moratorium ⓘ
An authorization to delay payment of money due, as by a bank or debtor nation.

Passive resistance ⓘ
Opposition to a government or occupying power by refusal to comply with orders.

Hyperinflation
Severe increase in general price levels of goods, causing a decline in purchasing power.

were among the most affected by the crisis, as their savings lost value and their economic activities saw a significant decline in profits. As a result, many joined those critical of the Weimar policies on both the extreme right and left.

STUDENT STUDY SECTION

RESEARCH ACTIVITY

The media worldwide exposed the effects of hyperinflation in Germany. Individually or in pairs, find one source that you think illustrates the effects of hyperinflation in Germany. With reference to its origins and purpose, discuss its value and limitation for an historian studying German policy towards the occupation of the Ruhr.

ToK Time

From the research activity opposite, share your source with the class. If the group was asked to select only two sources to illustrate the effects of hyperinflation in Germany, which would those be and why? Follow the guide:

- How did you make your choice and why?
- In what ways was the process used by the group similar and different to the way historians approach the problem of handling too much evidence?

What was the attitude of Britain towards the Ruhr Crisis?

Britain did not join France in the occupation of the Ruhr. The British government considered that only German acceptance of a status quo – as opposed to its imposition – could guarantee lasting peace. Britain also opposed any French attempt to dominate Europe and showed interest in the economic recovery of Germany. However, the British did not take explicit steps to oppose the occupation. Fear of war was a contributing factor to the British attitude.

SOURCE A

On 19 January the [German Chancellor] Cuno government ordered miners and railway workers to withhold their co-operation, hoping to make the occupation as costly as possible for France, undermining its finances and the franc on the foreign exchanges, and in the expectation that British and American diplomatic pressure would be brought to bear on Poincaré. This 'passive resistance' led France and Belgium to send in more troops and to extend their area of occupation… The number of occupying troops rose to 100,000. The French and Belgians were obliged to exploit the mines and operate the railways themselves. Nevertheless the French continued to exercise restraint which was criticised in France as a lack of forcefulness.

From John F. U. Keiger in Robert Boyce (ed.), *French Foreign and Defence Policy, 1918–1940: The Decline and Fall of a Great Power,* **1998**

STUDENT STUDY SECTION

QUESTION

According to Source A, what were the problems faced by France and Belgium as a result of the occupation of the Ruhr?

How was the crisis solved?

In September 1923, the new German Chancellor, Gustav Stresemann, was forced to call passive resistance off as a result of the collapse of the German economy. This move was sensed as a defeat by right-wing groups. Acts of violence broke out in several cities and Germany was placed under martial law. Yet Germany could no longer bear the burden of passive resistance and hoped for British and, perhaps, US intervention to solve the problem of reparations. The French economy had also suffered due to the cost of maintaining the occupation of the Ruhr. France's attempts to support separatist movements in the Rhineland and promote unrest in Germany had failed and there was no hope of either British or American support. Eventually, France joined negotiations to solve the crisis.

Raymond Poincaré

What were the consequences of the crisis?

It could be said that the French lost more than they gained from the Ruhr Crisis. If French action had been inspired by a feeling of isolationism, the invasion had only helped to strengthen such isolation. Although some material gains were made, the invasion confirmed to the British that France could not be trusted and that her actions were a significant threat to European stability. At home, Poincaré was attacked both by those who considered the occupation should have been extended, as well as by those who thought it had been a very risky policy that had done more harm than good to France.

Additionally, failure in the Ruhr taught France that it was impossible to impose the treaty by herself, which made the discussions on collective security that followed more productive. But ending French occupation was only part of the solution. The review of reparations was a step which, in the light of the situation in Germany, could no longer be postponed. The Dawes Plan (1924) addressed the issue of German reparations.

SOURCE B

It became clear that the occupation of the Ruhr constituted in fact a turning-point in the history of post-war Europe. It brought to a climax the Anglo-French conflict over the treatment of Germany and the application of the Treaty of Versailles; it signified the defeat of France and its slow subordination to British policy; it thereby pointed the way to the Treaty of Locarno and the resurgence of Germany… Lastly, the Ruhr occupation showed the inability of France, acting on its own, to produce any major change in the territorial integrity of Germany.

From Lionel Kochan, *The Struggle for Germany, 1914–1945*, 1963

● **Examiner's hint**
The key concept here is that of the Ruhr Crisis as a 'turning-point'. The source then continues to explain what issues made the Ruhr such a turning point. Carefully consider what the source says about each of the countries involved.

STUDENT STUDY SECTION

QUESTION
What, according to Source B, was the significance of the occupation of the Ruhr?

Dawes Plan (1924)

In 1924, the Dawes Plan – prepared by the USA, Britain, France and Germany – presented a new schedule for the payment of reparations and discussed the withdrawal of occupation troops in the Ruhr. The final figure for German reparations was not altered, but the annual payment figures were reduced. A two-year moratorium was granted and a loan of 800 million marks was made by the USA to Germany to help her overcome the crisis.

The Dawes Plan showed that, regardless of the US diplomatic policy of isolation, the nation could not turn its back on European economic affairs. American loans enabled Germany to pay reparations to Britain and France who, in turn, paid their war debts back to the USA. Between 1924 and 1930, Germany received in loans far more than it paid as reparations. The nation began to make reparation payments on time, but remained significantly indebted.

The plan contributed to stabilizing the economic situation for Germany, but many sectors of society saw it as an official acceptance of what they understood to be an unfair situation – reparations. This flow of money made European economies liable to crises if the USA faced one. If the USA stopped the loans to Germany, then Germany would have difficulties in paying France and Britain who, in turn, would have problems repaying their war debts. The following diagram illustrates the flow of capital:

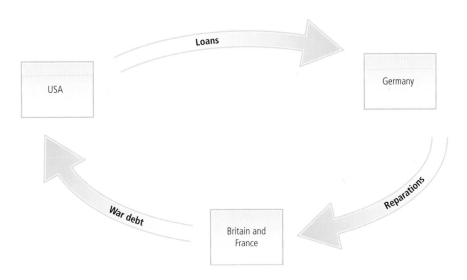

Young Plan (1929)

The Young Plan was designed as a continuation of the Dawes Plan to solve the problems caused by reparations.

- The Young Plan further reduced the total amount of German reparations.
- The Reparations Commission would no longer be able to impose sanctions.
- Like its predecessor, it contemplated extensive loans for Germany, linking the European economies to the USA even more.

Both the Dawes Plan and the Young Plan carried elements of potential instability in that they depended on foreign economic assistance to Germany. If the USA ceased to pour money into Germany, the European economies would suffer the effects. In turn, the payment of debts to the USA would cease.

STUDENT STUDY SECTION

QUESTION

'German reparations had a negative impact on international relations.' Using these sources and your own knowledge, evaluate this claim.

The Locarno Agreement (1925) and the Locarno Spring

Background information

The Ruhr Crisis marked the decline of the belief that the Treaty of Versailles could be imposed by the use of force. It was understood that policies of cooperation allowing some revision of the treaty would be more effective instruments to maintain peace in Europe. German inclusion in diplomatic talks and, eventually, its incorporation into the League of Nations, became a matter of discussions after 1923. This move partly responded to the idea that the nation would only contribute to peace if it accepted its terms, for which some revision of Versailles became necessary. Yet it was also hoped that the improvement of relations between Germany and its western neighbours would help to draw Germany away from the Soviet Union.

This section analyzes the relaxation of tensions following the Locarno Pact (1925) and the impact on international relations.

● **Examiner's hint**

Questions asking you to evaluate a claim expect you to give reasons as to why you agree or disagree with the view expressed. It is useful to ask yourself the following questions:

- Why could it be argued that reparations had a negative impact on international relations?

- What supporting evidence – either from the sources or my own knowledge – can I offer?

- Are there any reasons to claim they did not have a negative impact? If so, what are they? What evidence can I provide to support these claims?

Gustav Stresemann

The Locarno Pact (1925)

The Locarno Pact was a series of treaties signed by Germany, France, Belgium, Britain and Italy in 1925. The origin of the pact was a German proposal presented by Gustav Stresemann, now Secretary of Foreign Affairs, to accept Germany's western frontiers with France and Belgium in exchange for the withdrawal of foreign troops from the Rhineland. This proposal implied that Germany renounced its claims to French Alsace and Lorraine as well as Eupen and Malmedy in Belgium. Germany gained, on the other hand, assurance that events like the French invasion of the Ruhr would not occur again.

What were the terms of Locarno?

- Germany, France and Belgium promised to accept their 1919 frontiers as permanent and not to attack each other unless in self-defence.
- Any dispute over the terms was to be settled by the Council of the League of Nations.
- By the terms of the Treaty of Mutual Guarantee included in the Locarno Pact, Britain and Italy, as guarantors, agreed to come to the defence of any country victim of aggression in violation of these terms.
- Allied troops were to evacuate the Rhineland in stages and Germany was to apply for and take membership of the League of Nations.

What were the implications of Locarno?

- Germany renounced the use of force to recover territory from either France or Belgium.
- France had to respect German territorial integrity and abandon acts like the occupation of the Ruhr as well as any explicit encouragement of the separation of the Rhineland from Germany.
- France gained a guarantee of British assistance against a German attack. However, it was ruled that any major conflict would be directed to the Council of the League of Nations – where Germany occupied a permanent seat from 1926 – rather than allow direct British intervention. Therefore, British protection of France was not automatic.
- Locarno did not deal with Germany's eastern frontiers as Stresemann refused to recognize them as permanent. This meant Locarno was not to be equated to a German acceptance of all of the Treaty of Versailles.
- It did not benefit France's Eastern European allies as it would be more difficult for France to fulfil the terms of the Little Entente without violating German territory, thus breaking Locarno.

SOURCE C

For the German foreign minister, Stresemann, Locarno was the first step towards treaty revision, for his French colleague, Aristide Briand, it was the first step on the road to compliance; for the British foreign secretary, Austen Chamberlain, it was an assertion of British detachment. By guaranteeing the Franco-German frontier Britain implicitly repudiated responsibility for any other European frontier.

From Anthony Adamthwaite, *The Lost Peace – International Relations in Europe 1918–1939*, 1977

SOURCE D

The three powers had their reasons to be satisfied with their work, but the reasons were very different. Britain believed that France had been given sufficient reassurance so as not to be tempted to act foolishly as they had done in 1923. Germany saw the way open to revision for the eastern frontiers, eventually by force if necessary. France was lulled by such a comforting sense of security that it overlooked the fact that the country had undergone a serious loss of power and prestige.

From Martin Kitchen, *Europe Between the Wars*, 1998

STUDENT STUDY SECTION

QUESTION

Compare and contrast the views expressed about the Locarno Pact in Sources C and D.

Student Answer – *Karuna*

Both sources state that Locarno was a satisfactory Treaty and show that all countries gained from it. They both mention that Germany hoped for revision of Versailles. They both mention that France felt more secure after it. Both identify in Britain a sense of commitment, but also one of detachment.

However, Source D mentions German eastern frontiers and the possibility of German use of force. Source D mentions the French invasion of the Ruhr and the loss of prestige for France. None of this is stated in Source C.

Examiner's comments

The answer above provides some comparative structure – that is, the sources are not examined separately – as the candidate is trying to find ways in which they are similar and different. Similarities and differences are treated separately, which shows again a sense of structure and order. However, the use of the sources to support the similarities and differences found by the candidate needs to be made explicit. For each of the similarities identified in the first paragraph, the candidate should have included explanations of how and where the sources expressed similar views. The same could be said about the paragraph concerning the differences, which could gain marks by presenting other ways in which the sources differ. The student could have included a concluding remark summarizing how consistent the sources are in their views on Locarno.

ACTIVITY

Now that you have an opinion of the strengths and weaknesses of the answer, write your own response to the question.

Locarno was resented by the German nationalists, who felt Stresemann had acknowledged Versailles. It was also resented by those who did not want German foreign policy to upset relations with the USSR. It was therefore not easy for Stresemann to get the Reichstag (the German legislative assembly) to pass Locarno. However, it would be wrong to conclude that Stresemann had given up hopes to revise Versailles further.

SOURCE E

In my opinion there are three great tasks that confront German foreign policy in the immediate future. In the first place, the solution of the Reparations question in a sense tolerable for Germany, and the assurance of peace, which is an essential premise for the recovery of our strength. Secondly, the protection of Germans living abroad, those 10 to 12 millions of our kindred who now live under a foreign yoke in foreign lands. The third great task is the readjustment of our eastern frontiers; the recovery of Danzig, the Polish Corridor, and a correction of the frontier in Upper Silesia.

From a letter from Gustav Stresemann to the Crown Prince, 1925, taken from Anthony Adamthwaite, *The Lost Peace – International Relations in Europe 1918–1939*, **1977**

SOURCE F

Briand and Chamberlain tried to get [Stresemann] to guarantee Germany's eastern frontiers, but he would not agree to such undertaking. The most he would do was to state that the frontiers should not be altered by force, but he refused to put his signature to this promise… In fact, when Chamberlain informed the House of Commons that Germany had renounced the use of force in the east, he was promptly told by Berlin that this was not the case.

From Martin Kitchen, *Europe Between the Wars*, **1998**

● **Examiner's hint**

Many students jump into writing on the value and limitations of sources without having carefully considered their origins and purpose first. This is not just a repetition of the information about the source offered on the paper; you need to make your own deductions as well. For example, what does the fact that Source E is a letter to the Crown Prince say about the value and limitations of the source? How might it affect what is written?

STUDENT STUDY SECTION

QUESTION

With reference to their origin and purpose, discuss the value and limitations of Source E and Source F for historians studying German foreign policy in the Locarno years.

The Soviet Union witnessed the 'Locarno Spring' with great suspicion. The improvement of relations between Germany and Western Europe was seen as a factor that could throw the USSR back into isolation. The Dawes Plan was perceived as a capitalist strategy designed to delay a communist revolution in Germany. However, Stresemann believed that good relations with the West did not necessarily imply hostility towards the USSR and that the Soviets could offer Germany a guarantee in the East should Britain and France confront her in the West. At the same time that Germany joined the League of Nations (1926), the Treaty of Berlin was signed, reaffirming the Treaty of Rapallo for five years. As a new member of the League's Council, Germany agreed to abstain from any League measure to boycott the USSR or take arms against her under the obligations to Article 16 of the Covenant. Both nations guaranteed mutual neutrality in the case of an attack by a third power.

SOURCE G

The Pact of Locarno was concerned only with peace in the West, and it was hoped that what was called 'An Eastern Locarno' might be its successor. We should have been very glad if the danger of some future war between Germany and Russia could have been controlled in the same spirit and by similar measures as the possibility of war between Germany and France. Even the Germany of Stresemann was, however, disinclined to close the door on German claims in the East, or to accept territorial treaty positions about Poland, Danzig, the Corridor and Upper Silesia… Although our efforts were continued, no progress was made in the East. I did not at any time close my mind to an attempt to give Germany greater satisfaction on her eastern frontier. But no opportunity arose during these brief years of hope.

From Winston Churchill, *The Gathering Storm*, 1948

STUDENT STUDY SECTION

QUESTIONS

a) **According to Source G, which were the German claims in the east?**

b) **Using Sources C–G and your own knowledge, evaluate to what extent Locarno could be considered 'brief years of hope'.**

Student Answer (Question b) – *Jerome*

The Locarno Treaties were signed in 1925 by Germany, France and Belgium with Britain and Italy acting as guarantors of the agreements. The aim was to end disputes between France, Belgium and Germany by ratifying their borders of 1919. It opened a period of relaxation of tensions, for which it could be said to be a turning point in the inter-war period.

First of all, by the Locarno Treaty signatories renounced the use of force and recognized the authority of the Council of the League of Nations to settle disputes between them. Germany raised expectations for positive change. As stated in Sources C and D, Stresemann hoped that Locarno would initiate the revision of Versailles. France felt more secure thanks to the Treaty and particularly to the British guarantee as stated in Source D. Germany received promises for the quick end of the occupation of the Rhineland and was included in the League of Nations, which also brought significant hope.

There is some indication that Locarno did not change international relations for good and that it was only a peaceful interval after the Ruhr Crisis. The fact that Germany had vowed to respect her western frontiers exposed her weak, new eastern neighbours to greater risks. The Locarno years did not see any 'Eastern Locarno' (Source G) materialize. This is supported by Sources E and F. Also, the Soviets felt that Locarno had introduced an element of unrest in Europe as they feared Germany would give priority to the West and leave the USSR isolated again.

Examiner's comments

This answer uses both the candidate's knowledge and the sources to address the question. It also tries to look at the two sides of the issue, i.e. why Locarno brought hope and why Locarno introduced uncertainty. However, there are some very good points that have not been sufficiently developed to show the candidate's knowledge. Also, the use of the sources is not explicit; the candidate does not show the examiner exactly what part of the source referred to makes the point offered. It is important that you provide supporting evidence from the sources to make the point; this may be a sentence, a phrase or even a single word.

Kellogg–Briand Pact (1928)

Ten years after the end of World War I, the French Foreign Minister Aristide Briand proposed a treaty to the US government outlawing war between the two countries. Together with the American Secretary of State, Frank B. Kellogg, they agreed to 'the renunciation of war as an instrument of national policy'. This was extended to more than 60 nations.

The origin of the Kellogg–Briand Pact can be found in the principle of collective security. This treaty demonstrated the change in favour of collective security after the Ruhr; the idea that the best way to prevent conflict was if all nations acted collectively and renounced the individual use of force. However, the Kellogg–Briand Pact was little more than a statement of good intentions that contemplated no enforcement provisions. When Japan, Italy and Germany – signatories of the pact – breached the terms in the 1930s, nothing was done to reinforce it.

▲ Aristide Briand

◀ Frank B. Kellogg

SOURCE H

But, these treaties apart, the reality that we must not ignore if we do not wish to commit national suicide, the reality is this, my lords: that every country is arming itself! You should have no illusions about the general political climate in Europe. When the storm is approaching then it is that there is talk of calm and peace, as if because of a deep spiritual need. We ourselves do not wish to disturb the equilibrium in Europe but we must be prepared. None of you here, therefore, and nobody in the country will be surprised if, after a prolonged convalescence, I ask for another effort from the nation to bring up to scratch the forces of land, sea and air.

From a speech by Benito Mussolini to the Italian Senate, 6 December 1928, taken from E. G. Rayner, *The Great Dictators – International Relations 1918–39*, 1992

 ToK Time

- Do you think peace is a universal principle?
- Are norms and values capable of promoting international peace?
- What role do religious and cultural values, political beliefs and economic issues play in shaping a country's attitude towards peace?

SOURCE I

Cartoon by David Low, first published by *The Star* newspaper on 1 December 1925.

STUDENT STUDY SECTION

QUESTIONS

Read Source H and answer the following questions:

a) **What do you know about Benito Mussolini? What events have mentioned him earlier in this chapter? Do you consider this speech to be consistent with his actions in such events? Explain your answer fully.**

b) **To what extent is Source H consistent with Mussolini's role as guarantor of the Locarno Agreements?**

c) **What is the message conveyed by Source I?**

Student Answer (Question c) – *José*

Source I depicts Europe as a lady who has to cross a river and steps over stones to help herself. The stones are named after some international events of the inter-war period. She seems to have successfully used the Dawes Plan (stone) to advance. She is now standing on Locarno and hoping this stone will help her reach disarmament. The message conveyed is that Europe still has difficulties; that is shown by the fact that the lady has to cross a river and there is no shore in sight. The gap between Locarno and disarmament is very big and there is a risk that Europe may fall over. It is a message of hope in that some steps seem to have been successful (Dawes) but also, it shows that to reach disarmament, Europe will need to make a very big step.

Examiner's comments

This answer looks at all elements present in the cartoon (the woman, the river, the stones) and has interpreted each one of them to explain the message of the source. Pay attention to an effective approach for this particular type of question – a brief explanation of the elements followed by their interpretation.

QUESTIONS

a) **Compare and contrast the views about the future of Locarno expressed in Sources H and I.**

b) **Using the sources and your own knowledge evaluate whether international relations in Europe were more stable in 1928 than in 1923.**

Section III:

Depression and the threats to international peace and collective security: Manchuria (1931–33) and Abyssinia (1935–36)

Background information

The Great Depression marked the end of the atmosphere of international cooperation. The economic crisis caused by the collapse of the US financial markets in 1929 soon spread to American debtors as the USA started to call in their loans. In the world, productivity levels collapsed, **protectionist** policies were implemented and the **gold standard** abandoned.

The Dawes Plan and Young Plan had shown a larger involvement of the USA in European affairs, and America's entry into the Kellogg–Briand Pact had reinforced the US will to cooperate towards the goal of peace. However, the economic ties between the USA on the one hand and Germany, Britain and France on the other meant that what had started as an economic crisis in New York significantly affected the European economies and expanded the Depression to Europe and the world. The USA stopped the flow of money to Europe and began to ask to be repaid. Nations like Britain and France claimed they could not pay the USA back unless Germany paid them first. The greatest threat to international peace and collective security came from the social and political consequences of the Depression. The social unrest produced by situations of unemployment and low wages led to clashes between right and left political groups and to the rise of nationalist governments, which hoped to expand their frontiers to seize markets and raw materials.

The Depression marked the rise of economic protectionism, nationalism and international conflicts among the big powers. Japan saw the growing influence of a nationalist military in government, while the Depression contributed to the rise of Hitler and the Nazis in Germany. Italy – ruled by Benito Mussolini since 1922 – became a challenger of international order and adopted expansionist policies.

This section analyzes the causes of the Japanese invasion of Manchuria and the Italian invasion of Abyssinia and their effects on Europe, the League of Nations and international relations.

Protectionism
System of defending, promoting or developing domestic industries by protecting them from foreign competition through tariffs or quotas imposed on imports.

Gold Standard
Monetary system that backs its currency with a reserve of gold. The value of the currency of a given country under the gold standard is given by the amount of gold the country possesses.

The Japanese invasion of Manchuria (1931–33)

Background information

The dispute between China and Japan over the Chinese province of Manchuria needs to be understood in the context of the territorial changes that had been taking place in the region from the end of the 19th century. After the Russo-Japanese War (1904–05), Japan gained Korea, the Liaotung Peninsula containing Port Arthur, and the South Manchurian railway in China. During World War I Japan – an ally of Britain since 1902 – occupied former German colonies in the Pacific, which it received after the war. Like some other European nations, however, in the early 1920s the Japanese felt that their gains for their participation in the war were insufficient.

Despite feeling that it deserved more than it had obtained after World War I, Japan's position in the Pacific was still very strong. Neither Russia nor China could dominate Japan. In the 1920s, Japan's relations with the West produced a series of cooperative treaties such as the Washington Naval Treaties and the London Conference. An original member of the League of Nations, Japan joined the Kellogg–Briand Pact in 1928, renouncing the use of war. The country had clearly become an important player in international relations.

China, on the other hand, had been suffering internal problems and disintegration for many years. A combination of political instability and social and economic problems led many Chinese to turn to Marxism and follow the Bolshevik example. The Chinese Communist Party (CCP) confronted the nationalist Kuomintang (KMT) in a civil war that contributed to increase the weakness of the country.

STUDENT STUDY SECTION
RESEARCH ACTIVITY
Individually or in pairs, research the political situation in China and Japan in the years before the Manchurian Conflict.

Motives for Japan's aggressive foreign policy

The Great Depression brought the application of protectionist policies worldwide. Japan was at the time the world's largest silk producer, with silk constituting more than one third of her exports. These dropped nearly 40 per cent between 1929 and 1930 alone. The country's economy was also strained by a growing population, which challenged the nation's resources and made Japan dependent on imports it could hardly afford during the Depression. Moreover, Japanese immigrants were being turned away from countries like Australia and the USA as they became targets of anti-immigration laws.

The Depression brought political instability to Japan. The army – a highly prestigious institution in Japanese society – resented the government's decision to cut military spending in favour of disarmament. Right-wing sectors of the military were willing to rule and apply a policy of self-sufficiency to guarantee raw materials and space for their population based on the application of an expansionist policy. Manchuria produced almost half the world's supply of soya beans and had large supplies of coal and iron. These resources made it attractive to Japan for economic as well as strategic reasons.

SOURCE A

Behind Japan's urge to expansion are a number of impelling forces. There is the explosive pressure of rapidly increasing population in a land that is already overcrowded. There is the feeling of being unfairly treated in the world distribution of territory and raw materials. There is the exceptionally strong position of the fighting services vis-à-vis the civil authorities. There is the high-flown sense of nationalism, which for many Japanese has all the force of religious conviction. There is the mystical idea of Japan's Pan-Asian mission, very popular with retired army officers and nationalist theoreticians, which envisages Japan as the leader of an Asia from which 'white imperialism' has been banished.

From W. H. Chamberlin, *Japan over Asia*, 1938. Chamberlin was Tokyo correspondent for the *Christian Science Monitor* and author of books on inter-war Japan.

STUDENT STUDY SECTION
QUESTION
What, according to Source A, were the reasons for Japanese expansion?

The conflict

The Japanese presence in China was very strong. Victory in the Russo-Japanese War of 1905 had granted Japan the lease of the South Manchurian railway together with the right to protect it with a military force, known as the Kwantung Army. By the time of the outbreak of the Chinese Civil War in 1927, China received nearly 80 per cent of Japanese investment and seven out of 10 foreigners living in China were Japanese.

During the Chinese Civil War, many acts of hostility against foreigners and their interests in China took place. Inspired by Chinese nationalism, strikes and boycotts against Japanese companies and attacks on Japanese citizens in China became frequent and constituted a cause of concern for the Japanese. The Chinese authorities often did not investigate these incidents, which worried the Japanese as they feared for their assets and citizens in China. Other investors in China, like Great Britain, shared these concerns with Japan, which implied that at an international level, there was some sympathy for the need of Japan to protect its citizens and investments in China. Japan was viewed sympathetically also because it was considered a valuable ally against the communist expansion that now threatened China.

The Mukden Incident (1931)

On 18 September 1931, a bomb exploded near Mukden, on the South Manchurian railway. The Japanese accused the Chinese of sabotage. There is evidence to believe, however, that the Japanese planted the bomb themselves to cause friction with the Chinese. As a reprisal for the incidents, Japanese forces quickly advanced into areas of Manchuria beyond the railway. The Manchurian Crisis had begun. As a member state victim of an act of aggression, China appealed to the League of Nations.

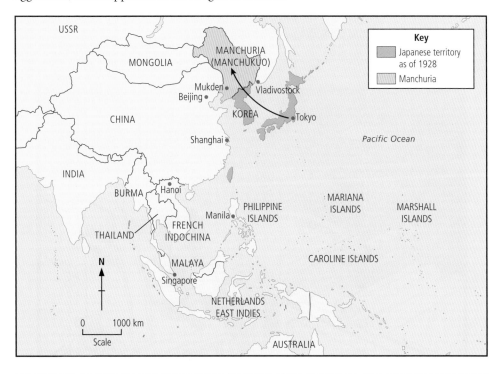

Map 5
Japanese invasion of Manchuria, 1931

SOURCE B

Although Japan has undoubtedly acted in a way contrary to the principles of the Covenant by taking the law into their own hands, she has a real grievance against China. This is not a case in which the armed forces of one country have crossed the frontiers of another in circumstances in which they had no previous right to be on the other's soil. Japan owns the South Manchurian railway and has been entitled to have a body of Japanese guards upon the strip of land through which the railway runs. Japan's case is that she was compelled by the failure of China to provide reasonable protection for Japanese lives and property in Manchuria in the face of attacks of Chinese bandits, and of an attack upon the line itself, to move Japanese troops forward and to occupy points in Manchuria which are beyond the line of the railway.

From a memorandum of Sir John Simon, Foreign Secretary, to the British Cabinet, 23 November 1931

ToK Time
How can it be determined whether an action that is defined as unjust by the international community is truly unjust? What elements could be considered in order to arrive at a decision?

STUDENT STUDY SECTION

QUESTIONS

a) **What is the attitude of the British Foreign Secretary towards Japan and China?**

b) **With reference to their origin and purpose, discuss the value and limitations of Source A and Source B for an historian studying the causes of the Manchurian Crisis.**

The League of Nations and the Lytton Report

The League of Nations was very cautious about developments in Manchuria and held several meetings to try to find a solution that would be fair to both the Chinese and the Japanese. Japan was a permanent member of the Council, while China had recently taken a seat as a non-permanent member. The USA, though not a League member, was invited to send representatives to the Council and attend the sessions, in which Manchuria was discussed.

While the Japanese government seemed willing to cooperate with the League, the Japanese Army continued to move across Manchuria. One thing became clear – the Japanese government no longer controlled its own army. These events prompted the League to send a Commission of Enquiry under the command of Lord Lytton (Great Britain) and formed from representatives of the USA, France, Germany and Italy.

SOURCE C

'Will the League stand up to Japan?' by David Low, first published by the *Evening Standard*, a British newspaper, in November 1931.

WILL THE LEAGUE STAND UP TO JAPAN ?

● **Examiner's hint**
To consider all the relevant elements in a cartoon, you can draw arrows identifying them and include brief comments to help you focus your writing about their meaning and significance. This should help you check that you have not left important elements out.

STUDENT STUDY SECTION

QUESTIONS

a) **Why do you think the USA was invited to form part of the Lytton Commission?**

b) **What is the message conveyed by Source C?**

It took months before the Lytton Commission arrived in the area to investigate the Manchurian incident. It then spent several months in the region gathering information and interviewing witnesses. These delays worsened the situation for China. While the Commission was engaged in fact finding, the Japanese Army continued its move across Manchurian territory, arguing that they were acting to protect their property and nationals from revenge by the outraged Chinese. By March 1932, Manchuria had became a Japanese puppet state called Manchukuo, with Pu Yi, the last Chinese Emperor, as ruler by name.

What were the conclusions of the Lytton Report?

The Lytton Report recognized that Japan had special rights in the region. It considered China was responsible for the deterioration of relations with Japan as its internal instability had affected Japanese economic interests. However, it rejected the use of force by the Japanese and refused to see this as part of 'police operations' to protect Japanese in Manchuria. Other conclusions of the Lytton Report were:

- It refused to recognize Manchukuo as an independent state and rejected the Japanese explanation that it was a result of independence movements in the region.
- It recommended that Japan withdraw its troops and recognize China's sovereignty over Manchuria.
- It recommended Manchuria adopt self-government while remaining under Chinese sovereignty.
- It recommended that Japan and China open negotiations.

STUDENT STUDY SECTION

ACTIVITY
In class, discuss to what extent the Lytton Report effectively addressed the causes of the Sino-Japanese conflict. Start by making a list of the causes of the conflict and, using information on the Lytton Report, decide to what extent the causes were addressed.

In February 1933, the Lytton Report was approved by all members of the League except Japan, who claimed that, in the past, many countries had used force against China and none had been condemned for it. In his address, Matsuoka, leader of the Japanese delegation, stated that Manchuria belonged to Japan by right and that Japan had created the prosperity of the region: 'Read your history. We recovered Manchuria from Russia. We made it what it is today.' Compromise over Manchuria – he said – was out of the question. Given that Japan and the League had very different views on the issue, Matsuoka stated that the Japanese government had reached the limit of their efforts to cooperate with the League with regard to Sino-Japanese differences. The Japanese withdrew from the League of Nations Assembly in March 1933.

The impact of the Manchurian Crisis on the League of Nations

- Even when the League of Nations had tried hard to determine fairly what had happened in Manchuria, and had approved the Lytton Commission report with full support from its members as well as US agreement, nothing changed for China. Confrontations with Japan on Chinese territory continued throughout the 1930s, with large-scale fighting breaking out in 1937.

ToK Time
'In Manchuria alone, we received approximately 1550 letters in Chinese and 400 letters in Russian, without mentioning those written in English, French or Japanese.' (Lytton Report as quoted in Manley O. Hudson, *The Verdict of the League: China and Japan in Manchuria; the Official Documents*, 1932)

- What does this source tell you about the difficulties in deciding 'what really happened' in Manchuria?
- How does this situation help illustrate some of the difficulties historians face in their research?

- Failure to prevent Japanese expansion in China improved Japan's economic and strategic position, as Japan gained access to timber, coal and iron resources, as well as suitable land for agriculture.
- Failure to address Manchuria collectively may well have encouraged Mussolini's invasion of Abyssinia in 1935.

Why was the League of Nations not effective?

- The Lytton Commission took very long to prepare their report. By the time their findings were presented, Manchuria had been turned into Manchukuo and was firmly under the control of Japan.
- Neither France nor Great Britain, the two most important members of the League, felt they could confront Japan. Any plan to engage in conflict against Japan would have clearly been met with hostile public opinion at home. Both countries were severely affected by the Depression, and either economic sanctions or military intervention would have put a lot of strain on their economies. Also, having interests in the Far East, there was some degree of sympathy with the Japanese, as the situation of chaos and civil war in China affected economic interests at a very sensitive time, due to the Depression.
- Although the USA played some part in the diplomatic efforts to solve the crisis, President Hoover made it clear that the USA would not use economic sanctions against Japan.
- The fear of communism, prompted by civil war in China, was another reason why there was little consensus about going to war against Japan, which was at the time viewed as a strong ally that could help contain the regional expansion of communism.

The Manchurian Crisis, however, also showed the weaknesses of other instruments of international diplomacy. Japan disregarded the Kellogg–Briand Pact and the Nine Power Treaty signed at the Washington Naval Conference in 1922, by which all signatories were bound to respect the integrity of China.

STUDENT STUDY SECTION

RESEARCH ACTIVITY

Refer back to the information on the Washington Naval Conference in Chapter 2 and explain why it is claimed that Japan violated the agreements reached at the Conference.

QUESTION

'Too little, too late.' Using these sources and your own knowledge, examine whether this is a fair judgement of the role of the League of Nations in the Manchurian Crisis.

Italian invasion of Abyssinia (1935–36)
Background information

After the Corfu incident (1923), Italian foreign policy under Mussolini underwent a great transformation as the country drew closer to the West. In 1925 Italy played a part in consolidating collective security by guaranteeing the Locarno Pact. In 1928, Mussolini joined the Kellogg–Briand Pact renouncing war, while in 1934 he helped prevent Hitler's expansion into Austria. Perceived as a valuable ally against Nazi Germany, Mussolini was invited by Britain and France to sign the **Stresa Front** in 1935 to contain German expansion. However, Italian foreign policy was about to take another sudden change. Later in 1935, Britain and Germany signed the **Anglo-German Naval Agreement**. Britain had not informed her Stresa allies of this intention. Not long after that, Italy invaded Abyssinia. By the following year, Mussolini had joined Hitler in the **Rome–Berlin Axis**.

Stresa Front
Britain, France and Italy formed a common front against Nazi Germany following Hitler's announcement of German rearmament.

Anglo-German Naval Agreement
This treaty allowed Germany to build a navy 35 per cent the size of the British navy. The agreement revised the disarmament clauses of the Treaty of Versailles and was a major triumph for German diplomacy.

Rome–Berlin Axis
An understanding between Hitler and Mussolini on cooperation in foreign policy.

● **Examiner's hint**
Take a few minutes to plan your answer before you start writing. You need to consider two aspects of the League's actions in Manchuria: (a) Why could it be said that the League did too little? (b) Why could it be argued that its eventual actions were 'too late'? Make sure you address both elements in the question and that you provide material from both the sources and your own knowledge for each. Remember to consider exactly what the League could reasonably be expected to do.

Why did Mussolini invade Abyssinia?

Abyssinia (Ethiopia) was an independent country situated between the two Italian colonies of Eritrea and Somaliland and ruled by Emperor Haile Selassie. In 1896 its army defeated an Italian invasion at the battle of Adowa. Mussolini sought to redress this humiliation, obtain overseas territories for Italy and transform it into an imperial power. Under the effects of the Depression in Italy, he developed an aggressive foreign policy aimed at gaining access to raw materials, markets and territory for the growing Italian population.

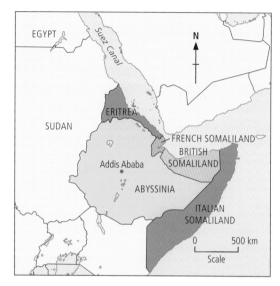

◀ **Map 6**
Abyssinia, 1934

▲ Benito Mussolini

STUDENT STUDY SECTION

QUESTION

Look at the map above and explain why you think Mussolini had interests in Abyssinia. Explain your answer fully.

In 1934, Italian troops provoked a clash at the Wal Wal oasis near the Abyssinian border with Italian Somaliland. Mussolini demanded from the Abyssinian government both the Wal Wal oasis and compensation for the deaths of 30 Italian soldiers in the incident.

Haile Selassie, the Emperor of Abyssinia, hoped that, should Italy attack, the international community would defend his country, which was a member of the League of Nations. Throughout 1935 he repeatedly asked the League to send neutral observers to arbitrate in the conflict with Italy. Mussolini, however, refused arbitration and began preparations for an invasion of Abyssinia.

In May 1935, an arms embargo was placed on both Italy and Abyssinia, aiming at preventing further escalation of the conflict. However, the arms embargo affected the Abyssinian Army far more than the Italian Army. Abyssinian forces could not obtain weapons, a situation that only served to stress the inferior position of the Abyssinian forces compared to that of the Italians.

Later that year the League declared that any discussion of the conflict would exclude issues of sovereignty over the disputed territories. Reluctance to discuss the issue of sovereignty denied Abyssinia the opportunity to use the instruments of the League of Nations and meant surrender to Mussolini's demands. Britain and France, acting independently, offered Mussolini territorial concessions in the region to prevent a war, but they were rejected. Yet this gesture showed the readiness with which Britain and France were prepared to make concessions to avoid war and probably only contributed to feed Mussolini's ambition.

▲ Haile Selassie

In October 1935, Italian troops invaded Abyssinia. The League declared Mussolini an aggressor and imposed economic sanctions in an attempt to deprive him of necessary goods and force the Italians out of Abyssinia. However, sanctions were not effectively applied:

- They took too long to be implemented.
- They excluded valuable goods such as coal, oil and steel.
- Not all countries respected the measure but rather continued to trade with Italy. Sanctions were not fully implemented by the USA and were ignored by Japan and Germany.
- Britain kept the Suez Canal open so Italy had ways to supply the troops in Africa.

One of the reasons why economic sanctions were not imposed more forcefully was British and French keenness not to lose Mussolini as an ally against Hitler. They feared that if the Italian economy was affected by the sanctions, Mussolini might decide to go to war over the issue, a chance they were unwilling to take. Mussolini considered it was unfair that sanctions were applied to Italy after the Japanese had not been punished for the invasion of Manchuria. He was aware of how important Italy had become to the Allies since Hitler's rise and was prepared to use that in his favour.

SOURCE D

The oil sanction was the crucial question. I have no doubt now that in their handling of this the British Government made a most serious mistake of judgement. By early December, most member states of the League had said they would support the embargo if others did likewise, and President Roosevelt was trying to put pressure on the American oil companies not to increase their exports to Italy. Some Ministers feared that imposition of the oil sanction would drive the Duce to war with us.

From a memorandum by Sir Anthony Eden in 1935, taken from *Facing the Dictators: The Memoirs of Anthony Eden, Earl of Avon*, 1962

SOURCE E

With Ethiopia we have been patient for forty years! It is time to say enough! In the League of Nations there is talk of sanctions instead of recognition of our rights. Until there is proof to the contrary, I shall refuse to believe that the real and generous people of France can support sanctions against Italy... Similarly, I refuse to believe that the real people of Great Britain, who have never had discords with Italy, are prepared to run the risk of hurling Europe along the road to catastrophe for the sake of defending an African country universally branded as a country without the slightest shadow of civilization.

From a speech by Benito Mussolini, 1935, taken from *Scritti e Discorsi di Benito Mussolini*, vol. IX

STUDENT STUDY SECTION

QUESTIONS

a) **What reasons does Source D give for economic sanctions against Italy being weak?**

b) **What is the significance of Source E for an historian studying Mussolini's policy during the Abyssinian crisis?**

c) **With reference to their origins and purpose, discuss the value and limitations of Source D and Source E for an historian studying the Abyssinian crisis.**

Student Answer (Question c) – *Dominic*

Source D is a memorandum by Sir Anthony Eden, who at the time served as British Minister for the League of Nations under Prime Minister Baldwin. It was written at the time of the crisis and published in 1962 in his memoirs. The purpose is to express his critical views about British policy towards sanctions on Italy and to explain that Britain had not been harder on Italy because some Ministers feared it would lead to a war with Italy.

The value of the source is that Eden was part of the British government at the time of the invasion of Abyssinia. As such, he provides an historian with valuable information such as the fact that Roosevelt was trying to contribute to the effectiveness of the embargo on Italy or that British Ministers feared war. We can also learn about his personal view on the issue, which becomes particularly relevant when we consider he was part of the government at the time and is nonetheless critical of the policies. Published in 1962, the source may have benefited from hindsight.

However, Eden admits the British made 'a crucial mistake'; he expresses his negative opinion on how the situation was handled and his stand could be taken as a limitation in his objectivity to present the evidence. The memorandum was published in 1962 in his memoirs. We cannot be certain that he has not altered it to reflect a better image of his role during the crisis.

Source E is a speech by Mussolini at the time of the invasion of Abyssinia. It is a primary source and it is therefore reliable. The purpose of the speech is to encourage the audience to support him in Abyssinia and to explain that it was a fair cause. The purpose is also to pass a message to Britain and France about how he expects them not to oppose him and to announce that, should they join sanctions against Italy, they may be 'hurling Europe to catastrophe'.

The value of this source is, as we have mentioned, that it is a primary source. We find out from Mussolini himself what his views about Abyssinia, France and Britain are. The limitation is that it could be propaganda and that the translator may have made mistakes.

Examiner's comments

The candidate has addressed all aspects of the question. However, the level of performance is better for Source D. Source D has been well handled, particularly in the comments the candidate has made on the origins and purposes. His own knowledge on Eden is used to make relevant comments on the usefulness of the source. (If there is anything relevant you know about the author of a source, use it in your source evaluation.) There's also awareness that although the source is a memorandum, it was published later in time, and the student links this issue effectively to the values and limitations. The candidate refers explicitly to what an historian studying the Abyssinian Crisis could learn from Source D.

Source E is not as well handled as Source D for two reasons. In the first place, the evaluation of Source E makes some assumptions that are not entirely supported/correct. Also, the time spent on D may have prevented the candidate from writing a more detailed evaluation of E. Although some imbalance can be allowed, make sure you have enough time to look at all aspects of both sources in similar depth.

One of the assumptions made in relation to E is that because it is a primary source, it is reliable. The first problem with this statement is that the question does not ask you to determine reliability, but usefulness. Next, there is no rule against identifying sources as primary or secondary, but you need to show explicitly how the nature of a source relates to its value and limitations. Avoid saying that a source is valuable because it is primary. It may be the case, it may not; it will largely depend on valuable 'for what'.

The second assumption made is that because this is a translation of the speech, it has limitations. Avoid these comments unless you have specific evidence that this is the case. It is something which could be said of many sources on exam papers and it does not necessarily demonstrate your skills to evaluate sources.

What were the reactions to the invasion of Abyssinia?

Italy was strategically important to Britain and France, the strongest countries in the League of Nations. If the organization was to act in defence of Abyssinia, it needed their full support. But they both had important reasons to want to prevent confrontation with Italy.

- Britain did not wish to engage in confrontation in the Mediterranean, because this might have affected her naval bases in Malta and Gibraltar. After the Japanese aggression in China, Britain wished to keep her navy strong for a potential conflict against Japan in the Pacific.
- A friendly Italy could also help protect the French Mediterranean coast. Additionally, in the event of war against Germany, a neutral Italy meant that there would be no requirement to station French troops in the Alps.
- Italy was a corridor through which French assistance could be sent to the Little Entente countries.
- Public opinion on both sides of the Channel was against war, and it played a part in determining the appeasing approach of Britain and France towards the conflict. Even within those groups ready to stand by the League, there was certain feeling that they were prepared to go, in Baldwin's phrase, for 'all sanctions short of war'.

SOURCE F

On 7 January 1935 Laval and Mussolini signed the Rome Agreements... The most controversial of agreements was a secret one on Abyssinia. With minor reservations France signed over to Italy her economic interests in Abyssinia. In a private conversation with the Duce, Laval used the phrase a 'free hand'. The Italian leader interpreted this gloss as meaning that France would turn a blind eye to the military conquest of Abyssinia, whereas Laval probably assumed Italy would stop short of war. No record of this colloquy was kept and the ambiguity was no doubt intentional.

From Anthony Adamthwaite, *The Making of the Second World War*, 1977

ToK Time

'Laval used the phrase a "free hand". The Italian leader interpreted this gloss as meaning that France would turn a "blind eye". Do you think there could have been a problem of interpretation? One of translation? Is the way we communicate more important between statesmen and diplomats than between ordinary citizens?

STUDENT STUDY SECTION

QUESTION

What, according to Source F, were the reasons for the Italian invasion of Abyssinia? What does Source F reveal about French foreign policy?

The Hoare–Laval Pact

In December 1935, in an attempt to solve the Abyssinian Crisis and appease Italy, Sir Samuel Hoare (British Foreign Secretary) and Pierre Laval (French Prime Minister) secretly offered Mussolini large parts of Abyssinia, some of which would come under direct Italian control and other under Italian economic influence. They proposed to compensate Haile Selassie by giving him territory from British Somaliland with an outlet to the sea. Details of the Hoare–Laval Pact leaked out the next day and there was public outcry in Britain and France at the double game their governments were playing by combining sanctions with the promise of concessions. It cost both Hoare and Laval their posts.

The following map illustrates the proposals made under the Hoare–Laval Pact.

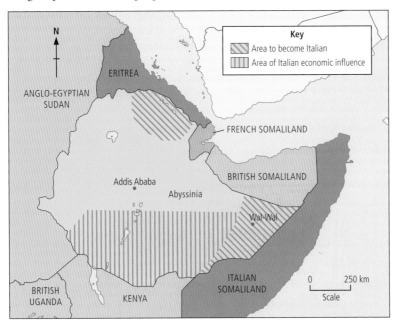

◀ **Map 7**
Proposals of the Hoare–Laval
Pact, 1935

SOURCE G

[To accept the British–French plan] would not only be a cowardice towards our people but a betrayal of the League of Nations and of all the States which have shown they could have confidence up to now in the system of collective security. These proposals are the negation and the abandonment of the principles upon which the League of Nations is founded. For Ethiopia they would consecrate the amputation of her territory and the disappearance of her independence for the benefit of the State which has attacked her. They imply the definite interdiction for her own people to participate usefully and freely in the economic development of about a third of the country, and they confide this development to her enemy, which is now making the second attempt to conquer this people. A settlement on the lines of this proposal would place a premium upon aggression and upon the violation of international engagements.

From a speech by Haile Selassie, taken from George W. Baer, *Test Case: Italy, Ethiopia, and the League of Nations*, 1976

STUDENT STUDY SECTION

QUESTIONS

a) How, according to Source G, would the League of Nations be affected by the Hoare-Laval Pact?

b) Compare and contrast the map of the Horn of Africa (page 83) before the invasion of Abyssinia with that illustrating the proposals of the Hoare–Laval Pact. Explain how this can help provide a better understanding of Source G.

Open confrontation in Abyssinia devastated the country, whose military resources could not match the Italian Army and Air Force. Italian troops massacred civilians, attacked ambulances and used mustard gas against Abyssinians in open violation of international conventions on warfare. Haile Selassie protested to the League about these violations and asked for the arms embargo to be lifted so that the Abyssinian troops could have access to weapons to fight the Italian advance. Nothing effective was done about this by the League, who admitted failure in the dispute in April 1936. Mussolini continued his advance and in May the King of Italy, Victor Emanuel III, was proclaimed Emperor of Abyssinia. The League abandoned economic sanctions.

SOURCE H

It is collective security: it is the very existence of the League of Nations. It is the confidence that each State is to place in international treaties. It is the value of promises made to small States that their integrity and their independence shall be respected and ensured. It is the principle of the equality of States on the one hand, or otherwise the obligation laid upon small Powers to accept the bonds of vassalship. In a word, it is international morality that is at stake. Have the signatures appended to a Treaty value only in so far as the signatory Powers have a personal, direct and immediate interest involved?

From Haile Selassie's appeal to the League of Nations, June 1936

SOURCE I

Cartoon 'On the Throne of Justice', first published by the *Evening Standard* on 24 July 1935.

ON THE THRONE OF JUSTICE.

STUDENT STUDY SECTION

QUESTION

With reference to their origins and purpose, discuss the value and limitations of Sources H and I to an historian studying the role of the League of Nations in the Abyssinian Crisis.

Effects of the Abyssinian Crisis

- The Abyssinian Crisis shattered any hopes that either the League or collective security could protect nations against acts of aggression.
- The Stresa Front ended and the relations of France and Britain with Italy became tense.
- Italy approached Germany, signed the Rome–Berlin Axis (1936) and abandoned the League of Nations (1937).
- There is a link between the Abyssinian Crisis and Hitler's invasion of the Rhineland, as the latter took place while the Abyssinians were suffering their last major defeat

in March 1936. As a consequence of the Abyssinian Crisis, Mussolini left the Stresa Front, which meant he would not join Britain and France in actions to stop Hitler. A. P. Adamthwaite also suggests that Hitler took advantage of British and French distraction over Mussolini and Abyssinia to send troops to the Rhineland. 'While Britain and France were distracted, Hitler made his first major territorial move, sending a force of 22,000 men into the demilitarised Rhineland' (Adamthwaite, *The Making of the Second World War*, 1977). The invasion of the Rhineland in March 1936 could have led Britain and France, scared of Hitler's moves in the West, to be more willing to negotiate with Mussolini over Abyssinia.

STUDENT STUDY SECTION

QUESTION

Using the sources and your own knowledge, assess the claim that the failure of the League of Nations should be attributed mainly to the policies of its most powerful members.

Summary

This section has focused on the attempts to apply the principle of collective security through the League of Nations and has assessed the successes and challenges for the organization by analyzing some of the early attempts at peacekeeping as well as the Manchurian and Abyssinian Crises of the 1930s. It has also analyzed significant events of the inter-war period such as the French invasion of the Ruhr. It has evaluated the impact of the Ruhr Crisis on international relations by analyzing the Locarno Spring period. Finally, it has assessed the effects of the Depression on international affairs. The Depression not only brought economic instability to world affairs. It also contributed to the rise of Hitler and the Nazis in Germany, the collapse of the Disarmament Conference in Geneva, the Japanese occupation of Manchuria, the Italian invasion of Abyssinia and Hitler's occupation of the Rhineland. In these conflicts, national interests were placed before collective security and the Covenant of the League was broken by its members, whether by acting against it or by failing to apply the instruments to keep peace through collective security.

REVIEW SECTION

Assess the importance of each of the following factors in explaining the weaknesses of the League of Nations:

- The absence of the USA
- The conflicts between Britain and France
- The withdrawal of Japan
- The policy towards the Italian invasion of Abyssinia
- The Locarno Spring and why was it short-lived

Add brief notes to the following bullet points to analyze how each of these events contributed to the development and outcome of the Manchurian incident:

- Wall Street Crash
- The role of the Lytton Commission
- Creation of the state of Manchukuo
- Japanese withdrawal from the League

Sample exam for Prescribed Subject 1: Peacemaking, Peacekeeping – International Relations 1918–36

These sources relate to the Treaty of Versailles, 1919.

SOURCE A

From Zara Steiner, *The Lights that Failed – European International History 1919–1933*, 2005

Germany was not destroyed. Nor was it reduced to a power of the second rank or permanently prevented from returning to great-power status. Outside of Russia, it remained the most populous state in Europe. With the disintegration of Austria-Hungary and the fall of Tsarist Russia, the application of the nationality principle left Germany in a stronger position than before the war. It was now surrounded on almost all its borders by small and weak states, none of which, including Poland, posed a danger to its existence… Germany's productivity capacity and industrial potential were left intact. Despite the loss of Saar coal and Lorraine iron ore, Germany remained Europe's 'industrial power house', able, in a remarkably short time, to dominate the trade of the central and eastern European states.

SOURCE B

From the private diary of Colonel E. M. House, advisor to President Wilson and member of the US delegation at Versailles

I am leaving Paris, after eight fateful months, with conflicting emotions. Looking at the conference in retrospect, there is much to approve and yet much to regret. It is easy to say what should have been done, but more difficult to have found a way of doing it. To those who are saying that the treaty is bad and should never have been made and that it will involve Europe in infinite difficulties in its enforcement, I feel like admitting it. But I would also say in reply that empires cannot be shattered, and new states raised upon their ruins without disturbance. To create new boundaries is to create new troubles. The one follows the other. While I should have preferred a different peace, I doubt very much whether it could have been made, for the ingredients required for such a peace as I would have were lacking at Paris.

SOURCE C

'The Easter offering', cartoon published in *Punch*, British magazine, April 1919. Cartoon caption: Mr Lloyd George (fresh from Paris). 'I don't say it's a perfect egg; but parts of it, as the saying is, are excellent.'

SOURCE D

From the *Deutsche Zeitung* (a German newspaper), 28 June 1919

Vengeance German nation! Today in the Hall of Mirrors at Versailles a disgraceful treaty is being signed. Never forget it! On that spot where, in 1871, the German Empire in all its glory began, today German honour is dragged to the grave… The German people, with unceasing labour, will push forward to reconquer that place among the nations of the world to which they are entitled. There will be vengeance for the shame of 1919.

SOURCE E

From David A. Andelman, *A Shattered Peace – Versailles 1919 and the Price We Pay Today*, 2008

In the end, Versailles proved a colossal failure for Woodrow Wilson, for the United States, and for the future of a world that had hoped it might be governed by principles of freedom and self determination – even today… Covenants of peace were not openly arrived at. Freedom of the seas was not secured. Free trade was not established in Europe; indeed, tariff walls wound up being erected, higher and more numerous than any yet known. National armaments were not reduced. German colonies and the land of its allies, Austria Hungary and the Ottoman Empire, were distributed among the victors as spoils – from the Saar to Shantung, from Serbia to Syria – the wishes, to say nothing of the interests, of their population flagrantly disregarded. Russia was not welcome in the society of nations… Territorial settlements in almost every case were mere adjustments and compromises between the claims of rival states. Even the old system of secret treaties remained untouched.

STUDENT STUDY SECTION

QUESTIONS

1a) **What, according to Source E, were the reasons why Versailles proved 'a colossal failure'?**

1b) **What message is conveyed by Source C?**

2) **Compare and contrast the views expressed in Sources A and B about the Treaty of Versailles.**

3) **With reference to their origin and purpose, discuss the value and limitations of Source D and Source E for historians assessing the Treaty of Versailles.**

4) **'The Treaty of Versailles was too harsh.' Using these sources and your own knowledge, assess the validity of this claim.**

Prescribed Subject 2:
The Arab-Israeli Conflict 1945–79

PALESTINE AND ISRAEL 1945–56

This Prescribed Subject addresses the development of the Arab-Israeli conflict from 1945 to 1979. You will need to know and understand the importance of the role played by foreign powers in the conflict. You will also need to be able to understand the background to the conflicts and be aware of the causes and consequences of the four wars between the Arabs and the Israelis, which occurred in 1948, 1956, 1967 and 1973. You will also have to be aware of the various political, social and economic issues that have arisen between the Palestinians, the Arabs and the Israelis and how these have affected the inhabitants of the region. Also covered is the nature and extent of social and economic developments within the territory of Palestine/Israel within the time period and their impact on their respective populations. Although the end date for the Prescribed Subject is 1979, it will be useful for you to study what has happened since 1979 in order to decide whether or not any of the issues that led to the first war between the Arabs and the Israelis in 1948 have been resolved.

This particular chapter will discuss the historical and religious background to the Arab-Israeli conflict and analyze the consequences of World War I on the region. It will then examine the reasons behind the creation of the State of Israel in 1948 and the consequences this had for Zionists, Palestinians and Arabs. Finally, this chapter will look at the reasons behind the outbreak of the 1956 Suez War and the consequences that this crisis had for the Middle East.

Timeline – 66 CE –1956

Note: CE = Common Era

66–73	Romans destroy Jerusalem
570	Mohammed, prophet of Islam, born in Mecca
638	Jerusalem and Palestine under Islamic rule
1896	*The Jewish State* is published by Theodor Herzl
1897	First Zionist Congress in Basle
1914	Outbreak of World War I
1915	McMahon–Hussein Letters
1916	Sykes–Picot Agreement
1917	The Balfour Declaration promises a national home for the Jews in Palestine
1918	World War I ends
1920	San Remo Conference – mandates approved
1921	Transjordan, the eastern part of Mandatory Palestine, promised to Abdullah
1923	League of Nations approval of British and French mandates
1929	Wailing Wall riots
1933	Hitler becomes Chancellor of Germany
1935	Nuremberg Laws passed in Germany
1936	The Arab Revolt breaks out in Palestine
1937	The Peel Commission visits Palestine
1938	Peel promises a two-state solution
1939	The Mufti rejects the White Paper that promises Arab control over immigration
1940	Stern Gang formed

1942	The systematic mass extermination of Jews commences in occupied Europe
	Biltmore Conference in New York
1945	League of Arab States formed
1946	Anglo-American Committee of Inquiry report published
1947	UNSCOP Report: second partition of Palestine into Jewish and Arab states
1948	Arab-Israeli War: the State of Israel proclaimed by the Jews during the War of Independence
	The Nakba brings defeat, flight, expulsion and exile for many Palestinian Arabs
1949	First Israeli elections – Ben-Gurion becomes Prime Minister
1950	France, Britain and the USA agree to restrict arms sales to Middle East
1952	Officer's coup in Egypt
1954	Nasser becomes leader of Egypt
1955	Gaza Raid
	Czech Arms Deal
1956	Suez Crisis; Eisenhower Doctrine

Section I:
Context and background for the Arab-Israeli conflict

There have been many explanations given for the conflict between the Arabs and Israelis over what will be called Palestine in these chapters, a conflict that developed after 1945. The two most common explanations have to do with a) 'who was there first', i.e. who has the claim of territorial ownership of the land, and b) claims based on religious books such as the Bible, the **Torah** and the **Koran**.

Around 1000 BCE, a Kingdom of Israel was formed through a merging of 12 tribes under one king, Saul. This kingdom later split into two, with Judah in the south and Israel in the north. These kingdoms were invaded by the Assyrians and, over time, the two kingdoms attempted several revolts with the result that, in 586 BCE, many Jews from Judah were exiled to Syria. When this Babylonian kingdom was overthrown by Persia, the Jews returned to Judah and established the province of Judaea around 330 BCE. In 63 BCE, Judaea was invaded by the Romans and in 70 CE, after a Jewish revolt, Jerusalem was taken and its Temple was destroyed. The Romans' punishment for the uprising was merciless. Thousands were killed. The name Judaea was banned and the land became known as Syria Palaestina, which is where the name Palestine comes from. Many Jews were forced to leave in the **Diaspora** and no Jew was allowed to live in Jerusalem.

While this was happening, other descendants of Canaan (the ancient territory that encompassed Palestine) were co-existing alongside the Jewish people. Thus, these descendants that we term 'Palestinian' today are also descended from the Canaanites. In the words of Gregory Harms: 'Palestinian is a regional ethnic term for a people who have lived in the land of Palestine for thousands of years… The Palestine-Arab culture of today is a result of a later seventh century influx of Arab tribes who brought with them the religion of Islam' (*The Palestine-Israel Conflict*, 2005). (For an excellent historical overview of this subject see Chapter 1 in Harms' book.) By the end of the 7th century, the Arabs controlled Palestine.

The religious claims to Palestine based on Christianity, Judaism and Islam are easy to trace. The Bible states that Abraham had two sons. The first was Ishmael, through Hagar his slave, as his wife Sarah believed that she was barren. The second was Isaac through Sarah. God promised to give the land of Canaan (Palestine) to 'the child of

 Torah
The Torah (Hebrew for 'learning') is the most sacred writing in the Jewish religion. It is also known as the Pentateuch or Five Books of Moses, which basically corresponds to Genesis, Exodus, Leviticus, Numbers and Deuteronomy (these are anglicized from the Hebrew names) in the Old Testament. The exact date of its origin is not known, but it is believed to have been compiled around 500–330 BCE.

Koran
The Koran or Qur'an (Arabic for 'the recitation') is the major religious text in Islam. Islam maintains that the Koran was retold to the prophet Muhammed by the angel Jibrīl (Gabriel) between 610 and 632 CE. It was initially retold by word of mouth and became a written text around 650 CE.

Diaspora
The dispersion of the Jews in the Roman Empire.

 ToK Time
What is an historical fact? Most Europeans know that the battle of Hastings took place in AD 1066 (AD is now often termed Common Era or CE). But this simple statement has a few problems. First, the battle took place a few kilometres away from Hastings at a site called Senlac Hill. Second, the date 1066 is actually inaccurate, as it is based on a dating system that was changed in the 18th century. Third, the term AD or CE is a Christian dating system that has little relevance in a world that is predominantly non-Christian. How does this simple analysis influence what you take to be an historical fact?

promise' – Isaac's descendants (Galatians 12:4–7). The problem is that the Koran teaches that Ishmael was 'the child of promise' (Sura 19:54) and so Muslims believe that God's promises were meant for Ishmael's descendants, not Isaac's. The prophet Muhammed was descended from Ishmael and so Muslims seek to lay claim to these covenant promises, namely the land of Palestine.

What is clear is that there has been no continuous dispute between the Arabs and the Israelis since ancient times. The conflict that exists today is essentially a modern conflict involving Arab and Jewish nationalism, with its roots in the late 19th and early 20th century. The origin of Jewish nationalism, or **Zionism**, in Western Europe is usually traced back to the publishing in 1896 of *The Jewish State* by **Theodor Herzl**. Zionism had existed among the Jews of Poland and Russia beforehand, but Herzl popularized the idea of the founding of a Jewish state. The Ottoman Empire had controlled Palestine for centuries, although there had been some Jewish emigration in the 1880s. Herzl's proclamation of the Basle Declaration at the First Zionist Congress in Basle 1897 defined Zionism's aim as follows: 'Zionism seeks for the Jewish people a publicly recognized legally secured homeland in Palestine.'

The Congress resolved, among other decisions, to implement the following:

2. *The organization and uniting of the whole of Jewry by means of appropriate institutions, both local and international, in accordance with the laws of each country.*

3. *The strengthening and fostering of Jewish national sentiment and national consciousness.*

4. *Preparatory steps toward obtaining the consent of governments, where necessary, in order to reach the goals of Zionism.*

The effect of World War I on the region

It would take 50 years for Herzl's dream of an Israeli state to become reality, and only after a lengthy and bloody struggle. The catalyst for the establishment of Israel is to be found in the outbreak of World War I in 1914 and its consequences after 1918.

During World War I, the Ottoman Empire was allied to the Central Powers of Germany and Austria-Hungary against Britain, France and Russia. It became obvious to these three Allied powers that any attempt to destabilize the Middle East would seriously weaken the Ottoman Empire's military capability. In addition, the recent discovery of oil reserves in the region gave the **Triple Entente** further motivation to try to get the Arab tribes to rise up against their enemy and become independent. In 1915, Henry McMahon, the British High Commissioner for Egypt between 1915 and 1917, promised **Sharif Hussein** that 'Great Britain is prepared to recognize and support the independence of the Arabs in all the regions within the limits demanded by the Sharif of Mecca.' The Arabs took the 'regions' to include Palestine, and in June 1916 they declared war on the Ottoman Empire. Secretly, however, in October 1916 Britain and France, in the **Sykes–Picot Agreement**, decided that they would divide the land occupied by the Ottoman Empire between themselves after the end of the war.

At the same time, Britain began to realize that support from Zionist sympathizers for the Allies would be a tremendous help in a war that had dragged on far longer than any of its participants believed would be the case in August 1914. By 1917, Britain needed money and, with the entry into the war of the USA in April, it was realized that more than four million Jews living on its east coast might provide a source of income to finance the war. On

Zionism
A nationalistic Jewish movement. In these chapters the term is used to describe those who wanted the establishment of a Jewish state in Palestine.

Theodor Herzl
An Austro-Hungarian Jew, who is considered by many to be the father of modern-day Zionism. Influenced by the anti-Semitism he saw in France as a result of the 1894 Dreyfus affair, Herzl decided that the only solution to discrimination against Jews was to push for the existence of a national state – a homeland for the Jewish people. Herzl believed that this could only be resolved internationally through political pressure with the result that, after the publication of his ideas in *Der Judenstaat* (1896), he called for an international meeting in Basle in 1897 to discuss his ideas. This meeting was to lay down the fundamental requirements for the creation of a modern Jewish state.

Triple Entente
Agreement between France, Britain and Russia, signed in 1907. It opposed the Triple Alliance of Germany, Austria-Hungary and Italy signed in 1882 and created a dangerous 'Armed Camp' in Europe whereby conflict between any member of the Alliance against a member of the Entente would involve all of the other powers. It was to be one of the main causes of World War I.

2 November 1917, the following declaration was sent by the British Prime Minister to Lord Rothschild, one of the foremost British Zionists.

SOURCE A

Dear Lord Rothschild,

I have much pleasure in conveying to you, on behalf of His Majesty's Government, the following declaration of sympathy with Jewish Zionist aspirations which has been submitted to, and approved by, the Cabinet.

His Majesty's Government view with favour the establishment in Palestine of a national home for the Jewish people, and will use their best endeavours to facilitate the achievement of this object, it being clearly understood that nothing shall be done which may prejudice the civil and religious rights of existing non-Jewish communities in Palestine, or the rights and political status enjoyed by Jews in any other country.

I should be grateful if you would bring this declaration to the knowledge of the Zionist Federation.

Yours sincerely,

Arthur James Balfour

This letter became known as the Balfour Declaration. When World War I ended in November 1918 with the defeat of the Central Powers, including the Ottoman Empire, the British government had to decide which of the three contradictory statements they had made would be their policy. Not surprisingly, both the Arab leaders and the Zionists believed that Palestine had been promised to them. Britain and France had already decided that they would take over the territories, as proposed under the Sykes–Picot agreement, ignoring Arab and Zionist claims. The seeds of the Arab-Israeli conflict had been sown.

The League of Nations and the Mandated Territories

The future of the defeated Central Powers was decided at the Paris Peace Conferences that were held between 1919 and 1923. One decision, based on a memorandum written by **General Jan Smuts**, was that some form of territorial adjustment was needed to deal with the territories that belonged to Austria-Hungary, Russia and Turkey. Smuts proposed that these should be put under the administration of the League of Nations. His plan met with some objections, although the principle of a mandate (stemming from the Latin *mandatum*, where property was entrusted to people for safekeeping) was adopted for Germany's former colonies and the non-Turkish parts of the Ottoman Empire. As we saw in Chapter 2, Article 22 of the Covenant of the League of Nations set up three types of mandated territory, which later became known as the A, B and C Mandates.

 Sharif Hussein
Sharif and later Emir of Mecca, the Muslim holy city, between 1908 and 1917. During World War I, the Turkish-dominated Ottoman Empire allied with the Central Powers against the Triple Entente. Sharif Hussein allied with the British and French, initiating the Great Arab Revolt in June 1916 against the Ottomans with the idea of creating an independent and unified Arab state in the Middle East.

Sykes–Picot Agreement
An agreement named after a British and a French diplomat, who signed the agreement that determined British and French spheres of influence in the Middle East.

 Jan Smuts
Smuts was a Prime Minister of South Africa between 1919 and 1924 and later from 1939 until 1948.

STUDENT STUDY SECTION

QUESTION
Look back at the Article 22 quotation in Chapter 2 (page 45). What are some difficult words? It is important that you understand what the implications of the League of Nations mandates were to be. Look up any word you do not know and then attempt to paraphrase in three or four sentences the intention behind the setting up of mandates.

The mandatory power had the 'dual mandate' of administering the territory and ensuring that all nations had equal access to these territories. At a 'Supreme Council' meeting in San Remo attended by Britain, France, Italy and Japan on 25 April 1920, it was decided that France would be given mandates over Syria and Lebanon, while Britain was to receive the mandates over Transjordan, Iraq and Palestine. Britain and France were to report regularly to the Mandates Commission of the League of Nations (see Map 8).

Map 8
European mandates in the Middle East, 1920.

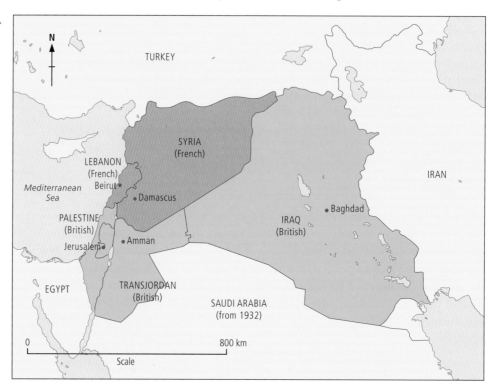

Thus, Britain and France went back on the promises they had made during World War I and, in essence, adopted the Sykes–Picot Plan of 1916.

Britain found itself in something of a dilemma, as it was responsible for ensuring freedom and security for the Jews but guaranteeing the Arabs that there would not be a major flood of Jewish immigration. The mandate clearly reflected the Balfour Declaration of 1917, with its promise of a 'National Home for the Jewish People' allowing Jewish immigration into Palestine. It also required that Britain establish two self-governing bodies, one for the Jews and one for the Arabs. **Autonomy** would naturally favour the Arabs as they comprised the majority of the population. In 1918 Gilbert Clayton, the head of British Military Intelligence, estimated that there were 512,000 Muslims, 61,000 Christians and 66,000 Jews in Palestine. Any establishment of a self-governing Arab state would certainly prohibit the establishment of a Jewish state in Palestine. The contradictory attitude of the British government is best represented by George Curzon, its Foreign Secretary, who wrote in 1920:

Autonomy
Independent self-rule.

> *The Zionists are after a Jewish state with the Arabs as hewers of wood and drawers of water. So are many British sympathizers with the Zionists. Whether you use the word Commonwealth or State that is what it will be taken to mean. That is not my view. I want the Arabs to have a chance and I don't want a Hebrew State.*

From Ritchie Ovendale, *The Origins of the Arab-Israeli Wars*, 2004

In June 1922, a White Paper was published by the British government and passed by the House of Commons. It was to be the basis of British policy towards Palestine for the next 10 years.

SOURCE B

Unauthorized statements have been made to the effect that the purpose in view is to create a wholly Jewish Palestine. Phrases have been used such as that Palestine is to become 'as Jewish as England is English'. His Majesty's Government regard any such expectation as impracticable and have no such aim in view. Nor have they at any time contemplated, as appears to be feared by the Arab delegation, the disappearance or the subordination of the Arabic population, language, or culture in Palestine. They would draw attention to the fact that the terms of the Declaration referred to do not contemplate that Palestine as a whole should be converted into a Jewish National Home, but that such a Home should be founded 'in Palestine'.

From the White Paper of 1922

STUDENT STUDY SECTION
QUESTION
What is the White Paper actually saying? Write it out in your own words.

This White Paper responded to some Arab concerns that had resulted in Arab uprisings in 1920 and 1921. Yet it also disappointed Zionist hopes for a national home, particularly as Churchill had identified Palestine as being west of the River Jordan with the creation of a separate Transjordan under the leadership of **Abdullah** (see Map 8). The Zionists somewhat reluctantly agreed to the White Paper, but it was rejected by Arab nationalists because of its acceptance of the principles behind the 1917 Balfour Declaration. Between 1922 and 1928 there was relative calm in the region. Jewish immigration did increase, although not to the extent that the Arabs had feared, as many Jews preferred to emigrate to the USA instead. By 1929 there were approximately 150,000 Jews in a total population of 990,000 in Palestine.

The British mandate between 1922 and 1939

Between 1922 and 1928, the status of Transjordan under the mandate was resolved. After 1922, Britain administered the part west of the River Jordan as Palestine, and the part east of the Jordan as Transjordan, although legally they were part of a joint mandate. In May 1923, Transjordan was granted limited independence, but by 1928 Transjordan was still not fully independent, as the British still maintained some administrative control there. A key factor behind this decision was the building of an oil pipeline from Iraq through Transjordan to ports in Palestine. This situation continued until 1946, when Transjordan became fully independent under the rule of King Abdullah and, after the 1948 war, Transjordan was renamed the Hashemite Kingdom of Jordan.

Iraq was the only British mandate to become fully independent between 1920 and 1935. In 1929, Britain made a recommendation to the League that Iraq should be released from the mandate and be allowed to become an independent state. The Mandates Commission appointed a committee to investigate whether Iraq met the conditions for statehood, having sufficient financial resources to provide a functioning government. On 3 October 1932, the mandate in Iraq ended and the country became a fully fledged member of the General Assembly of the League of Nations.

Meanwhile, in Palestine the relative calm was ended by riots in Jerusalem. The British, on the request of the Arabs, had removed a screen at the **Western Wall** in Jerusalem. The screen had been placed there to separate Jewish worshippers by gender, and its removal led to serious clashes between Jews and Arabs. By August 1929, 133 Jews and 116 Arabs had been killed and Jewish settlements in Hebron had been attacked. The British sent two commissions to investigate, which concluded that Arab concern at the extent of Jewish immigration into Palestine was the root of the problem. The commission suggested limiting

Abdullah
Abdullah was the ruler of the British mandate Transjordan, and later Jordan, between 1921 and 1951. He was the son of Sharif Hussein and played an important part in the 1916 Great Arab Revolt against Ottoman rule. Abdullah was eventually assassinated by a Palestinian who feared that he was intending to negotiate a peace with Israel after the creation of the Israeli state in 1948.

The Western Wall
The Western Wall refers to a section of an ancient wall situated on the western flank of the Temple Mount in the Old City of Jerusalem. It is sometimes referred to as the 'Wailing Wall' and is one of the most important Jewish religious sites. In around 19 BCE Herod began a massive temple-building project on the Temple Mount. This temple was mostly destroyed by the Romans along with the rest of Jerusalem in 70 CE, leaving the Western Wall standing.

Jewish immigration to 20,000 per year. This outraged the Zionists, eventually causing the British government to withdraw the proposal. The reversal of the immigration policy by the British was greeted by the Arabs with dismay.

In January 1933, **Adolf Hitler** came to power in Germany and passed the **Enabling Act** of March 1933, establishing his Nazi dictatorship with its clearly anti-Semitic policies, as outlined in Hitler's book *Mein Kampf*. Hitler began to exclude Jews from many areas of public life and by 1935, after the proclamation of the 'Reich Citizenship Act' and the 'Law for the Protection of German Blood and Honour' at Nuremberg, it was clear that more extreme anti-Semitic measures were to follow. There resulted a wave of Jewish emigration that, accompanied by further anti-Semitism in Poland and Romania, led to a flood of refugees. The USA placed restrictions on the number of Jews allowed into the country, which meant that Palestine became the only option for many emigrants. By 1936 Jewish immigration into Palestine had resulted in an increase in their numbers to 370,000 out of a Palestinian population of 1.3 million. The Arabs feared that further Jewish immigration would result in their losing much of their land. In 1936 the **Mufti** of Jerusalem called for a general strike in protest against Jewish immigration. The British government sent a commission under Lord Peel (a Conservative Party politician) to investigate. The commission resulted in the publication of a 1937 report, which was to lay the framework for the future. It introduced the idea of partition.

Adolf Hitler
Chancellor and later *Führer* (leader) of Germany between 1933 and 1945.

Enabling Act
Law passed by the Reichstag that allowed Hitler to pass laws in Germany without needing Parliamentary approval.

Mufti
An Islamic scholar who interprets Islamic law. The most important Islamic cleric in Jerusalem.

SOURCE C

The advantages to the Arabs of Partition on the lines we have proposed may be summarized as follows:

(i)   *They obtain their national independence and can co-operate on an equal footing with the Arabs of the neighbouring countries in the cause of Arab unity and progress.*

(ii)   *They are finally delivered from the fear of being swamped by the Jews, and from the possibility of ultimate subjection to Jewish rule….*

The advantages of Partition to the Jews may be summarized as follows:

(i)   *Partition secures the establishment of the Jewish National Home and relieves it from the possibility of its being subjected in the future to Arab rule.*

(ii)   *Partition enables the Jews in the fullest sense to call their National Home their own; for it converts it into a Jewish State. Its citizens will be able to admit as many Jews into it as they themselves believe can be absorbed. They will attain the primary objective of Zionism – a Jewish nation, planted in Palestine, giving its nationals the same status in the world as other nations give theirs. They will cease at last to live a minority life.*

From the Peel Commission Report, 1937

● **Examiner's hint**
When answering this question, think about how the British government's policies towards the Palestine question have changed over time.

STUDENT STUDY SECTION

QUESTION

What do you think the reaction of the Arabs and the Zionists would be to the Peel Commission's report?

Hardly surprisingly, the Arabs protested vigorously against what they saw as the theft of their land. This protest then spread into a full-scale Arab revolt in October 1937, which resulted in the dispatch of 20,000 British troops to Palestine at a time when the situation in Europe was rapidly deteriorating. It was at about this time that the Munich Conference of 1938 had resolved the question of the Sudetenland in Hitler's favour, and it was becoming more and more clear that war was imminent. The British knew that they would need Arab support in any war with Germany and were afraid that the Arab states might even ally with Hitler against Jewish interests. In some areas, there was concern expressed that the Arabs were being forced to accept changes in Palestine because of events elsewhere in the world. George

Antonius' *The Arab Awakening* pointed out that it was unfair to make the Arabs in Palestine a scapegoat of Hitler's policies. He argued that it was the Arabs who were being persecuted rather than the Jews. It was in response to these claims that the Colonial Secretary Malcolm MacDonald produced a White Paper in May 1939 which was strongly pro-Arab.

SOURCE D

His Majesty's Government believe that the framers of the Mandate in which the Balfour Declaration was embodied could not have intended that Palestine should be converted into a Jewish State against the will of the Arab population of the country...

...(1 a) For each of the next five years a quota of 10,000 Jewish immigrants will be allowed, on the understanding that a shortage in any one year may be added to the quotas for subsequent years, within the five-year period, if economic absorptive capacity permits...

...(3) After the period of five years no further Jewish immigration will be permitted unless the Arabs of Palestine are prepared to acquiesce in it...

From the MacDonald White Paper, May 1939

STUDENT STUDY SECTION

QUESTION

Read through Sources B, C and D again. Is the British government being consistent in the policies it is following? You should try to imagine how the Arabs and Zionists are viewing the changing direction of the policies of the British government.

The 1939 White Paper was rejected by both the Arabs and the Zionists. The former demanded independence while the latter protested that its terms contradicted the mandate. The apparent change in British attitude and the outbreak of World War II were to have a key effect on Zionist tactics, as they began to focus on the USA rather than the mandatory power, Britain.

The effect of World War II on the region

Germany's invasion of Poland on 1 September 1939 was the spark that caused World War II, when Britain and France declared war on Germany on 3 September. The Arab states remained officially neutral while events in Germany made it essential for the Zionists to join the Allied forces. Despite their irritation at the inconsistency of the British, it was obvious that a truce had to be called to deal with the greater threat of Nazi Germany. A Jewish legion was created from Palestinian Jews, despite their opposition to the White Paper, and fought against Hitler in the Middle East. Nazi oppression increased in Europe and the *Endlösung* or '**Final Solution**' was decided upon by Hitler after the invasion of the Soviet Union in July 1941. This was finalized in January 1942 at the **Wannsee Conference** near Berlin and the plight of European Jews became all too clear. The existence of the death camps in Poland, such as Auschwitz, and the extent of the genocide carried out by the Third Reich against the Jews, only became evident when the Allies liberated the camps and obtained access to Nazi documents and archives. After the end of World War II in Europe (8 May 1945), the number of Jewish immigrants into Palestine increased significantly.

One important consequence of Hitler's Holocaust, with its murder of more than six million Jews, was to strengthen the Zionist call for the establishment of a Jewish state in Palestine for the survivors of the concentration camps. The mandatory power, Britain, was bankrupt after the war and was faced with a disintegrating empire. It was clear that it was only a matter of time before Britain would have to give up control over its mandate.

Final Solution
Nazi Germany's plan for the systematic genocide of European Jews during World War II. By 1945, a total of six million Jews had been murdered in concentration and extermination camps, and in field executions by SS murder squads.

Wannsee Conference
A meeting where Reinhard Heydrich, head of the Reich Main Security Office, presented a plan for the Jewish population of Europe to be deported to German-occupied areas in Eastern Europe to work on construction projects and then be killed.

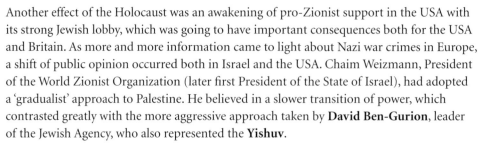

David Ben-Gurion

Ben-Gurion was a Zionist leader who played an important role in the creation of the State of Israel and became Israel's first Prime Minister in 1948.

Yishuv

Yishuv (Hebrew 'settlement') is the name given to a Jewish resident in Palestine before the establishment of the State of Israel in 1948. The term was first used in the 1880s, referring to settlers who had lived in Palestine before 1882, at which time about 25,000 Jews, mostly from Russia, emigrated there. Yishuv is still used today to refer to any pre-1948 settler in Israel.

Franklin D. Roosevelt

President of the USA between 1933 and 1945 for four terms. In regard to the Middle East, Roosevelt was seemingly inconsistent. On the one hand he wanted to end the mandate system and was totally against the idea of colonialism. He therefore supported the withdrawal of Britain from Palestine and encouraged the establishment of a Jewish state. On the other hand Roosevelt was a little ambivalent in his statements, appearing to support both Arab and Jewish claims to Palestine.

ToK Time

An assassination takes place in 1950. There are three accounts of it: 1) an account written by the assassin; 2) an account written by an observer at the time who saw the shooting; 3) an account written by someone writing in 2000. Which of the three accounts actually 'knows' what happened and why? What do you think? Explain your answer.

Another effect of the Holocaust was an awakening of pro-Zionist support in the USA with its strong Jewish lobby, which was going to have important consequences both for the USA and Britain. As more and more information came to light about Nazi war crimes in Europe, a shift of public opinion occurred both in Israel and the USA. Chaim Weizmann, President of the World Zionist Organization (later first President of the State of Israel), had adopted a 'gradualist' approach to Palestine. He believed in a slower transition of power, which contrasted greatly with the more aggressive approach taken by **David Ben-Gurion**, leader of the Jewish Agency, who also represented the **Yishuv**.

The British had opposed Weizmann's plan to create a Jewish military division in Palestine to help fight against the Germans. Britain rightly suspected that this would give the Yishuv a strong bargaining position when World War II was finally over.

Back in May 1942, the American Zionists decided to hold a conference at the Biltmore Hotel in New York. The aim was to unite, in one group, all of the pro-Zionist groups in the USA in order to create a strong political lobby and to raise money to support Palestinian Jews and European refugees. The resolutions passed at the Conference wanted to open Palestine to Jewish immigration, which would be overseen by the Jewish Agency and, following Weizmann's proposals, also called for the creation of a Jewish commonwealth in Palestine.

The Biltmore Program was successful in uniting American Jews and, as details of Nazi atrocities became more widespread in early 1943, membership of Zionist organizations increased dramatically. Until this time the US policy towards Palestine had been to leave it to Britain to deal with. But, by 1943, due to the tremendous lobby of pro-Zionist groups, the US position changed. Three groups were particularly influential in this lobby: The American Palestine Committee, the Christian Council on Palestine and the Zionist Emergency Council. In February 1944, the American Palestine Committee managed to get a resolution introduced into the US Senate calling for the establishment of a Jewish commonwealth in Palestine. Although the resolution was defeated, it was to intensify the debate in the USA about British government policy in Palestine.

In Britain, there was concern about the growing Zionist agitation in the USA as the British felt that this might create a split between the USA and Britain at a crucial time in the war, with the upcoming invasion of Normandy. However, 1944 was a presidential election year in the USA and, under intense Zionist pressure, **Franklin Roosevelt** promised in October 1944 to help create 'the establishment of Palestine as a free and democratic Jewish Commonwealth'. By November 1944 both the Democratic and Republican political platforms made reference to a Jewish commonwealth in Palestine. The proposals made by the Biltmore Program seemed to have been widely accepted. One of the reasons for this was the Jewish lobby. It would have been impossible for any politician to win an election in Illinois, New York or Pennsylvania without Jewish support, as there were more than four and a half million Jewish voters in these three states alone. Later, in August 1945 after Roosevelt's death in April, the new President **Harry Truman** wrote to the British Prime Minister, **Clement Attlee**, concerning the lifting of quotas on Jewish immigration and requested the immediate admission of 100,000 Jewish refugees into Palestine. Some members of the US State Department thought that Truman's pro-Zionist sentiments might offend the Arab states. Truman replied: 'I am sorry gentlemen, but I have to answer for hundreds of thousands of those who are anxious for the success of Zionism; but I do not have hundreds of thousands of Arabs among my constituents.' American domestic politics would ultimately play an important role in the events leading to the 1948 Arab-Israeli War. Somewhat ironically, the Biltmore Program had a negative consequence for the Zionist leadership. A split developed between Weizmann and Ben-Gurion over the direction that the World Zionist Agency Organization and the Jewish Agency should take, which eventually escalated into a direct power struggle between the two leaders. Weizmann wanted to negotiate with London and tried to reintroduce the Peel Commission's partition plan, whereas Ben-Gurion wanted direct action in Palestine supported by US-based Zionist groups.

Between 1939 and 1945, the Arabs in Palestine were in some disarray. The Mufti had fled from Palestine during the Arab Revolt and was officially banned from entering Palestine. The British attempted to get his support for the 1939 White Paper, as they were scared of a pro-German Arab alliance. The Mufti rejected the British proposals and, instead, travelled to Axis Europe where he attempted to persuade Hitler to support him in overthrowing the British in the Middle East. Here he was unsuccessful and instead turned to intensive anti-British propaganda in Palestine, with the intention of creating an Arab uprising. His pleas fell on deaf ears and the Middle East remained relatively peaceful until the end of the war, when the Palestine Arab Party became the leading political party in Palestine. The other Arab states attempted to create some form of Arab unity, but little was achieved until late 1944.

Section II:
The last years of the British mandate; UNSCOP partition plan and the outbreak of civil war

By the end of 1945, the British government found itself in an impossible position. It was increasingly aware of Soviet interests in the Middle East, particularly in Turkey and Iran, and wanted to remain friendly with the Arab states. This would be difficult if Britain were to agree to the establishment of a Jewish state in Palestine. There were still large numbers of refugees following World War II, many of whom wanted to relocate to Palestine. The League of Nations mandate in Palestine had not worked, as what the Zionists wanted was exactly the opposite of what the Arabs wanted. The aims and objectives of the two sides were simply irreconcilable. The main concern of the British Foreign Secretary, **Ernest Bevin**, was British interests in the Middle East. Personally, he believed that the Jewish refugee problem was not going to be solved by the partition of Palestine and supported the idea of a Palestinian state under some sort of United Nations trusteeship, with Britain retaining a degree of administrative control. Bevin also proposed that a joint Anglo-American Committee of Inquiry be set up to investigate the matter further.

Neither the Arabs nor the Zionists supported Bevin's announcement. The Arab leaders disagreed about which actions to take, but insisted on Palestine remaining Arab. The leaders had already met in Alexandria in October 1944 to discuss how best to unify the policies of the Arab states. They decided to create a **League of Arab States**, which eventually came into existence in March 1945. They also issued a statement on Palestine:

SOURCE A

The Committee is of the opinion that Palestine constitutes an important part of the Arab World and that the rights of the Arabs in Palestine cannot be touched without prejudice to peace and stability in the Arab World…

The Committee also declares that it is second to none in regretting the woes which have been inflicted upon the Jews of Europe by European dictatorial states. But the question of these Jews should not be confused with Zionism, for there can be no greater injustice and aggression than solving the problem of the Jews of Europe by another injustice, i.e., by inflicting injustice on the Arabs of Palestine of various religions and denominations.

From the Alexandria Protocol, 8 October 1944

Harry Truman
Truman became President of the USA after Roosevelt's death in 1945 and served until 1953. As regards the Middle East, and as a result of Nazi Germany's anti-Semitic policies in Europe, Truman's sympathies were firmly with the Jews. He accepted the 1917 Balfour Declaration, in principle, arguing that it supported the idea of national 'self-determination'. Truman also supported the UNSCOP Partition Plan and was one of the first leaders to recognize the new State of Israel in May 1948.

Clement Attlee
Attlee was a British politician, who served as Prime Minister of the United Kingdom from 1945 to 1951. Attlee's government publicly declared in early 1947 that Britain's mandate in Palestine had become 'unworkable'.

Ernest Bevin
Bevin opposed the creation of a Jewish state and supported the idea of an Arab-controlled western Palestine partly as a consequence of attacks on British groups by Zionist groups such as Irgun and LEHI. However, Britain's weakness after World War II and Attlee's decision to give up Palestine forced Bevin to agree with the handing over of the British mandate of Palestine to the United Nations.

League of Arab States
The Arab League was founded in 1945 by Egypt, Iraq, Transjordan, Syria, Yemen, Saudi Arabia and Lebanon, and was aimed at representing Arab interests in the region.

STUDENT STUDY SECTION

QUESTION
What are your reactions to the last sentence of Source A starting 'But…..'?

The Arab League made the support of the Palestinian claims an essential part of their programme, but did little else. The Zionists, on the other hand, decided to take direct action. David Ben-Gurion believed that the only way to rid Palestine of the British was through armed resistance. To this end he received financial support from the USA to buy weapons and arm Zionist paramilitary groups. There were three main groups at this time. There was the Haganah, which was a full-scale underground army with more than 12,000 members. The Haganah was initially formed to protect Jewish farms and **Kibbutz** residents from Arab attack in 1920. It later became an underground paramilitary force that was to form the basis for the creation of the Israel Defense Forces (IDF). After 1929, the Haganah reformed itself into a much more coordinated body, but its policies were seen by some Zionists as being too cautious. There were two more radical groups: the Irgun and the Lohamei Herut Israel (Fighters for the Freedom of Israel; LEHI). The Irgun Tsvai Leumi (Israeli National Military Organization), simply known as Irgun, had set itself up in 1931, but was still relatively small, with about 500 members in 1944. It believed in using terrorist tactics to achieve its aims and declared war against the mandate, committing itself to the expulsion of Britain from Palestine. The Stern Gang, later to become the LEHI, had been created in 1940 by members of the Irgun, who believed that the Irgun's policies were not effective enough to remove the mandate. Condemned as a terrorist group by the British, it assassinated the British Minister to the Middle East, Lord Moyne, in November 1944. The killing of Moyne, a personal friend of Winston Churchill, was to backfire on the LEHI and the Irgun, as the murder created a split between these two groups and the Haganah until the middle of 1945. During this time, the Haganah began to take action against members of both LEHI and Irgun, rounding up their leaders and turning them over to the British authorities.

The Anglo-American Committee of Inquiry

While the Jewish underground groups continued their revolt against the British, the Anglo-American Committee of Inquiry finally met in Washington on 13 November 1945. It was made up of six Britons and six Americans and the committee was then moved to Europe to carry out interviews with displaced persons following World War II. It finally issued its report in May 1946, calling for the issuing of 100,000 immigration certificates, which were to be given to Jewish refugees in order that they could emigrate to Palestine. The committee also recommended that a system of trusteeship be set up with the backing of the United Nations. Somewhat ironically, neither the British nor the US government endorsed these recommendations, nor did the Arabs, nor the Zionists. In April 1946, Bevin rejected the idea of issuing the 100,000 immigration certificates. There was a further attempt to break the deadlock with the **Morrison–Grady Plan** in July 1946, which called for the creation of Arab and Jewish provinces under a trusteeship. This disappointed both Arabs and Zionists and, after a further series of meetings that resolved none of the issues, President Truman rejected its proposals in August.

Kibbutz

A collective community in Israel that was traditionally based on agriculture. The kibbutz is a form of communal living that combines socialism and Zionism.

Morrison–Grady Plan

Herbert Morrison was Deputy Prime Minister of Britain between 1945 and 1951. Henry Grady was an American diplomat, later to become US ambassador to India.

SOURCE B

The British devised a committee that would attempt to solve the immigration/refugee impasse: the Anglo-American Committee of Inquiry (AAC).
Six British and six American delegates formed the twelve man committee, which would

interview Jewish refugees in America and Europe. What they decided (May 1946) was the following: 100,000 immigration certificates to be issued; rejection of partition of Palestine; relaxed future immigration; removal of restriction on Jewish land purchases; and the illegalization of discriminatory Zionist labor laws. Great Britain would continue the role of administrator, thus continuing the British Mandate.

From Gregory Harms, *The Palestine–Israel Conflict*, 2005

SOURCE C

But as for the future of Palestine, the report remained intentionally vague. 'Any attempt to establish either an independent Palestinian state or independent Palestinian states would result in civil strife such as might threaten the peace of the world.' Consequently, Palestine should remain under the British Mandate 'pending the execution of a Trusteeship agreement under the United Nations'. The committee seemed to envisage a binational state in which neither Arab nor Jew could dominate the other, but beyond support for admission of 100,000, it made no recommendations for future immigration, thus leaving that matter in British hands. No one was pleased, especially Bevin, who had conceived the committee as a means to draw the Americans into the problem and to compel them to share responsibility for any future actions regarding Palestine.

From Charles D. Smith, *Palestine and the Arab-Israeli Conflict*, 2007

STUDENT STUDY SECTION

QUESTION

Compare and contrast the views expressed in Sources B and C about the report of the Anglo-American Committee of Inquiry of 1946. Here are three student answers. Which is best and why?

Student Answer A – *Abelia*

Source B explains the formation of the Anglo-American Committee of Inquiry and its role in solving the immigration/refugee issue of the Jewish and Palestinian people. The source reveals how the decisions made by the committee were supportive of Jewish people. For instance, the committee agreed to relax future immigration, remove restriction on Jewish land purchases and make illegal the discriminatory Zionist labour laws. Also the source expresses the view that the committee made some effective decisions to solve the issue of Palestinian and Israeli conflict. According to the source, the Arab-Israeli immigration conflict would continue to be administered by Great Britain.

Unlike Source B, Source C expresses the view that the newly set up Anglo-American Committee did not provide any substantial report that suggests a solution to the conflict. According to the source, the committee failed to make recommendations for future immigration and the 'binational state of Palestinian and Israeli land'. Also, the source expresses the view that Britain wanted to shift over their responsibility for the Palestinian issue by working with the Americans.

In conclusion, the views expressed by Source B contrast with the views expressed by Source C. While Source B reveals the idea that the AAC provided recommendations to solve the issue of Arab-Israeli conflict, Source C disapproves of this. Also, Source B specifically states that the committee decided to maintain the 'relaxed future immigration,' but Source C says that 'no recommendations for future immigration' were provided by the committee. Moreover, Source B contrasts with Source C as it suggests that the committee agreed to 'reject the partition of Palestine' whereas Source C expresses the idea that the committee wanted to create 'a binational state controlled by British-American force'.

● **Examiner's hint**
Look at the different approaches used by the three students.

Student Answer B – *Daisy*

The two sources concerning the Anglo-American Committee of Inquiry of 1946 express separate views of the committee's decision, but base these views on similar grounds and reasoning. One of the main ideas that the two sources have in common is the agreement that the British mandate will be maintained. Source B expresses this by recognizing the decisions made, and then stating that 'Great Britain would continue the role of administrator, thus continuing the British Mandate'. Similarly, Source C states that 'Palestine should remain under the British Mandate'. Source C also states that the British wanted to share responsibility with the Americans, and that this was the reason for the AAC.

However, the two sources express different interpretations of the decisions made by the AAC. Both sources state that the immigration of 100,000 was to be supported and certificates were issued, but the mention of future immigration in the two sources differs. Source B states that the AAC agreed on 'relaxed future immigration'. However, this view is contrasted with Source C as it states that 'no recommendations [were made] for future immigration'.

Sources B and C also have different statements on the other decisions made by the AAC. For example, the decision made about the removal of restriction on Jewish land purchases is mentioned in Source B, but not at all in Source C. In conclusion, Source B basically states the terms of the agreement of the AAC, whereas Source C focuses on immigration and the independence of Palestine, and discusses them more in depth.

Student Answer C – *Sean*

Both Sources B and C discuss the aim of the Anglo-American Committee of Inquiry of 1946 and the role it had in Palestine in order to keep the conflict at peace. Source B claims that the Anglo-American Committee of Inquiry, or the ACC, had a big role in the peacemaking of Palestine to solve the immigration impasse. Both Americans and British men formed the committee and would work against the immigration, rejection of Palestine and the immigration certificates needed to be issued. Source B, written in London, is not biased towards Britain and therefore includes the Americans in the ACC and their plan to support Palestine.

Source C, however, complains about the involvement of Britain in Palestine and argues that America does not take a major part in the peacemaking in Palestine. The source, however, explains, like Source B, how all the steps taken by Britain were against the immigration. Source C, written by an American in Boston, therefore shows the contradictions between the British and the Americans as to who had the ability to establish order and who had the responsibility for any actions. Both sources therefore agree on the actions taken by the ACC but disagree on the the countries' real involvement in the actions.

Examiner's comments

Abelia's is not a good approach to take. The first two paragraphs have no direct linkage between the two sources. The last paragraph is much better, but comes too late.

Daisy's answer is much better and is an excellent model for this type of question. It links Sources B and C together and is stylistically very elegant. A point is taken from Source B and is then either supported or refuted by Source C. The examiner can therefore clearly see the use of 'compare and contrast' in this approach. It is much stronger than the answers given by Pat and Sean.

In Sean's answer there is considerable reference here to material that is in the sources, but Sean has not used the information very well. The first paragraph quickly makes a comparison, but then loses focus. The last sentence is a value judgement. The second paragraph makes the same sort of mistake. There is not enough direct linkage between the two sources.

In the meantime, the situation in Palestine had become more critical. The Haganah, the **Palmach** commanders, LEHI and Irgun unified their command and began to collaborate from October 1945. A full-scale terrorist campaign was carried out against British troops and institutions. This culminated in July 1946 with the blowing up of the King David Hotel in Jerusalem by the Irgun, killing 91 people and injuring many more. During the rest of 1946, attacks were made on bridges, railway lines, banks, power stations and military camps.

The British position in Palestine was becoming impossible for the government. There were more than 100,000 British troops stationed there and public opinion at home was strongly against the continued existence of British forces in Palestine. By October 1947, 127 British soldiers had been killed and 133 others wounded. On 4 October 1946, President Truman called for the partition of Palestine and, coming under increasing political and economic pressure both at home and abroad, Bevin hosted a conference in London in February 1947. The United Nations (UN), formed between April and June 1945, had taken over from the League of Nations as the administrator of mandated territories, and Bevin was keen to hand the issue over to the new organization. Delegations from both the Zionists and Arabs met with the British government and it was soon clear that the two sides had two completely opposite proposals. Ben-Gurion wanted partition, which Bevin was against, while the Arabs wanted to prevent any further Jewish immigration and wanted their own state. Initially Bevin offered to place the territories under a trusteeship for five years with the intention of creating an Arab state with a Jewish minority and limiting Jewish immigration. This the Zionists rejected out of hand and Ben-Gurion suggested a return to the pre-1939 status quo, a proposal that the Arab states immediately turned down. Unable to come to any compromise with the Zionists and the Arabs, Bevin decided to hand the whole matter over to the UN to resolve, and on 18 February made a speech to the House of Commons in which he explained the decision of the British government.

> **Palmach**
> Palmach is short for *Plugot Machats*, i.e., crushing battalions or literally 'strike force'. It was established by the British and Haganah in 1941 with the intention of protecting Palestine from any German invasion.

SOURCE D

For the Jews, the essential point of principle is the creation of a sovereign Jewish State. For the Arabs, the essential point of principle is to resist to the last the establishment of Jewish sovereignty in any part of Palestine... His Majesty's Government have of themselves no power, under the terms of the Mandate, to award the country either to the Arabs or to the Jews, or even to partition it between them...

It is in these circumstances that we have decided that we are unable to accept the scheme put forward either by the Arabs or by the Jews, or to impose ourselves a solution of our own. We have, therefore, reached the conclusion that the only course now open to us is to submit the problem to the judgment of the United Nations…

We shall then ask the United Nations to consider our report, and to recommend a settlement of the problem. We do not intend ourselves to recommend any particular solution.

From Bevin's speech, 18 February 1947

STUDENT STUDY SECTION

QUESTION

Bevin's statement makes it clear that Britain decided to give up the mandate over Palestine. The reasons should be clear to you why this was the case in the Middle East, but find out for yourself, by research, what other global factors influenced the British decision to leave.

The UNSCOP partition plan

The UN decided to set up a UN Special Committee on Palestine (UNSCOP) to investigate the problem. Representatives of 11 countries stayed in Palestine during June and July 1947. During their stay, two British soldiers were kidnapped by the Irgun and held as hostages against three Irgun members. When the British executed the Irgun prisoners, the Irgun hanged the British soldiers and booby-trapped their bodies. Also during this time, British treatment of the passengers of a ship called the *Exodus* (originally the *President Garfield*) horrified the world. The ship, carrying 4550 refugees from Europe, attempted to sail to Palestine. It was seized by the Royal Navy and taken to Haifa in Palestine. The British then returned the ship to Marseilles, from where the refugees were shipped back to Germany and detained in a displaced persons camp amid worldwide condemnation.

The UNSCOP plan was submitted to the General Assembly in New York in August 1947 and was unanimous in calling for the ending of the British mandate. There was, however, disagreement about the nature of the state that should replace the British mandate. The majority of the committee wanted partition into a Jewish and an Arab state, with Jerusalem becoming an international city. Other members wanted an independent federal state under UN administration. The report made a number of recommendations:

SOURCE E

PART I. Plan of partition with economic union justification
1. *The basic premise underlying the partition proposal is that the claims to Palestine of the Arabs and Jews, both possessing validity, are irreconcilable, and that among all of the solutions advanced, partition will provide the most realistic and practicable settlement, and is the most likely to afford a workable basis for meeting in part the claims and national aspirations of both parties.*
2. *It is a fact that both of these peoples have their historic roots in Palestine, and that both make vital contributions to the economic and cultural life of the country. The partition solution takes these considerations fully into account.*
3. *The basic conflict in Palestine is a clash of two intense nationalisms. Regardless of the historical origins of the conflict, the rights and wrongs of the promises and counter-promises, and the international intervention incident to the Mandate, there are now in Palestine some 650,000 Jews and some 1,200,000 Arabs who are dissimilar in their ways of living and, for the time being, separated by political interests which render difficult full and effective political co-operation among them, whether voluntary or induced by constitutional arrangements.*
4. *Only by means of partition can these conflicting national aspirations find substantial expression and qualify both peoples to take their places as independent nations in the international community and in the United Nations.*

From UN Special Committee on Palestine, Recommendations to the General Assembly, A/364, 3 September 1947

STUDENT STUDY SECTION

QUESTION

Find a blank map of Palestine in 1947. Pretend that you are a member of UNSCOP. Taking into account the population figures cited above, how would you divide up the territory and Jerusalem? Draw the boundaries of the Arab and Jewish states taking into account access to drinking water, sea access, access to fertile areas, religious concerns etc. The following map of settlements might help you (Map 9).

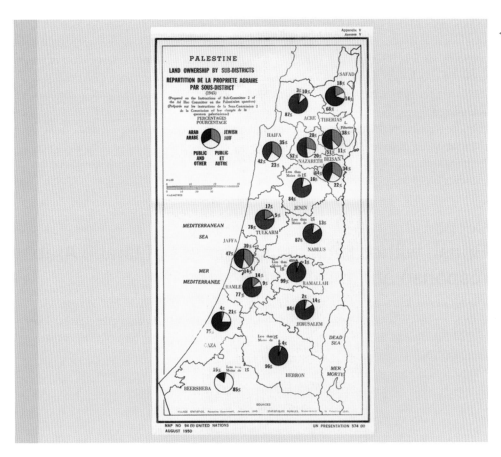

◀ **Map 9**
A map produced by the
Palestine government in
1945, and republished by the
United Nations in 1950

An Ad Hoc Committee on the Palestinian Question was set up by the General Assembly to
hear reactions from both Arabs and Jews to UNSCOP's proposals. The Arab state rejected
the proposals in their entirety. The Arabs believed:

SOURCE F

*… that Palestine was an integral part of the Arab world and that from the beginning its
indigenous inhabitants have opposed the creation in their country of a Jewish national home.
They also insisted that the United Nations, a body created and controlled by the United States
and Europe, had no right to grant the Zionists any portion of their territory. In what was to
become a familiar Arab charge they insisted that the Western world was seeking to salve its
conscience for the atrocities of war and was paying its own debt to the Jewish people with
someone else's land.*

From Mark Tessler, *A History of the Israeli-Palestinian Conflict*, 1994

STUDENT STUDY SECTION

QUESTION
**Take each of the three sentences in the above quotation from Tessler. Do you
agree with the points he is making? What evidence is there to support his
claims?**

The Zionists generally supported UNSCOP's recommendations, but there was concern that,
even with the support of the USA, the resolution would not receive the two-thirds majority
in the General Assembly needed to pass. It was believed that the Arabs would find support
for their cause from the USSR (particularly after the USA published the Truman Doctrine
of March 1947 and the Marshall Plan of June 1947, which virtually cemented the Cold War

in Europe) and that other African and Asian countries would also support the Arabs. The vote was to take place on 27 November 1947, but was postponed. Pressure was brought on countries such as Liberia by US corporations (concerned about a potential boycott of their goods by pro-Jewish supporters), which attempted to influence their votes. Eventually, on 29 November 1947 with a vote of 33 for, 13 against and 10 abstentions, UN Resolution 181 was passed. The USSR voted for the resolution, surprising many observers. The reasons for the vote were strategic. The Soviets aimed to limit US influence in the area, make links with the Arab states that would oppose partition and establish themselves as a potential force in the Middle East. Twelve days later, Ernest Bevin announced that Britain would end her mandate on 15 May 1948.

Section III:
British withdrawal; establishment of Israel; Arab response and the 1948/49 war

The result sparked wild scenes of celebration in New York and Tel Aviv, but was greeted with anger by the Arabs. They could not understand how the UN could give almost 57 per cent of Palestine to the Jewish settlers, who comprised about 30 per cent of the population (see Map 10).

Map 10

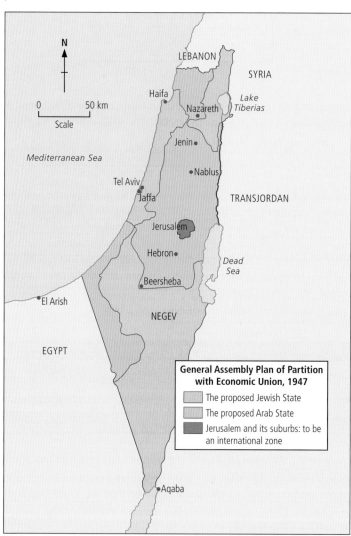

General Assembly Plan of Partition with Economic Union, 1947

- The proposed Jewish State
- The proposed Arab State
- Jerusalem and its suburbs: to be an international zone

STUDENT STUDY SECTION

QUESTION

Look carefully at the map. What problems can you see with the UN partition plan? Explain your answer carefully. Why do you think that the UN partitioned Palestine in this way? How does the UN partition of Israel agree with your partition of the territory?

The immediate result was the calling of a general strike by the Arabs for 2–4 December 1947, which gradually escalated into violence. Between the UN vote in November 1947 and the day that Israel was created (14 May 1948), a bloody civil war erupted between Palestinian Arabs and the Zionists. The UN decided against installing any temporary peacekeeping force in Palestine and the British forces turned a blind eye to the fighting between the two groups.

At first the Arab forces were successful in attacking many Jewish convoys and settlements, thereby cutting off the delivery of supplies to larger Jewish cities. In March 1948, the Haganah changed tactics and adopted a new strategy based on their Plan Dalet (or Plan D), which had two objectives. The first was to defend Jewish settlements and ensure that the territory designated to become Jewish by the proposed partition plan was under Jewish control. Its second objective was to drive Arab settlers from the land that had been promised to the Palestinian Arabs.

SOURCE A

(d) Operational Objectives

1. *Self-defense against invasion by regular or semi-regular forces. This will be achieved by the following:*
   A fixed defensive system to preserve our settlements, vital economic projects, and property, which will enable us to provide governmental services within the borders of the state (based on defending the regions of the state on the one hand, and on blocking the main access routes from enemy territory to the territory of the state on the other). Launching pre-planned counter-attacks on enemy bases and supply lines in the heart of his territory, whether within the borders of the country [Palestine] or in neighboring countries.
2. *Ensuring freedom of military and economic activity within the borders of the [Hebrew] state and in Jewish settlements outside its borders by occupying and controlling important high-ground positions on a number of transportation arteries.*
3. *Preventing the enemy from using frontline positions within his territory which can easily be used for launching attacks. This will be effected by occupying and controlling them.*
4. *Applying economic pressure on the enemy by besieging some of his cities in order to force him to abandon some of his activities in certain areas of the country.*
5. *Restricting the capability of the enemy by carrying out limited operations: occupation and control of certain of his bases in rural and urban areas within the borders of the state.*
6. *Controlling government services and property within the borders of the state and ensuring the supply of essential public services in an effective manner.*

From Plan Dalet, 10 March 1948

STUDENT STUDY SECTION

QUESTION

After the 1948 war, Plan Dalet was heavily criticized by Palestinian Arabs as they argued it was a deliberate plan to expel all Arabs from Palestine – an Arab Diaspora. Read through the extract above and make a list of which sentences in it could justify this claim.

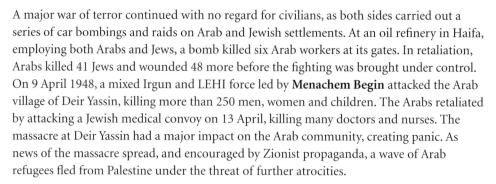

Menachem Begin
Menachem Begin was the sixth Prime Minister of the State of Israel. Before the establishment of the state, he was the leader of the Irgun, playing a central role in Jewish resistance to the British Mandate of Palestine. Begin's most significant achievement as prime minister was signing a peace treaty with Egypt in 1979, for which he won the Nobel Prize for Peace together with Anwar Sadat.

A major war of terror continued with no regard for civilians, as both sides carried out a series of car bombings and raids on Arab and Jewish settlements. At an oil refinery in Haifa, employing both Arabs and Jews, a bomb killed six Arab workers at its gates. In retaliation, Arabs killed 41 Jews and wounded 48 more before the fighting was brought under control. On 9 April 1948, a mixed Irgun and LEHI force led by **Menachem Begin** attacked the Arab village of Deir Yassin, killing more than 250 men, women and children. The Arabs retaliated by attacking a Jewish medical convoy on 13 April, killing many doctors and nurses. The massacre at Deir Yassin had a major impact on the Arab community, creating panic. As news of the massacre spread, and encouraged by Zionist propaganda, a wave of Arab refugees fled from Palestine under the threat of further atrocities.

By the time the mandate ended in May, it is estimated that more than 300,000 Palestinian Arabs had fled to other areas in Palestine or to other Arab states. This issue was to become a legacy of the 1948 war and was to prove impossible to resolve. On 14 May 1948, David Ben-Gurion proclaimed the existence of the independent State of Israel according to the UNSCOP partition plan. The new state was immediately recognized by both the Soviet Union and the USA. The next day the armies of Egypt, Syria, Transjordan, Lebanon and Iraq attacked the embryonic Israeli state. Saudi Arabia supported the other Arab states, but only in a limited way.

SOURCE B

Accordingly we, members of the People's Council, representatives of the Jewish Community of Eretz-Israel and of the Zionist Movement, are here assembled on the day of the termination of the British Mandate over Eretz-Israel and, by virtue of our natural and historic right and on the strength of the resolution of the United Nations General Assembly, hereby declare the establishment of a Jewish state in Eretz-Israel, to be known as the State of Israel.

From the Israeli Proclamation of the State of Israel, 1948

STUDENT STUDY SECTION

QUESTION
This extract from the Israeli Proclamation of Independence on 14 May 1948 refers three times to 'Eretz Israel'. Find out what this term means. Why do you think that this term was used and not any other?

The 1948 Arab-Israeli War

The 1948 war can be divided into two clear stages. They date from 15 May to 11 June, at which point a temporary truce was declared, and from 6 July to 19 July. The Arab armies were superior in air power and heavy weapons, but their land forces were not trained for sustained campaigns. The Egyptian Army was really only an armed police force, and the only effective army was that of Transjordan whose King, Abdullah, was put in command of the entire Arab armies. The Arab states were also not united in their policies and each country had its own particular objectives. Thus the creation of a separate Palestinian state was not really the motivation behind the Arab states going to war. King Abdullah was keen to annex the West Bank (a territory on the west bank of the River Jordan), while both Syria and Egypt hoped to acquire some land for themselves. Abdullah had already accepted the UN partition plan and ordered his troops to defend Arab land, but not to undertake any military action in the land that had been given to Israel. There was, therefore, no coordinated military leadership among the Arab states.

Despite this situation, the early campaigns saw Arab forces penetrate Israeli positions and the Arabs had managed to secure some territory around Jerusalem. The Israeli forces, though outnumbered three to one, were better trained and superior in tactics. The core of the IDF was made up of members of the Haganah and Irgun who had become battle-hardened fighting the British. Count Folke Bernadotte, a Swedish UN negotiator, arranged for a month-long truce on 11 June. During this truce, an arms blockade was in force but, despite this blockade, the Israelis bought large quantities of arms from Czechoslovakia, largely with US assistance.

When Syria and Egypt restarted the war on 6 July it was clear that the Israeli forces were in a much stronger military position than they had been before and they were soon making huge land gains, particularly around Galilee. Hundreds of thousands of Palestinians became refugees. By the time that the second truce was declared on 18 July, the Israelis had greatly expanded their territory at the expense of the Palestinians. Count Bernadotte worked tirelessly to find a diplomatic solution to end the war. By September he had worked out a proposed agreement: Jerusalem was to be an international city; Israel was to retain Galilee; and Palestinian refugees were to be allowed to return to the land from which they had fled. The Israelis objected vigorously to these proposals which were, in principle, accepted by the British and the Americans. Jordan also rejected the plan as Abdullah was hoping to acquire some more territory for himself.

On 17 September 1948, Bernadotte was murdered by members of LEHI. The Israeli government condemned the assassination, but still rejected the giving up of any territory gained in the war. In October the IDF regained control of the Negev Desert and pushed the Egyptian Army back to the Gaza Strip. Eventually an armistice was signed in January 1949, which was concluded on 24 February. Territorially Israel controlled more than 75 per cent of Palestine and about half of the Arab state proposed in the 1947 UN Partition Plan had been lost (see Map 11).

Map 11

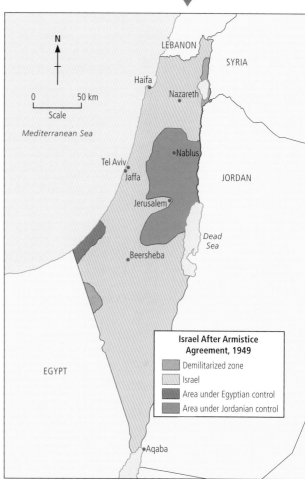

Israel After Armistice Agreement, 1949
- Demilitarized zone
- Israel
- Area under Egyptian control
- Area under Jordanian control

STUDENT STUDY SECTION

QUESTION
Compare this map with the UN Partition Plan (Map 10) above. What are the differences between the two maps?

SOURCE C

The state of Israel came into being because, in the end, two of the Great Powers, Russia and the United States, for conflicting reasons, strategic and domestic, thought it would be in their interests. Britain, concerned to maintain its paramountcy in the Middle East, opposed the move. British morale was eroded by a combination of Zionist terrorism, and a feeling that an American President dictated a policy in the interests of Zionism and his re-election, that led to the deaths of British troops. In any case this was the period of the twilight of the British Empire and the replacement of the pax Britannica by the pax Americana. After May 15 1948 the situation in the Middle East was not determined just by Great-Power politics, but by a local fight for possession of land. Britain's imperial position there, established between 1917 and 1923, was eroded.

From Ritchie Ovendale, *The Origins of the Arab-Israeli Wars*, 2004

● **Examiner's hint**

When studying the student answers here, look for three sentences or two well-developed sentences with good structure.

STUDENT STUDY SECTION

QUESTION

Why, according to Source C, did the State of Israel come into being?

Compare your answer to each of the three student answers below.

Student Answer A – David

It came into being because Russia and the USA thought it would be in their interests for this to happen and the British Empire was in decline and Britain was losing influence in the Middle East.

Student Answer B – Adelah

Britain was no longer in control of the mandate and, after the Second World War, the influence of former colonial powers, such as Britain, was being replaced by a Cold War struggle in the Middle East between the Soviet Union and the USA. The continued terrorist campaigns against Britain, resulting in the deaths its soldiers, and strong US support for Zionism were also contributory factors behind the creation of the State of Israel.

Student Answer C – Sam

It came into being because 'Russia and the United States, for conflicting reasons, strategic and domestic, thought it would be in their interests'. Britain was facing a combination of Zionist terrorism, and a feeling that an American President now dictated policy. It was also 'the twilight of the British Empire and the replacement of the *Pax Britannica* by the *Pax Americana*'.

Examiner's comments

David's answer is simply too short and does not demonstrate much understanding of the issues involved. Sam has simply copied large sections from the source, some in quotation marks and some direct text, and while the points he makes are reasonable there is not much understanding of the text. He needed to have paraphrased the ideas – not simply copied them down word for word.

Adelah has a very sound understanding of the issues, has rephrased the ideas in the source and has clearly done enough to receive maximum marks.

The Israeli victory is easily explained. The IDF had the support of all of the Jews in Israel and were unified in their aims. Their forces were well equipped and well organized and, apart from Transjordan's Arab Legion, the Arab forces were not well trained and were without a cohesive command structure. The ceasefire did not lead to a formal peace settlement and technically the two sides were still at war until the 1967 Six-Day War. The proposal put forward by the UN Partition Plan to create Jerusalem as an international city was formalized on 9 December 1949. Israel immediately rejected this resolution and declared that the Israeli part of Jerusalem would become the capital of the new State of Israel.

SOURCE D

(1) To restate, therefore, its intention that Jerusalem should be placed under a permanent international regime, which should envisage appropriate guarantees for the protection of the Holy Places, both within and outside Jerusalem, and to confirm specifically the following provisions of General Assembly Resolution 181 (II) 3/ (1) the City of Jerusalem shall be established as a corpus separatum under a special international regime and shall be administered by the United Nations; (2) the Trusteeship Council shall be designated to discharge the responsibilities of the Administering Authority... ; and (3) the City of Jerusalem shall include the present municipality of Jerusalem plus the surrounding villages and towns...

From United Nations General Assembly Resolution 303

STUDENT STUDY SECTION

QUESTION
**What precisely is meant by 'the Holy Places, both within and outside Jerusalem'?
What does the Latin term *corpus separatum* mean?**

Section IV:

Demographic shifts: the Palestinian Diaspora 1947 onwards; Jewish immigration and the economic development of the Israeli state

The refugee question

One of the most important consequences of the 1948 war was the dispersion or Diaspora of the Palestinian Arabs, still known today as *al-Nakba* or 'The Catastrophe'. There is considerable disagreement as to how many Palestinians left Palestine between 1947 and 1949. Not surprisingly, the Israelis tend to underestimate the number, while the Arabs appear to overestimate how many refugees were forced to flee. The UN has estimated that 750,000 had left by January 1949, with approximately 940,000 leaving by June 1949. These figures would leave somewhere between 130,000 and 150,000 Palestinians remaining inside the expanded Israeli state. Some refugees settled in the Egyptian-controlled Gaza Strip, others went to the Jordanian-controlled West Bank, but the majority settled in refugee camps in Jordan, Syria and Lebanon.

SOURCE A

Palestinian Refugee Camp, 1949

● **Examiner's hint**
You should spend no more than about five minutes on this question. There are two easy points. Can you find them?

STUDENT STUDY SECTION

QUESTION

What message is conveyed in Source A?

Here are two student sample answers. Can you do better?

Student Answer A – *Ken*

The message conveyed in Source A is that the Palestinians in the refugee camps are suffering. The women are queuing up, probably for food, and are being guarded by an Israeli soldier. This gives the viewer the impression that the Palestinians are the victims and the Israelis the aggressors.

Student Answer B – *Alan*

The photograph shows a line of Palestinian women waiting for food distribution. They are being watched by an armed guard and the compound is surrounded by barbed wire. There appear to only be women in the line, who seem to have been waiting for some time, suggesting that there is a shortage of food. Palestinians did not have, by that time, a land that belonged to them and they are therefore in camps. This situation, however, takes some of their identity away from them as they do not know to which country they belong and where their homes are.

Examiner's comments

Ken's answer is a sympathetic summary, but one that is unlikely to earn full marks as Ken has not fully utilized the images in the photograph. He is also making an assumption that might not be entirely justified. Compare this with Alan's answer. This is clearly a better analysis initially, with some perceptive observations in it. However, the last sentence is simply opinion and cannot be determined by the images in the photograph.

Israeli flag

Palestinian flag

STUDENT STUDY SECTION

QUESTION

What was the political status of Palestinians living in the Gaza Strip, the West Bank and Israel? There were, in fact, four classes of Palestinian. Use the Internet or your library to find out what these were.

What do the symbols and colours on the flags of Israel and Palestine represent? Why do you think these were chosen?

A key point to establish is why the refugees left Palestine. If they decided to leave by themselves, with no direct influence from any other factor, then Israel could legally argue that they had no right of return and must stay in their chosen state. If, on the other hand, they were illegally expelled by Israeli forces, as the Palestinian Arabs claimed, then Israel had a duty of care to allow them to return to their homes. Naturally, an influx of Palestinian refugees back into Israel would upset the political and economic stability of the new state. The Israelis maintain that the Arab armies had encouraged the Palestinian Arabs to leave temporarily to allow freedom of military action. Those refugees who did so would therefore have no right of return, as they left their homes voluntarily.

The Arabs argue that Israel systematically forced the refugees out through a methodical programme of terror and violence. They point to the Deir Yassin massacre and the existence of Plan Dalet as proof of their claims. The plight of these refugees and their attempt to return to what they still see as their homeland is an issue that is yet to be resolved. The refugees' desires and Israel's determination to resist them are still at the heart of the continuing Middle East conflict.

One immediate effect of the refugee problem in the 1940s was the creation of an international agency to try to deal with the problem. In December 1948, the UN established the Palestine Conciliation Commission, which was set up to reach agreement on the question of the refugees. Finally, in December 1949, the **UN Relief and Works Agency for Palestine Refugees (UNRWA)** was created as a temporary measure to aid the refugees. Still in existence today in June 2009, UNRWA estimates that there are over 4.6 million displaced Palestinian refugees.

UNRWA
The UN Relief and Works Agency (UNRWA) administers the only registration system for Palestinian refugees. UNRWA records, however, only include those refugees displaced in 1948 (and their descendants) in need of assistance and located in UNRWA areas of operation – West Bank, Gaza Strip, Jordan, Lebanon and Syria. Other figures from the UN High Commissioner for Refugees (UNHCR) are higher.

SOURCE B

A photograph of Palestinian refugees in al-Nakba (the Catastrophe), 1948.

STUDENT STUDY SECTION

QUESTIONS
What message is conveyed in Source B?

● **Examiner's hint**
You should spend no more than about five minutes on this question. There are two easy points. Can you find them?

The immediate consequences of the 1948 war for Israel

In 1949 Israel held its first election. A proportional system of representation was used, which meant that each of the approximately 20 parties would receive the same proportion of seats in the **Knesset** as their share of the total votes cast. David Ben-Gurion of the **Mapai Party** received the largest number of seats in the Knesset and formed a coalition government with some smaller parties, becoming Israel's first Prime Minister. Chaim Weizmann was given the ceremonial position of President. A constitution was never developed, partly because this might have upset groups within Israel, and partly as this would have had to define Israel's territorial borders – something Ben-Gurion preferred to leave open. The government dissolved the Irgun and the Palmach with the intention of creating a strong centrally controlled military base and introduced compulsory conscription for all Jewish young people regardless of gender. The new Jewish state also made it clear that a place existed in Israel for any Jew who wished to live there. In reality this was a call for all those who left in the Jewish Diaspora to return. In July 1950, the Knesset passed the following measure:

 Knesset
The Knesset is the Israeli parliament. It first met on 14 February 1949 after the elections which were held in January 1949. Members are elected to it every four years by citizens of Israel who are at least 18 years old. The Knesset passes laws and elects the President. At the moment there are 120 members of parliament in the Knesset.

Mapai Party
Left-wing political party founded in 1930. It formed a coalition in 1968 and became the Israeli Labor Party.

Aliyah and oleh

Aliyah means immigration of Jews, and *oleh* (plural: *olim*) means a Jew immigrating into Israel.

SOURCE C

*Right of **aliyah***

1. *Every Jew has the right to come to this country as an oleh.*

***Oleh**'s visa*

2. (a) *Aliyah shall be by oleh's visa.*

    (b) *An oleh's visa shall be granted to every Jew who has expressed his desire to settle in Israel, unless the Minister of Immigration is satisfied that the applicant*

        (1) *is engaged in an activity directed against the Jewish people; or*

        (2) *is likely to endanger public health or the security of the State.*

From *The Law of Return*, 5 July 1950

STUDENT STUDY SECTION

QUESTION

What effect do you think the passing of this law would have on Jews living outside Israel, Jews living within Israel and Palestinians? On 14 July 1952, Israel passed the First Nationality Law. Use the Internet or your library to find out what consequences this would have for Jews and Palestinians.

Naturally the Law of Return encouraged immigration. Between 1949 and 1952, Israel's population doubled to about 1.4 million. This population was made up of two large groups, European Jews (Ashkenazim) and Middle Eastern/Asian Jews (Sephardim). The former tended to have family and relatives in Israel and found it relatively easy to integrate into society. The latter group often lacked skills to find jobs. Many of them ended up in camps and settlements. A two-class society began to emerge, as many European Jews considered themselves superior. The new immigrants initially supported Ben-Gurion's Mapai Party, but as time passed and Ben-Gurion's negative attitude towards the Sephardim became apparent, they began to switch their allegiance to the opposition party, **Likud**, led by Menachem Begin.

Likud

Likud is the major centre-right political party in Israel and was founded in 1973 as a coalition party. Its victory in 1977 was the first time the left-wing parties in Israel had lost power. Likud lost support in the 1990s but, following the 2009 elections, it led the Israeli government under Prime Minister Netanyahu.

SOURCE D

A photograph of a camp for Jewish immigrants, 1952.

QUESTION
What message is conveyed in Source D?

The new State of Israel had to try to resolve some major problems. It had an increasing population, a shortage of water and a shortfall in food supplies. Additionally, Israel possessed few natural resources, including oil or coal. Before 1948, Israel had imported oil from the Arab states that now refused to trade with her. The Arab states also closed sea access to the Red Sea and the Gulf of Aqaba. It was therefore essential for Israel to try to get foreign aid.

After 1948 the two major sources of funding for Israel were the American Export-Import Bank and the United Jewish Appeal – both of which were US based. Yet as Israel emerged victorious from the war, less and less money was coming into Israel from these sources. In 1950 Israeli politician **Golda Meir** travelled to the USA to appeal for a renegotiation of Israel's debts. Somewhat ironically, a new source of income was found that proved to be difficult for some Israelis to accept. In 1951, the German Chancellor, Konrad Adenauer, announced that Germany would pay compensation to Israel for Germany's treatment of Jews under the Nazi regime. The German government agreed on the manner of reparations at almost exactly the time that Israel was in a state of financial collapse. The influx of materials and money from Germany, as well as compensation payments made to individuals, was to provide the basis for the agricultural and industrial recovery of Israel. The Reparations Treaty between Germany and Israel was finally signed in Luxembourg in September 1952.

The consequences of the 1948 war for the Arab states

For the Arab states, defeat in the 1948 war and the problem of the Palestinian refugees were a catastrophe and they had immediate effects in every state. The leaders were universally blamed for the Arab humiliation, and nationalist and military groups saw the chance to seize the initiative. In Syria, there were three military coups in 1949 alone. In Jordan the Palestinian Arabs blamed King Abdullah for not taking a stronger stand against Israel and he was heavily criticized for signing a non-aggression agreement with Israel in 1950. In July 1951, a Palestinian assassinated Abdullah as he left a mosque. He was replaced by his son Talal, who himself was overthrown in 1953 by **Hussein**. The Lebanese Prime Minister was assassinated in 1951 and the President was overthrown by a military coup in 1952.

Perhaps the most significant change came in Egypt. The country, under King Farouk, was suffering domestic turmoil. Nationalist groups were demanding total independence from Britain and the removal of the 70,000 British troops still stationed in Egypt, guarding the Suez Canal. Following disturbances in Cairo in early 1952, which were started by the **Muslim Brotherhood**, Farouk was overthrown in a bloodless coup by a group of young army officers. Two years later, after a power struggle with the first President of Egypt, General Muhammed Naguib, **Gamal Abdul Nasser** became the new President.

Nasser was intensely nationalistic and was determined to improve the living conditions of the Egyptian people. He rapidly reached an agreement with the British government by which British troops would withdraw from their bases close to the Suez Canal by June 1956. Nasser had little experience in international affairs, but was seen by the USA as a leader who would not provoke conflict with Israel. In fact between 1952 and 1954 relations between Egypt and Israel were relatively peaceful.

● **Examiner's hint**
You should spend no more than about five minutes on this type of question. Try to find two clear points.

 Golda Meir
Member of the Knesset between 1949 and 1974 as a member of the Mapai Party. She was Foreign Minister in 1956 in David Ben-Gurion's government and Prime Minister of Israel from 1969 to 1973, playing a key role in Israel's actions taken during the 1973 Yom Kippur War. She merged the Mapai Party with two other parties to create the Israeli Labor Party in 1967. In August 1970, Golda Meir accepted a US peace proposal attempting to end the War of Attrition, and consequently lost her support in the Knesset.

King Hussein
King of Jordan from 1953 until his death in 1999. He expelled the Palestine Liberation Organization (PLO) from Jordan and signed a peace treaty with Israel in 1994.

Muslim Brotherhood
The world's oldest and largest Islamic group, first founded in Egypt in 1928. It is a movement, not a political party, although separate political parties have been created in several countries. It has supported the use of violence to achieve its goals and strongly opposes Western colonialism. The Muslim Brotherhood is extremely influential in many Arab countries, although officially it is banned in some Arab nations and follows traditional, conservative, interpretations of the Koran.

Gamal Abdul Nasser
Former soldier and Prime Minister of Egypt in 1954. President between 1956 until his death in 1970.

SOURCE E

The Palestinians who fled from their homes during this conflict could have been spared this tragedy if their fellow Arabs had accepted the authority of the United Nations. And so they should have. What point is there to being part of a democratic body – the United Nations – if its decisions are accepted only if they agree with one's own views? By rejecting the majority decision to partition Palestine, the Arab nations had placed themselves above the fundamental democratic process on which the United Nations is based. Since the creation of Israel over fifty years ago, Arab nations have repeatedly denied Israel's right to exist. Hatred and bloodshed have been the result of such intransigence. While Jews have sought peace with their neighbours, the Arabs have waged war.

A Jewish Perspective by Dan Cohn-Sherbok, from Dan Cohn-Sherbok and Dawoud El-Alami, *The Palestinian-Israeli Conflict,* **2002**

SOURCE F

As the situation stands, the law of this state supposedly created as a moral reaction to religious and ethnic discrimination incorporates a 'Right of Return' that gives any Jew from any part of the globe the right to settle in Israel. Immigrants do not have to be victims of discrimination or persecution who are seeking a place of safety. At the same time the indigenous population has been uprooted and scattered. Hundreds of thousands still live as refugees or stateless persons. The total number of Palestinians in the Diaspora is in the region of four million. They have no right of return. How can this ever be the basis of a just society? From a Palestinian perspective it seems that Israelis, non-Israeli Jews and indeed the world are oblivious to or simply do not care about what has been done to the Palestinians. How can the Jewish people, whether in the Holy Land or elsewhere, a people themselves so badly wronged within living memory, in conscience accept that the creation of the Jewish state has been achieved by the displacement and the continued agony of another people?

A Palestinian Perspective by Dawoud El-Alami, from Dan Cohn-Sherbok and Dawoud El-Alami, *The Palestinian-Israeli Conflict,* **2002**

● **Examiner's hint**

Make sure you link the two sources right from the beginning. Start your answer 'In Source E…' and then 'whereas [or 'this is supported'] in Source F…'

STUDENT STUDY SECTION

QUESTION

Read Sources E and F. Compare and contrast the two viewpoints. When you have finished, try analyzing the following cartoon according to the question rubric.

SOURCE G

Cartoon from the *Seattle Post Intelligencer* by David Horsey in 2002.

STUDENT STUDY SECTION

QUESTION

What is the message conveyed by Source G?

● **Examiner's hint**
Make sure that you include as many different aspects of this message as you can: size, colour, expression, text and so on.

Student Answer A – *Dawn*

Source G is a political cartoon from the Seattle Post Intelligencer by David Horsey from the year 2002. The cartoon is titled 'The Pawn' and shows a chessboard. The figures which are involved in the game are labelled as Arab countries such as Saudi Arabia, Egypt, Libya, Iraq and Jordan. The faces of these figures can be identified as prominent leaders of these nations, as for example Saddam Hussein or Gaddafi. Israel and Palestine are also represented in the game. Israel is represented as a rook in the game in the form of a black soldier with a machine gun. Palestine, white as all other Arab nations, is a pawn threatened by the Israeli rook. Saudi Arabia is looking at the situation and encouraging the Palestinian pawn 'Go ahead! He took your square – take it back!' The message conveyed is that Palestine stands no real chance against heavily armed Israel. Even if Israel seeks to occupy Palestinian territory, without the help of the Arab nations, Palestine has no realistic opportunity of reconquering the land.

Student Answer B – *Amy*

The corner of a chessboard is shown. In the corner is a black figure which is pointing a gun at a very small white figure next to it. Due to their differing colours one can assume that they are on opposing sides; against each other. The soldier figure is labelled Israel, and the small figure labelled Palestine. As Israel is portrayed as bigger, and being armed, Palestine is shown to be the weaker of the two – in fact, it looks ridiculously defenceless. In a rough semi circle behind Palestine are other white figures labelled as Arab countries such as Saudi Arabia, Egypt, Libya, Iran, etc. These can be assumed to be on Palestine's side because they are also white. Unlike Palestine, however, they are shown to be very large in size. As such, the white group of 12 figures largely outnumbers Israel, and yet Israel is shown to be powerful. A quote just beneath the pictures says 'Go ahead! He took your square – take it back!' The cartoon shows that although the Arab countries are meant to be supporting and helping their fellow Palestine, they are not only watching Israel threaten to kill Palestine, but are even encouraging it.

Examiner's comments

Dawn has too much summary of content here. Only the last three lines actually answer the question. This is one of the most common errors made by students with this sort of question. Without the last three lines, Dawn would score zero. Here she will probably get 1 mark.

Amy has provided an interesting and perceptive analysis of the cartoon. Do you agree with the last sentence or is Amy mistaken? If you do not agree with her would this analysis still be worth 2 marks? The examiner would look at the mark scheme and then see whether or not Amy had done enough to achieve 2 marks by making two clearly identifiable points. In this case it is probable that she would, as examiners are told to credit what is there, rather than penalize the student.

 ToK Time
James W. Loewen is the author of a book entitled *Lies My Teacher Told Me: Everything Your American History Textbook Got Wrong*, in which he claims that much of what is taught in history classes in school is simply untrue. One of his examples is that Columbus was the first European to discover America. Can you think of any examples where you have been taught historical information that was 'wrong'? Get in groups of three and discuss your findings.

Section V:

The Suez Crisis of 1956: role of Britain, France, the United States, the USSR, Israel and the UNO; Arabism and Zionism; emergence of the PLO

While Nasser was establishing his control over Egypt, a series of developments was transforming the Cold War. These events would have an important impact on the Middle East, and eventually lead to the 1956 Suez Crisis. In 1950 Britain, France and

Radford Plan

After the Korean War, and as part of National Security Council policy statement 162, Admiral Radford and the Joint Chiefs of Staff aimed to reduce the level of US troops deployed overseas and replace them with local forces supported militarily by the USA, up to and including nuclear deterrent.

NATO members

NATO's members included Belgium, the Netherlands, Luxembourg, France, Great Britain, the USA, Canada, Portugal, Italy, Norway, Denmark and Iceland.

SEATO members

The members were the USA, France, United Kingdom, New Zealand, Australia, the Philippines, Thailand and Pakistan.

Baghdad Pact

The Baghdad Pact is sometimes known as the Middle Eastern Treaty Organization (METO) and became the Central Treaty Organization (CENTO) in 1959.

the USA agreed to limit arms shipments to Egypt and Israel in an attempt to minimize the possibilities of further conflict in the area. At the same time, partly as a result of the ending of the Korean War in 1953 and partly as a result of the **Radford Plan**, the US government was changing the thinking behind its foreign policy. The aim was still to contain communist expansion as envisaged in the March 1947 Truman Doctrine, but the means by which this was to be done had shifted emphasis. The aim was to put a 'ring around the Soviet Union' by establishing treaties with countries bordering on the southern parts of Soviet territory and which were considered to be strategically important to the West. The North Atlantic Treaty Organization (**NATO**) had already been established in 1949 and Turkey became a member in February 1952. Following Mao's accession to power in China in October 1949, the North Korean invasion of South Korea in June 1950 and the defeat of the French in Indochina in 1954, another pact was signed in September 1954. The South East Asian Treaty Organization (**SEATO**) was signed between eight nations and aimed to limit any further communist expansion into Asia.

Hardly surprisingly, the Middle East was seen as a region where Soviet influence might need to be contained. John Foster Dulles, the US Secretary of State and a fervent anti-communist, was in favour of a 'northern tier' concept. In this concept, those non-Arab countries that lay on the Soviet Union's southern borders would sign a treaty that would be supported by the West along the same lines as NATO and SEATO. It was clear that Nasser was not in favour of the establishment of US military bases in Egypt and the USA sought to find other nations with which it could ally itself. The USA had supported the coup in Iran and now signed agreements with Turkey and Pakistan. Britain was against the extension of US influence in the region, particularly with countries it saw as being part of its own sphere of influence. In 1955 a mutual security agreement called the **Baghdad Pact** was signed by Great Britain, Turkey, Iran, Iraq and Pakistan, aiming to consolidate Britain's position in the Middle East. The USA did not join the pact formally, but was allowed to have observer status instead. As time passed it was obvious that the policies and actions of the Soviet Union, Great Britain and the USA would play ever-increasing roles in the region.

SOURCE A

Military blocs in the Near and Middle East are needed, not by the countries of that area, but by those aggressive American circles which are trying to establish domination there. They are also needed by those British circles which, by means of these blocs, are trying to retain and restore their shaken positions, in spite of the vital interests of the peoples of the Near and Middle East who have taken the road of independent national development...

Of course, the Soviet Union cannot remain indifferent to the situation arising in the region of the Near and Middle East, since the formation of these blocs and the establishment of foreign military bases on the territory of the countries of the Near and Middle East have a direct bearing on the security of the USSR. This attitude of the Soviet government should be all the more understandable since the USSR is situated very close to these countries – something which cannot be said of other foreign powers, for instance, of the United States, which is thousands of kilometres from this area…

From a statement by the Soviet Ministry of Foreign Affairs on Security in the Near and Middle East, 16 April 1955

STUDENT STUDY SECTION

QUESTION

What are the origin, purpose, value and limitations of Source A?

Student Answer A – *Sebastian*

The origin of the source is a statement by the Soviet Ministry of Foreign Affairs on security in the Near and Middle East on 16 April 1955. The purpose of the source is to state that the situation in the Middle East does affect the Soviet Union and that it will not tolerate American domination of the area. A value of the source is that it shows the Soviet view and policies towards the Middle East. It shows Soviet fears for its security due to American military bases in the East. A limitation of the source is that it is politically biased as the USA was the enemy of the USSR at this time during the Cold War. It will aim at presenting the United States in a bad light. It thus is not an objective account of the situation in the Middle East.

Student Answer B – *Carl*

The passage originates from a statement by the USSR Ministry of Foreign Affairs on Security in the Near and Middle East on 16 April 1955. Its main purpose is to account for and explain the stance of the USSR towards the situation in the Near and Middle East. It also makes plans as to aspects that are needed to limit the aggressive American and British circles. The greatest value is that it is part of an original and official statement of the policies the USSR had towards the USA and UK as well as an explanation for the policies. The biggest limitation of the source is that just because it's official, one cannot assume that these were the actual policies taken on by the USSR. Although these were the policies and explanations that were published, the actual reasoning and aims are often not enclosed in such documents.

Examiner's comments

Sebastian provides a very sound analysis of the source, although he should be careful in his use of the word 'biased'. The reason for this is that weaker students use the term 'biased' all the time, but are unable to provide any justification as to why this is so – or they assume that any Israeli source writing about the Palestinian issue will automatically be negative towards the Palestinian cause and is therefore automatically 'biased'.

Which of these two would receive the higher mark or should they both receive the same mark? Explain your answer. Although both Sebastian and Carl have made different points they have both included a clear attempt at following the rubric of origin, purpose, value and limitations. Sebastian relies too much on the content, whereas Carl's analysis is a little deeper. Carl would probably receive a mark more than Sebastian (4 against 3).

● **Examiner's hint**
Be very careful when you use the word 'biased' in your answer – make sure that your judgement is justified. Also try to see if you can answer this question by not using the terms 'primary' and 'secondary' (see Chapter 1).

Nasser was furious at the signing of the Baghdad Pact and was particularly angry with Iraq's leader, **Nuri al-Said**, whom Nasser saw as rejecting Arab nationalist interests and potentially upsetting the fragile peace that existed between Egypt and Israel. Nasser perceived himself as the leader of Arab nationalism, and it was clear that sooner or later his objectives would result in a clash with the Western powers, particularly as Britain and France still technically owned the Suez Canal.

In the meantime, the Palestinian Arabs had become better organized and their *fedayeen* guerrillas were carrying out raids on Israeli positions. Between 1950 and 1954, 186 Israelis were killed and 279 wounded. The Israeli government decided to take a hard line against the *fedayeen* and began to strike back in retaliation, creating a new anti-terrorist force, Unit 101. On 13 October 1953, as revenge for an attack that killed an Israeli mother and her children, Ben-Gurion ordered an attack on the Jordanian village of Qibya during which 69 people were killed, many of them women and children. This raid was condemned by the USA and the Arab world. It would also be one of the reasons behind a gradual deterioration of the relationship between Egypt and Israel. In 1954 a hard-liner, Pinhas Lavon, became the Israeli Minister of Defense. Lavon was worried that the impending departure of British troops from the Suez Canal, effectively removing the buffer between Egypt and Israel, would be a military threat to Israel. He devised a scheme whereby American and

 Nuri al-Said
Nuri served as Prime Minister of Iraq many times, and was its leader between 1954 and 1957. In 1930 he was instrumental in negotiating a treaty with Britain recognizing Iraq's independence. After World War II, Iraq joined the Baghdad Pact, which served to alienate Nuri from many Arab nations, who saw Iraq as being too pro-Western. Eventually, in 1958, following the army revolt that overthrew the monarchy, Nuri was killed in the coup d'état.

Fedayeen
Means 'resistance forces' or 'commandos' in Arabic. The term specifically refers to Palestinian guerrilla fighters.

British buildings, such as banks, would be bombed by Israeli agents. He thought that this would force the British to keep their troops in the region to protect British interests, thus removing any potential Egyptian threat. The plan failed and Lavon was forced to resign, but the incident damaged Egyptian-Israeli relations.

Nasser and the 1956 Suez Crisis

The turning point came in February 1955. The number of raids from Gaza into Israel had been steadily increasing. In one such raid an Israeli was killed by an Egyptian squad. In retaliation Ben-Gurion, who had returned as Minister of Defense, ordered a major strike on Gaza on 28 February. Thirty-eight people were killed and the raid was clearly intended as a message to Nasser and the West, showing the strength of Israel's military capability. Nasser became much more hostile towards Israel, supporting *fedayeen* attacks in early 1955.

His next reaction was to turn to Washington and ask for the USA to supply Egypt with weapons in order that they could defend themselves if there were any further Israeli aggression. President **Dwight D. Eisenhower** decided to follow the Arms Limitation Agreement, which the USA, Britain and France had signed in 1950, and refused Egypt's request. To Nasser it seemed as if he could not get any support from the West and, following the Bandung Conference of non-aligned states in March 1955, began to look elsewhere. In September an agreement was reached with Czechoslovakia (in reality the agreement was with the USSR) who would sell 300 tanks, 200 armoured personnel carriers, 200 MiG-15 fighters and 50 Ilyushin bombers to Egypt. This massive arms shipment threatened to tip the military scales against Israel in favour of Egypt. The Czech arms deal with Egypt immediately spurred Israel into action and Israel entered into an arms agreement with France, which was opposed to Nasser's Arab nationalism and his support of **FLN** guerrillas in French Algeria. Through the arms agreement, Israel was to be supplied with tanks and aircraft in November 1955. It seemed as if a war was imminent.

Interestingly enough, it was the actions of the USA that were to be the catalyst for the Suez War of 1956. One of Nasser's major dreams was the building of a dam at Aswan, on the River Nile, to generate hydroelectric power and provide badly needed irrigation for the area. The intention was to increase the amount of land that Egypt had for the cultivation of its crops. The cost of the dam was financed by loans from the World Bank, the USA and Britain. Suddenly, without warning, the USA announced that it would no longer provide any more money for the building of the dam. Britain also told Nasser that it too would no longer make any more loans available. For Nasser, the Aswan Dam was one of his most important and prestigious projects. It would raise his profile in the Arab world and provide the basis for an agricultural and industrial transformation of the Egyptian economy. Nasser's reaction to the US and British decisions was swift. On 26 July he announced that Egypt had nationalized the Suez Canal, putting it under the control of the Egyptian government. He stated that all revenue from it would now belong to Egypt, not the French- and British-controlled Suez Canal Company.

Dwight D. Eisenhower
One of the USA's great war leaders from World War II, and President of the USA between 1953 and 1961.

FLN
FLN stands for *Front de Libération Nationale* – the National Liberation Front (in Algeria). It was set up on 1 November 1954 to gain independence for Algeria from France. The FLN is a socialist group, but sees itself as representing Arab Socialism, rather than Marxist-Leninism. It is still a powerful force in Algerian politics and in the 2007 elections the FLN received 136 seats in Parliament, remaining the largest party in Algeria and forming a coalition government with other parties.

SOURCE B

The uproar which we anticipated has been taking place in London and Paris. This tremendous uproar is not supported by reason or logic. It is backed only by imperialist methods, by the habits of blood-sucking and of usurping rights, and by interference in the affairs of other countries. An unjustified uproar arose in London, and yesterday Britain submitted a protest to Egypt. I wonder what was the basis of this protest by Britain to Egypt? The Suez Canal Company is an Egyptian company, subject to Egyptian sovereignty. When we nationalized the Suez Canal Company, we only nationalized an Egyptian limited company, and by doing so we exercised a right which stems from the very core of Egyptian sovereignty. What right has Britain to interfere in our internal affairs…

From a speech by President Nasser justifying the nationalization of the Suez Canal Company, 28 July 1956

● **Examiner's hint**
Are all four parts of the rubric included in the answers?

STUDENT STUDY SECTION

QUESTION

According to its origin and purpose, what are the value and limitations of Source B for historians studying the Suez Crisis? (6 marks would be awarded for two documents, so this should be marked out of 3 or 4.)

Student Answer A – *Ted*

The source is an extract from a speech by President Nasser on 28 July 1956 and has the purpose to affirm Nasser's justification for the nationalization of the Suez Canal Company, but more importantly to stress Britain's interference in Egypt's affairs, condemning them for their imperialist methods which employ neither reason nor logic. Nasser provokes the reader with an image of a greedy and selfish Britain, displaying his antipathy.

The speech's value lies in the fact that it provides the reader with a first-hand speech experience by Nasser to demonstrate his opinion of the nationalization of the Suez Canal Company. Thus the reader can assess the extract in respect to international interferences into the internal affairs of Egypt and acquire a subjective view of the country. The book's limitations are distinguished in its subjectivity of speech, enforcing political bias. Therefore, the reader is confronted with one perspective of the issue instead of an objective view, which limits the reader's evaluation of the big picture.

Student Answer B – *Mark*

The origin of the source is a speech by President Nasser made on 28 July 1956. Its purpose is to justify the nationalization of the Suez Canal. Furthermore, it is aimed at convincing the public that the act was justified in the face of British and French claims on Egyptian land. Nasser thus wants to make clear that Britain and France have no rights over Egyptian territory. The value of the source is that it shows how the nationalization of the canal was presented to the Egyptian public. It demonstrates that the foreign countries Britain and France were presented as 'imperialist' powers. A limitation of the source is that it is politically biased and only shows the views of the Egyptian president, which will be subjective, especially because the speech aims at shaping the Egyptian public's opinion. Other views which may see the event more objectively are not considered.

Student Answer C – *Pablo*

Because of the source's purpose, it should not be regarded as flawless and its limitations must be considered. Of course, an historian would not be able to extract from the speech the nature of Britain and France's intervention, and so the extent of Egyptian right to the Canal cannot be determined. Nasser simply makes claims to the area, but the accuracy of his sole right to it cannot be determined from this source because of the president's aims to convince. The source is limited in the information it reveals, and thus its main strength is that it can convey the extent of Egypt's anger towards Britain and France. Through the source, historians can discover to what extent Nasser believed his actions justified and his claim to the Canal region undeniable. This, of course, would generally allow for an interpretation of why he believed British and French intervention in the area was unjustifiable. A general explanation of Arab nationalism at the time can be discovered.

Examiner's comments

Look at the style, tone and use of language when answering this type of question. There are three very different approaches here. Which is better and why? Pablo does not follow the rubric (the instructions in the question) and ignores the origin. His line of argument is hard to follow. Ted writes in a rather wordy way, which tends to hide what he means and it can be a little hard to follow what he is saying, although some of his points are good. Mark is succinct and easy to follow, but has he done enough for full marks? Yes, he has. The four parts of the rubric are easily identifiable, there is a clear understanding of the source and Mark has analyzed the source well, although his last sentence does not add to his analysis.

Nasser's decision to nationalize the Suez Canal was the last straw for France. It had decided, early in 1956, that Nasser needed to be deposed and now seriously began to find a means to achieve this goal. Naturally Britain might be willing to assist, but an attack on Egypt by two permanent members of the Security Council of the UN would be seen as unacceptable by the Arab states and the rest of world opinion. Another country that was keen to see the overthrow of Nasser was Israel and it was in Israel's direction that the French decided to go. By the end of September 1956, an agreement had been reached between the two countries that action against Egypt should be taken as soon as possible. But this action would need the support of the British, particularly as it had bases in the Mediterranean that could provide support for any military operation.

SOURCE C

A 1956 photograph of the Suez Canal showing the actions taken by the Egyptian government.

● **Examiner's hint**

Try to find two clear points and give some explanation to show your understanding of them.

STUDENT STUDY SECTION

QUESTION

What message is conveyed by Source C?

The involvement of Britain, France and Israel in the Suez Crisis

The British government's attitude towards Nasser was clear. The seizure of the Suez Canal had been damaging to British influence in the Middle East and had severe financial implications, as most of the oil that was supplied to Britain had to pass through the canal. At the same time, Nasser's refusal to join the Baghdad Pact and his negotiation of the Czech arms deal seemed to imply that Nasser was becoming closer to the USSR, further threatening British interests in the region. The relationship between Britain and Israel was somewhat strained, but eventually, by October 1956, Britain had realized that it was in her best interests to enter into a three-way agreement with France and Israel. At a secret meeting in Paris, attended by Ben-Gurion, Britain, France and Israel came up with a plan.

SOURCE D

The results of the conversations which took place at Sèvres from 22–24 October 1956 between the representatives of the Governments of the United Kingdom, the State of Israel and of France are the following:

1. *The Israeli forces launch in the evening of 29 October 1956 a large scale attack on the Egyptian forces with the aim of reaching the Canal Zone the following day.*
On being apprised of these events, the British and French Governments during the day of 30 October 1956 respectively and simultaneously make two appeals to the Egyptian Government and the Israeli Government on the following lines:

2. A. *To the Egyptian Government*
   a) halt all acts of war.
   b) withdraw all its troops ten miles from the Canal.
   c) accept temporary occupation of key positions on the Canal by the Anglo-French forces to guarantee freedom of passage through the Canal by vessels of all nations until a final settlement.

   B. *To the Israeli Government*
   a) halt all acts of war.
   b) withdraw all its troops ten miles to the east of the Canal.
   In addition, the Israeli Government will be notified that the French and British Governments have demanded of the Egyptian Government to accept temporary occupation of key positions along the Canal by Anglo-French forces.
   It is agreed that if one of the Governments refused, or did not give its consent, within twelve hours the Anglo-French forces would intervene with the means necessary to ensure that their demands are accepted.

   C. *The representatives of the three Governments agree that the Israeli Government will not be required to meet the conditions in the appeal addressed to it, in the event that the Egyptian Government does not accept those in the appeal addressed to it for their part.*

3. *In the event that the Egyptian Government should fail to agree within the stipulated time to the conditions of the appeal addressed to it, the Anglo-French forces will launch military operations against the Egyptian forces in the early hours of the morning of 31 October.*

4. *The Israeli Government will send forces to occupy the western shore of the Gulf of Aqaba and the group of islands Tirane and Sanafir to ensure freedom of navigation in the Gulf of Aqaba.*

5. *Israel undertakes not to attack Jordan during the period of operations against Egypt. But in the event that during the same period Jordan should attack Israel, the British Government undertakes not to come to the aid of Jordan.*

6. *The arrangements of the present protocol must remain strictly secret.*

7. *They will enter into force after the agreement of the three Governments.*

From The Sèvres Protocol, October 1956

STUDENT STUDY SECTION

QUESTION

This document has been widely regarded by most observers as one of the most cynical of the 20th century. Make a list of any of its terms you would refer to in order to agree with this statement. It is also very difficult to find the original copy of it in Britain. Why do you think this is?

The plan was based on an Israeli attack into the Sinai Peninsula, initially to destroy *fedayeen* camps that existed there. The Israelis would advance to the Gulf of Aqaba, seemingly to open up the Red Sea to allow Israeli ships free access to its waters. The British would then issue an ultimatum to both Israel and Egypt to withdraw to positions 16km (10 miles) from either side of the Suez Canal. It was predicted that Nasser would refuse to withdraw his forces, which would give Britain and France the excuse to intervene militarily to protect the Suez Canal, with the result that Nasser would be removed from power either by the joint Franco-British force, or by the Egyptians themselves. Israel would then be able to occupy the entire Sinai Peninsula. The fatal mistake of Britain, France and Israel was their determination to go ahead with the attack without having received support from Washington.

SOURCE E

Ministers had already considered at several meetings the ways in which the situation might develop. These had also been canvassed with the French. On October 25th the Cabinet discussed the specific possibility of conflict between Israel and Egypt and decided in principle how it would react if this occurred. The Governments of France and the United Kingdom should, it considered, at once call on both parties to stop hostilities and withdraw their forces to a distance from either bank of the canal. If one or both failed to comply within a definite period, then British and French forces would intervene as a temporary measure to separate the combatants. To ensure this being effective, they would have to occupy key positions at Port Said, Ismailia and Suez. Our purpose was to safeguard free passage through the canal, if it were threatened with becoming a zone of warfare, and to arrest the spread of fighting in the Middle East.

From Anthony Eden, *Full Circle – The Memoirs of the Rt. Hon. Sir Anthony Eden*, 1960

● **Examiner's hint**

Question (a) – this question is invariably the first type of question you will see on Paper 1. Find three points and try to paraphrase the source. Question (b) – this question is invariably the second question on Paper 1 after 1a) and 1b). Remember to link the sources.

STUDENT STUDY SECTION

QUESTIONS

a) **What, according to Source E, were the actions that the British government would take in 1956?**

b) **Compare and contrast Sources D and E.**

On 29 October, Israel dropped a paratroop force into the Sinai. On 31 October, Britain and France issued the agreed-upon ultimatum, which Israel followed and, as anticipated, Nasser ignored. On 5 November a combined British-French force attacked Port Said. The invasion was greeted by an international protest, not least by British public opinion. In Washington, Eisenhower was furious at the actions that had been taken by Britain, France and Israel, particularly as he was involved in his own presidential election campaign. He was also very concerned that the Soviet Union might use the crisis as an excuse to intervene in the Middle East and the US government issued the following warning.

SOURCE F

If power-hungry Communists should either falsely or correctly estimate that the Middle East is inadequately defended, they might be tempted to use open measures of armed attack. If so, that would start a chain of circumstances which would almost surely involve the United States in military action. I am convinced that the best insurance against this dangerous contingency is to make clear now our readiness to cooperate fully and freely with our friends of the Middle East in ways consonant with the purposes and principles of the United Nations. I intend promptly to send a special mission to the Middle East to explain the cooperation we are prepared to give.

From US Department of State Press Release 604, 29 November 1956

The United States proposed a resolution to the UN Security Council on 30 October calling for the ending of military actions, a proposal that was quickly vetoed by Britain and France. The USA then went directly to the General Assembly where, on 1 November, a resolution was passed by a vote of 64 to 5 calling for an immediate ceasefire and condemning the aggressor nations. Britain and France ignored the UN action and continued their military campaigns. Despite being involved in the Hungarian uprising, the Soviets made it known that they were considering taking military action against Israel. Eisenhower and Dulles then put tremendous pressure on the British Prime Minister, **Anthony Eden**, to end the operation. The USA threatened to cut off oil supplies to Britain, withdraw US funds from London banks and block any loans from the International Monetary Fund to aid Britain's depleted sterling reserves. In the face of such opposition, Britain informed France that it would no longer support their actions and on 6 November Britain and France agreed to a ceasefire, although Israeli forces still remained in the Sinai.

SOURCE G

The Suez crisis has haunted British governments ever since 1956 – it hung over Margaret Thatcher during the 1982 Falklands War, and its ghost now moves between the Foreign Office and Downing Street, between Jack Straw and Tony Blair. For Suez destroyed a British prime minister – along, almost, with the Anglo-American alliance – and symbolised the end of the British Empire. It killed many civilians – all Egyptian, of course – and brought shame upon the allies when they turned out to have committed war crimes. It rested on a lie – that British and French troops should land in Egypt to 'separate' the Egyptian and Israeli armies, even though the British and French had earlier connived at Israel's invasion. Colonel Gamal Abdul Nasser was described by the British Prime Minister, Anthony Eden, as 'the Mussolini of the Nile' even though, scarcely a year earlier, Eden had warmly shaken Nasser's hand in an exchange of congratulations over a new Anglo-Egyptian treaty… In the end, British troops – poorly equipped and treating their Egyptian enemies with racial disdain – left in humiliation, digging up their dead comrades from their graves to freight back home lest the Egyptians defiled their bodies.

From Robert Fisk, 'New Crisis, Old Lessons – The Suez Crisis of 1956', an article in *The Independent*, a British newspaper, 15 January 2003

 Anthony Eden
British Prime Minister between 1955 and 1957. He supported the joint invasion of Egypt by France, Britain and Israel in the Suez Crisis of 1956, but severely underestimated the attitude of the USA, who put intense pressure on Eden's government resulting in the withdrawal of British troops from the area. Eden's reputation was severely damaged by the policies he followed during the Suez Crisis, which was universally considered as disastrous for Britain, and a clear sign of the end of Britain's status as a superpower.

 ToK Time
What makes a statement 'historical'? Give three examples of statements that are truly historical and three examples of statements that are not. What do you think is the difference between them?

STUDENT STUDY SECTION

QUESTION
Answer this question first, and then look at the Examiner's Comments afterwards. According to its origin and purpose, what are the value and limitations of Source G for historians studying the Suez Crisis? (6 marks would be awarded for two documents, so this should be marked out of 3 or 4.)

Student Answer – *Julian*

Source G is an extract from the article 'New Crisis, Old Lesson – The Suez Crisis of 1956', by Robert Fisk from The Independent. Its purpose is to inform readers of the crises the Suez Canal has provoked in Britain in the past. Furthermore it examines the attitude of British leaders towards the situation in the Middle East during the Suez Crisis of 1956. The value of Source G lies in its origin. The article originates from 2003, thus being quite recent, and allows for an examination of the Suez Crisis from several points of view as well as from the later historical context of the United Kingdom. The actions of the British government during the Suez Crisis have come under intense scrutiny. The limitations of the source lie in its tone and the type of language used in it. The journalist, Robert Fisk, has a critical stance to the actions of the British during the Suez Crisis. This has an effect on the tone of the document which is rather judgemental, and thus makes the source biased. This makes it difficult for historians to obtain objective information from Source G.

Examiner's comments

This is the sort of extract that is very common in the IB Paper 1 examination. One of the points to note is the year in which it was written. Is this a value, or a limitation, or both, depending on which way you view it? Explain your answer. The comments about the tone of the article should be noted, as the language and tone of a source can help you to judge its values and limitations. What words used by Fisk would show that his position might not be truly objective?

QUESTION
Do you agree with Fisk's analysis of the Suez Crisis? Explain your answer.

The consequences of the 1956 Suez Crisis

The Suez Crisis had important and long-lasting consequences for all of the countries involved. The biggest losers were certainly Britain and France. Eden was forced to resign in January 1957 and his denials of responsibility damaged the credibility of Britain in the eyes of the world. Britain and France lost a considerable amount of influence in the Middle East and, following France's defeats in Algeria, were soon to become of minor importance in the region. Guy Mollet's government resigned in May 1957 (Mollet was the French Prime Minister between 1956 and 1957). Britain and France's influence in the Middle East was taken over by the USA and the USSR, who began to pursue a more active role there.

In 1957, Eisenhower proclaimed the existence of 'the Eisenhower Doctrine', which promised military and economic aid to Middle Eastern countries who needed it to contain any communist expansion. Eisenhower's rationale behind this doctrine was that 'the existing vacuum in the Middle East must be filled by the United States before it was filled by the Soviet Union' (Charles Smith, *Palestine and the Arab-Israeli Conflict*, 2007).

The United States further insisted on a complete withdrawal of Israeli troops from the Sinai Peninsula and supported the UN in the installation of a UN Emergency Force (UNEF) to replace them as a buffer between Egypt and Israel. The USA supported Israel diplomatically, although Suez had shown how much leverage the USA could exercise in the region, and the Soviet Union continued its implicit support of Egypt.

The Middle East had now become a part of the Cold War. While not having gained anything territorially from the Suez War, Israel was well satisfied by the outcome, as now Israel's own borders were guaranteed by UNEF. It also gained access for Israeli shipping into the Gulf of Aqaba from Eilat, providing Israel with a Red Sea port. Israel's military victory demonstrated what a potent force its armed forces had become and the Israelis learned several key military lessons that were to be useful in the future.

Somewhat ironically, although Nasser was on the losing side in the war, Egypt gained considerably. It had taken over control of the Suez Canal from Britain and France and had also seized a considerable number of British assets in the area. The Aswan Dam project continued its course and Egypt began to develop economically. UNEF also provided protection from any aggressive Israeli military action. To the Arab world, Nasser was the first leader successfully to challenge the West and for some years to come he was seen as the voice of Arab nationalist aspirations. In 1958, Egypt joined with Syria to create the United Arab Republic, a union that the Israelis saw as threatening. As you will see later, the immediate consequences of the 1956 Suez Crisis, which resulted in the decision to open both the Straits of Tiran and the Gulf of Aqaba to Israeli shipping, were to be instrumental in causing the next war to break out between the Arabs and the Israelis in June 1967.

SOURCE H

Cartoon in the Swiss satirical magazine *Nebelspalters* in Zurich, 28 November 1956.

STUDENT STUDY SECTION

QUESTIONS

a) **Study this cartoon carefully. Look at each of the six panels and, in as much detail as you can, summarize the message conveyed by each panel. The man on the left is President Nasser of Egypt. What is the overall message of the cartoon?**

b) **Using Sources B, D, E, G and H in this section, and your own knowledge, analyze to what extent the actions of the British and French governments in October 1956 were merely to 'separate the Egyptian and Israeli armies' (Source G). (8 marks)**

Student Answer (Question b) – *Debby*

Although the British and French governments claimed that their actions and policies were to act as mediators between the Egyptians and Israelis, in reality their motives were clearly aimed at weakening Nasser and re-establishing control of the Suez Canal.

In 1956 Nasser had nationalized the Suez Canal Company exercising, what he saw, as a 'right which stems from the very core of Egyptian sovereignty' (Source B). The British and French governments saw this as a deliberate attempt to destabilize their position in the Middle East. Britain was worried about oil supplies in Iraq and France had been expelled from Indochina by Ho Chi Minh. Although Britain claimed that its purpose was to 'safeguard free passage through the canal … and arrest the spread of fighting in the Middle East' (Source E), it is clear from the secret Sèvres protocol signed between itself, France and Israel that Britain was far from being a neutral observer. The Protocol clearly shows in term 2A clause c) that the aim was to re-establish a military presence in Egypt (Source D). It was apparent that all three signatories of the Protocol were aware that Egypt would not agree to its terms, which would give them an excuse to invade – Clauses 3 and 4 (Source D). The date of 25 October in Source E is also important as the Cabinet is meeting *after* the Sèvres Protocol had been signed, which clearly shows that it knew of the agreement between the three governments before making its statement about the purpose of its actions – and this therefore seems to support Fisk's claims (Source G).

Nasser's popularity among the Arab states and the increase of nationalism had become the justification for Western powers to desire his overthrow. The fact that he had bought arms from Czechoslovakia and the USSR meant that, to the west, the Soviets were establishing a proxy base in the Middle East. The USA was extremely concerned about this increasing Soviet presence in the region. It is interesting to note that Source H, from a Swiss magazine, supports the idea that Nasser was provoking Israel by his actions, being supported by some other Arab states, whereas Source G blatantly accuses France, Britain and Israel as acting together to weaken Nasser. Fisk maintains that they 'connived at Israel's invasion' (Source G) indicating a clear intention behind their actions.

Thus, despite claims that the actions of the British and French were to ensure stability in the region, it seems clear that their real intention was to destabilize Nasser and regain control of the Suez Canal.

Examiner's comments

This is an excellent answer. All of the sources are used, even with Source H's counter-argument, and there is a focused attempt to answer the question. The sources have been used to support the claims made by Debby and are not simply mechanically applied. There is also good use of Debby's own knowledge. This would certainly receive top marks.

REVIEW SECTION

This chapter has dealt with the historical causes of the conflict between the Arabs and the Zionists/Israelis, has analyzed the significance of the establishment of the State of Israel in 1948 and has explored the causes, course and consequences of the 1948 and 1956 wars between the Arab states and Israel. Respond to the following questions/activities briefly using information from the text, the sources and your own knowledge.

Review questions

1. What are the major issues which separate the Arabs and the Israelis? Where do these originate?

2. Analyze the reasons behind the UNSCOP plan for the partition of Palestine. In your opinion was there an alternative solution?

3. Draw up a table to compare the 1948 and 1956 wars. Use the headings: Causes and Consequences.

5

Prescribed Subject 2:
The Arab-Israeli Conflict 1945–79

WARS AND PEACE 1963–79

This particular chapter will analyze the causes of the Six-Day War and examine the consequences it had for the region. It will then go on to look carefully at the causes of the 1973 war and assess the importance of this conflict for movements towards peace in the Middle East. This chapter will then analyze events in the region since the Egyptian-Israeli peace treaty of 1979 up to 2009, to see whether or not there have been any significant changes in the relationship between the Arabs and the Israelis. The chapter will finally examine the present status of Palestinian claims to the West Bank and Gaza Strip.

Timeline – 1967–2009

1967	Nasser sends troops into Sinai and closes the Straits of Tiran to Israeli shipping
	Six-Day War
	UN Security Council Resolution 242 issued
1968	Yasser Arafat elected chairman of the executive committee of the PLO
	Egyptian-Israeli War of Attrition
1970	Palestinian National Council declares an independent Palestinian state
1972	Black September organization seizes Israeli athletes at Munich Olympics. Nine Israelis die in airport shoot-out
1973	Egypt and Syria launch full-scale war against Israeli forces occupying the Sinai Peninsula and Golan Heights
1974	Summit meeting of Arab leaders in Rabat declares the PLO the only legitimate representative of the Palestinian people
1977	Sadat goes to Jerusalem for peace offer
1978	Camp David Accords signed by Egypt, Israel and the USA
	Israel–Jordan Peace Treaty: White House lawn handshake between Rabin, Peres and Arafat, who are jointly awarded the Nobel Peace Prize
1979	Egypt and Israel sign peace treaty
1981	Sadat assassinated by Egyptian militants during a military parade celebrating victory in the 1973 war
1987	First Palestinian Intifada begins in the Israeli-occupied Gaza Strip and the West Bank
1988	Hamas founded
	Palestinian National Council (PNC) declares the creation of a Palestinian state
1990	Arafat recognizes Israel and renounces terrorism before the UN at Geneva
	Iraq invades Kuwait
1991	Middle East Peace Conference in Madrid
1993	Israeli-Palestinian declaration of principles on interim self-government
1994	Palestinian self-rule starts in Gaza Strip and Jericho
1995	Oslo II agreement
	Rabin assassinated by Jewish extremist at a peace rally in Tel Aviv
1996	Palestinian Self-Governing Authority elected
	Benjamin Netanyahu becomes Prime Minister
1998	Wye River Agreement between Netanyahu and Arafat
2000	Second Camp David summit
2003	Mahmoud Abbas becomes Prime Minister of the Palestinian Authority

2004 Death of Yasser Arafat
2005 Mahmoud Abbas becomes President of the Palestinian Authority
2006 Hamas wins parliamentary elections in the Gaza Strip
2009 Israel invades the Gaza Strip

Section I:
The Six-Day War of 1967: causes, course and consequences

Towards the outbreak of war

In 1967, another war was fought between the Arabs and the Israelis. One of the main reasons for this conflict was the growth of Arab nationalism, which occurred as a consequence of the 1956 Suez Crisis. The Arab nations of Syria, Jordan and Egypt found it difficult to agree among themselves upon common goals for the region. Syria and Egypt joined together to form the United Arab Republic in 1958, which was partially caused by Jordan's refusal to join the other nations in pressing for the recovery of Palestine for the Arabs. This Republic was short-lived and lasted only three years.

In 1948, a 7-year-old Palestinian boy named Mahmoud Darwish, and his family, abandoned their home in western Galilee, fleeing from the advance of Israeli forces. Mahmoud and hundreds of other refugees walked to the Lebanon. Some years later, however, Mahmoud journeyed to a poetry festival in Nazareth, in Israel. There he read out one of his poems, which was well received by the crowd, who asked for more material. Mahmoud then recited a few lines scribbled on a piece of paper, written to capture the experience of renewing his travel pass with the Israeli police.

Mahmoud Darwish, the 'voice of Palestine', died on 9 August 2008, aged 67.

The poem included these lines:

SOURCE A

Write down!
I am an Arab
You have stolen the orchards of my ancestors
And the land which I cultivated
Along with my children
And you left nothing for us
Except for these rocks…

STUDENT STUDY SECTION

QUESTION

Find out some more about Mahmoud Darwish. Research using the Internet and try to discover some more of his poems. What are the value and limitations of poetry as an historical source?

The existence of 700,000 Palestinian refugees following the creation of the Jewish state in 1948 caused many problems for those countries to which the Palestinians had fled. Jordan took in so many that these refugees outnumbered the Jordanian citizens. Should they be housed and provided with social services such as education and social welfare? If the refugees became **assimilated** into their host country they would lose their Palestinian identity, virtually destroying any possibility of their gaining their own state, and so the temporary refugee camps became permanent homes and the majority of the Palestinian refugees stayed in them.

There was a desperate need for the creation of an organization to give the Palestinians some degree of unity. In 1957 a group of Palestinians, including Yasser Arafat, founded a movement in Kuwait, which quickly became known as **Fatah**, and whose goal was the liberation of Palestine from Israeli control. By the early 1960s, the Arab League had decided to sponsor the creation of an organization that would represent Palestinians and in January 1964, at a summit meeting of Arab leaders, the Palestine Liberation Organization (PLO) was formed under the leadership of an Egyptian lawyer named Ahmed Shukhairy. The PLO's stated goals were the uniting of the Palestinian refugees and the regaining of the land lost in the 1948 war.

Below is an extract from the Covenant of the PLO written on 28 May 1964. It had 29 articles that outlined the aims and objectives of the organization.

SOURCE B

Article 17. The partitioning of Palestine in 1947 and the establishment of Israel are illegal and false regardless of the loss of time, because they were contrary to the wish of the Palestine people and its natural right to its homeland, and in violation of the basic principles embodied in the charter of the United Nations, foremost among which is the right to self-determination.

Article 18. The Balfour Declaration, the Mandate system and all that has been based upon them are considered fraud. The claims of historic and spiritual ties between Jews and Palestine are not in Agreement with the facts of history or with the true basis of sound statehood. Judaism because it is a divine religion is not a nationality with independent existence. Furthermore the Jews are not one people with an independent personality because they are citizens of the countries to which they belong.

Article 19. Zionism is a colonialist movement in its inception, aggressive and expansionist in its goals, racist and segregationist in its configuration and fascist in its means and aims. Israel in its capacity as the spearhead of this destructive movement and the pillar for colonialism is a permanent source of tension and turmoil in the Middle East in particular and to the international community in general. Because of this the people of Palestine is worthy of the support and sustenance of the community of nations.

From the Covenant of the PLO, 28 May 1964

ToK Time
The role of the individual in history has been the subject of much debate. There are many people who believe that history is made by 'Great Men and Women'. To some the Russian Revolution was caused by Lenin, and Hitler started World War II. How do you react to this line of argument? Is there any truth in it?

Assimilated
Assimilated means completely integrated into another country socially and culturally.

Fatah
Palestinian guerrilla organization. The word means 'opening' or 'conquest' in Arabic. Fatah was founded in 1954 by a group of Palestinian exiles, including Yasser Arafat. Its main aim was the liberation of Palestine by violence. Fatah became part of the Palestine Liberation Organization (PLO) in 1967 and has been a key force in the Middle East since then, having led or supported many radical groups such as Black September and the al-Aqsa Martyrs' Brigades. Since 2006 there has been intense conflict between Fatah and Hamas (sometimes referred to as the Palestinian Civil War) in the Gaza Strip, where fighting began after Hamas won control over the area in recent elections.

● **Examiner's hint**
Is it possible to identify the value and limitations of a source without knowing its purpose?

STUDENT STUDY SECTION

QUESTION

Study Source B. Look up any words you do not know in a dictionary. How do you think that a) the Palestinian refugees and b) the Israeli government would react to these articles? Be sure to give reasons for your answers. What limitations does this source have? Why? What values do you think it has?

Nasser's real motives behind the establishment of the PLO were to set up an organization over which he could exert his personal influence and to try to keep the *fedayeen* and Fatah under some degree of control. Nasser found that this was not possible and gradually *fedayeen* raids against Israel began to increase, reinforcing Israel's sense of vulnerability. At the same time Syria, believing that Nasser and Egypt were being too soft towards Israel, began openly to support Fatah's activities. The Syrian media called for all Palestinians to join in a war of popular liberation against Israel. By 1966 the PLO had also begun to give its backing to both Fatah and the *fedayeen*.

Ba'athist
Belonging to the Ba'ath Party, which formed in Syria in 1947 and became very influential in Iraq, Jordan and the Lebanon. The Ba'athists eventually came to power in Syria and Iraq. The word is from the Arabic for 'resistance'.

In February 1966, the government in Syria changed, bringing a more radical **Ba'athist** regime into power, a change that worsened Syrian-Israeli relations. In August, Israeli and Syrian forces clashed in a military encounter. Nasser reversed his former policies and stated that he wanted to liberate Palestine in a revolutionary manner and not in a traditional way. He then signed a mutual defence pact with Syria that seemed to threaten Israeli security. The signing of this agreement was one of the key factors that would lead to war the following year. Egypt's support of Syria would give the latter confidence in any conflict with Israel and would also ensure that Nasser would be deeply involved in the increasingly tense relationship between Syria and Israel.

In response to *fedayeen* raids and increasing Arab propaganda, Israel launched a retaliatory raid against Samu, a town in the West Bank. The IDF destroyed buildings and killed 18 people. By the end of 1966, therefore, tensions were running high. King Hussein of Jordan was caught between the Israelis and the Syrians, being unable to counter Israeli attacks or prevent raids by the *fedayeen*. Nasser was seen as being weak, as he was unable to protect Arab states from continued Israeli military action. The fact that UNEF still patrolled the Sinai Peninsula also contributed to the perception that Nasser and Egypt were unwilling to take direct action to support the Palestinians in their demands for land.

In April 1967, Israel and Syria again clashed militarily around the Golan Heights on the Syria–Israel border, with the result that six Syrian MiG fighters were shot down. This action could have brought Egypt into the dispute through the 1966 defence pact it had signed, but Egypt took no direct action. Nasser's reputation and prestige among the Arab states was falling.

Anwar Sadat
Former soldier and Egyptian politician. Sadat followed Nasser as President in 1970 and was assassinated by his own soldiers in 1981.

The spark that was to lead directly to war, strangely enough, came from the USSR. On 13 May 1967, the Soviet President informed Nasser, through **Anwar Sadat**, that Israel intended to attack Syria and was massing its forces on Syria's border. Although this Soviet message was later found to be untrue, Nasser decided to take action. (No clear explanation has ever been given for the Soviet action. Some observers have suggested that the USSR was trying to help the Syrians to withstand increasing Israeli pressure.)

On 14 May, Nasser moved 100,000 Egyptian troops into the Sinai Peninsula and four days later informed the UN that Egypt would defend its own borders in future. He demanded that UNEF immediately withdraw from Egyptian territory. The UN suggested to Israel that the UN troops be allowed on its side of the border to create a buffer zone, but Israel refused. Finally, on 21 May, Nasser closed the Straits of Tiran to all shipping heading towards Israel, thus cutting off all Israeli oil imports. He also threatened to sink any Israeli ships that attempted to enter the Gulf of Aqaba through the Straits of Tiran.

SOURCE C

N

0   50 km

Scale

STUDENT STUDY SECTION

QUESTION

Look at the map. Can you identify the following?

The Sinai Peninsula, the Suez Canal, the Red Sea, the Gulf of Aqaba, the Straits of Tiran, Eilat, Egypt, Israel, Saudi Arabia, Syria, Lebanon and Jordan.

Carefully explain what you think the result would be of a) Egypt requesting that UNEF withdraw from the Sinai Peninsula; b) Egypt closing the Straits of Tiran.

SOURCE D

2. *We have repeatedly stated that Israel has no interest in the strip of land overlooking the western coast of the Gulf of Aqaba. Our sole purpose has been to ensure that, on the withdrawal of Israeli forces, continued freedom of navigation will exist for Israel and international shipping in the Gulf of Aqaba and the Straits of Tiran. Such freedom of navigation is a vital national interest for Israel, but it is also of importance and legitimate concern to the maritime Powers and to many States whose economics depend upon trade and navigation between the Red Sea and the Mediterranean...*

11. *The Government of Israel believes that the Gulf of Aqaba comprehends international waters and that no nation has the right to prevent free and innocent passage in the Gulf and through the Straits giving access thereto, in accordance with the generally accepted definition of those terms in the law of the sea....*

13. *Interference, by armed force, with ships of Israel flag exercising free and innocent passage in the Gulf of Aqaba and through the Straits of Tiran, will be regarded by Israel as an attack entitling it to exercise its inherent right of self-defence under Article 51 of the United Nations Charter and to take all such measures as are necessary to ensure the free and innocent passages of its ships in the Gulf and in the Straits.*

From a speech by Israeli Foreign Secretary, Golda Meir, to the United Nations, 1 March 1957

● **Examiner's hint**
Look at the words used and their tone. This will usually help you to analyze any source.

Levi Eshkol
Eshkol was an Israeli politician and served as Prime Minister from 1963 to 1969. He was elected to the Knesset in 1951 as a member of the Mapai Party and served as Minister of Agriculture, Finance Minister and Mapai Party Chairman until his appointment as Prime Minister. Eshkol was the first Israeli Prime Minister to go on an official state visit to the USA, in May 1964. His decision to ignore military pressure to attack Egypt early in 1967 is seen by many observers as contributing to the success of the Six-Day War, as it allowed the Israeli forces to reach optimum strike readiness.

Moshe Dayan
Dayan was an Israeli soldier and politician. He was leader of the IDF in the 1950s and Defense Minister during the 1967 Six-Day War.

STUDENT STUDY SECTION

QUESTION
Read the above source and make a list of what you think are the most important sections. You should be selective. Do not list everything – just the most important words.
What is the purpose of this source?

On the Egyptian side, Nasser did not believe that his actions in requesting UNEF to withdraw and closing the Straits of Tiran would necessarily result in war. The intention behind his actions was the desire to improve his own position among the Arab states and achieve a political rather than a military victory. He insisted that Egypt would not attack first and that Israel would be the aggressor.

Despite the claims made by Golda Meir in her 1957 speech to the UN, there was also caution on the side of the Israeli government. Although the military establishment in Israel pushed for immediate action, Prime Minister **Levi Eshkol** was hesitant to go to war without being assured of international support. He sent representatives to the USA, France and Great Britain seeking assurances of their approval for any future military action. The US government wanted to avoid war in the Middle East and informed Israel that they would try to intervene to get Nasser to reopen the Straits of Tiran. On 27 May, the Eshkol administration voted not to go to war but to wait for two weeks, as requested by the USA, while it tried to get international support to put pressure on Egypt.

Eshkol's uncertainty about what sort of action to take led to increasing criticism in Israel and a decline in his popularity. His generals, on the other hand, pushed for action. They were convinced that they would win any conflict with the Arab states and saw the opportunity to expand Israeli territory into the Gaza Strip, the West Bank and finally win the coveted prize of Jerusalem. On 30 May, Nasser signed a joint defence pact with King Hussein of Jordan and the following day Eshkol gave in and created a Government of National Unity, appointing **Moshe Dayan** as Minister of Defense and giving Menachem Begin a place in the cabinet. It seemed certain that a war would start; the only questions were when and by whom? A key factor was the news, on 2 June, of the decision by Nasser to send an Egyptian representative to Washington on 7 June. The Eshkol government had received notification of support for an attack from the **CIA** and officials from the Pentagon and on 4 June the Israeli cabinet approved Moshe Dayan's plans to attack Egypt the next day.

SOURCE E

Moshe Dayan, the celebrated commander who, as Defense Minister in 1967, gave the order to conquer the Golan... [said] 'many of the firefights with the Syrians were deliberately provoked by Israel, and the kibbutz residents who pressed the Government to take the Golan Heights did so less for security than for the farmland... They didn't even try to hide their greed for the land...We would send a tractor to plow some area where it wasn't possible to do anything, in the demilitarized area, and knew in advance that the Syrians would start to shoot. If they didn't shoot, we would tell the tractor to advance further, until in the end the Syrians would get annoyed and shoot.

'And then we would use artillery and later the air force also, and that's how it was...The Syrians, on the fourth day of the war, were not a threat to us.'

From *The New York Times*, 11 May 1997, published on a website called 'Jews for Justice in the Middle East – A revisionist history': http://www.cactus48.com/1967war.html

STUDENT STUDY SECTION

QUESTIONS

According to its origin and purpose, what are the value and limitations of this source for historians studying the 1967 war?

Here are two answers. Which do you think would receive the higher mark? Why? (See Examiner's Comments below.)

Student Answer A – *Simon*

The origin of the source is a New York Times article dated 11 May 1997, published on a website called 'Jews for Justice in the Middle East – A revisionist history'. Its purpose is to show the motives behind the Israeli conquering of the Golan Heights. The value of the source lies in that it is a statement by the Israeli Minister of Defense who speaks openly about the reasons behind the war over the Golan Heights. The fact that it was published on a Jewish website although it portrays Israel in a bad light, speaks for its value. The limitation of the source is that the interview was conducted 30 years after the actual war with Syria.

Student Answer B – *Soraya*

The origin of this source is an excerpt from the New York Times, which was originally published on 11 May and is now part of a revisionist website. The purpose of this source is to reveal that the firefights with Syrians and Israelis on the Golan Heights were deliberately provoked by Israel. The value of this source is that it includes the Defense Minister's explanation of the incident. Since he was directly involved in the firefights, his accounts could provide first-hand information about the course of the fight. Also, considering that he is Israeli makes the source valuable to the historians as his account reveals Israel's general view on the Golan Height Confrontation. However, the fact that this source was taken from a website called 'Jews for Justice ... A revisionist History' suggests a number of limitations. For instance, the source might contain biased information as the revisionists attempt to provide counter-ideas and arguments to orthodox view points. Also, since the source is mainly focused on Moshe Dayan's account, it fails to provide a Syrian's perspective on the same issue.

Examiner's comments

Naturally Soraya's answer is the better of the two. The four parts of the question are very clearly identified and her comments indicate a good historical awareness of the issues involved in analyzing sources. While Simon's analysis is solid, some of his explanations are a little unclear and he needs to clarify the point he is making about the purpose.

CIA
Central Intelligence Agency. Formed in 1947 in the USA, the CIA's main function is collecting and analyzing information about foreign governments, corporations and persons in order to advise US policymakers.

Revisionist
'Revisionist' history is history writing that challenges official or orthodox portrayals of the past.

● **Examiner's hint**
Look at how well the student has identified the purpose of the source. That will be a key determinant of its value and limitations.

 ToK Time
'The charges which I have found to be substantially true include the charges that Irving has for his own ideological reasons persistently and deliberately misrepresented and manipulated historical evidence.'
An excerpt from High Court Judge Charles Gray's ruling in the David Irving libel suit, guardian.co.uk, 11 April 2000.

Discuss, using examples, ways in which historians' accounts of events could be seen as having 'deliberately misrepresented and manipulated historical evidence'.

The Six-Day War

The Israeli Air Force struck at 7:00am on 5 June. Within three hours almost the entire Egyptian Air Force had been destroyed on the ground, airfields in Syria and Jordan had been hit and it was already clear that an Israeli victory was likely as the Arab forces had no air support and the Israeli Air Force could strike at will. Almost simultaneously, the Israeli Army attacked the Sinai Peninsula and, despite strong Egyptian resistance, was already pushing forward towards the Suez Canal by the end of the first day of fighting. Israeli troops also attacked the West Bank, heading for the River Jordan. Syria, Egypt and Jordan counterattacked on the same day.

The UN Security Council called for a ceasefire but the Arab states refused, believing that they still had a chance of victory. In the Mitla Pass much of the retreating Egyptian Army was surrounded and captured. The war with Egypt effectively ended when the IDF occupied Sharm-al-Sheikh, which opened the Gulf of Aqaba and the Straits of Tiran to Israeli shipping. Egypt requested a ceasefire. This was ignored and instead Israel mounted an attack on East Jerusalem, which it occupied on 7 June, and the Israeli Army moved towards the River Jordan. King Hussein asked for a ceasefire on the same day. In the meantime, Syria had only carried out limited artillery fire from the Golan Heights and had mounted several small-scale raids into Israel. After defeating the Egyptian and Jordanian armies, General Dayan moved against Syria on 9 June, with the result that the Syrians requested a ceasefire the next day. The 1967 war was over.

Why were the Israelis able to so comprehensively defeat three Arab nations in far less time than it had taken in 1948? The single most important factor was Israeli air superiority and the pre-emptive attack, which wiped out the Arab air force strike capability. A second reason, as in 1948, was the inability of the three Arab states to coordinate their military forces. This enabled Israel to carry out three separate military actions independently rather than having to fight a three-front war against Egypt, Jordan and Syria.

SOURCE F

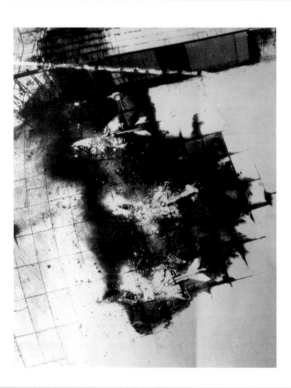

Egyptian aircraft destroyed by Israeli air strikes in the Sinai Peninsula during the Six-Day War.

STUDENT STUDY SECTION

QUESTION
What do you think are the limitations of photographs as historical evidence? Do they have any value? If so, what? What is missing here from this source? It is really important!

The consequences of the 1967 war for Israel

The territorial gains made by Israel were huge. Within a week it had taken Egypt's Sinai Peninsula, the Gaza Strip, Jordan's West Bank, Syria's Golan Heights and East Jerusalem.

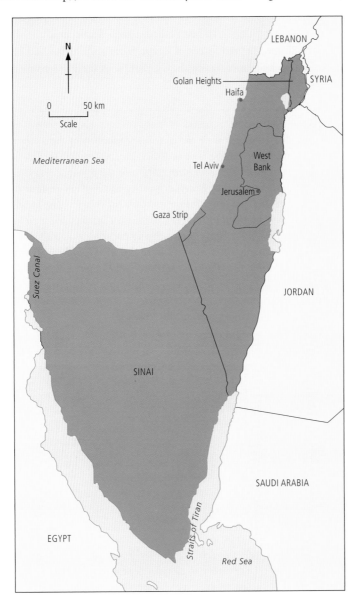

◀ **Map 12**
Israel after the 1967 war.

Results of the Six-Day War:
- Israel had gained over 180,000 square kilometres of land, which became known as the '**Occupied Territories**'.
- The Straits of Tiran were now open again, giving free access to the port of Eilat, while at the same time the eastern bank of the Suez Canal was in the hands of Israeli troops.

Occupied Territories
The Israeli-occupied territories are the territories captured by Israel from Egypt, Jordan and Syria during the Six-Day War of 1967, consisting of the West Bank and East Jerusalem, the Gaza Strip and the Golan Heights, and, until 1982, the Sinai Peninsula.

- Sharm-al-Sheikh, the gateway to the Gulf of Aqaba and the Gulf of Suez and a tremendously important strategic military site, was in Israeli hands.
- In the north, the Golan Heights were taken from Syria, thus preventing the possibility of artillery shelling into Israel from Syria.
- East Jerusalem was added to the State of Israel.

The Israeli gains created a serious refugee problem, as more than 300,000 Arabs moved out of the Golan Heights, the West Bank and Israel into neighbouring territories. Many of these were forced out of their homes as Arab villages in important strategic areas were bulldozed to the ground. For example, the **Maghrebi Quarter** opposite the Western Wall in East Jerusalem was demolished, displacing more than 600 Arab residents. By now there were more Palestinians living under Israeli occupation (1.6 million) than there were living in the neighbouring Arab countries (1.5 million). Casualty figures vary according to the source, but approximately 18,000 Egyptians had been killed. Israeli deaths amounted to around 1000. Militarily, the combined armed forces of Egypt, Syria and Jordan had been almost eliminated and the Israelis had, once again, shown that they could overcome any threat from the Arab states.

Maghrebi Quarter
The Maghrebi Quarter of Jerusalem, dating back to 1320 CE, was the second smallest quarter located within the old city walls.

SOURCE G

The long-range causes of the 1967 war were the continued inability of the Arabs to recognize and accept the political sovereignty of the Jews in Israel, the antagonism and desire for revenge that had been fuelled by defeats and humiliation in the previous wars, as well as by Israel's excessive retaliations; Arab fear of Israeli aggressiveness and expansionism; and Israeli 'hawkishness' and the determination to maintain military superiority. The inability to find a solution for the plight of the Palestinian refugees, because of intransigence on both sides, provided the raison d'être [reason for being] and rallying point for the Arab crusade against Israel. The short-term and more proximate causes were the arms build-up on both sides in the previous decade; Soviet meddling; the volatile situation in Syria; Nasser's brinkmanship; the defense pacts that linked together Egypt, Syria, and Jordan; and the failure of the international community to prevent war through diplomacy. All sides thus must share the blame for the outbreak of hostilities and for the consequences that followed.

From Ian Bickerton and Carla Klausner, *A Concise History of the Arab-Israeli Conflict,* **2001**

STUDENT STUDY SECTION

QUESTIONS

a)   What do the words 'hawkishness', 'intransigence' and 'brinkmanship' mean?

b1)   According to its origin and purpose, what are the value and limitations of Source G to an historian studying the causes of the 1967 Arab-Israeli War?

b2)   In your own opinion what are the strengths and weaknesses of this extract as an explanation as to why the 1967 war started?

You should notice that Questions (b1) and (b2) are not identical! Why? Now look at the Examiner's Comments below...

Examiner's comments

Question b1 uses the wording common to all IB history exam source papers. A common mistake made by students answering this type of question is that they spend far too much time discussing the content of the sources rather than their origin, purpose, value and limitations. That is the major difference between Question b1 and b2. Question b2 requires you explicitly to examine the content to make a judgement on the strengths and weaknesses of the source, whereas question b1 will require you to apply the content to answer what the question is actually asking.

SOURCE H

Try to remember some details. For the world
is filled with people who were torn from their sleep
with no one to mend the tear,
and unlike wild beasts they live
each in his lonely hiding place and they die
together on battlefields
and in hospitals.
And the earth will swallow all of them,
*good and evil together, like the followers of **Korah**,*
all of them in their rebellion against death,
their mouths open till the last moment,
praising and cursing in a single
howl. Try, try
to remember some details.

From Yehuda Amichai, 'Try To Remember Some Details'

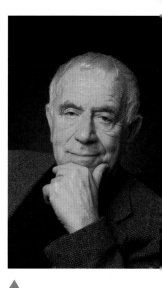

▲ Born in Germany, Yehuda Amichai emigrated to Israel when he was 12. He is considered to be one of the greatest Israeli poets of modern times and he died in 2000.

Korah
In the Jewish scriptures, Korah was the son of Izhar. Korah rebelled against Moses, and was punished for his rebellion when the earth opened and swallowed up all those who had rebelled.

STUDENT STUDY SECTION

RESEARCH ACTIVITY

Find out some more about Yehuda Amichai. Research using the Internet and try to discover some more of his poems, particularly 'Seven Laments for the War-Dead'. He also read a poem at the Nobel Peace Prize ceremony with Peres, Rabin and Arafat. Compare and contrast this poem with that of Darwish on page 132. You would not get an activity like this on an IB exam, but it is interesting to see how the two poets view the Arab-Israeli conflict.

The consequences of the 1967 war for the Arab states

For the Arabs the 1967 war was a disaster. They had been crushed militarily in a humiliating defeat lasting less than a week. Nasser immediately resigned from his position as President of Egypt, but returned to office following a massive display of support from the Egyptians. His position, as perceived leader of the Arab states, was severely weakened and his policies were seen by many as misguided. With the Arab states in some disarray, as each attempted to salvage something from the debacle, there was no immediate Arab unity.

- King Hussein moved closer to the USA, attempting to enlist their support for the restoration of the West Bank to Jordan.
- Egypt threatened retaliation, which was in reality an empty threat, and it moved closer to the Soviet Union. Egypt's major aim was the removal of Israeli soldiers from the east bank of the Suez Canal and the reopening of it to shipping (this was to take until 1975).
- Syria moved away from the other Arab states and eventually suffered a military coup in 1968.

This division of the Arab states had further key consequences in the region – the resurrection of Palestinian demands for their own territory and further debate about the unresolved question of the Palestinian refugee problem.

One fact was certain; the Arab states were determined never to recognize the existence of the State of Israel. Nasser became more closely allied with King Hussein and tried to re-establish his position as leader of the Arab world. In August 1967, a conference of Arab leaders was held in Khartoum. This was attended by the majority of states, although Syria boycotted the meetings. The most important of the eight resolutions that were passed was the following:

SOURCE I

3. *The Arab Heads of State have agreed to unite their political efforts at the international and diplomatic level to eliminate the effects of the aggression and to ensure the withdrawal of the aggressive Israeli forces from the Arab lands which have been occupied since the aggression of June. This will be done within the framework of the main principles by which the Arab States abide, namely, no peace with Israel, no recognition of Israel, no negotiations with it, and insistence on the rights of the Palestinian people in their own country.*

From Khartoum conference resolutions, August 1967

This became known as 'The three No's of Khartoum' – 'No peace, no recognition and no negotiations' was to be the general policy followed by the Arab states towards Israel for the next 10 years.

STUDENT STUDY SECTION

QUESTION

Read Source I carefully. What do you notice about the first and second sentences?

Answer: They contradict themselves.

President Lyndon Johnson

Lyndon Johnson, often referred to as LBJ, was the 36th President of the United States (1963–69). He came into office after the assassination of Kennedy in 1963 and successfully won the 1964 election. The Vietnam War and domestic concerns would dominate his presidency. Johnson was a strong supporter of Israel both during the 1967 war and in the United Nations debates that followed. During his administration Israel received a number of arms shipments that would prove invaluable in helping to defeat Egypt in June 1967.

President Richard Nixon

Richard Nixon was the 37th President of the United States (1969–74). Nixon was noted for the final withdrawal of US troops from the conflict in Vietnam, and he was the only President to ever resign the office, following the Watergate scandal.

The consequences of the 1967 war for the USA, the Soviet Union and the United Nations

The USA supported the UN Resolution, which condemned Israel for annexing East Jerusalem, but US policy under Presidents **Johnson** and **Nixon** had two faces. There was a tremendous amount of public support for Israel in the USA, which meant that publicly the USA supported Israeli actions and policies, whereas behind the scenes the US position was not nearly so clear cut. On the one hand, the USA supported Israel's position that there would be no removal of Israeli forces from the Occupied Territories. On the other hand, it is clear that the USA expected that these lands would be given up by Israel and that any border changes resulting from the 1967 war would be minor. Privately the US administration made it abundantly clear to Israel that it expected almost all Israeli forces to be withdrawn from the land occupied during the war and that it wanted to return to the pre-1967 territorial status quo. This was something that Israel was unwilling to do.

SOURCE J

By any calculation, Israel had gained one of the most spectacular victories of recent history. Not only had the armed forces of Egypt, Jordan and Syria been decimated, but Israel now controlled the future of East Jerusalem, the West Bank, the Sinai Desert and the Golan Heights, and enjoyed the overwhelming support of Western public opinion…While those on the right, notably the followers of Menachem Begin, held that the West Bank was an inalienable part of the Jewish inheritance, the initial view of Eshkol and Eban was that most of the conquered land was negotiable in return for peace settlements. There was a widespread sense of relief that Israeli towns and cities were for the time being far removed from any attack, but few believed that these new positions would become the country's long-term frontier.

From T. G. Fraser, *The Arab-Israeli Conflict*, 2004

SOURCE K

If… the Israeli victory of 1967 meant that Israel got more than it bargained for in terms of the newly acquired territories and the Palestinian Arab populations of the West Bank, Arab East Jerusalem (including the old city) and the Gaza Strip, there was also evidence of splits within the political establishment over what strategy to adopt next. While it is true that the Israelis have remained in continuous occupation of these lands ever since, there have always been opposing arguments for the maintenance of Israeli control (or sovereignty) of such territories. From a strategic point of view, by holding on to the West Bank, for example, Israel could better defend its borders and major centres of population. On the other hand, there were some who believed that if land were traded for peace with its Arab neighbours, then relinquishing the West Bank or elsewhere would be worth it.

From Beverley Milton-Edwards and Peter Hinchcliffe, *Conflicts in the Middle East Since 1945*, 2004

STUDENT STUDY SECTION

QUESTION
Compare and contrast Sources J and K.

Here are two answers to the question you have just answered. Which do you think would receive more marks and why?

Student Answer A – *Julia*

Sources J or K are both similar and different in multiple ways. Source J shows that the Israeli victory was extremely successful and that Israel captured East Jerusalem, the West Bank, the Sinai Desert and the Golan Heights. According to this source there was considerable argument over whether to relinquish or retain the captured Arab territories. Those Israelis who wanted to retain the territories believed that the land was an 'inalienable part of the Jewish inheritance'. Those who wanted to relinquish the captured Arab territories felt that this would be necessary in order to negotiate peace settlements with the Arabs. Lastly, Source J claims that most Israelis felt that these borders would not remain for long. Source K claims the Israeli victory was successful, saying that Israel 'got more than it bargained for.' However, it states that Israel apparently captured the West Bank, East Jerusalem, and the Gaza Strip.

Both sources mention the viewpoint that Israel should relinquish the territories in favour of Arab peace settlements. However, although Source K also mentions the viewpoint that the land should be retained, different reasons are given for this point of view: supporters of this argument want the land for strategic/defensive reasons

Student Answer B – *Rajid*

The two sources J and K are similar in their assertion that the 1967 war resulted in great Israeli territorial gains. In both sources, Israel is shown to have been uncertain about whether to relinquish or keep the conquered Arab territories in the aftermath of the war. In both sources, it is made clear that some Israelis believed that if 'the conquered land was negotiable in return for peace settlements' (Source J) then 'relinquishing the West Bank or elsewhere would be worth it' (Source K).

The sources disagree over what territories Israel captured. Source J claims that Israel captured East Jerusalem, the West Bank, the Sinai Desert and the Golan Heights, while Source K names the West Bank, East Jerusalem, and the Gaza Strip. Both sources show that some Israelis wanted to keep the territories, but they cite different reasons for this. Source J says that these territories were valued as an 'inalienable part of the Jewish inheritance', while Source K says these territories were strategically significant. Lastly, Source J shows that the borders were only considered to be short term and does not mention the long-term. However Source K emphasizes that the new borders were retained in the long term.

> ● **Examiner's hint**
> Do not look at the answers and the Examiner's Comments below until you have tried this question yourself.

Examiner's comments

Rajid's answer is the better of the two. Julia has spent too long on describing the content of the two sources. There is no linkage until her third paragraph. The former is what examiners term the 'end-on' approach – comments on one source, followed by comments on a second source. A third paragraph is needed because there is no linkage made between the two sets of comments.

International negotiations

The position of the USSR as the ally of Egypt and Syria had been severely damaged and it began slowly to rebuild the Egyptian military forces by supplying them with arms shipments and the support of Soviet technical experts. The Soviets were optimistic that they might be able to gain a warm-water port by supporting the Arab cause, although privately Nasser was against this option.

Despite the Cold War, and US involvement in Vietnam, the USSR and the USA both attempted to find some common ground that would provide the basis for a framework for peace talks. The two countries eventually sponsored a draft agreement in July 1967, which they saw as a possible basis for the resolution of the territorial gains made by Israel. This initial agreement was to have a profound influence upon what is agreed upon by most authorities to be the most significant UN resolution passed relating to the Middle East. Its terms have become the basis for all attempts at resolving the Arab-Israeli disputes, even today. Security Council Resolution 242, passed on 22 November 1967, included some of the points made in the Soviet-US draft of July. The British had refused to support the initial draft, which the Arab states thought was too beneficial to Israel. Diplomatic efforts by the British Ambassador to the UN, Lord Caradon, resulted in Resolution 242 gaining limited Arab and Israeli support.

● **Examiner's hint**
This is one of the most important documents relating to the Arab-Israeli conflicts. You must know all of its terms.

SOURCE L

The Security Council,
Expressing its continuing concern with the grave situation in the Middle East,
Emphasizing the inadmissibility of the acquisition of territory by war and the need to work for a just and lasting peace in which every State in the area can live in security,
Emphasizing further that all Member States in their acceptance of the Charter of the United Nations have undertaken a commitment to act in accordance with Article 2 of the Charter,

1. *Affirms that the fulfilment of Charter principles requires the establishment of a just and lasting peace in the Middle East which should include the application of both the following principles:*
   Withdrawal of Israeli armed forces from territories occupied in the recent conflict;
   Termination of all claims or states of belligerency and respect for and acknowledgement of the sovereignty, territorial integrity and political independence of every State in the area and their right to live in peace within secure and recognized boundaries free from threats or acts of force;

2. *Affirms further the necessity*
   For guaranteeing freedom of navigation through international waterways in the area;
   For achieving a just settlement of the refugee problem;
   For guaranteeing the territorial inviolability and political independence of every State in the area, through measures including the establishment of demilitarized zones;

3. *Requests the Secretary General to designate a Special Representative to proceed to the Middle East to establish and maintain contacts with the States concerned in order to promote agreement and assist efforts to achieve a peaceful and accepted settlement in accordance with the provisions and principles in this resolution;*

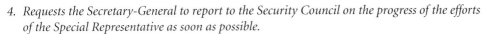

4. *Requests the Secretary-General to report to the Security Council on the progress of the efforts of the Special Representative as soon as possible.*

Security Council Resolution 242

The resolution was accepted by Jordan, Egypt and Israel. The key debate was about the word 'territories' in Clause 1, Point 1. To the Israelis this meant only those territories that would ensure that Israel's security concerns would be protected i.e. *some* territories, but to Egypt and Jordan 'territories' meant *all* of the land that Israel had seized in the 1967 war. The Israeli government was also concerned that the resolution did not include the term 'Israel'. Resolution 242 was rejected in its entirety by Syria and the PLO, who wanted Palestine to be liberated through force.

The Secretary-General of the UN, **U Thant**, appointed **Gunnar Jarring** to be the Special Representative to the Middle East. Jarring worked untiringly until 1970 to try to bring Israel and the Arab states closer together, but was ultimately unsuccessful. Both sides were more concerned with their own issues.

STUDENT STUDY SECTION

QUESTION
Read through Source L carefully. Make a list of any terms that you think would be unacceptable to the Israelis. Make another list of any terms you think would be unacceptable to the Arab states (except Syria). Finally, make a list of any terms that you think would be unacceptable to Syria and the PLO. Do you think that Resolution 242 is a realistic basis for peace in the Middle East? Explain your answer.

Despite Resolution 242, there was little success in any peace moves. Neither side was willing to give ground. Israel retained the territories it had gained in 1967 and the severity of the defeat meant that the Arab states were not ready to make any compromises with Israel. Similarly, neither the USA nor the USSR was able to introduce any peace initiatives. There was a stalemate in the Middle East. In the USA, President Johnson decided not to contest the 1968 presidential election and Richard Nixon duly became the new President. Between March 1968 and August 1970, a 'War of **Attrition**' existed between Israel and Egypt. To some extent it was a continuation of the 1967 war, but on a much smaller scale. The Israelis completed a line of fortifications along the eastern side of the Suez Canal, the Bar Lev Line, and Nasser was determined to destroy it and try slowly to reduce the size of the Israeli forces in the Sinai Peninsula. In response the new Prime Minister in Israel, Golda Meir, travelled to Washington and was promised military supplies by President Nixon. In January 1970, Israeli aircraft began a series of raids on Egypt, even attacking Cairo itself. Nasser in turn visited Moscow to ask for arms and aircraft. The Soviet Union was not prepared to supply any military equipment to Egypt, as **Leonid Brezhnev** feared an escalation of violence in the Middle East that might bring the Soviets into conflict with the USA. Eventually Nasser threatened to resign and guarantee that any new Egyptian president would turn away from the Soviet Union and open the way for the USA to support Egypt. Nasser told Brezhnev: 'I'm a leader who is bombed every day in his own country, whose army is exposed and whose people are naked. I have the courage to tell our people the unfortunate truth, that whether they like it or not, the Americans are masters of the world. I am not going to be the one who surrenders to the Americans. Someone else will come in my place and have to do it.'

As Nasser had thought, the Soviet Union was not willing to lose its ally in the Middle East and Brezhnev promised to provide Egypt with surface-to-air missiles (SAM-3 type),

U Thant
Burmese diplomat and the third Secretary-General of the United Nations, from 1961 to 1971. He was critical of American involvement in the Vietnam War and was heavily criticized by both Israel and the USA for agreeing to Nasser's request to remove UNEF from the Sinai Peninsula in 1967. U Thant made an unsuccessful attempt to persuade Nasser not to go to war with Israel by intervening personally.

Gunnar Jarring
Jarring was a Swedish diplomat. After the 1967 Arab-Israeli War and the adoption of UN Security Council Resolution 242, Jarring was appointed by the UN Secretary-General as a special envoy for the Middle East peace process, the so-called Jarring Mission.

Attrition
The act of weakening or exhausting an enemy by constant harassment or attack.

Leonid Brezhnev
Leonid Brezhnev was General Secretary of the Communist Party of the Soviet Union (and thus political leader of the USSR) from 1964 to 1982, serving in that position longer than anyone other than Joseph Stalin.

technicians and aircraft. In exchange for these shipments, Nasser allowed the Soviets access to Egyptian air and naval facilities, giving them a base in the region and even allowing them to establish a massive military presence in Egypt.

The new Soviet presence in Egypt alarmed the USA, which was afraid that the continuation of Israeli air strikes on Egypt might bring the US into direct conflict with the Soviet Union. Washington began to put pressure on Golda Meir to stop the raids and threatened to cut off financial and military supplies to Israel. The US Secretary of State **William Rogers** proposed a ceasefire, which was supported by the Soviet Union. On 8 August, under considerable US pressure, Israel agreed to stop the bombing of Egypt and Nasser agreed to halt artillery bombardments. This ceasefire was also supported by King Hussein of Jordan. The War of Attrition was over, although the agreement signed between Nasser, Arafat and Golda Meir was to have serious consequences for the region later on.

> **William Rogers**
> William Rogers served as Secretary of State under President Nixon from 1969 to 1973, and initiated efforts at a lasting peace in the Arab-Israeli conflict through the so-called Rogers Plan.

Arabism and Zionism; emergence of the PLO

Soon after the Six-Day War, the PLO began to reorganize itself into a more coherent group with broadly unified aims. The Palestinian issue had regained momentum as a result of the war. There were about one million Palestinians living in the Gaza Strip and the West Bank in the Occupied Territories, and a huge refugee population living in the countries that neighboured Israel. The Palestinians, who had been under Jordanian and Egyptian control before June 1967, now found themselves under Israeli occupation. If Israel were to follow the terms of Resolution 242, which called for their withdrawal from Gaza and the West Bank, the Palestinians saw the chance of becoming a more unified group with clear objectives.

Before June 1967, the PLO had been perceived as a fragmented group under weak leadership, and Fatah's regular attacks on Israel seemed, to many Palestinians, to be the direction to take in the future. In December 1967, several members of the PLO's executive committee demanded that Shukhairy resign as its leader. He rejected their demands and the PLO began to lose financial support. Shukhairy asked Nasser for help, but he refused and Shukhairy was forced to resign. An interim leader was selected but, more importantly, several of the military sub-groups, including Fatah, were merged into the PLO. Yasser Arafat was to become the leader of the PLO in February 1969 as Fatah gradually assumed control of the majority of seats in the Palestine National Council, holding 33 of the 57 seats allocated to the paramilitary groups. Arafat's main aim was to shape the PLO into a unified political and military organization, which he hoped would find support from the Arab states.

One of the factors that helped Arafat to assume the leadership of the PLO was the battle at Karameh. In March 1968, Israel attacked the Jordanian town of Karameh in retaliation for an attack on an Israeli bus, which was blown up by a mine. Karameh was the site of a Palestinian refugee camp and was also the headquarters of Fatah. An intense battle took place, and although Fatah was finally defeated Israel suffered many casualties. The Palestinians had been joined by the Jordanian Army at Karameh and its defence became a rallying point for Arab nationalists, with the result that thousands of Arabs joined Fatah and the *fedayeen*. Karameh had another important consequence for the PLO, as it led to direct cooperation between Egypt and Fatah. This connection was to bring Arafat into contact with the Soviet Union, and he joined Nasser in a visit to Moscow in July 1968. By October 1968, as a consequence of Soviet military support, the Egyptian Army was already larger and better equipped than it was at the beginning of the June war. The Egyptians now began equipping and training the Palestinian fighters of Fatah.

A revision of the PLO Charter in 1968 indicated the future direction of PLO actions when it stated that 'Armed struggle is the only way to liberate Palestine.' This was later to be reaffirmed in 1974 when the PLO made the following statement concerning Resolution 242: 'The Liberation Organization will struggle against any proposal for a Palestinian entity the price of which is recognition, peace, secure frontiers, renunciation of national rights, and the deprival of our people of their right to return and their right to self-determination on the soil of their homeland.'

The PLO and Jordan

The August 1970 agreement proposed by Secretary Rogers, and signed by Hussein, Nasser and Golda Meir, brought the War of Attrition to a temporary halt, but was greeted with shock and horror by the PLO. They considered that the Palestinian cause had been betrayed by Egypt and Jordan. They were determined that this ceasefire must be broken as quickly as possible and that the best way to do so would be to overthrow King Hussein. The PLO had almost created a 'state within a state' in Jordan, and Palestinian–Jordanian relations had been deteriorating rapidly throughout 1970.

Two assassination attempts on Hussein failed in September, but the catalyst for the eventual breakdown of relations between the PLO and the Jordanians was the hijacking of four aircraft by a PLO-affiliated group. Three of them were forced to land at Dawson Field, an airstrip approximately 50km from Amman. The group demanded the release of *fedayeen* from prisons in Britain, Germany and Switzerland, but they were told that no prisoners would be released until the passengers were freed. The hijackers responded by blowing up the planes (the passengers were taken off first), but received no concessions. King Hussein decided to take action against the PLO and on 17 September ordered the Jordanian Army to attack PLO positions in Jordan. Syria had invaded Jordan with tanks in support of the PLO. Washington requested that Moscow put pressure on its ally to withdraw and Israel seemed ready to intervene in the Golan Heights. Syria withdrew and Hussein was condemned by other Arab states. The conflict finally ended on 22 September with more than 3000 Palestinians killed and 11,000 wounded. This incident became known as 'Black September' by the PLO and was to lead to the formation of a similarly named radical group of Palestinians, with disastrous consequences for the future. The PLO was forced to leave Jordan in 1971 and established itself in Lebanon, making it the centre of PLO operations against Israel. In the middle of negotiations on 28 September, Nasser collapsed and died of a heart attack. He was succeeded by Anwar Sadat, who had been his deputy.

One of the Black September terrorists, seen at the Munich Olympics.

The Munich Massacre (1972)

Between 1971 and 1973, terrorist groups carried out a number of international attacks. In November 1971, four members of Black September assassinated the Jordanian Prime Minister in Cairo as revenge for Jordan's expulsion of the PLO. In September 1972, the group turned its attention to the Munich Olympics. In 1972 the XXth Olympic Games were held in Munich, Germany. On 5 September 1972 eight members of Black September managed to infiltrate themselves into the Olympic village where the athletes were being housed. They took control of one of the buildings after killing two Israeli team members and took another nine Israeli athletes hostage. The terrorists then demanded an exchange of prisoners, requesting the release and safe passage of over 200 Palestinians and non-Arabs in Israeli prisons, along with the release of Andreas Baader and Ulrike Meinhof, the founders of the German Red Army Faction, who were imprisoned in Germany. It became clear that neither Israel nor Germany would agree to these demands and the Black September members requested transport to an airport and a plane to take them to Cairo. A bus was provided which took the terrorists and their captives to two helicopters, waiting to take them to a NATO airbase. The German government organised a rescue attempt at the airport, although they had no specially trained hostage rescue force. The Germans also underestimated the number of terrorists, believing that there were only two or three of them, rather than the real number – eight. The rescue attempt failed. In the fighting five Black September members were killed and the remaining three were taken prisoner. All nine of the Israeli athletes were killed along with one German policeman.

SOURCE M

After hours of tense negotiations, the Palestinians, who it was later learned belonged to a PLO faction called Black September, agreed to a plan whereby they were to be taken by helicopter to the NATO air base at Fürstenfeldbruck where they would be given an airplane to fly them and their hostages to Cairo. The Israelis were then taken by bus to the helicopters and flown to the airfield. In the course of the transfer, the Germans discovered that there were eight terrorists instead of the five they expected and realized that they had not assigned enough marksmen to carry out the plan to kill the terrorists at the airport. After the helicopters landed at the air base around 10:30 p.m., the German sharpshooters attempted to kill the terrorists and a bloody firefight ensued. At 11, the media was mistakenly informed that the hostages had been saved and the news was announced to a relieved Israeli public. Almost an hour later, however, new fighting broke out and one of the helicopters holding the Israelis was blown up by a terrorist grenade. The remaining nine hostages in the second helicopter were shot to death by one of the surviving terrorists. Five of the terrorists were killed along with one policeman, and three were captured.

From Mitchell Bard, *The Munich Massacre,* http://www.jewishvirtuallibrary.org/jsource/Terrorism/munich.html

● **Examiner's hint**
By looking at the tone of language and the use of the words in Source M, can you find more than one purpose?

STUDENT STUDY SECTION

QUESTION
According to its origin and purpose, what are the values and limitations of Source M to historians studying the Munich Massacre of 1972?

Following Munich, other terrorist groups began to form, which began to copy Black September's tactics. Attacks were made on the international airports at Rome and Athens. The result was a loss of support for Arafat and the PLO – Saudi Arabia even withdrew funding – and Arafat tried to redirect the actions of some of these extremist groups by stating that the target of any terrorist attacks should be Israel.

Section II:
October War of 1973: causes, course and consequences

Background information

President Sadat had broadly the same political aims as his predecessor Nasser – to regain the Sinai Peninsula and re-establish control over the Suez Canal. However, Sadat had more far-reaching economic goals. Egypt was in a disastrous state economically. The costs of both the 1967 war and the War of Attrition had left the country almost bankrupt. Nasser's policy of state capitalism had also resulted in a stagnant economy. Sadat was convinced that

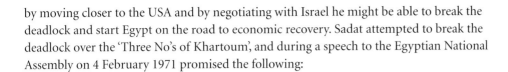
by moving closer to the USA and by negotiating with Israel he might be able to break the deadlock and start Egypt on the road to economic recovery. Sadat attempted to break the deadlock over the 'Three No's of Khartoum', and during a speech to the Egyptian National Assembly on 4 February 1971 promised the following:

SOURCE A

We add to all the efforts aimed at solving the crisis a new Egyptian initiative as a basis according to which any work will be considered the true yardstick of the desire to implement the Security Council Resolution.

We demand that during this period of withholding fire a partial withdrawal of the Israeli troops on the eastern bank of the Suez Canal will be realized as a first step in a timetable to be laid down with a view to implementing the rest of the provisions of the Security Council Resolution.

If this is realized during this period, we are ready to start at once in clearing the course of the Suez Canal in order to reopen it for international navigation and to serve world economy.

From Anwar Sadat, speech to Egyptian National Assembly, 4 February 1971

Sadat also promised to restore diplomatic relations with the USA and to sign a peace agreement with Israel.

STUDENT STUDY SECTION

QUESTION
Some observers have commented that this initiative was a real opportunity to move forward with the peace process. Do you think this is true? Why do you think that Israel ignored Sadat's proposals?

Following Israel's rejection of this proposal, Sadat decided to pursue a rather different line of action. One of the first moves that he made was to break away from the Soviet Union. He knew that Washington considered this as a prerequisite for moving forward with the peace process. On 8 July Sadat notified Moscow that all 15,000 of its advisors and technicians were to leave Egypt within a week. This change in policy was intended to satisfy the USA without unduly upsetting the USSR. It also responded to demands from his own military leaders that they be allowed to have direct control over the entire Egyptian military force rather than being under Soviet control. The expulsion of the Soviet advisors had the unexpected result of speeding up arms shipments, and Sadat received a new delivery of SAM missiles from the Soviet Union to bolster Egypt's defensive position along the Suez Canal.

Sadat also began to build bridges with the other Arab states. With the help of **President Assad** of Syria, he helped to resolve the dispute between Syria and Jordan over Hussein's treatment of the PLO in 1970. In private, Assad and Sadat began to prepare for a war with Israel. Sadat was annoyed with Israel's refusal to entertain any notion of compromise and decided that the only way to make the Israelis start peace negotiations was to go to war – a war that he knew he could not win. By taking direct action against Israel, Sadat also hoped to gain territory and prestige within the region and his own country. He wanted to take back the Suez Canal and the Sinai Peninsula, which were still under Israeli occupation.

President Assad had similar aims to those of Sadat. His position as President of Syria was still rather uncertain and he wanted to regain the Golan Heights, which were lost to Israel in the 1967 war. A conference in Cairo in 1973 led to the resolution of the quarrel between Jordan and Syria over the PLO, creating a tripartite agreement between Egypt, Jordan and Syria. Assad and Sadat realized that events in the USA, such as the Vietnam War and **Watergate**, meant that Israel's ally was distracted and they decided to attack Israel, hoping that the USA and the USSR would intervene before either side could claim victory.

 President Assad
Hafez al-Assad was the President of Syria for 30 years. Assad's rule stabilized and consolidated the power of the country's central government after decades of coups and counter-coups. He was succeeded by his son and current president Bashar al-Assad in 2000.

Watergate
'Watergate' refers to a series of American political scandals during the presidency of Richard Nixon, which resulted in the indictment of several of Nixon's closest advisors, and ultimately his resignation on 9 August 1974.

The Israeli position seemed secure. Israeli inflexibility was bolstered by its perception of Egyptian weakness. Egypt seemed to have broken with the Soviet Union, and was perceived as being militarily weak after the events of 1967 and the War of Attrition. On the other hand, Israel was confident of strong US political and military support and, following the Munich massacre of 11 Israeli athletes in September 1972 by the radical Black September group, was certain of international sympathy. Israeli intelligence observers dismissed the warning signs, not realizing until too late that an attack was close.

The 1973 war

At 2:00pm on 6 October 1973, Egypt and Syria launched Operation *Badr*, attacking Israeli forces in the Sinai and Golan Heights simultaneously. It was the day of a Jewish religious celebration, **Yom Kippur**, one of the holiest days in the Jewish calendar. Although many Israeli soldiers were not in their bases, and the main Israeli radio station was closed, it was relatively easy for the Israelis rapidly to mobilize their forces. The Egyptian and Syrian forces were well supplied with Soviet weapons. Surface-to-air missiles and hand-held anti-tank missiles resulted in heavy Israeli losses of aircraft and tanks.

The first week of fighting brought success to the Arab states, forcing Israel to retreat from some of its military positions. Israel appealed to Washington for weapons and, following a massive Soviet shipment to Egypt, the USA agreed to airlift military supplies to Israel. Israel counterattacked against Syria, pushing back the Syrian Army, and was soon closing in on the Syrian capital, Damascus. The Israeli Army was also having success in the Sinai Peninsula, driving back the Egyptian forces. In response to the US support of Israel, the Arab members of **Organization of Petroleum Producing Countries (OPEC)** stopped oil shipments to the USA and any European nations that were helping Israel. OPEC reduced its oil exports by 25 per cent globally, creating a world shortage. A new weapon had been discovered in the Middle East – the use of oil as a means of creating pressure internationally.

Yom Kippur

Yom Kippur is one of the most solemn and important of the Jewish holidays. Its central themes are atonement and repentance. Jews traditionally observe this holy day with a 25-hour period of fasting and intensive prayer, often spending most of the day in synagogue services.

OPEC

The Organization of Petroleum Exporting Countries (OPEC) is a cartel of 12 countries made up of Algeria, Angola, Ecuador, Iran, Iraq, Kuwait, Libya, Nigeria, Qatar, Saudi Arabia, the United Arab Emirates and Venezuela.

SOURCE B

A cartoon by Yaakov Kirschen, an Israeli cartoonist, 16 October 1973.

Dry Bones

STUDENT STUDY SECTION

QUESTION

a) What is the message portrayed by the cartoon?

Interestingly, my students found this very hard to identify. Can you work out what it is saying? See the Examiner's hint for the answer.

QUESTION

b) What are the value and limitations of this cartoon as a historical source?

It was at this point, during the third week of October, that the superpowers decided to get involved. **Henry Kissinger**, the American Secretary of State, was invited to go to Moscow, where he drafted a plan for ending the war with the Soviet leader, Leonid Brezhnev, whereby the Security Council of the UN would mediate. Israel and the Arab states initially rejected any proposals for a ceasefire, until the USA and the Soviet Union threatened to intervene directly in the conflict. A ceasefire was agreed on 22 October 1973, although fighting continued until 24 October.

SOURCE C

October 22, 1973
The Security Council
1. *Calls upon all parties to the present fighting to cease all firing and terminate all military activity immediately, no later than 12 hours after the moment of the adoption of this decision, in the positions they now occupy;*
2. *Calls upon the parties concerned to start immediately after the ceasefire the implementation of Security Council resolution 242 (1967) in all of its parts;*
3. *Decides that, immediately and concurrently with the ceasefire, negotiations start between the parties concerned under appropriate auspices aimed at establishing a just and durable peace in the Middle East;*

From United Nations Security Council Resolution 338

This resolution was passed unanimously, with China abstaining.

SOURCE D

Cartoon produced from 'Cartooning for Peace', an initiative born on 16 October 2006 at the UN headquarters in New York. Twelve of the most renowned political cartoonists from all over the world participated in a two-day conference to help us 'Unlearn intolerance'. The artist, Baha Boukhari, is a Palestinian cartoonist.

● **Examiner's hint**
The cartoon is by an Israeli cartoonist. Its message is that the Arab states need to galvanize their members into war by music and calls to go to war, whereas for the Israelis the protection of their children and families is sufficient motivation to fight.

Question (b) is the type of question you can expect to see on Paper 1.

Henry Kissinger
Henry Kissinger was US National Security Advisor (1969–75) and Secretary of State (1973–77). In 1973, Kissinger negotiated the end to the Yom Kippur War, during which the US military conducted one of the largest military airlifts in history.

● **Examiner's hint**
Question (b): Try to work
out why all the images are
included, but do not start your
answer by simply listing them.

STUDENT STUDY SECTION

QUESTIONS

a) **Read through Source C carefully. Make a list of any terms that you think would be unacceptable to the Israelis. Make another list of any terms you think would be unacceptable to the Arab states. Finally, make a list of any terms that you think would be unacceptable to the PLO. Do you think that Resolution 338 is a realistic basis for peace in the Middle East? Explain your answer.**

b) **What is the message portrayed in the cartoon?**

Here are three student answers to Question (b).

Student Answer A – *Peter*

The traditional peace dove slightly wounded is depicted in a UN soldier's outfit. Bullets are flying around it but still it is running to try to establish peace. The message conveyed by this cartoon is that the peace troops of the UN were in support of the Arab nations and tried to solve the conflict in their favour.

Student Answer B – *Susan*

This cartoon from 1967 shows the Palestinian point of view regarding the war. A white dove carrying an olive branch in its beak – a common symbol for peace world wide – is shown wearing body armor and a helmet. The artist has clearly voiced his opinion regarding the Israelis and how the rest of the world has reacted to their attack. The dove is fleeing for its life away from speeding bullets – this shows both the arrogance and carelessness of the opposing sides of the war towards the ultimate institution of world peace and cooperation, the United Nations. It is also apparent, however, that the UN is not up to the challenge and not willing to take real measures against the violence in the Middle East of the time.

Student Answer C – *Midori*

The cartoon shows a bird with an olive branch in its beak. The white bird symbolizes peace. It also represents the United Nations. The bird is wearing a bullet-proof vest and a helmet to protect itself from the bullets that are being shot at it from all sides. The United Nations is trying to mediate between the nations at war and to come to a peaceful agreement. The countries, however, do not want to stop fighting and the UN will be hurt, too, if it does not get out of their way. Alternatively, the UN could also be the target of the fighting countries.

Examiner's comments

Peter has understood part of the cartoon, but has mistaken the message. There is no evidence to support his assertion that the UN troops were supporting the Arab nations. Susan has described the content of the cartoon. She has also assumed that the bullets are Israeli as the cartoonist is Palestinian. She also makes a claim about the UN that is not entirely supported by the cartoon. She says that it is fleeing for its life from the bullets. The point is that the UN (Dove) is caught in a crossfire between the bullets and is not running away from them. Susan also has an incorrect date for the cartoon. Midori's answer is the best of the three. This would be a very clear 2 mark maximum. Notice that it is shorter than Susan's answer.

The consequences of the 1973 war for the Arab states and Israel

It is generally agreed that, despite the military setbacks, the Arab states and Sadat were the victors of the Yom Kippur War. Although they had begun to suffer military reverses, the Arab armies were not defeated for the first time since 1948. The Arab states had also succeeded in overcoming their many differences and emerged from the war more united than they had been for years. This new-found unity was to give the Arabs a fresh weapon in their attempt to influence events in the Middle East – that of oil. The oil embargo, as we have seen, had started in 1973 and continued until January 1974. Yet the price of oil, which had increased by as much as 70 per cent in October 1973, did not come down after the embargo was lifted, and OPEC began to use its control of oil supplies as an economic bargaining tool. One effect of this new policy was a statement from the **European Economic Community (EEC)** which, in 1973, affirmed that the rights of Palestinians must be considered in any settlement of the Arab-Israeli conflict.

Sadat had become the 'new Nasser' and had emerged as an international statesman of some renown, something that Nasser had always wanted but never managed to achieve. In fact, Sadat managed to accomplish his goal of giving Egypt a more visible presence in international affairs. Despite suffering military reversals in the war, Egypt managed to attain increased political status in the region.

SOURCE E

Following the wars of 1967 and 1973 the two superpowers realized the wisdom and necessity of détente, having very nearly come into direct nuclear confrontation via their local protégés during the 1973 hostilities. Yet the Soviet Union was still willing to maintain its influence with its allies – taking Egypt's side during the conflict in Yemen. During this period the Soviets enjoyed a fairly strong relationship with the 'progressive' or 'radical' Arab states (Egypt, Syria, and Iraq), but it was already clear that they were mainly reacting to developments that they did not really control…

From Beverley Milton-Edwards and Peter Hinchcliffe, *Conflicts in the Middle East Since 1945*, 2004

> **European Economic Community (EEC)**
> The European Economic Community, also referred to as the 'European Community', or the 'Common Market', was an international organization created in 1957 to bring about economic integration between Belgium, France, Germany, Italy, Luxembourg and the Netherlands. It was enlarged in the 1970s and 1980s with six other states, and since the creation of the European Union in 1993 it grew to include another 15 countries by 2007.

> ● **Examiner's hint**
> A question that is worth 3 marks will probably require a three-sentence answer.

STUDENT STUDY SECTION

QUESTION
What does Source E say about superpower policies after 1973?

Here are two answers to the same question. Which is better and why?

Student Answer A – Sophie

After being at the brink of direct nuclear confrontation in 1973, both superpowers realized the necessity for a relaxation. They were both moving towards disarmament. The Soviet Union did not stop fighting in the Cold War altogether, but were reactive rather than proactive and simply supported their allies such as Egypt, Syria and Iraq in conflicts.

Student Answer B – David

Both superpowers (US and USSR) reacted to the wars with the same realization. They both believed that a relaxation of tension was necessary in the Middle East, especially because the conflict of 1973 almost resulted in a nuclear escalation between the two superpowers. The Soviet Union, however, remained involved in its allies' conflicts. The Soviet Union stood on Egypt's side in the conflict with Yemen and enjoyed good relationships with the radical Islamic states of Egypt, Syria and Iraq.

Examiner's comments

Although David's response seems better on first reading, he is only making two points. There is some repetition in the last two sentences. Sophie, on the other hand, has three clear points – the third one being that the Soviet Union only reacted to developments. Both students have paraphrased the source quite well and have not just copied, word for word, what the source says.

Yitzhak Rabin

Yitzhak Rabin was an Israeli politician and general. He was the fifth Prime Minister of Israel, serving two terms in office, 1974–77 and 1992 until his assassination in 1995. In 1994, Rabin won the Nobel Peace Prize together with Shimon Peres and Yasser Arafat.

Map 13

Occupied Territories (in green), 1982

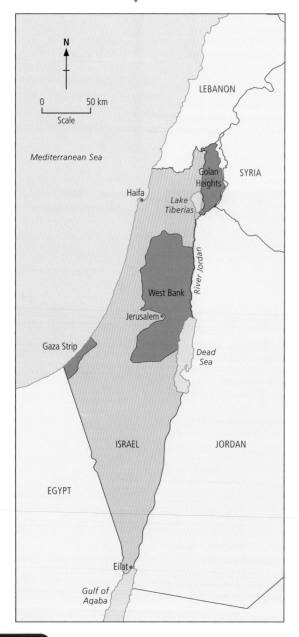

In technical terms Israel had won the war, but only with huge US military support. Public confidence in the government was shaken and an internal political quarrel followed, which was ultimately to force the Israeli Prime Minister Golda Meir and Defense Minister Moshe Dayan to resign in April 1974. **Yitzhak Rabin** took over the leadership of the government. For the first time in the Middle East, Israeli soldiers were taken as prisoners of war. Almost 3000 Israeli troops were killed and 8000 wounded (comparable figures for the Arab states were 8500 killed and 20,000 wounded). In Israel the public reaction to these figures was to lead to the establishment of a movement towards peace within the country.

The role of the United States, the PLO and the United Nations

Attempts by the international community to resolve the tensions in the region came to nothing. The Geneva Conference held in December 1973 failed to make any progress. A new, key figure was soon to emerge, the American Secretary of State Henry Kissinger. He knew that Sadat was willing to work with the Israelis, who had rejected any attempts he had made to open negotiations. Kissinger was also concerned about any potential action by OPEC to reduce or even cut off oil supplies. So he undertook a series of visits to the Middle East in an attempt to persuade Israel to withdraw some of its forces from the Occupied Territories. At the same time, Kissinger suggested to the Palestinians that any partial withdrawal of Israel might lead to a more comprehensive withdrawal in the future. This 'shuttle diplomacy', which lasted almost two years, was eventually to succeed as the Israelis gradually withdrew from the Suez Canal, part of the Golan Heights and parts of the Sinai. By 1982, following the 1978 Camp David Agreement, Israel was to withdraw further from its 1967 gains, leaving the Gaza Strip, the West Bank and the Golan Heights to be the only territories still under Israeli occupation.

Another group to gain from the 1973 war was the PLO. Arafat had begun to believe in the possibility of the existence of a separate Palestinian state and a separate Israeli state. This Palestinian state would be comprised of the West Bank and the Gaza Strip. At the Arab League meeting in Rabat in October 1974, the PLO was declared 'the sole and legitimate representative of the Palestinian people', who had 'the right to establish the independent state of Palestine on any liberated territory'.

King Hussein also agreed to give up claims to the West Bank and the parts of Jerusalem that Jordan had gained in 1948, but which were seized by Israel in 1967. The UN Security Council decided to hold a debate on the Palestinian question and invited Arafat to speak to the UN on behalf of the PLO. This seemed to be something of an about-turn by the UN, which had supported the Partition Plan in 1947 in favour of Israel. The Israelis were furious. Wearing an empty holster on his hip, Arafat spoke to the General Assembly thus, receiving a standing ovation:

SOURCE F

In my formal capacity as Chairman of the Palestine Liberation Organization and leader of the Palestinian revolution I appeal to you to accompany Our people in its struggle to attain its right to self-determination. This right is consecrated in the United Nations Charter and has been repeatedly confirmed in resolutions adopted by this august body since the drafting of the Charter. I appeal to you, further, to aid Our people's return to its homeland from an involuntary exile imposed upon it by force of arms, by tyranny, by oppression, so that we may regain Our property, Our land, and thereafter live in Our national homeland, free and sovereign, enjoying all the privileges of nationhood. Only then can we pour all our resources into the mainstream of human civilization. Only then can Palestinian creativity be concentrated on the service of humanity. Only then will Our Jerusalem resume its historic role as a peaceful shrine for all religions.

I appeal to you to enable Our people to establish national independent sovereignty over its own land.

Today I have come bearing an olive branch and a freedom fighter's gun. Do not let the olive branch fall from my hand. I repeat: do not let the olive branch fall from my hand.

From Arafat Speech to UN, 13 November 1974

STUDENT STUDY SECTION

QUESTION
What do you think would be: a) international reaction to Arafat's speech; b) the reaction of Israel; c) the reaction of the Arab states?

In his response to Arafat's speech the Israeli ambassador to the UN, Yosef Tekoah, summed up his nation's feelings as follows:

SOURCE G

On 14 October the UN hung out a sign reading 'Murderers of children are welcome here.' Today these murderers have come to the General Assembly, certain that it would do their bidding. Today this rostrum was defiled by their chieftain, who proclaimed that the shedding of Jewish blood would only end when the murderers' demands had been accepted and their objectives achieved.

From Charles Smith, *Palestine and the Arab-Israeli Conflict*, 2007

Despite Israel's opposition to the PLO invitation, the General Assembly proceeded to pass two resolutions. The first, Resolution 3236 on 22 November 1974, spelt out the UN's intentions:

SOURCE H

The General Assembly
Recalling its relevant resolutions which affirm the right of the Palestinian people to self-determination,
1. Reaffirms the inalienable rights of the Palestinian people in Palestine, including:
   (a) The right to self-determination without external interference;
   (b) The right to national independence and sovereignty;

From UN Resolution 3236

This was followed on the same day by Resolution 3237:

SOURCE I

The General Assembly

1. *Invites the Palestine Liberation Organization to participate in the sessions and the work of the General Assembly in the capacity of observer;*
2. *Invites the Palestine Liberation Organization to participate in the sessions and the work of all international conferences convened under the auspices of the General Assembly in the capacity of observer;*

From UN Resolution 3237

STUDENT STUDY SECTION
QUESTION
What do you think would be a) international reaction to the UN resolutions; b) the reaction of Israel; c) the reaction of the Arab states?

The PLO and Arafat's presence had been legitimized by the UN. Israel was furious, but could do nothing about it. The PLO was now the official representative of the Palestinian people and had received international recognition. The Palestinian question was firmly back on the international agenda, and it was here to stay. Palestinians began to believe in the reality of a Palestinian state for the first time since 1948.

Camp David and the Egyptian-Israeli peace agreement

Rabin's government in Israel was the first Likud government to be elected to power since 1948. Its Prime Minister, Menachem Begin, was considered by the Arab states to be a hardliner who was unlikely to make any concessions towards the Palestinians. There was also domestic discontent, because many Sephardic Jews were beginning to express their discontent at their treatment by the Ashkenazim. The election was seen by many in the region as a clear change of policy in Israel. It was feared that any possibility of a dialogue between Israel and the Arab states would be impossible. Likud's ideological background indicated that any giving up of the West Bank and the Gaza Strip to the Palestinians would be a betrayal of Israel's sovereignty over the territory. Begin's election was seen as a setback to any peace initiatives in the region.

In the meantime, **Jimmy Carter** had replaced **Gerald Ford** as President in the USA. Carter had the intention of reaching a 'comprehensive' settlement in the Middle East. By this he meant a single, one time, settlement that would resolve the disputes over the Occupied Territories and create a national home for the Palestinians. After his inauguration in January 1977, he travelled to Syria to test the waters for himself. He was surprised to find that President Assad did not support the idea of an independent Palestinian state, but wanted a Syrian-controlled, PLO-supported state in the region that would be a rival to Egypt. Carter's aims for a simple settlement seemed to be shattered when Begin publicly supported the idea of the establishment of more Israeli settlements in the West Bank. Begin even compared Arafat with Adolf Hitler. However, Begin's public statements were contradicted by his secret approaches to the USA, indicating that there might be the possibility of a reopening of peace negotiations.

In November 1977, President Sadat suddenly announced to the Egyptian National Assembly that he was willing to be the first Arab leader to travel to Israel and address the Knesset. He told the government that:

Jimmy Carter
Jimmy Carter served as the President of the United States from 1977 to 1981 and was the recipient of the 2002 Nobel Peace Prize in foreign affairs. Carter pursued the Camp David Accords and he negotiated a peace treaty between Israel and Egypt in 1979.

Gerald Ford
Gerald Ford was President of the United States from 1974 to 1977. He became President upon Richard Nixon's resignation on 9 August 1974.

SOURCE J

I am ready to go to the ends of the earth if this will prevent a soldier or an officer of my sons from being wounded – not being killed, but wounded. Israel will be astonished when it hears me saying now before you that I am ready to go to their house, to the Knesset itself and to talk to them.

This announcement was greeted with shock by extremists on both sides. Sadat was denounced by some Arab states and the PLO as being a traitor to the Palestinian cause. The USA treated the announcement with some scepticism believing that without an intermediary nothing would break the deadlock between the Arab states and Israel. On 19 November 1977, Sadat travelled to Jerusalem as a guest of the Israeli government. The following day Sadat addressed the Knesset, inviting the Israelis 'to shape a new life and to establish peace' and suggesting that both sides could achieve a 'durable and just peace'.

Sadat's proposal was not based on any bilateral agreements between Egypt and Israel, but was to include a solution to the Palestinian issue. The talks did not create the breakthrough that Sadat had hoped for. He wanted an Israeli withdrawal from the lands occupied in 1967 as well as some guarantee for the Palestinians. Begin's reaction to Sadat's proposal was noncommittal. Begin wanted a bilateral agreement that would allow for a withdrawal from the Sinai, but not give up control over the West Bank and Gaza Strip. Thus something of an impasse was reached.

The major impact of the meeting was simply the fact that an Egyptian leader had gone to Israel, which some observers saw as groundbreaking. To Syria and the PLO, Sadat was a traitor to the Arab cause. The visit certainly led to increased US pressure on Egypt and Israel to arrive at an agreement. In March 1978, 35 civilians were killed by Palestinians in two bus attacks, resulting in a retaliatory strike by Israel into Lebanon. It seemed as if the movements towards peace had broken down. President Carter, desperate to revive talks between Egypt and Israel, invited both Begin and Sadat to **Camp David** in Maryland. This was a real attempt by the USA to restart the peace process, and the leaders travelled there in September 1978.

Camp David
Camp David is the mountain retreat of the President of the United States in Maryland.

Left to right: President Sadat of Egypt, President Carter of the USA and Prime Minister Begin of Israel.

The conference was a bad-tempered affair with frequent clashes between Begin and Sadat. It appeared as if nothing would be achieved, but suddenly, on 15 September, after Sadat had threatened to return to Egypt, the two leaders began to find some common ground. The result was the signing of the Camp David Accords on 17 September 1978. The first called for Israel, Egypt, Jordan and the Palestinian people to resolve issues relating to the West Bank and the Gaza Strip over a period of five years. The second was a proposal for a peace treaty whereby Israel would withdraw from the Sinai in exchange for free passage of Israeli ships through the Gulf of Suez and the Suez Canal. These accords were finally ratified in March 1979, with the signing of a 'Treaty of Peace between the Arab Republic of Egypt and the State of Israel' at a White House ceremony.

ToK Time

'Where Does History Come From'? Alun Munslow

History Today, Vol 52, Issue 3 (March 2002) pp.18–20

Where does history come from? This may seem like an odd question. Surely history comes from the traces of the past that historians find in their sources? However, we might get a different answer if we put the question in another way. What happens if we choose to view history as what, from one perspective at least, it plainly is: a narrative written about the past constructed by the historian in the present? This is clearly not the way history is conventionally defined. To be technical for a moment, it is more usually described as an **empirical** and analytical undertaking – a source-based and inferential activity concerned with the study of change over time. I am posing this question – Where does history come from? – because I think historians still tend to ignore the role of narrative in studying history.

What do you think? What is the role of the historian and how does that affect historical knowledge?

Empirical
Knowledge based on experimentation and observation rather than pure theory.
Autonomy
Independent self-rule.

SOURCE K

The historic initiative of President Sadat in visiting Jerusalem and the reception accorded to him by the parliament, government and people of Israel, and the reciprocal visit of Prime Minister Begin to Ismailia, the peace proposals made by both leaders, as well as the warm reception of these missions by the peoples of both countries, have created an unprecedented opportunity for peace which must not be lost if this generation and future generations are to be spared the tragedies of war…

Framework

Taking these factors into account, the parties are determined to reach a just, comprehensive, and durable settlement of the Middle East conflict through the conclusion of peace treaties based on Security Council resolutions 242 and 338 in all their parts. Their purpose is to achieve peace and good neighborly relations. They recognize that for peace to endure, it must involve all those who have been most deeply affected by the conflict. They therefore agree that this framework, as appropriate, is intended by them to constitute a basis for peace not only between Egypt and Israel, but also between Israel and each of its other neighbors which is prepared to negotiate peace with Israel on this basis.

From the *Camp David Accords*, 17 September 1978

The following matters are agreed between the parties:
1. *the full exercise of Egyptian sovereignty up to the internationally recognized border between Egypt and mandated Palestine;*
2. *the withdrawal of Israeli armed forces from the Sinai…*
4. *the right of free passage by ships of Israel through the Gulf of Suez and the Suez Canal on the basis of the Constantinople Convention of 1888 applying to all nations; the Strait of Tiran and Gulf of Aqaba are international waterways to be open to all nations for unimpeded and nonsuspendable freedom of navigation and overflight…*

From a Framework for the Conclusion of a Peace Treaty between Egypt and Israel

---

STUDENT STUDY SECTION

QUESTION
What do you consider to be the key terms of these two documents? Make a list of them.

Despite the apparent settling of long-term grievances, these accords would not, in reality, lead to the desired consequences implied by the Treaty of Peace. It is true that Camp David brought peace between Egypt and Israel, which has lasted over 30 years. But the key issues of the Occupied Territories were unresolved and no progress was made on the question of the **autonomy** of the West Bank. The Gaza Strip, the West Bank, the Golan Heights and East Jerusalem remained under Israeli control and, in fact, the number of Israeli settlers in some of these areas increased significantly. The other Arab states had to decide what their own position was going to be regarding the bilateral agreement. Most of them refused to become involved, primarily because of the neglect of the Palestinian question in the Accords. Sadat was severely condemned by the Arab world as a traitor with the result that, in October 1981, he was assassinated by his own soldiers when attending a parade commemorating the crossing of the Suez Canal. Both the Arab League and the PLO suspended diplomatic relations with Egypt. The League went so far as to impose an economic boycott on all Egyptian goods. Egypt was no longer seen as the leader of the Arab world and the PLO began to gain in membership and support. In 1982, *Time* magazine held a poll indicating that 98 per cent of the inhabitants of the Occupied Territories wanted an autonomous state, and 86 per cent thought that this should be governed by the PLO (*Time*, 24 May 1982).

The year 1979 was to prove a difficult one in the Middle East. Already in February the Shah of Iran, **Mohammad Reza Pahlevi**, was overthrown by the **Ayatollah Khomeini** in the Iranian Revolution and an Islamic republic was proclaimed in Iran. Iran became more and more anti-American with the result that, on 4 November 1979, the US Embassy in Tehran was invaded and 68 Americans were taken hostage. This hostage crisis was to last 444 days, and included a disastrous US hostage rescue mission. Finally, in December, the Soviet Union invaded Afghanistan. The USA turned away from the Arab-Israeli question to resolve its own domestic and foreign concerns. President Carter was soundly defeated in the 1980 US presidential election, winning only six states (and Washington D.C.) and was replaced by Ronald Reagan.

Palestinians and Israelis 1979–2009

The IB History programme for the Arab-Israeli Prescribed Subject has 1979 as its end date. However, to understand what has happened in the region and to see if any progress has been made between the two sides, a brief overview of events up to 2009 is needed.

Following the defeat of the PLO in Lebanon, it was forced to move its headquarters from Beirut to Tunis in Tunisia. On 8 December 1987, an Israeli Army vehicle crashed into a lorry in Gaza, killing four Palestinian workers and wounding seven. The funerals turned into a protest against Israel and the IDF fired on the protesters, killing one of them. The 'shaking off' (*Intifada*) of the Israeli presence had begun. Youths threw stones, leaflets were distributed, roads were blocked and tyres were set on fire.

Despite military superiority, the Israelis were unable to control the *Intifada*. Radical Islamic groups such as **Hamas** and **Islamic Jihad** were formed, whose aims included the establishment of an Islamic state in Palestine through **Jihad**. The *Intifada* was to continue until 1993 and its lasting effect was to strengthen Palestinian claims for autonomy in the West Bank and the Gaza Strip.

SOURCE L

Article 13
Initiatives, the so-called peaceful solutions, and the international conferences to resolve the Palestinian problem, are all contrary to the beliefs of the Islamic Resistance Movement. For renouncing any part of Palestine means renouncing part of the religion; the nationalism of the Islamic Resistance Movement is part of its faith, the movement educates its members to adhere to its principles and to raise the banner of Allah over their homeland as they fight their Jihad... There is no solution to the Palestinian problem except by Jihad.

From Hamas Charter, August 1988

STUDENT STUDY SECTION

QUESTION
What reaction do you think Israel would have to the Hamas Charter? Explain your answer.

The ending of the Cold War in 1990 led to a change of attitude and policy in the Middle East, and by 1993 relations had even begun to improve between Israel and the PLO. A meeting was held in Norway in January 1993, which resulted in the 1993 Declaration of Principles (more commonly known as the Oslo Accord). This was not a peace treaty, but it did allow Israel and the PLO to negotiate together. This agreement was signed at the White House on 13 September 1993 by the Israeli Prime Minister Yitzhak Rabin and PLO Chairman Yasser Arafat.

Mohammad Reza Pahlevi
Mohammad Reza Shah Pahlevi, Shah of Iran, was the monarch of Iran from 16 September 1941, until his overthrow during the Iranian Revolution on 11 February 1979.

Ayatollah Khomeini
Ayatollah Khomeini is usually known as 'Imam Khomeini' ('Iman' denotes an Islamic leader) inside Iran and 'Ayatollah Khomeini' outside of Iran. He installed a theocratic political state in Iran.

Intifada
Intifada is an Arabic word for 'shaking off', though it is generally translated into English as rebellion or uprising. It is the term given to the Palestinian uprising against the Israelis which began on 9 December 1987 and was followed by a second Intifada on 28 September 2000.

Hamas
Hamas is an Islamic Palestinian political and social organization that includes a paramilitary wing. Hamas was created in 1987 at the beginning of the First Intifada. Since June 2007, Hamas has governed the Gaza Strip.

Islamic Jihad
The Islamic Jihad Movement in Palestine is a militant organization whose goal is the destruction of the State of Israel and its replacement with a Palestinian state. This group defines *jihad* as acts of war against Israelis. Palestinian Islamic Jihad also opposes many other Arab governments, whom they see as being insufficiently Islamic and too Western.

Jihad
Arabic for 'struggle'. Often translated as a 'Holy War' against any foreign occupation or unjust rule.

The Oslo Accord was an historic landmark in Middle East relations and, for most observers, seemed to point to a resolution of many of the issues that had remained unresolved since 1948. It was later followed by the Cairo Agreement, in May 1994, which allowed for Israeli withdrawal from the West Bank and the Gaza Strip and an increase in the role of the Palestinian National Authority (PNA). As a result of these agreements, in December 1994 Rabin, Arafat and Israeli Foreign Minister **Shimon Peres** were awarded the Nobel Peace Prize for their work to achieve peace in the region.

Arafat, Peres and Rabin after receiving the Nobel Peace Prize.

Hezbollah
Hizbollah or Hezbollah is an Islamic political and paramilitary organization based in Lebanon. It was founded in 1982.

Shimon Peres
Shimon Peres became President of the State of Israel in 2007, having served twice as Prime Minister. Peres was elected to the Knesset in November 1959 and, except for a three-month period in early 2006, served continuously until 2007, when he became Prime Minister.

Benjamin Netanyahu
An Israeli politician who has been the Prime Minister of Israel since March 2009. He previously held the same position from June 1996 to July 1999 and is currently the Chairman of the Likud Party. Netanyahu's policies towards the Palestinian question have varied. As Prime Minister he has supported the policy of settlements in the West Bank, rejected US peace talks, has negotiated with Yasser Arafat, rejected withdrawal from the Golan Heights and most recently, on 14 June 2009 in a speech to the Knesset, supported the idea of a Palestinian state co-existing with an Israeli state.

In September 1995, Oslo II was signed at the White House. It created three zones in the West Bank and proposed how these were to be controlled. It was also agreed that elections would be held in January 1996 for what became known as the Palestinian Authority, creating a form of autonomous state for the Palestinian people.

The radicals on both sides, however, were furious with the national leaders. Palestinian suicide bombings increased (between April 1994 and January 1995, 65 Israelis were killed), and on 4 November 1995, at a peace rally in Tel Aviv, Rabin was assassinated by Yigal Amir, an Israeli law student and a devout follower of the Torah. Shimon Peres became the new Prime Minister and immediately began implementing the terms of Oslo II. Israeli forces withdrew from parts of the West Bank by the end of 1995.

In January 1996, the promised Palestinian elections were held. Arafat received more than 88 per cent of the votes cast and a Palestinian Authority legislature was created. It seemed as if an embryonic Palestinian state was in the process of being created. The apparent optimism on the Palestinian side, however, was soon to be destroyed by events. Israel assassinated Yahya Ayyaash, an expert Hamas bomb-maker. In retaliation, suicide bombings increased and in turn Peres launched Operation *Grapes of Wrath* in April 1996, attacking **Hezbollah** camps and Lebanese roads and power stations.

In the Israeli elections that followed, Peres was defeated by **Benjamin Netanyahu**, who condemned the Oslo agreements and decided to allow **Israeli settlers** to occupy land in the West Bank. He vowed that he would not allow the Palestinians to regain any more land

and would not negotiate with Arafat. A stalemate ensued, but eventually some common ground was found with the signing of the Hebron Agreement in 1997, in which both sides agreed that Israel would withdraw from the territory in exchange for a Palestinian promise to reduce terrorist acts. This was followed by the Wye River Memorandum in 1998, which continued to implement some of the Oslo proposals. Netanyahu's position in the Knesset, and internationally, became more and more difficult and in the May 1999 elections he was replaced as Prime Minister by Ehud Barak. With the defeat of Netanyahu, the possibility of the opening of the peace process seemed bright. This was ultimately confirmed by the meeting of Barak and Arafat with President Clinton at Camp David in July 2000. Hopes of further progress were dashed by Arafat's inflexibility, which resulted in the failure of the summit.

The Middle East exploded in September 2000. Likud leader **Ariel Sharon** insisted on visiting the Temple Mount in Jerusalem, one of the holiest sites in Islam. Protesters attempted to block his access and the IDF opened fire, killing four protesters. The **al-Aqsa** or Second *Intifada* broke out with extreme violence. Between late September and December, 365 people were killed and almost 1100 were wounded. Arafat's decision to support the *Intifada* was ultimately to lead to a rejection of the Oslo process.

Ariel Sharon became Israeli Prime Minister in February 2001 and adopted a hardline approach to the peace process. He wanted a new basis for discussion and a fresh proposal was put forward by the USA, Russia, the UN and the European Union, which became known as the 'roadmap'. This was intended to provide the basis for an end to violence and a territorial settlement that both sides would accept. The Palestinian Authority and Israel did accept the basic terms of the roadmap, although Israel had several reservations. Neither side fully implemented the proposals. Although the roadmap was initially supported by Sharon, he had other goals as well. These included the weakening of Arafat and the targeting of radical Palestinian groups through the assassination of their leaders. Sharon also wanted to build a wall between the West Bank and Israel to separate the two territories. Work was started in 2002 on the wall, which would be more than 700km long and, at the time of writing (June 2009), is not yet fully completed.

Arafat was unable to control the extremist elements among the Palestinians. Hamas, in particular, received more and more support, which resulted in a direct clash with Fatah. The Palestinian Authority was seen as being less and less effective, as it was unable to do anything about the continued Israeli occupation of the West Bank and the Gaza Strip. Arafat died in November 2004, but his successor **Mahmoud Abbas** was also unable to provide the Palestinian Authority with sound leadership. The Second *Intifada* had created one positive achievement for the Palestinians, however. It brought about the evacuation of the Gaza Strip by Israel, although it was no surprise that in the elections of January 2006 Hamas gained control of the Palestinian Authority, winning 74 seats out of 132. This Hamas victory strengthened Israel's determination not to surrender land, and Fatah would not accept the result of the election.

In spring 2007, the Hamas government collapsed and Abbas began to meet again with the Israeli government. Both sides have endorsed the roadmap, but little concrete progress has been made towards its implementation. The continued firing of rockets by Hamas into Israel in 2008 and the suspected smuggling of weapons from Egypt to Gaza through specially built tunnels prompted Israel to invade Gaza in January 2009, killing more than 1000 Palestinians. As ever, the situation remains tense. But, can we look forward to any major changes in the attitudes of the two sides in the future? Both Israelis and Palestinians seem sceptical of a peaceful resolution of the issues.

Israeli settlers
This issue of Jewish settlers in the West Bank was to become one of the thorniest problems between the Israelis and the Palestinians. Even today this is unresolved.

Ariel Sharon
Ariel Sharon is a former Israeli Prime Minister and military leader. Sharon served as Prime Minister from March 2001 until April 2006, but suffered a disabling stroke on 4 January 2006.

al-Aqsa
The Temple Mount in Jerusalem is also the site of the al-Aqsa Mosque, from which the uprising takes its name after Ariel Sharon's visit in 2000.

Mahmoud Abbas
Mahmoud Abbas was named the first Prime Minister of the Palestinian Authority in March 2003. He resigned as Prime Minister on 6 September 2003. Following the death of Yasser Arafat, the Palestinian Authority held an election for his successor, an election won by Abbas.

REVIEW SECTION

This section has dealt with the causes and consequences of the 1967 and 1973 wars between the Arabs and the Israelis. Answer the following questions briefly using information from the text, the sources and your own knowledge.

Review questions

1 Draw up a table to compare the 1967 and 1973 wars. Use the following headings: causes, course and consequences.

2 Why, do you think, has there been no major war between the Arab states and Israel since 1973?

3 Do you think there has been any significant progress in the relationship between the Palestinians and the Israelis?

Sample exam for Prescribed Subject 2: The Arab-Israeli Conflict 1945–79

SOURCE A

From a Telegram from Valeriu Georgescu, Extraordinary Envoy and Plenipotentiary Minister of Romania in Tel Aviv, to Petru Burlacu, Deputy Minister of Foreign Affairs of the Socialist Republic of Romania, 20 June 1967

S. Mikunis replied [to the Soviet Ambassador] that the war was the result of actions undertaken by Nasser for the evacuation of the UN troops, the closing of the Tiran Straits, troop movements at the Israeli border, and war-like declarations by Egyptian leaders.

Israel had to mobilize its entire military force to defend its right to exist.

The Israeli Government made declarations in favor of an immediate cessation of combat actions, in favor of negotiations between the sides involved in the conflict, against territorial annexations, without naming an aggressor. Israel carried out the war to defend the very existence of the state, a war imposed by the Arab Nations. The Soviet Union, instead of adopting a constructive position to prevent the war and maintain peace, [instead of] having an essential role in this direction, was the catalytic factor which instigated Egypt against Israel.

SOURCE B

From Sandy Tolan, 'New Lessons from the Six-Day War', 11 June 2006. Sandy Tolan is director of the Project for International Reporting at the Graduate School of Journalism at the University of California, Berkeley. This is adapted from his book *The Lemon Tree: An Arab, A Jew, and the Heart of the Middle East,* 2007

That same day [26 May 1967], however, Israel sent urgent word to Secretary of State Dean Rusk, indicating imminent attack from Egypt and Syria. 'Our intelligence,' Rusk reiterated, 'does not confirm this Israeli estimate.' During this time, Nasser was reiterating to Westerners his reluctance to engage Israel – despite his heated rhetoric for the Arab masses. On May 31 in Cairo, he told former American Treasury Secretary Robert Anderson, a longtime acquaintance, that he would not 'begin any fight.' The two men discussed the possibility of a visit to Cairo by Vice President Hubert Humphrey, and laid the groundwork for a secret visit to Washington by Egyptian Vice President Zakariya Moheiddine. On June 2, Nasser told the British MP, Christopher Mayhew, that Egypt had 'no intention of attacking Israel.' The Soviets, meanwhile, continued to urge Nasser away from war; at one point, the Soviet ambassador to Cairo made a personal visit to Nasser's residence at 3 a.m., underscoring Moscow's concern.

SOURCE C

From 'Why Diplomacy Failed to Avert the Six Day War', a speech by Moshe Raviv to The Washington Institute's symposium marking the 40th anniversary of the 1967 war between Israel and its Arab neighbours, 4 June 2007. Moshe Raviv served as an aide to Israeli Foreign Minister Abba Eban in 1967.

We now embarked on the crucial visit to Washington. When we landed in Washington on May 25, the assessment in Jerusalem was that the Egyptian deployment was offensive and an attack on Israel was imminent. Eban was instructed by the prime minister to request urgently an American declaration that an attack on Israel is equivalent to an attack on the U.S. The hope was that such a declaration would deter Nasser from attacking. Within hours Eban was received by the secretary and transmitted the request. Rusk said that the foreign minister had raised questions that involved constitutional decisions. He promised to transmit the request to the president and cautioned against Israel being the first to open hostilities. The U.S. initiated a comprehensive intelligence assessment of the situation and the Egyptian ambassador was invited to the State Department and given a stern warning against attacking Israel.

SOURCE D

From a US government memorandum, National Archives and Records Administration, RG 59, Central Files 1967–69, POL UAR-US, 26 May 1967

At 4:10 p.m. today, Friday, May 26, 1967, Mr. James E. Birdsall telephoned the following message. This is the message from Nasser: 'Now is the time when all Arab people are waiting to see an act of friendship on the part of the USA.' His urgent request is that the U.S. undertake no direct military action in the form of landings, shifting of naval fleet, or otherwise. Nasser assured Siddiqui [a personal friend of Nasser] that the UAR [United Arab Republic of Egypt and Syria] had no intention of fighting. What they are doing is returning to the 1956 frontier. He assured Siddiqui that this matter would soon be terminated without any fighting. He informed Siddiqui that his current actions were intended only to prove to the Arab world that Saudi Arabia and Jordan are false friends. And the Arabs should follow Nasser who is their friend. He also wishes to prove that President Johnson is impartial as between the Arabs and Israel and that he will not take any sides in the present war of nerves. If President Johnson can grant Nasser's request, he can be assured that Nasser will place his entire services at President Johnson's disposal.

SOURCE E

Cartoon by Zapiro in the Mail and Guardian, **a South African newspaper, June 2007.**

STUDENT STUDY SECTION

QUESTIONS

1a) What does Source C say about the USA's response to Eban's visit? (3 marks)

1b) What is the message portrayed in Source E?

2)   Compare and contrast the explanation given in Sources A and D about the reasons for the outbreak of war.

3)   According to their origin and purpose what are the value and limitations of Source B and Source C to an historian studying the causes of the 1967 war?

4)   Using the sources and your own knowledge, to what extent do you agree that 'Israel carried out the war [1967 Six-Day War] to defend the very existence of the state'? (Source A)

ToK Time

Gary Latuff is a Brazilian cartoonist

What is the message of this cartoon? Why is it so difficult to find an objective cartoon on the Arab-Israeli crisis? Is it ever possible to find an objective cartoon? Explain your answer.

Latuff on Gaza: Western Logic, 11 March 2008.

6

Prescribed Subject 3:
Communism in Crisis 1976–89

THE FALL OF COMMUNISM: THE USSR AND EASTERN EUROPE 1976–89

Introduction

This Prescribed Subject looks at the late 20th century in China and also the USSR, along with its Eastern European satellite states of Poland, Czechoslovakia and the German Democratic Republic (East Germany).

In Russia (part of the future Soviet Union), a communist regime came to power after the Revolution of 1917. The Bolsheviks promised widespread change and the establishment of a Marxist state that would fulfil Karl Marx's vision of a communist utopia. Lenin, as the first ruler of the Soviet Union, experimented with various economic and social policies, but it was Josef Stalin, after controlling the Soviet Union for almost 25 years, who left behind a firmly entrenched system that was to become the model for other communist states. Creating the communist utopia proved extremely difficult, however, and by the time of Stalin's death in 1953, living conditions were still very hard for the majority of the people. Stalin's successor, Nikita Khrushchev, saw the need for reform, although he found it almost impossible to change the Soviet Union. The 1960s and 1970s were marked by 'stagnation' as economic growth slowed down. Between 1976 and 1989, the USSR was in a period of crisis, with similar problems affecting its satellite states.

China, the other great communist superpower, would also encounter challenges at the end of the 20th century. Established in 1949, the People's Republic of China, under the leadership of Mao Zedong, borrowed heavily from the Soviet model. Like Stalin, Mao encouraged **collectivization** and **Five Year Plans**, but he also faced similar problems. These included the challenge of how to keep the economy growing, how to maintain the aims of the revolution and how to keep up with the West. After Mao's death in 1976, new economic policies were introduced to find ways to modernize and to make the planned economy more efficient. Both China and the USSR would discover that encouraging economic growth meant allowing greater economic freedom and that this also meant dealing with demands for more political freedom.

Here was the 'crisis of communism' and the next two chapters will look at how this was addressed by the Soviet Union and China. Communism collapsed in the former state, while it is still in existence in the latter.

 Collectivization
Collectivization was introduced by Stalin in 1928 and was applied to agriculture. Individual peasant plots were too small for machinery to be used and the pooling of land and labour was intended to make farming more efficient. The political motive was also important, as people working as a collective unit rather than individuals would help put the ideals of communism into practice. Another 'benefit' would be to extend the control of the Communist Party over the population in the countryside.

Five Year Plans
Stalin introduced the First Five Year Plan in 1928. These plans were intended to give fixed targets that the Soviet economy would achieve over a period of five years. This model was copied by most other communist states.

Timeline – 1976–89	
1977	A new constitution is introduced in the USSR
	Leonid Brezhnev replaces Nikolai Podgorny as head of state
	Charter 77 is established in Czechoslovakia
1978	A revolutionary coup takes place in Afghanistan
	Pope John Paul II is elected as head of the Catholic Church
1979	President Carter and Leonid Brezhnev sign SALT II in Vienna
	The Shah is overthrown in Iran
	US embassy in Tehran is attacked and diplomats are taken hostage
	The Soviet invasion of Afghanistan begins

1980	Moscow Olympic Games are boycotted by the USA
	The Carter Doctrine warns the Soviets against expansion into the Persian Gulf
	Jimmy Carter loses US presidential election to Ronald Reagan
	Solidarity is established in Poland
	US Senate does not ratify SALT II
	Soviet Premier Alexei Kosygin dies
1981	Martial law is imposed in Poland
1982	Leonid Brezhnev dies and is succeeded by Yuri Andropov
1983	Flight KAL 007 is shot down over Sakhalin Island
	NATO exercise Able Archer 83
1984	Yuri Andropov dies and is succeeded by Konstantin Chernenko
1985	Konstantin Chernenko dies and is succeeded by Mikhail Gorbachev
	Gorbachev meets Reagan in Geneva
1986	27th Party Congress takes place in the USSR
	Limited electoral reforms are introduced for regional Soviets
	There is an accident at the nuclear powerplant in Chernobyl
	Gorbachev meets Reagan in Reykjavik
1987	President Reagan visits Moscow
	Gorbachev visits Washington – INF treaty is signed
1988	Law of State Enterprises comes into effect in the USSR
	Geneva Accords on Soviet withdrawal from Afghanistan
	Constitutional changes – Gorbachev amends the 1977 Constitution
1989	Multi-candidate elections to Congress of People's Deputies in USSR
	Hungary opens its border with Austria
	Berlin Wall opened
	Multi-party elections in Poland
	The Velvet Revolution in Czechoslovakia

Section I:

Domestic and foreign problems of the Brezhnev era: economic and political stagnation; Afghanistan

This section will focus on the final years of Leonid Brezhnev's time as leader of the Soviet Union. It was decided, after the removal of Nikita Khrushchev in 1964, that no other leader could be both First Secretary of the Party as well as Chairman of the Council of Ministers (Prime Minister). In other words, no one person was meant to lead both the Party and the government/state, although Brezhnev was to end up as both General Secretary and President.

The Soviet Union After 1976

Background Information

Since 1929, the Soviet Union had achieved great things under the **command economy** system. Within the framework of the Five Year Plan, Stalin had used central control, propaganda and terror to industrialize a Soviet Union that was able to defeat Nazi Germany, become a nuclear superpower and expand its borders farther than those of the Tsarist Empire.

Command or planned economy system
The Soviet economy was organized by the state. Gosplan (State Planning Committee) made decisions about what products would be produced and in what quantities as well as how resources would be distributed.

Josef Stalin died in March 1953, leaving the legacy of a rigidly planned economy, a subservient workforce and gulags full of prisoners. After short-lived interregnums led by Georgi Malenkov (1953–55) and Nikolai Bulganin (1955–58), Nikita Khrushchev became both First Secretary (head of the Party) and Prime Minister (head of state). A convinced and enthusiastic believer in communism, Khrushchev was sure that the USSR could compete with and overtake the West and that people living in Moscow could enjoy the same standard of living as the people of London, Paris and New York. To do this, the Soviet Union needed to produce more consumer goods. It needed to provide a better quality of life for its citizens, and it could achieve this only with economic reform. Yet population growth was slowing down, resources were running out, machinery was becoming obsolete and agricultural output was falling, so the Soviet Union would have to change.

Both Khrushchev and his successor, Leonid Brezhnev, knew that the Soviet economy needed to be more efficient. Workers had to work harder and more productively, managers had to manage more efficiently and the centrally planned economy had to be more flexible. The problem was that the Soviet Union also had to remain a single-party, communist state with workers and managers trained to fulfil targets set for them by the central government.

How far could the economic system of a communist state be modified before it turned into a free market state? Was there room for reform?

In his book, *Armageddon Averted*, the American historian Stephen Kotkin summed up the state of the Soviet Union in this way:

SOURCE A

Since the 1930s the Soviet Union had rapidly industrialised, captured Hitler's Berlin, launched Sputnik, banged its shoe on the podium of the UN, and boasted it would bury capitalism. But by winning the Second World War, and therefore having no necessity or feeling no desire, to change fundamentally, to compete in the transformed post-war international context, the Soviet Union, in a way, doomed itself… right in the midst of its great 1970s oil boom, the socialist revolution entered a decrepit old age.

From Stephen Kotkin, *Armageddon Averted*, 2001

STUDENT STUDY SECTION

QUESTION

What, according to Source A, were the reasons for the decline of the Soviet Union?

Student Answer A – Jan

According to Source A, the Soviet Union went into decline because being successful in the Second World War, it did not feel the need to change or adapt to a different post-war environment. Hence, it fell behind its rival.

Student Answer B – Emily

The Soviet Union went into decline because it did not feel the need 'to compete in the transformed post-war international context'. The USSR had won the Second World War and this gave it the confidence to feel that it no longer needed to compete. The 1970s had an oil boom that benefitted the USSR, but it still did not make use of this to make necessary changes and so went into 'decrepit old age', meaning it could no longer be revived.

● **Examiner's hint**

When you are asked to look for an answer in a source, underline the relevant points and then focus on the information that you need to answer the question. Don't list everything, only what is relevant.

Presidium
The Presidium was the new name given in 1952 to the Politburo. This was the highest level of the Central Committee of the Communist Party of the Soviet Union (CPSU). It met frequently to make policy decisions. During Stalin's rule, the Politburo did not meet frequently. After Stalin died in 1953, his successors restored the weekly meetings of what was now known as the Presidium. Its membership was increased to nine full-time and three candidate members, as well as a permanent chairman.

The Council of Ministers
The Supreme Soviet was the highest body of the Congress of Soviets. It consisted of the ministers for all the governmental departments. The Chairman of the Council of Ministers was also known as the Prime Minister. He was the head of the government and the head of state.

Nomenklatura
The members of the nomenklatura formed the 'ruling class' of the Soviet Union. These were the senior officials of the Party, the ones who made the policies. The name came from the list of jobs that were available within the Party. Once appointed to leading positions, these officials remained in those jobs until they retired. They had better accommodation, better health care, better education for their children and access to scarce goods and resources. They were a kind of aristocracy.

Cadre
A cadre is a party official.

Apparat
Apparat is an abbreviation of *apparatchik*, meaning a Party man.

Examiner's comments
Notice that Jan does get to the main part of the answer and mentions how the USSR felt that after winning World War II, it did not need to adapt. He does not go further, though, and explain that it failed to make the most of the oil boom in the 1970s and so missed a chance to recover. Emily gives a fuller answer and makes this connection and so has read the source more carefully looking for more points to make.

Brezhnev's leadership

Leonid Brezhnev was appointed General Secretary of the Communist Party in 1964. He was a member of the **Presidium** that removed Nikita Khrushchev from power and replaced him with a 'collective leadership'. Andrei Kosygin was appointed Chairman of the **Council of Ministers** (Prime Minister). As was the case after the death of Lenin in 1924 and of Stalin in 1953, 'collective leadership' did not last for long. Brezhnev emerged as a dominant personality and by the time he died in 1982, he was not only General Secretary of the Party but also President of the Soviet Union.

After the removal of Nikita Khrushchev, policies were introduced to restore the Soviet Union to a more stable and predictable leadership. Many of Khrushchev's radical initiatives were reversed and Brezhnev, in many ways, personified a more passive and more conservative administration. He presided over a period in the Soviet Union known as 'stagnation'. This referred to the slowing down of economic growth and the 'inertia' that gripped the leadership.

The *nomenklatura* liked Brezhnev. Unlike Khrushchev, he was predictable and was unlikely to be captivated by ideas that he would insist upon implementing. Many of the officials in the higher levels of government wanted a quiet time after the dramas of the Khrushchev years.

SOURCE B

Brezhnev believed that his main forte [strong point] was personnel policy. He was Comrade **Cadres** *(this nickname reflected Brezhnev's eagerness to support the party officials rather than to disturb the system by introducing change). Hence policy making was of secondary importance… Brezhnev never took great risks since he lacked the political imagination of a Khrushchev. He never tried to force legislation through the Politburo if there was a majority against it. He knew, as a master* **apparat** *man, that contentious [controversial] legislation cannot be successfully implemented, and the nomenklatura knew where it was with him.*

From Martin McCauley, *The Soviet Union 1917–1991*, 1996

SOURCE C

Brezhnev's Politburo was composed mainly of Stalin's ageing promotees [the people he had promoted into important jobs]. Their fundamental attitudes to politics and economics had been formed before 1953. They were proud of the Soviet order and present achievements. Change was anathema [hateful] to them… Indeed, the contemplation of change would have required a concentration of intellectual faculties that hardly any of them any longer possessed.

From Robert Service, *A History of Modern Russia*, 2003

STUDENT STUDY SECTION

QUESTION
To what extent are the views in Source B about Brezhnev's leadership supported by the views expressed in Source C?

● **Examiner's hint**
Find and list phrases in both
sources that convey the
same or different impressions
of Brezhnev. You could use
different colour pens to
indicate similar views and
different views. If asked to do
so, always be sure to compare
and also to contrast.

Student Answer – *Elizabeth*

Source B mainly focuses on Brezhnev's inability to force legislation through the Politburo. It focuses on how 'policy making' was of secondary importance and that Brezhnev 'never took great risks'. In contrast, Source C focuses on the rigid idea of the Politburo as opposed to weaknesses of Brezhnev. It points out that the members' attitudes to politics and economics had been formed before 1953! Though both sources are discussing the time of Brezhnev's rule and the lack of political imagination, Source B lays the blame with Brezhnev's character, while Source C lays the blame with the aged Politburo.

Examiner's comments

Elizabeth has done quite well here and focused on the main contrast – in Source B the emphasis is on Brezhnev's style of leadership, while in Source C the emphasis is on the members of the Politburo. She has also attempted a comparative format and although she begins by summarizing Source B and then goes on to summarize Source C, she does make links between them. It would be better to begin by saying, 'Sources B and C disagree…' and then to explain how they differ. She has also hinted at a comparison by saying that both sources discuss the time of Brezhnev's rule but then goes on to mention a contrast.

Be sure that you use a comparative format and that you find ways to both compare and contrast the sources when answering this question. Here, Elizabeth could have mentioned that both sources discuss the resistance to change. Source C states that the members of the Politburo did not like change, while Source B states that Brezhnev understood their resistance to change and this made him a skilful leader.

Brezhnev: The cult of personality

Even though it was said of Brezhnev that his was a 'personality cult without a personality', he was easily recognized and well known throughout the Soviet Union.

How was he able to do this?

- He made sure that his name was frequently mentioned in newspapers and on the TV.
- Photos or posters of him were placed in public spaces.
- He made sure that he remained in power and was well known for removing his rivals and surrounding himself with supporters.
- When Nikolai Podgorny left the Politburo in 1977 and resigned as Chair of the Presidium of the Supreme Soviet, Brezhnev took this role and became head of state.
- When Prime Minister Alexei Kosygin, who had resigned because of ill health, died in December 1980, the announcement of his death was delayed to enable Brezhnev to celebrate his birthday.
- Brezhnev's love of honours was well known and he was made Marshal of the Soviet Union in 1976, as well as receiving his 5th Order of Lenin medal and his 2nd Hero of the Soviet Union medal.

There are many different opinions of Brezhnev's leadership. As mentioned earlier, it has been said that he wanted a quiet time and so avoided doing anything controversial. Yet he took the Soviet Union into a period of **détente** and into a foreign war. Robert Service notes how Brezhnev was 'kept alive' by his supporters or 'cronies' such as Chernenko and Tikhonov, and that even Foreign Minister Gromyko and Defence Minister Ustinov, neither of whom liked Brezhnev, thought it wiser to keep him in power rather than to have to choose a successor. Mikhail Gorbachev, who was to become General Secretary in 1985, was appointed to the Politburo in 1980 at the age of 49, but he was among its very few 'young' members.

Détente (an easing of tension)
Détente is the term used to describe the nature of the relationship between the USA and the USSR from around 1969 to 1979. Some historians may argue that détente began with the signing of the Test Ban Treaty in 1963, but the term is usually applied to the late 1960s. By the mid 1970s, détente was already losing popularity and it ended when the Soviet invasion of Afghanistan in 1979 worsened relations between the superpowers.

SOURCE D

ТАК ПОЙДЁМ ЖЕ СМЕЛО ВПЕРЁД
ПО ПУТИ, ВЕДУЩЕМУ К КОММУНИЗМУ!

A propaganda poster. Caption: 'And so we will go bravely forward on the way to communism!'

● **Examiner's hint**
If you are asked to explain a cartoon or a photograph, always read the caption and try to say something about this. Look carefully at all the detail and include as much as you can in your answer.

STUDENT STUDY SECTION

QUESTION
What is the message conveyed by Source D?

Student Answer – *Kristian*

This propaganda poster shows Brezhnev, who was Khrushchev's successor. As the caption confirms, he wanted to continue to carry out communist ideals. It is interesting to note that the poster suggests his interest in returning to Lenin's ideals as behind him is a flag with Lenin's picture on it. The image suggests that Lenin is behind Brezhnev almost like a stern guardian. To have Lenin's picture on the poster reminded people that Brezhnev was a 'student' of Lenin and the cult of Lenin was still very important. The words 'we will go bravely forward on the way to communism' tell us that the Soviet Union was not communist yet but still on the 'way' to communism.

Examiner's comments

Kristian has given a good answer here. He has paid attention to the detail in the poster and the caption and tried to say something about all the different parts. He has not included too much of his own knowledge, though, and described only what the poster shows. This is good, as it means he has not 'read' more into the poster than what is actually shown.

Brezhnev's economic policies

Industry – Stagnation (Failure to grow)

During the 1970s, the Soviet economy started to slow down despite efforts to increase production, especially of consumer goods. The command economy had some advantages if there were major goals to achieve, like the industrialization of the Soviet Union or fighting World War II. It was not, however, an effective model for producing consumer goods because production levels and prices were not determined by the forces of supply and demand.

Despite all this, the Five Year Plan remained the model for economic planning and Prime Minister Kosygin was responsible for economic policies during:

- The Eighth Five Year Plan (1965–70)
- The Ninth Five Year Plan (1971–75)
- The Tenth Five Year Plan (1976–81)

The Eighth Five Year Plan was relatively successful. Kosygin wanted to make the economy more dynamic and to increase the production of goods. He tried to reduce the involvement of central planning authorities and to allow managers of factories to make more decisions. Unfortunately, decades of central planning and working to achieve targets handed down by Moscow made it very unlikely that managers would turn into entrepreneurs. There were some increases in production in the Eighth Five Year Plan, but the results of the Ninth and Tenth Five Year Plans were disappointing. For instance, production was predicted to rise by 5.7 per cent in 1979, but the actual increase was only 3.4 per cent. There was also a decline in the production of coal, still a major source of power in the Soviet Union. After the oil crisis of 1973, there was pressure on the manufacturing industries in the USA and Western Europe to come up with new ways to reduce oil consumption, but the USSR had plenty of oil and so there was no incentive to innovate.

The Oil Crisis of 1973

The increase in oil prices resulting from the Arab oil embargo had a huge impact on the world economy and led to a recession in the West. (See Chapter 5 regarding the 1973 war in the Middle East.)

Reasons for weak industrial growth:

- The machinery was obsolete. Money was spent on repairing old, worn-out machinery rather than replacing it with new technology.
- Workers were not willing to be paid for what they produced rather than for the time they spent at work.
- Managers set very low targets that they knew they could achieve, rather than trying to increase production.
- There was a falling birth rate and so workers were in short supply.
- There was no incentive to reform because the USSR benefited from increased oil and gold prices. This meant that badly needed reforms became less important and so could be postponed.
- The arms industry (known as the 'steel eaters') took up huge quantities of resources for the arms race with the USA.

SOURCE E

Unwittingly, the oil-producing Arab states had rescued the Soviet state budget in 1973 by increasing the world-market prices for oil… The 1973 oil shock initially had seemed to doom capitalism's remarkable post-war run but it definitely pushed capitalism further on the path to deep, structural reforms. These changes would soon cast the USSR's greatest ostensible achievement, its hyper fossil-fuel economy, upon which its superpower status rested, into a time warp, which its institutional framework could not or would not manage to confront... Only very dimly were Brezhnev and his colleagues aware that doing nothing was a recipe for political disaster.

From Robert Service, *A History of Modern Russia*, 2003

● **Examiner's hint**

Who is Robert Service? Can you find out something about how he interprets the history of the Soviet Union? Don't forget origin and purpose when you evaluate a source. It is often tempting to rush into describing its value and limitations, but you need to understand where a source comes from (origin) and who it is written for (purpose) before you can decide on its value. Also, be careful, in this case, not just to describe the extract.

STUDENT STUDY SECTION

QUESTION

With reference to its origin and purpose, discuss the value and limitations of Source E for historians studying the Brezhnev era.

SOURCE F

The maturity of the system posed a further problem for Brezhnev and his colleagues: by the late 1980s much of the industrial capital stock was very old; most of it was technically out of date, and much of it was physically worn out as well. This was just one aspect of a larger problem, which also grew worse over time: the Soviet economy was an economy without an exit. Plants were rarely closed, the service lives of machinery and equipment were far too long, and too little attention was paid to obsolescence.

From William Tompson, *The Soviet Union Under Brezhnev,* **2003**

Agriculture – Stagnation

Agriculture played a very important part in the Soviet economy. Since well before the Bolshevik Revolution of 1917, an emphasis was placed on improving agricultural production, both to feed the population and also to increase exports. During the Russian Civil War (1918–20,) Lenin experimented with 'War Communism' as a way to force peasant farmers to hand over grain to the state and to push through the rapid introduction of communism, but relented when this led to famine and political opposition. In 1921, Lenin brought in the New Economic Policy to encourage rather than force the peasants to produce more food crops. By 1928, determined to bring food production under the control of the state, Stalin introduced collectivization and the establishment of the *kolkhoz* and *sovkhoz*. It was this **land system** that was inherited by Stalin's successors. Khrushchev tried to increase agricultural production by giving more control back to the local collective farms and also by his Virgin Lands campaign. Brezhnev restored central control over agricultural planning but retained the larger collective farms set up by Khrushchev. He also increased the size of private plots.

Like Khrushchev, Brezhnev believed that bigger *kolkhozi* would mean more efficient farming. By the late 1970s collective farms received 27 per cent of all state investment, not including farm machinery and chemical fertilizers. By 1980, gross agricultural output was 21 per cent higher than the average for 1966–70. Cereal crops production rose 18 per cent in the same period. Brezhnev also believed that the workers on the *kolkhozi* needed to be given more incentives to work hard. Although food prices for consumers were kept low, the prices paid to the *kolkhozi* for their production were increased. For instance, the state subsidy for meat was so high that it was sold to the consumer at half its cost to the state. Life on the collective farm improved under Brezhnev, as workers were now paid a regular wage instead of having to wait until the end of the year to see if there was a profit and how this would be shared out. If you worked on a collective farm (and 40 per cent of the Soviet population still worked on the land) then you would, for the first time, get a pension as well as an internal passport that allowed you to travel to the city. But there were still problems.

When the government gathered statistics to assess agricultural production, only the figures for the grain harvest were used. These statistics also failed to show that cereals were imported as 'fodder crops' (food for farm animals) or that the sugar beet harvest declined by 2 per cent in the same period. Another problem was that although investment in agriculture was rising and the *kolkhozi* were paid more for their produce, the cost of fuel and machinery also rose.

Land system

A *kolkhoz* (pl. *kolkhozi*) was a large area of farmland controlled by a group of Communist Party officials. A *sovkhoz* (pl. *sovkhozi*) was a state farm. Private plots were small areas of land on which peasants were allowed to grow food for their families. By 1978, Brezhnev increased the area of land that a peasant was allowed to farm individually to half a hectare.

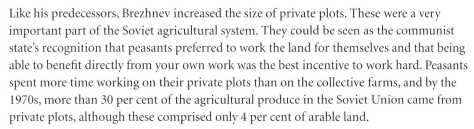

Like his predecessors, Brezhnev increased the size of private plots. These were a very important part of the Soviet agricultural system. They could be seen as the communist state's recognition that peasants preferred to work the land for themselves and that being able to benefit directly from your own work was the best incentive to work hard. Peasants spent more time working on their private plots than on the collective farms, and by the 1970s, more than 30 per cent of the agricultural produce in the Soviet Union came from private plots, although these comprised only 4 per cent of arable land.

Reasons for weak agricultural growth:
- The collective farms were too big and inefficient.
- The labour supply was shrinking.
- Maintaining farm machinery was a problem and so tractors, for instance, were often out of service.
- It was difficult to store food and to transport it to the cities.

Production of consumer goods

Brezhnev wanted workers to feel that their lives were improving and he didn't want the state to be challenged by unhappy workers. He was aware of growing discontent in Poland and did not want to face the same kind of confrontation in the Soviet Union, so he made an effort to increase the production of consumer goods. In 1970, 32 per cent of households owned a refrigerator and this increased to 86 per cent by 1980. In 1970, 51 per cent of households owned a television and this figure went up to 86 per cent by 1980. The cost of food staples such as bread, potatoes and meat continued to be heavily subsidized by the state and apartment rents and the cost of gas for heating and cooking were kept down. In fact, it is estimated that these costs were barely higher than during the First Five Year Plan (1928–32).

SOURCE G

ECONOMIC PERFORMANCE 1955–87						
Average annual growth (%)						
	1955–65	1966–70	1971–75	1976–80	1981–83	1984–87
Population growth	1.6	0.9	0.9	0.8	0.9	0.9
GNP	5.4	5.2 (5.0)	3.7 (3.1)	2.7 (2.2)	2.3	1.6
Industry	7.5	6.3	5.9 (5.4)	3.4 (2.6)	1.5	2.1
Agriculture	3.5	3.5 (3.7)	−2.3 (−0.6)	0.3 (0.8)	4.2	0.8
Services	4.0	4.2	3.4	2.8	2.1	–
Consumption	4.7	5.3	3.6	2.6	1.7	2.4
Investment	9.1	6.0	5.4	4.3	4.2	3.0

Sources: 1955–80: US Congress, Joint Economic Committee, *USSR: Measures of Economic Growth and Development, 1950–80* (1982); *1981–87: Handbook of Economic Statistics* (1983 and 1988); figures in brackets: recalculations from 1988 publication; Population: *Narodnoe Khozyaistvo SSR*, various years, from Martin McCauley, *The Soviet Union 1917–1991* (1996)

STUDENT STUDY SECTION

QUESTIONS

a) **How reliable are the statistics used in Source G?**

b) **How successful was Leonid Brezhnev in dealing with the economic problems of the Soviet Union after 1976? Using both the sources and the material you have read so far, write a short essay that answers this question.**

 GNP
In the table, 'GNP' stands for Gross National Product, representing the total output of goods and services in the Soviet Union in a year. This measure shows a marked decline from 1966 onwards, with subsequent recalculations reinforcing the trend. The decline was spread across all sectors of the economy, with agricultural production actually falling in the 1971–75 time period following two bad harvests in 1972 and 1975.

● **Examiner's hint**
Before you answer Question (a), be sure to read carefully what the source information says about where these numbers came from and why, in some cases, there are additional numbers included. With Question (b), first of all plan your essay. To do this you need to write an outline that includes all the arguments you will make and how you will support these. Jot down quotes from the sources you want to use and do not forget to state which sources these come from. An examiner will want to see which sources you have used. Then, note all the details you will need to explain your point of view. Do not forget that in the mini-essay you always need both sources and your own information.

Brezhnev and political stagnation – the 1977 constitution

Brezhnev introduced a new constitution in 1977, the year of the 60th anniversary of the Bolshevik Revolution. Since the time of Stalin, the Soviet Union had been 'on the road to socialism', but it was now claimed that the **proletarian** revolution had succeeded. So the Soviet Union could now be referred to as 'the socialist state of the whole nation', while 'The Soviet of the Working People's Deputies' was renamed 'The Soviet of People's Deputies'.

The role of the Communist Party was clearly outlined in Article 6 of the constitution and the overall supremacy of the Party was recognized in a more concrete way than ever before. The constitution also re-enforced the ban on any political opposition. The elections of delegates to the Supreme Soviet would now be held every five instead of every four years. This increase was intended to bring elections in line with the start and finish of Five Year Plans. The preamble of the 1977 constitution stated that the Soviet Union had achieved 'developed socialism'. Article 13 (see below) also mentioned the right to personal property and that such a right would be protected by the state. Of course, individual rights such as freedom of speech could be enjoyed only when they did not interfere with the wellbeing of the state.

Developed Socialism

Developed Socialism was a term first used in 1966 because it was thought that a system that had already achieved great things, such as the 1917 Revolution, victory in World War II and a series of Five Year Plans, had reached a significant point on the journey towards communism. It was given an official definition in the 1977 constitution.

SOURCE H

Article 6 of the Soviet Constitution of 1977
(1) The leading and guiding force of the Soviet society and the nucleus of its political system, of all state organizations and public organizations, is the Communist Party of the Soviet Union. The Communist Party of the Soviet Union exists for the people and serves the people.
(2) The Communist Party, armed with Marxism-Leninism, determines the general perspectives of the development of society and the course of the home and foreign policy of the USSR, directs the great constructive work of the Soviet people, and imparts a planned, systematic and theoretically substantiated character to their struggle for the victory of communism.

Article 13 of the Soviet Constitution of 1977
(1) Earned income forms the basis of the personal property of Soviet citizens. The personal property of citizens of the USSR may include articles of everyday use, personal consumption and convenience, the implements and other objects of a small-holding, a house, and earned savings. The personal property of citizens and the right to inherit it are protected by the state.
(2) Citizens may be granted the use of plots of land, in the manner prescribed by law, for a subsidiary small-holding (including the keeping of livestock and poultry), for fruit and vegetable growing or for building an individual dwelling…
(3) Property owned or used by citizens shall not serve as a means of deriving unearned income or be employed to the detriment of the interests of society.

From the Soviet constitution, 1977

Proletarian
This is a term that was used by Karl Marx to describe the working class or the class that worked for a wage and did not own the means of production. The term would have been used to describe workers in factories, for instance.

STUDENT STUDY SECTION

QUESTION

With reference to its origin and purpose, discuss the value and limitations of Source H for historians studying the political changes during the Brezhnev Era.

Section II:
Brezhnev's foreign policy after 1976

The Cold War entered a period of détente at the end of the 1960s. This era of 'understanding' was symbolized by such events as the signing of Strategic Arms Limitation Treaty (SALT) I in 1972 and the border, trade and human rights agreements of the Helsinki Final Act of 1975. By 1976, however, the mood was changing. The USA felt that détente benefited mostly the USSR, especially as there was an expansion of Soviet influence into Africa at this time.

Arms control and SALT II

It was always intended that **SALT I** would be the beginning of a series of treaties about strategic weapons.

The SALT I Treaty dealt mostly with obsolete weapon systems and, for instance, ignored the new **MIRV** technology, so agreement was reached fairly easily. It was harder to discuss the more advanced, highly valued weapon systems and to agree on how to limit these. There was also disagreement over what 'strategic' meant. The USSR said that all weapons that could reach the USSR were 'strategic' and so this included weapons that could be deployed from France or Britain.

By 1977, the USSR had SS-20s (MIRV) rockets based in Eastern Europe, and the USA responded in 1979 by putting Cruise and Pershing missiles in Western Europe. Relations between the Soviet Union and the USA were becoming less friendly by the end of the 1970s. The arms agreements had gone as far as either side was prepared to go and, in the USA, there was a feeling that all the gains had been made by the Soviet Union. On reflection, it did seem that, regardless of détente, the Soviet Union under Brezhnev had adopted a more expansionist foreign policy. There was a Soviet presence in the Horn of Africa and the invasion of Afghanistan in 1979 worsened relations. The mood was not very promising for negotiations and although SALT II was signed in 1979, it was not ratified (approved) by the US Senate.

The USSR, Africa and Asia

The USSR tried to expand its influence in the Third World during the 1970s. There was an upsurge of post-colonial movements that were communist in ideology, and many of these were either a cause or a consequence of civil wars that broke out in both Asia and Africa.

The Vietnam War ended in 1975 with the takeover of the whole country by the North Vietnamese Army (NVA). Vietnam was now united under a communist government. There was a communist government in Laos and also in Cambodia, where the Khmer Rouge under the leadership of Pol Pot took control and changed its name to the People's Republic of Kampuchea. The USSR continued to support Vietnam even when it invaded Kampuchea in 1978. China, angered by this invasion, demonstrated its opposition by invading Vietnam in 1979 to 'teach Vietnam a lesson'. This also indicated that adopting communism did not always unite countries, but could be a source of division. The Sino-Soviet split was not as

● **Examiner's hint**
Consider what value this source has if you want to know more about the Soviet Union during the 1970s. What do you think would be the limitations? When you are asked to evaluate an official document like this one, it is sometimes difficult to think of what you can say about its value and its limitations. In this case, the constitution is a public document and so it has been written to be published and to be read by everyone. Ask yourself what kind of image of the Soviet Union Leonid Brezhnev wanted to convey in 1977, not only to the people of the Soviet Union, but also to the world. Also, ask yourself whether or not the articles you have read were a realistic account of the rights of the people of the Soviet Union.

 ToK Time
Think about the way 'truth' was perceived in the Soviet Union. It is likely that a lot of Soviet citizens knew that what they were told by the government about the economy, foreign policy and their history was not true. Do you think this actually mattered to individuals? Was it important to a bus driver living in Leningrad in 1980 that he had access only to newspapers, journals, TV and radio broadcasts that were censored by the state?

 SALT I
SALT I was the Strategic Arms Limitation Treaty signed in 1972 by the USSR and the USA. Strategic weapons are defined as nuclear warheads and the missiles that could deliver these weapons.

MIRV
A MIRV is a Multiple Independently Targeted Re-Entry Vehicle (a rocket that can carry several warheads that can be programmed to attack different locations).

deep as it had been during the late 1960s, but it was still not to be taken for granted that the support of one communist superpower would guarantee the support of the other.

In Africa, the collapse of the Portuguese Empire in 1974 led to communist liberation movements coming to power, as with the governments of Guinea Bissau and of Mozambique. The handover of power was not as straightforward in Angola, where the USSR and Cuba supported the MPLA (Popular Movement for the Liberation of Angola) and the USA supported UNITA (National Union for the Total Independence of Angola) as well as the FNLA (National Front for the Liberation of Angola). This was the first time that a revolutionary movement so far away from the USSR received its active support. The USA complained, but the USSR maintained its right to support 'national liberation struggles'.

SOURCE A

Our Party supports and will continue to support peoples fighting for their freedom. Some bourgeois leaders affect surprise and raise a howl over the solidarity of the Soviet people with the struggle of other peoples for freedom and progress. This is either outright naivety or more likely a deliberate befuddling of minds. It could not be clearer after all, that détente and peaceful coexistence have to do with interstate relations. This means, above all that disputes and conflicts between countries are not to be settled by war… Détente does not in the least abolish the laws of the class struggle. We make no secret of the fact that we see détente as the way to create more favourable conditions for peaceful socialist and communist construction.

From a speech by Leonid Brezhnev at the Party Congress, February 1976

STUDENT STUDY SECTION

QUESTION
What does Source A tell you about the way that Brezhnev interpreted détente?

The USA interpreted the expansion of Soviet interests as taking advantage of détente to spread communism in areas that were not traditionally in the Soviet sphere of influence. By 1977, Colonel Mengistu, a communist guerrilla fighter, established control over Ethiopia and purchased arms from the USSR. The Soviet Union had already established good relations with both Somalia and Ethiopia, but when regional rivalry between these two countries would lead to conflict, the Soviet government chose to stand by Ethiopia. In June 1977, Somalia attacked Ethiopia and made inroads into the **Ogadon** region. It was anticipated that the USA would almost automatically offer support to an enemy of its enemy (i.e. Somalia), but the US President, Jimmy Carter, refused to arm Somalia until it withdrew to its own territory. Meanwhile, the USSR and Cuba reinforced Ethiopia with both arms and 10,000 Cuban troops. The Somalis were forced out of Ethiopia and Mengistu was given assistance to help recover Eritrea.

The response of the USA had not been very strong. It was concerned about the increase of Soviet influence in the strategically important Horn of Africa, but was not prepared to get involved in any show of force. It is possible that this apparent reluctance by the USA to commit to intervention in Somalia influenced the Soviet Union's decision to go ahead with the invasion of Afghanistan in 1979. It was assumed that if the USA did not openly challenge Soviet intervention in Africa, then it was unlikely to do so in Afghanistan.

Carter and Brezhnev

There was division within the White House and Jimmy Carter's National Security Advisor, Zbigniew Brzezinski, wanted a stronger show of US force to challenge the expansion of Soviet influence in Africa. He said 'détente is buried in the sands of Ogadon'.

Ogadon
Ogadon was a region claimed by both Ethiopia and Somalia and led to the escalation of conflict in the Horn of Africa.

Non-Aligned Movement
This movement grew out of a meeting in Bandung, Indonesia, in 1955. Led by India, Yugoslavia and Egypt, an agreement was reached to avoid being pulled too far into the sphere of influence of either the Soviet Union or the USA. In practice, the countries that joined the Non-Aligned Movement were more likely to lean towards the USSR.

Brzezinski implied that Brezhnev did not have the same respect for Carter as for President Nixon. Indeed, Brezhnev considered Carter's reluctance to arm Somalia to show weakness. President Carter's concern over the lack of human rights in the Soviet Union, whereas he did not seem to worry so much about the lack of human rights in South Korea or China, was also a source of annoyance. The Soviets were also put out by Carter's proposal in 1977 to restart the SALT II talks with offers of a much greater cutback in weapons than had already been decided in 1974.

Détente was dying and, as we will see, the invasion of Afghanistan was the final blow.

Brezhnev was not a well man at this time. He was suffering from a heart ailment and was not in full control of the government of the USSR. Meanwhile, Jimmy Carter lost the presidential election in 1980 and was succeeded by his Republican opponent, Ronald Reagan.

> **Brezhnev Doctrine (also known as 'The doctrine of limited sovereignty')**
> In 1968 after the Warsaw Pact invasion of Czechoslovakia, Brezhnev stated that Soviet support for any communist government was justified if socialism was under attack. This policy was viewed with suspicion by China, for instance, who saw the doctrine as an excuse for Soviet interventionism.

The Soviet invasion of Afghanistan 1979–89

Known as 'the Soviet Union's Vietnam', this description summed up many aspects of the Afghanistan conflict, which lasted for 10 years and contributed significantly to the collapse of the Soviet Union. It was ended by Mikhail Gorbachev, but it was started under the leadership of Leonid Brezhnev. Why did the USSR decide to send Soviet troops to Afghanistan?

Background to the war in Afghanistan

Afghanistan was linked to the **Non-Aligned Movement** until a coup carried out by the communist People's Democratic Party of Afghanistan (PDPA) in April 1978 killed President Mohammed Daoud. The USSR shared a border with Afghanistan and had previously given some limited assistance in the form of road-building and aid, but after the coup it became far more involved.

The PDPA itself was divided into two main factions: the moderate Parcham (Banner) led by Babrak Karmal and the dominant but more hard-line Khalq (People's Party) led by Hafizullah Amin and Nur Mohammed Taraki.

Soviet advisors were sent in to Afghanistan to help establish the new communist government, but almost immediately there were problems. There was internal division in the PDPA, but there was also popular resistance to 'un-Islamic' reforms such as collectivization of land and the education of women.

Nur Mohammed Taraki

Hafizullah Amin

Uprising in Herat

In March 1979, there was a major uprising in Herat and many Soviet advisors were killed, along with their families. The Soviet response was to send more advisors and to insist that Afghan government troops restore order. It is estimated that several thousand Afghan civilians were killed in the reprisals. By now, it was feared that there was a state of civil war in Afghanistan and President Taraki, quoting the **Brezhnev Doctrine**, asked for Soviet intervention. Prime Minister Kosygin refused to send troops because he thought that it would make the Soviet Union seem aggressive, and Brezhnev agreed with this decision.

The murder of President Taraki

The PDPA was torn apart by the rivalry between President Taraki and Defence Minister Amin, and a plot was hatched by Taraki to assassinate his rival. There is speculation that the USSR was involved in this, but the plan backfired and on 9 October it was not Amin but Taraki who was arrested and later killed in prison.

Babrak Karmal

In Moscow in September, Taraki told Brezhnev of the danger to his regime being posed by Amin, and asked for Soviet troops to be sent to Afghanistan: 'Without them we cannot defend the Afghan revolution.' In Andropov's presence, Brezhnev told Taraki that they 'would take responsibility for Amin' but urged Taraki to try to 'normalize' relations in the leadership for the sake of the revolution. While the KGB was trying to deal with Amin, Taraki decided to take matters into his own hands. Brezhnev soon received a report on what was happening in Kabul. Taraki had invited Amin, as his second in command, to his residence for a chat. Amin's supporters warned him that it was a trap but the Soviet ambassador, who was at Taraki's house, reassured Amin that he was under no threat.

From Dmitri Volkogonov, *The Rise and Fall of the Soviet Empire*, **1999**

SOURCE C

Soviet leaders recognized deep problems with the Afghan leadership itself, and rumors arose that Moscow was angling to replace the Khalqi Taraki-Amin regime with one headed by Babrak Karmal, head of the Parcham faction. Mutinies and rebel attacks continued, and Moscow began to increase its security presence in the country, though still short of sending military forces. In September–October 1979, tensions between Taraki and Amin and their supporters exploded into open warfare, ending with Amin in control and Taraki dead, a result clearly contrary to the Kremlin's wishes.

From *Cold War International History Project Bulletin*, Issue 4, Fall 1994

STUDENT STUDY SECTION

QUESTION
To what extent are the views about the involvement of the Soviet leadership in the removal of Amin expressed in Source B supported by Source C?

Soviet troops are sent in to Afghanistan

After the murder of Taraki, Amin became both General Secretary of the Party and Prime Minister. Brezhnev condemned what he called the 'treachery' of Amin and although Amin asked repeatedly to visit Moscow 'to explain everything', he was not invited. Popular unrest in Afghanistan increased, as Amin's policies were even more hardline than those of his predecessor. The Soviet leaders later claimed that Amin asked many times for Soviet troops to be sent to help him but, possibly frustrated by Moscow's refusal, he seemed to be moving closer to Pakistan, China and even the USA. The USSR feared the possibility of a Chinese or US-influenced Afghanistan, and after much debate in the Politburo, it was decided to send troops to restore order. Were they also sent in to kill Amin?

By 27 December 1979, there were 10,000 Soviet paratroopers in Kabul and Amin was killed following an attack on the presidential palace. Amin's replacement was Babrak Karmal from the Parcham wing of the PDPA, who returned from exile in the USSR. Within a month, another 40,000 Soviet troops were sent in.

The official Soviet account of these events stressed that Karmal was already in Kabul before the murder of Amin took place and that this 'coup' had been the work of the PDPA, with no Soviet involvement. Other sources, however, such as Vladimir Boukovsky, a Russian historian, claimed that documents in the Soviet archives indicate that 'Amin and his personal guard (100 to 150 men) were to be killed and no survivors left alive'.

Possible reasons for Soviet intervention

- Fear of losing control of Afghanistan.
- Fear of Iranian or Pakistani cross-border raids.

- Fear that a civil war in Afghanistan would result in an Islamic republic similar to that installed in Iran by the **Iranian Revolution**. Potentially, this would threaten the stability of Soviet republics with majority Muslim populations. Just as the USA feared the spread of communism and wanted to 'contain' it, so the USSR wanted to contain the spread of Islamic fundamentalism.
- Belief that the USSR had to support a regime that was openly communist.
- Confidence that the USA would not intervene.

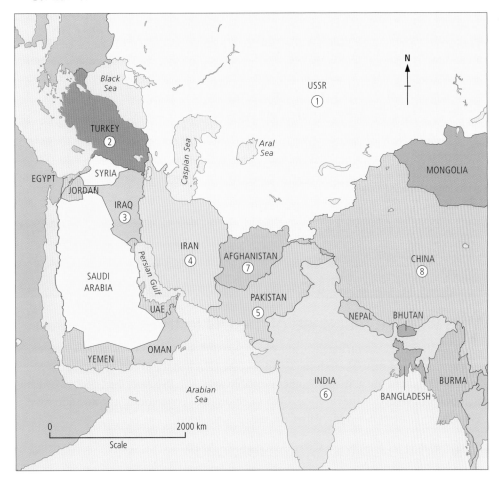

 Map 14

The USSR and its neighbours – 1979

① **USSR**: communist state
② **Turkey**: member of NATO
③ **Iraq**: One-party state led by Saddam Hussein at war with Iran 1980–88
④ **Iran**: Islamic state – revolution in 1979
⑤ **Pakistan**: Military coup in 1977. Opposed to Soviet invasion of Afghanistan
⑥ **India**: Democratic state – generally perceived to be pro-USSR
⑦ **Afghanistan**: communist state after April 1978
⑧ **China**: communist state but not closely allied to the Soviet Union

SOURCE D

Imperialism launched the present undeclared war against the Afghan revolution. That created a direct threat and a danger to our southern border. The situation compelled us to provide the armed assistance this friendly country was asking for… As for the Soviet contingent, we are ready to withdraw it in agreement with the Afghan government. For that to happen, the sending of counter-revolutionary bands into Afghanistan must cease altogether… Reliable guarantees are required that there will be no new intervention.

Brezhnev announcement at the 26th Party Congress in February 1981, from Dmitri Volkogonov, *The Rise and Fall of the Soviet Empire*, 1999

The Iranian Revolution

In 1979, the Shah of Iran was overthrown and driven into exile. He was replaced by the Ayatollah Khomeini, who proceeded to turn Iran into a theocracy by introducing Islamic law and carrying out a revolution that affected every aspect of political and social life. In the USSR, there was a fear that this kind of Islamic revolution would spread to neighbouring countries with large Muslim populations. Many of the Soviet Union's southern republics were predominantly Muslim.

STUDENT STUDY SECTION

QUESTIONS

a) **What did Brezhnev mean here by 'Imperialism launched the present undeclared war…'?**

b) **When would he be prepared to order the withdrawal of Soviet troops?**

It was still unclear what the Soviet Union hoped to achieve and the Carter administration in the USA wondered whether this was an occupation of Afghanistan or a Soviet expansion towards the Persian Gulf.

SOURCE E

Brezhnev: Not a day goes by when Washington has not tried to revive the spirit of the 'Cold War' to heat up militarist passions. Any grounds are used for this, real or imagined. One example of this is Afghanistan. The ruling circles of the USA and of China as well, stop at nothing, including armed aggression, in trying to keep the Afghanis from building a new life in accord with the ideals of the revolution of liberation of April 1978. And when we helped our neighbour Afghanistan, at the request of its government, to give a rebuff to aggression, to beat back the attacks of bandit formations which operate primarily from the territory of Pakistan, then Washington and Beijing raised an unprecedented racket. Of what did they accuse the Soviet Union[?]: of a yearning to break out to warm waters, and an intention to make a grab for foreign oil… In the Soviet act of assistance to Afghanistan there is not a grain of avarice. We had no choice other than the sending of troops. And the events confirmed that it was the only correct choice.

From minutes of the meeting of the plenum of the Central Committee of the Communist Party of the Soviet Union, 23 June 1980

● **Examiner's hint**
Is this a public or a private document, or somewhere in between? What kind of audience was it prepared for, do you think? How important was it that the information given was 'true'?

STUDENT STUDY SECTION

QUESTION
Assess the origin, purpose, value and limitations of Source E for an historian researching the origins of the Soviet-Afghan War.

What was the response of the UN to the invasion?

As was so often the case during the Cold War, it was difficult to pass resolutions in the Security Council of the UN. Both the USSR and the USA had the power of veto and if one superpower did not use it, then the other probably would. In this case, the USSR vetoed any resolution that criticized the invasion. Even so, resolutions condemning the invasion were passed in the General Assembly, where the veto did not apply.

How did the United States respond?

President Carter described the Soviet invasion as 'the greatest threat to world peace since the Second World War' and demanded a withdrawal. This was ignored by the leaders of the USSR, who thought it unlikely that the USA would intervene in Afghanistan. Also, détente was no longer so important and so the USSR was less concerned about the disapproval of the USA.

SOURCE F

… [this action of the Soviets] has made a more dramatic change in my own opinion of what the Soviets' ultimate goals are than anything they've done in the previous time I've been in office… We cannot be certain … if they seek colonial domination only in Afghanistan, or … other conquests as well. No President … can afford to gamble … upon wishful thinking about the present or the future intentions of the Soviet Union… There is no doubt that the Soviets' move into Afghanistan, if done without adverse consequences, would have resulted in the temptation to move again and again [towards the control of warm water ports and oil supplies].

President Carter outlining the US response, from J. P. D. Dunbabin, *The Cold War*, 1994

STUDENT STUDY SECTION

QUESTION

With reference to its origin and purpose, discuss the value and limitations of Source F for historians studying the Soviet-Afghan war.

President Carter now referred to an 'arc of crisis' that extended from Iran to Afghanistan. He was worried that the USSR was trying to gain control of the Persian Gulf. In January 1980, President Carter issued the **Carter Doctrine**. The USA applied sanctions and boycotted the 1980 Olympics that were held in Moscow. They also, rather more aggressively, began to look for ways to arm the guerrilla rebels in Afghanistan.

SOURCE G

A cartoon published during the Moscow Olympics, 1980

● Examiner's hint

When you study a source like this, consider why the President is making this speech and what he intends to achieve. It is a public address made to the American people but does he also have another audience in mind?

Carter Doctrine

President Carter stated that any attempt by an 'outside force' to impose its control over the Persian Gulf region would be interpreted as a challenge to the 'vital interests' of the United States and would be 'repelled by any means necessary, including military force.'

STUDENT STUDY SECTION

QUESTION

What is the message conveyed in this cartoon published at the time of the Moscow Olympics in 1980?

In fact, Soviet troops had been instructed not to cross any border under any circumstances and so American fears of a 'Soviet Persian Gulf' were unfounded. The Soviet leadership mistakenly assumed that all they needed to do in Afghanistan was to send in troops and heal the division between the Khalq and the Parcham factions and all would be well. By the end of 1980, the number of Soviet soldiers had grown to 100,000 and although Ustinov, the Soviet Minister of Defence, said the troops would stay no longer than 'a year and a half', it was very difficult to support and stabilize the unpopular Karmal regime. Yuri Andropov succeeded Brezhnev in 1982, but Afghanistan continued to be a drain on the USSR with no end in sight.

The Soviet Union's Vietnam

Like the USA's involvement in Vietnam, the Soviet Union was drawn into a war after the assassination of an unpopular leader, intending to restore order and prop up a '**client state**'. Also like the USA in Vietnam, the USSR found it easier to enter a conflict than to leave. Fighting against a well-armed guerrilla force supported by their ideological enemy was a very difficult task and by the time Soviet troops pulled out in 1989 more than 13,000 soldiers had been killed and almost 50,000 wounded.

Reagan's Presidency and its impact on the Soviet-Afghan War

President Ronald Reagan was determined to take a harder line towards the Soviet Union. He did not respond to attempts by Yuri Andropov to restart arms reduction talks and he referred to the USSR as 'the evil empire'. He also wanted to use every means possible to support the enemies of the Soviet Union, and so continued the policy of supplying arms to the *mujahedeen* (soldiers of God) who were fighting a guerrilla war inside Afghanistan against the Soviet troops. Many of the *mujahedeen* were recruited in Afghan refugee camps inside Pakistan, where the CIA was also able to make contact with them. Care was taken to supply them only with Chinese-made arms that could not be traced back to the United States.

In 1985, the US stepped up its support of the *mujahedeen* and gave them Stinger shoulder-mounted surface-to-air missiles that made a huge difference to their capability to shoot down Soviet helicopters.

Client state

This would refer to a state that, during the Cold War, was under the influence of and dependent on economic or military support from one or other of the superpowers.

SOURCE H

● **Examiner's hint**
Look carefully at the photograph. What is the man holding? Where, do you think, did this weapon come from? Does it change your perception of guerrilla warfare? Also, notice the background. This is a tough environment in which to fight. How would the winter snow influence the nature of the war. Would it help the guerrillas or the Soviet Army?

STUDENT STUDY SECTION

QUESTION
What does this photograph tell you about the nature of guerrilla war in Afghanistan?

The Soviet strategy in Afghanistan

The Soviet strategy was to bomb areas of known resistance, such as the Pansher Valley and also routes into Afghanistan from Pakistan and Iran that were used by guerrilla forces. More than a third of the Afghan population fled: an estimated three million became refugees in Pakistan and two million in Iran. The Soviet Union sent in its Special Forces, the *spetznaz*, who fought an aggressive ground campaign and were flown by helicopter to remote villages, where guerrillas were thought to be hiding, to clear these areas of inhabitants. The mines they placed on paths and roads killed or maimed not only guerrillas, but also many refugees and civilians.

Mohammed Najibullah replaced Karmal as leader of the PDPA in 1985 and as President in 1986. There was pressure from the Soviet Union to stabilize the situation in Afghanistan, and it was felt that Karmal was not providing strong leadership. Najibullah was elected President and proceeded to try to negotiate some kind of shared power, but he was unable to reach agreement with the *mujahedeen*.

Gorbachev and Afghanistan: the beginning of the end

When Mikhail Gorbachev came to power in 1985, he referred to the Afghan war as a 'bleeding wound' and stated that unless it had been won within 12 months the Soviet Union would begin a withdrawal. A total of 8,000 troops were withdrawn in 1986, but Gorbachev knew that he needed the support of the USA to end the war. There could not be an end to the war while the USA continued to supply the *mujahedeen* with weapons.

The Geneva Accords

Discussions began in Geneva by 1988 involving the USSR, the USA, Pakistan and Afghanistan. Gorbachev explained to the USA that the war would come to an end, but that some kind of assurances were needed to make sure that the post-war government was not overthrown and replaced by an Islamic republic. By April 1988, it was agreed that:
- Afghanistan and Pakistan would not interfere in each other's affairs and would not train or allow armed men to move from one country to the other.
- This provision would come into effect 30 days after the signing of the accord and Soviet troops would then begin their withdrawal.
- All the troops would have left by April 1989. All aid to the *mujahedeen* would cease once the withdrawal had begun.
- These 'instruments' were guaranteed by both the USA and USSR.

The Soviets now focused on consolidating the regime of President Najibullah, so that it would survive after they left. This policy of 'National Reconciliation' brought the regional commanders (tribal chiefs in many cases) into an agreement not to fight the government.

SOURCE I

On 24 January, 1989, the Foreign Minister, Eduard Shevardnadze reported on his visit to Kabul and declared: 'In withdrawing from Afghanistan, we must recognize that we are leaving that country in a lamentable state, in the literal sense of the word: its cities and villages have been destroyed, the capital is starving, the economy is virtually paralysed. Hundreds of thousands of people have perished…' Gorbachev replied, 'It is important that this regime and its cadres are not swept away altogether. We must not appear before the world in our underpants or even without any. A defeatist position is not permissible.'

From Dmitri Volkogonov, *The Rise and Fall of the Soviet Empire*, 1999

STUDENT STUDY SECTION

What does Source I tell you about the differences in opinion between Gorbachev and Shevardnadze regarding Soviet withdrawal from Afghanistan?

Student Answer A – *Annabel*

Source I says that Shevardnadze said that Afghanistan was in a 'lamentable state', 'its cities and villages destroyed', 'the capital is starving', 'the economy is virtually destroyed'. Gorbachev says what the USSR must not be is 'defeatist'.

Student Answer B – *Lisa*

In Source I we can see that Shevardnadze and Gorbachev have different points of view. Shevardnadze who has just come back from Kabul says that the country is in a very bad state. He calls it 'lamentable'. Also, he says the economy almost doesn't exist anymore and that people are not getting food. Gorbachev does not disagree with this, but he does say that the USSR must not show the world that this is the condition of Afghanistan. He talks about the USSR not appearing 'before the world in its underpants or even without any', meaning that it cannot show that the condition of the country is very poor.

Examiner's comments

Annabel has some idea of what is needed here. She has selected relevant quotations from Source I to show what Shevardnadze said, but it is not enough just to quote from a source. You need to show that you understand what is being said so it is best to put it in your own words. Also, Annabel mentions that Gorbachev does make a response, but simply including a quotation does not answer the question.

Lisa has written a much better answer. She explains in her own words what Shevardnadze has said. She shows that she understands the content of the source by doing this. Also, she explains Gorbachev's reaction quite clearly. She does quote the source, but then shows she understands what is being said by explaining the metaphor about the USSR and its underpants.

The end of the conflict

The *mujahedeen* continued to fight. They included not only Afghanis, but also recruits from Africa, Asia, Europe and the Middle East. By February 1989, although all Soviet troops had been withdrawn, the USSR continued to supply the government of President Najibullah and the USA continued to supply the *mujahedeen*. The civil war continued and did not end until the collapse of the Soviet Union in 1991. All Soviet aid to the Najibullah government came to an end and so the USA stopped supplying the *mujahedeen*.

President Najibullah was overthrown in 1992 and the Islamic State of Afghanistan was set up. This was led by a group of fighters from the north of Afghanistan, the Jamiat-i-Islami (Islamic Society), which was hostile to Pakistan. This regime was quickly challenged by fighters from southern Afghanistan, supported by Pakistan and known as the Taliban.

ToK Time
'Those who don't study the past are condemned to repeat it.' (George Santayana)

How could you use what you have just read about the Soviet-Afghan War to support this judgement?

STUDENT STUDY SECTION

QUESTION
Using the sources and the information in the text, write a short essay on the following topic: 'To what extent would you agree with the judgement that the Soviet-Afghan War was 'the USSR's Vietnam'?

Dark humour

The role of terror in making Soviet citizens compliant was lessened after the death of Stalin, although random arrests, torture and incarceration in psychiatric clinics were still commonplace. Oddly enough, the Brezhnev era became renowned for the jokes that were told about him. Brezhnev was known to be fond of receiving medals, for instance, and it was said that by the time of his death he had been awarded 110. This was one of many jokes told:

> *The Brezhnev family are having dinner and, suddenly, the whole building shakes like an earthquake. 'Oh my God, what's that?' asks his daughter Galina.*
>
> *'Don't worry,' says her mother, 'that's just your father's jacket falling on the floor.'*

Other jokes made fun of Brezhnev's physical state, and the elderly leaders that ran the Soviet Union at this time:

> *The government of the Union of Soviet Socialist Republics has announced with great regret that, following a long illness and without regaining consciousness, the General Secretary of the Central Committee of the Communist Party and the President of the highest Soviet, Comrade Leonid Brezhnev, has resumed his governmental duties.*
>
> *What has forty teeth and four legs? A crocodile.*
>
> *What has four teeth and forty legs? The Central Committee of the Communist Party.*

After being ill for many years, Brezhnev died in 1982 and this joke made the rounds. 'What were Brezhnev's last words? Leave the plug alone, Yuri.' ('Yuri' was a reference to Yuri Andropov, Brezhnev's successor.) (Jokes from Ben Lewis, *Hammer and Tickle*, 2008.)

It seems that Brezhnev knew that the jokes were made about him. He did not seem to mind and considered them to be a mark of affection. 'They do it because they love me.'

 ToK Time
Think about how important humour can be in helping people deal with living in a single party state. Why, do you think, were there so many jokes told about Brezhnev?

REVIEW SECTION

You have been reading about the Brezhnev Era. Write brief answers to the following questions, supporting your arguments with information both from the text and the sources.

Review questions

1. What do you consider to have been the main problems with the Soviet economy by the end of the 1970s?
2. How, and with what success, were these problems addressed?
3. To what extent was poor leadership an obstacle to successful reform during the Brezhnev Era?
4. How did the relationship between the USSR and the USA change after 1976?

Section III:

Gorbachev and his aims/policies (*glasnost* and *perestroika*) and consequences for the Soviet state

This section deals with the policies of Mikhail Gorbachev, the last leader of the Soviet Union. The state established by Lenin imploded in 1991 when the Soviet Union broke up into independent republics. The Communist Party of the Soviet Union lost power and seemed oddly old-fashioned. It was as if the political movement that had appeared so dynamic and revolutionary in 1917 had entered a deeply conservative and authoritarian old age.

Gorbachev – aims

If Vladimir Illich Lenin was the father of the Soviet Union, Mikhail Sergeevich Gorbachev was its gravedigger.

From Martin McCauley, *The Soviet Union 1917–1991*, 1996

Leonid Brezhnev died on 10 November 1982. He was succeeded by Yuri Andropov (head of the KGB), who was confirmed as General Secretary in December 1982. Andropov was only in office for 15 months and, for most of this time, he suffered from ill health.

Unlike Brezhnev, Andropov wanted to reform the USSR. He felt that much of the idealism of Bolshevism had been lost and that change was needed in order to save the revolution. The first step was to change the *nomenklatura*, as Andropov wanted to bring into the government people who were willing to carry out changes. With this in mind he replaced one fifth of all city and local party secretaries, one fifth of Soviet ministers and one third of all department heads in the Central Committee Secretariat.

In order to tackle the slowdown in economic growth, Andropov tried to improve production by making sure workers turned up and, just as important, stayed at the workplace to do a full day's work. He also tried to improve the quality of goods produced by encouraging workers to take pride in their work. Another aim was to reduce the level of alcoholism, as this was a huge problem in the USSR. Andropov did not have much opportunity to make far-reaching changes, however, as he died in February 1984.

Although Andropov had hoped the young Mikhail Gorbachev would succeed him, it was Konstantin Chernenko who became General Secretary, although he was already very sick. So many members of the Politburo were old that it was jokingly said that when Chernenko brought 94-year-old Vyacheslav Molotov back into the Party (he had been expelled in 1957 by Nikita Khrushchev), it was because he intended to make him his successor! The Soviet Union was ruled by a 'gerontocracy' intent only on dying in their beds. That, in itself, was quite an achievement for a generation that had survived Stalin.

Chernenko died in 1985 and Gorbachev was appointed General Secretary. For the first time in many years, the USSR had a leader who was relatively young and in good health. A protégé of Andropov, Gorbachev knew only too well the true state of the Soviet Union's economy and how difficult it would be to push through reforms. On the eve of his appointment, he told his wife, Raisa Gorbachev, 'Things cannot go on as they are.' It was just over 60 years since Lenin's death but, for Gorbachev, the intervening years had been a betrayal of the revolution. The time had come to set things straight and to restore the legacy of Lenin.

SOURCE A

Gorbachev found inspiration in what he saw as Lenin's willingness to learn and develop and, concretely, in his New Economic Policy launched in 1921. He seemed inclined to believe that Lenin had turned from being a revolutionary to a reformer in his last years. Gorbachev had always had an idealised view of Lenin who in reality was scarcely less ruthless than Stalin, although unlike Stalin, he did not employ the weapon of terror against members of his own party. It was, therefore, psychologically important for him, especially in the earliest years of his General Secretaryship, to persuade himself that what he was doing was in line with Lenin's thought before it had been distorted by Stalin.

From Archie Brown, **The Gorbachev Factor**, 1997

SOURCE B

One idea that he expressed reflects an essential aspect of Gorbachev's political personality. He declared, 'We must not change our policy. It is a true, correct and genuinely Leninist policy. We have to raise the tempo, move forward, expose shortcomings and overcome them, and see our bright future clearly.' Thus at the outset of the new leadership the goal was still to attain the 'bright future' and with the help of true Leninist policy. In 1991 Gorbachev still believed in Lenin. Indeed, it was probably his attempt to combine his liberal reforms with Leninism that led to their failure. He was a Leninist because his whole life had made him one. Since his youth he had been held in the Party's close embrace and it was the Party that formed him into the person who would one day become its General Secretary, the last ruling Leninist.

From Dmitri Volkogonov, *The Rise and Fall of the Soviet Empire*, 1999

ToK Time

What does Volkogonov mean in Source B when he says that 'Gorbachev still believed in Lenin'? How does belief in Lenin (or communism) compare with a religious belief?

STUDENT STUDY SECTION

QUESTION

Compare and contrast the views expressed in these two sources.

● **Examiner's hint**

What do Sources A and B tell you about why Gorbachev admired Lenin?

From the outset, Gorbachev tried to push through change. He understood that there was no alternative to reform and he introduced three policies that would always be associated with his leadership. These were ***perestroika***, ***glasnost*** and ***uskorenie***.

Wanting to bring in change and actually achieving change were two different things, however. It was not long before Gorbachev realized that if he wanted reform then he needed the support of reformers. By 1986, Gorbachev added five of his own supporters to the Politburo, but 60 per cent of the Central Committee was still made up of Brezhnev's appointees. So, there was some change but not enough to make a difference. Gorbachev knew that the Party was probably his biggest obstacle to reform.

Perestroika, glasnost and uskorenie

Perestroika meant 'reconstruction' or 'restructuring'. Gorbachev talked of the need for a reconstruction of not only the economy, but the entire Soviet system. *Glasnost* was 'openness'. This was a vague term, but had the possibility of meaning freedom of speech and the right to publish. *Uskorenie* meant 'acceleration' and Gorbachev used this term to indicate that he wanted a rapid increase in the quantity of goods produced.

Chernobyl

The first crisis Gorbachev had to deal with was the Chernobyl disaster. In April 1986, during a routine cleaning session, the core of one of the reactors at the nuclear power station in Chernobyl began to overheat. Inadequate safety procedures meant that the plant was not immediately closed down and a massive explosion released radioactive particles into the atmosphere. The authorities at the nuclear plant did not reveal the full extent of the disaster to the Kremlin and all information was kept secret. Radioactive clouds drifted over Western Europe and it was not until he was questioned by the alarmed governments of neighbouring countries that Gorbachev realized the full extent of the disaster.

Brave firemen had been sent in, without adequate protection, to tackle the blaze at the reactor and the evacuation of civilians was hampered by procedures that were slow and secretive. No one seemed accountable and no one seemed capable of acting on their own initiative. Chernobyl became symbolic of many of the problems that plagued the Soviet Union and Gorbachev later referred to it as a 'turning point'.

SOURCE C

According to the dissident Soviet Marxist historian Roy Medvedev, General Secretary Mikhail Gorbachev wanted to adopt a policy of giving 'correct information' about the nuclear power plant accident at Chernobyl; but, at a Politburo meeting on April 28, two days after it occurred, he was supported by only two other members, the Premier of the Russian Republic and the head of the KGB, while all the others wanted 'a limitation of news'. Only later, when the scope of the accident became clearer and the chorus of protests from Western countries increased in intensity, did Gorbachev 'succeed in imposing his line,' as manifested in the television address in which he gave the Soviet people and the outside world what were claimed to be the available facts about the accident. This version of what occurred was given by Medvedev in an exclusive interview granted to the Italian communist journalist Alberto Jacoviello, on the staff of the centre-left newspaper La Repubblica. *Medvedev gave no source for his assertions.*

From a broadcast on Radio Free Europe by Kevin Devlin, 5 June 1986

STUDENT STUDY SECTION

QUESTION

With reference to its origin and purpose, assess the value and limitations of Source C for historians studying the Gorbachev era.

SOURCE D

The Chernobyl disaster, more than anything else, opened the possibility of much greater freedom of expression, to the point that the system as we knew it could no longer continue. It made absolutely clear how important it was to continue the policy of glasnost, and I must say that I started to think about time in terms of pre-Chernobyl and post-Chernobyl. The price of the Chernobyl catastrophe was overwhelming, not only in human terms, but also economically. Even today, the legacy of Chernobyl affects the economies of Russia, Ukraine, and Belarus. Some even suggest that the economic price for the USSR was so high that it stopped the arms race, as I could not keep building arms while paying to clean up Chernobyl. This is wrong. My declaration of January 15, 1986, is well known around the world. I addressed arms reduction, including nuclear arms, and I proposed that by the year 2000 no country should have atomic weapons. I personally felt a moral responsibility to end the arms race. But Chernobyl opened my eyes like nothing else: it showed the horrible consequences of nuclear power, even when it is used for non-military purposes.

From an interview given by Gorbachev on the 20th anniversary of Chernobyl

---

Gorbachev had spoken of the need for more openness (*glasnost*) in Soviet society and for its citizens to be kept informed of important events. Chernobyl showed quite clearly that this was not happening. The radioactive fall-out from this nuclear disaster affected many people who were neither adequately warned nor adequately protected by the state.

SOURCE E

In essence, the process of perestroika was an attempt to transform a sluggish, dogmatic, bureaucratic command system in the direction of a sort of liberalism. But it was no part of its architect's scheme to knock away its Communist supports. Its results were therefore limited, although they served as an important prerequisite for the democratic changes to come. Gorbachev could not have done more than he did. Nor could anyone else. Perhaps his most important achievement was to widen the avenues of public access to information of all kinds, thus giving people a view of many aspects of political life that had hitherto been closed to them. This was called glasnost – openness, publicity or just telling the truth. The process was begun by Gorbachev, but continued to evolve without regard to his decisions. The system based on the class lie was destroyed from within by glasnost.

From Dmitri Volkogonov, *The Rise and Fall of the Soviet Empire*, **1999**

● **Examiner's hint**

When you mention that a source is 'biased', you need to give an example to support your argument.

STUDENT STUDY SECTION

QUESTION

In Source E, what is Volkogonov's opinion of Gorbachev? Can you find examples in Source E of the author's personal views of the Soviet system? (Is he biased?)

Gorbachev – the economy

Consumer demands were growing during the 1970s, along with rising expectations for a better standard of living and better education. Although **socialism** had brought full employment, cheap housing and low food prices, it was difficult to see how these benefits could be sustained. By the mid 1980s, the price of essential goods such as basic foods was heavily subsidized and the country's economic growth was slowing down.

During the 1980s, labour shortages and low productivity continued to be a problem and efforts to improve the quality of consumer goods had little effect. In agriculture, although actual production was increasing, the USSR was importing grain not only from the USA but also from India. Inadequate storage, refrigeration and transportation facilities meant that even when there was enough food, it did not always reach the consumer.

Coal production was below planned estimates in 1985 but, even more seriously, so was oil and gas. Of course, the 'estimates' had been exaggerated but even so, the drop in production was a matter of serious concern. Between 1960 and 1965, GNP rose by around 5 per cent per annum, but this fell to 3.75 per cent by 1975, 2.5 per cent by 1980 and then to 2 per cent by 1985. Both Khrushchev and Andropov tried to address the problem of an economic slowdown, and now it was Gorbachev's turn to wrestle with reforming the system.

Like Andropov, Gorbachev tried to target problems in the workplace. All too often, workers would arrive at their place of work, 'clock in' and then leave to 'moonlight' as plumbers, carpenters or handymen. Women workers would also leave in order to queue at shops that were only open during working hours. As Andropov discovered when he had tried to end this absenteeism, when workers stayed at their place of work all kinds of other necessary jobs did not get done. The 'black economy' was actually vital for the day-to-day running of the Soviet Union.

Alcohol abuse was another problem. Large quantities of spirits like vodka were consumed and this was damaging to health and to efficiency at work. Like Andropov, Gorbachev used propaganda to raise awareness about the dangers of alcohol abuse and workers could be dismissed for habitual drunkenness, but the problem remained. One policy with unforeseen consequences was the cut-back in the production and sale of alcohol. Illegal distilleries sprang up producing just as much alcohol, but this alcohol was not taxed and so there was a loss of revenue for the state.

Gorbachev wanted some aspects of a command economy and some aspects of a free market, but how could he change the attitude of Soviet workers and managers? Gorbachev's economic reforms are described as taking place in two stages.

 Socialism

This term was used by Karl Marx to describe the period of the 'dictatorship of the proletariat' or the stage after the workers had seized power but before communism had actually come into being. The USSR was 'The Union of Soviet Socialist Republics' and still in the stage of socialism, but on the way to becoming a communist state. After World War II, many governments in Western Europe described themselves as 'socialist', meaning that they intended to re-distribute wealth through higher taxation, for example, or to nationalize the main industries. This was a different meaning from that of the Marxist term.

Perestroika I

Gorbachev began by trying to encourage the Party to accept change. This was very difficult, as he met a great deal of opposition from the *nomenklatura* who did not want change, especially if it meant reducing their privileges. They liked to do things in the way they had always been done and which guaranteed their privileges. For example, when Gorbachev tried to centralize all aspects of agricultural production under Gosagroprom (the State Committee for the Agro-Industrial Complex), it quickly became bogged down in bureaucracy and didn't improve efficiency. Another idea was to encourage peasant farmers to lease land from collective farms. Building on the idea of peasant plots, Gorbachev hoped this would increase production, but it turned out that collective farm managers were reluctant to lease any of their land. No one really wanted to deal with change. Over and over, Gorbachev was obstructed by state officials, but after Chernobyl he realized that he had to push through reform quickly.

He was also frustrated by the failure of *uskorenie* and the difficulty of pushing through effective reforms aimed at the production of more goods of a higher quality. For many, the idea of 'acceleration' only brought to mind the old ploy of demanding that a Five Year Plan be completed in four!

SOURCE F

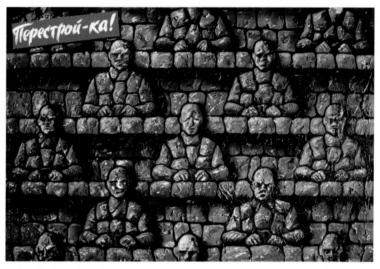

'Just try to re-build (and you will fail).' A wall whose 'bricks' are high-level party officials illustrates how difficult it was to get perestroika *moving. The poster by Kanstantsin Khatsyanouski was selected for the International Biannual Poster Exhibition in Warsaw in 1990 – 'Visual Code of the Time: post-Soviet poster art in Belarus'.*

STUDENT STUDY SECTION

QUESTION

'Perestroi-ka' is a play on the word *Perestroika*. So, rather than 'reconstruct' it means 'try to do this [reconstruct], but you will fail.' Why, do you think, did the artist choose this title?

This poster represents a problem that faced all the 'reformers', notably Khrushchev, Andropov and Gorbachev. It was the Communist Party that stood in the way and the brick wall was an apt metaphor for the difficulty of getting change through the Party officials who did not want to change.

Perestroika II

If Gorbachev could not get the Party officials to accept change, then he would need to change the Party officials. By stimulating political change, Gorbachev was hoping to push through economic reform.

In January 1987, at a Central Committee meeting, Gorbachev announced that members of local Soviets would now be elected by the people and not the Party and that there would be a choice of candidates. There would also be direct elections for several important Soviet posts. Gorbachev wanted to break the stranglehold of the Party over the state and to bring reformers who agreed with him into positions of authority.

In 1988, changes were made to the government of the Soviet Union. The Supreme Soviet would now consist of 400 members chosen from a Congress of People's Deputies. This

Congress would have two thirds of its members elected by universal **suffrage** and one third from 'people's organizations' that would include the Communist Party. The new style Supreme Soviet would meet regularly and act as a parliament.

In 1989, elections were held for the Congress of People's Deputies and these were 'semi-free' because there could be non-Party candidates. Although 88 per cent of successful candidates were from the Communist Party, prominent dissidents such as the physicist Andrei Sakharov were also elected. This was the beginning of the end of the Communist Party grip on Soviet politics, a lesson that was observed by the satellite states of Eastern Europe. The sessions of the new 'parliament' were televised and they made exciting viewing when the reformers, although only a minority, clashed with the conservatives.

Change did begin to happen and the Law on State Enterprises that came into effect in 1988 meant that 60 per cent of state enterprises moved away from state control and the remaining 40 per cent followed in 1989. Factories and businesses could now trade with each other and set their own prices. A quota of the goods produced still went to the state, but it was possible to sell the remainder at a profit. Small private businesses and workers' cooperatives were also set up.

There was still the problem of how to set prices and measure demand, however, and the USSR experienced shortages and severe economic problems.

> **Suffrage**
> This means the right to vote. Another term with the same meaning is 'franchise'.

What was the impact of all these changes?

- There was demand for more change in the Soviet Union and the introduction of multi-party elections to the Supreme Soviet.
- The Soviet republics began to ask for independence, with the Supreme Soviet of Georgia declaring sovereignty in November 1989.
- Economic reforms led not to an increase but to a shortage of goods in the shops. Shelves were empty and necessities such as soap, razor blades and washing powder disappeared.
- In July 1989, miners in the Kuzbass region went on strike when they had no soap to get washed at the end of their shift. The strike spread to include around 500,000 miners as well as 160,000 workers from other industries. Not only did they demand better working conditions, however, but also a trade union like Solidarity in Poland and greater political freedom.

Overview of Gorbachev's reforms

Gorbachev's constitutional changes had an impact at a local level, but these changes were not always as he expected. In many cases, the elections were not won by economic reformers but by nationalists, and so the demand grew for independence. Although Gorbachev wanted change, he was not always happy with the changes that took place. For example, Gorbachev introduced the new roles of President and Vice-President along with a Cabinet to replace the Council of Ministers. The intention had been to encourage the election of like-minded reformers who would help him to push through *perestroika* despite the resistance of the Party hierarchy. Gorbachev hoped that this new blood would enable him to move the Soviet Union in the 'right' direction and, furthermore, that changes to the structure of the government would add to this impetus for reform.

Gorbachev pushed for political change and the result was more democracy, but the end of the single-party system led to the growth of political parties hostile to communism. In 1988, the discontent of Party members led to 18,000 leaving the Communist Party and a further 136,000 left in 1989. Admittedly, this was a tiny drop in an ocean of 20 million members, but it was a new phenomenon and did not bode well for the future of the Party.

There was no smooth transition to democracy and political instability led to an economic slowdown, with production falling by 4 per cent in 1990 and by 15 per cent in 1991. Gorbachev wanted reform, but the freer market led to price increases, unemployment and shortages. The Soviet Union was in a critical situation, and Gorbachev refused to declare a state of emergency in 1991. In August, while on holiday in the Crimea, he was placed under house arrest by a group of hardline communists who tried to stage a counter-revolution. The coup failed and Gorbachev was rescued by **Boris Yeltsin**'s decisive action to protect the Russian (not the Soviet) parliament and to defy what he called the 'putschists' (a 'putsch' is an attempt to overthrow a government through violence). When the plotters realized this, they lost their nerve and although there was some violence, ultimately the army also decided not to fire on the demonstrators who came out to support Yeltsin.

Gorbachev returned to Moscow and seemed to think that little had changed. He proposed to go through with the new Union Treaty that he had put together, but found that the Communist Party had lost its authority to govern. Yeltsin placed a ban on the Russian Communist Party and Gorbachev resigned as General Secretary of the CPSU on 25 August. In December, the Ukraine, Russia and Belarus formed the Commonwealth of Independent States (CIS). The Union of Soviet Socialist Republics had ceased to exist.

Boris Yeltsin

A staunch member of the Communist Party, Yeltsin held senior positions and was promoted to the Politburo by Mikhail Gorbachev in 1985. Following a difference of opinion, Yeltsin was removed from the Politburo in 1987, but became famous for 'rescuing' Gorbachev during the August coup of 1991. By this time, Yeltsin was the President of the Russian Soviet Republic and determined, it seemed, on bringing about the break-up of the Soviet Union. He had achieved this by the end of 1991 and proceeded to move ahead with ambitious plans to transform the Russian economy. He served two terms as President, resigning in 1999 after a turbulent and controversial decade marred by ill health. He died in 2007.

Why did Gorbachev fail?

SOURCE G

Democratisation of production, satisfaction of the huge consumer demand, and improving quality were impossible in the context of old Bolshevik economic relations. The system Lenin had created had shown that it was not amenable to radical democratic reform. Communism with a democratic face, a free market and political pluralism, is not Communism. The paradox of Gorbachev, in other words, was that he believed it was possible to change that which could not be changed. What was needed was not a restructuring – perestroika – but a new structure – novostroika.

From Dmitri Volkogonov, *The Rise and Fall of the Soviet Empire*, 1999

STUDENT STUDY SECTION

QUESTION

Why, according to Source G, was *perestroika* bound to fail?

Student Answer – *Tom*

In Source G, Volkogonov says that it was not possible to reform communism. If it had democracy, a free market and more than one political party then it wouldn't be a communist state anymore. So, how can you reform something that cannot be reformed, is the question that he asks. Perestroika was supposed to reform communism, so Volkogonov is saying that it won't work because you cannot reform it. What you need is *novostroika*.

Examiner's comments

This is a good answer that gets straight to the point. Tom could have avoided repeating himself though, and also given some explanation for *novostroika*, or left this sentence out as it is not really necessary.

Did Gorbachev's criticism of the system inevitably lead to criticism of the ideology that lay at the heart of the system? Surveys taken in Russia during the 1990s showed that socialism was still popular, and for many the 'good old days' meant the Soviet Union under Brezhnev. Also, it has been argued there was no public outcry for competitive elections until Gorbachev introduced them.

Once he began the process of reform, however, it was impossible to restore the authority of the Communist Party. As Gorbachev had intended, *glasnost* encouraged discussion and it was hardly surprising that people grumbled about their government and, when given the opportunity, voted to remove it from power.

Economic reform failed and for many there were even fewer goods in the shops by 1990 than there had been in 1985. Incomes rose but output fell and shortages became worse – basic necessities like soap, salt, matches and washing powder were difficult to find and buy. Quality also fell, queues grew even longer, the black market flourished and by 1990 up to 25 per cent of the population was living below the poverty line.

Another problem that continued throughout the 1980s was the economic and moral weight of the Soviet-Afghan War. Not only was it a huge drain on the scarce resources of the Soviet Union, but it was also unpopular and so the war added to the tension that led to the collapse of the rickety structure of the state.

Another, less expected, but very significant factor in the collapse of the Soviet Union was the upsurge in nationalism. From 1987 onwards, there was an open call for increased autonomy and independence in the Transcaucasian and Central Asian republics – for example, Georgia and Kazakhstan – as well as in the Baltic States. If the Soviet Union could not deliver benefits to its population then independence offered a way out. By the end of 1989, the Soviet empire had given up its control over Poland, Hungary, Czechoslovakia, East Germany and the other Eastern European satellite states. It was not long before it also lost control over the republics that lay within its borders.

Gorbachev – foreign policy and *glasnost* abroad

When Gorbachev introduced *glasnost*, he intended to encourage more openness within the Soviet Union. *Glasnost* also meant the improvement in relations with the West. After the end of détente, relations between the USA and the USSR were once again rather frosty. Ronald Reagan was elected President of the USA in November 1980 and his administration wanted to take a stronger line against the USSR. A series of events in the early 1980s made matters worse:

- SALT II had not been ratified by Congress.
- Korean Airlines commercial flight KAL 007 was shot down after it strayed into Soviet airspace in September 1983.
- The NATO 'Able Archer' military exercises in 1983 were interpreted by the USSR as preparations for an actual invasion of the Eastern Bloc. The USSR was watching events in Western Europe very carefully and because 'Able Archer' was a high-level exercise meant to follow, as closely as possible, what an actual war against the Warsaw Pact forces would be like, there were doubts in Moscow that this really was an 'exercise' and not the real thing.

Yuri Andropov wanted to improve relations with the USA, but his ill health made it difficult for him to make this a priority. Chronic ill health also prevented Chernenko from doing anything to improve relations and so it was left up to Gorbachev to work towards a 'thaw'.

INF Treaty

This was the treaty to eliminate Intermediate Range Ballistic Missiles (IRBMs) that were placed in Europe by both the USSR and the USA. A decision was also made to limit the total numbers of IRBMs deployed by both superpowers.

Strategic Defense Initiative (SDI)

This was the plan to put a 'shield' in outer space that would protect the USA from incoming ballistic missiles. Approaching missiles would be destroyed outside the earth's atmosphere by lasers.

Intermediate Range Ballistic Missiles (IRBMs)

IRBMs did not have the range of an Intercontinental Ballistic Missile (ICBM), but had been located in both Eastern and Western Europe since the late 1970s.

For President Reagan, the Soviet Union was the 'evil empire' and he was disinclined to work towards a better understanding with a communist regime. His opinion changed with the appointment of Mikhail Gorbachev. Margaret Thatcher, the British Prime Minister, had met Gorbachev and decided that he was a man 'we could do business with'. Reagan agreed to meet Gorbachev for a summit in Geneva in November 1985 and this was the beginning of a strong personal friendship. Although nothing concrete came of the Geneva summit, a follow-up meeting in Reykjavik was planned for October 1986. Gorbachev wanted to show Reagan that he was serious about arms reduction and he made several proposals to reduce **Intermediate Nuclear Forces** (**INF**) drastically in Europe. He also said he would consider doing away with all nuclear weapons within 10 years on condition that the USA cancelled the **Strategic Defense Initiative** (SDI or 'Star Wars') anti-nuclear missile defence programme, but Reagan would not agree to this. The two leaders met again in Washington D.C. in December 1987 and agreed to an INF Treaty that removed **Intermediate Range Ballistic Missiles** (**IRBMs**) from Eastern and Western Europe.

By April 1988, agreements were reached on the withdrawal of Soviet troops from Afghanistan and there were two more summits before the end of Reagan's term as President in January 1989. These good relations continued during the subsequent presidency of George H. Bush.

By now, Gorbachev had built up a strong reputation abroad as a reformer and for being a very different kind of Soviet leader from his predecessors. He was very popular with the media and the people of Western Europe. He was also popular with the people, if not the leaders, of the Eastern European satellite states.

As we have seen, this admiration was not always shared by the people of the Soviet Union and Gorbachev would be remembered more warmly abroad than at home.

Did President Reagan end the Cold War?

One theory is that President Reagan put economic pressure on the Soviet Union, leading to its collapse. It may be more accurate to say that he applied pressure to a Soviet Union that was already about to keel over. The increased funding for an arms build-up in the USA and Reagan's rhetoric against the Soviet Union made the Soviet leaders realize that détente was over. By massively increasing US spending on arms, he applied economic pressure at a time when the Soviet Union was no longer able to compete. It had an ailing economy and a war it could not end, and it was falling behind in computer technology, a vital component in modern warfare.

What was more significant, perhaps, was that President Reagan helped Gorbachev build a reputation as a world statesman and this made it easier for him to impose change on the Soviet Union. Unintentionally, it was these changes that actually led to its collapse. In trying to save the Soviet Union, Gorbachev destroyed it and because the USA was left without an opponent, the Cold War came to an end. Many factors contributed to the collapse of the Soviet Union including, of course, the end of communism in the satellite states of Eastern Europe, but overwhelmingly it was Mikhail Gorbachev who destroyed what he had set out to save.

SOURCE H

Cartoon by Jeff Koterba.

SOURCE I

Cartoon by Cummings.

SOURCE J

'I can't believe my eyes!' – Cartoon by Edmund Valtman.

● **Examiner's hints**

For Source H, think about what this image implies about why the Cold War came to an end and also about the nature of the Soviet Union in the 1980s.

For Source I, try to say something about each one of the objects and don't forget to identify the man in the space capsule! Look at the soldier and all the medals hanging off his space suit. What, do you think is the irony of this? Also, notice there is a knot in the air pipe connecting him to the capsule. Why do you think the capsule is breaking apart?

For Source J, identify all the characters drawn here and describe their expressions. For instance, who is the bearded gentleman holding the hammer and sickle? Note that to help identify Gorbachev, cartoonists usually include his birthmark!

Don't forget that in Paper 1, the last question in each section is always a mini-essay. It is 'mini', but it still needs to be planned and you will need to refer to sources as well as your own knowledge. Here, you can use sources and material from the text.

ToK Time

Is it correct to say that 'Language is power'? In a single-party state, the government (or party) can take over language and change the meaning of words. What the Soviet state called 'truth' might be a lie; anyone who criticized the state was a 'criminal' or, in the time of Brezhnev, was diagnosed as suffering from a mental illness. See if you can find more examples from this chapter (especially in the sources) of ways in which words were misused. How, do you think, do ordinary people cope when the state steals language and uses it for its own purposes?

'I CAN'T BELIEVE MY EYES!'

STUDENT STUDY SECTION

QUESTIONS

a) **What is the message conveyed in Source H?**

b) **What is the message conveyed in Source I?**

c) **What is the message conveyed in Source J?**

Now that you have read this section, write a mini-essay:

QUESTION

How far would you agree with the assertion that Gorbachev was the 'grave digger' of the Soviet Union?

REVIEW SECTION

You have been reading about the Gorbachev Era. Give brief answers to the following questions using information from the text and from the sources.

Review questions

1   How far, do you think, did the Chernobyl disaster influence Gorbachev's determination to reform?

2   What did Gorbachev aim to do? In what ways was he successful?

3   What was the role of the USA in the ending of the Cold War?

Section IV:

Consequences of Gorbachev's policies for Eastern European reform movements: Poland – the role of Solidarity; Czechoslovakia – the Velvet Revolution; the fall of the Berlin Wall

This section deals with the impact of Gorbachev's policies on developments in Eastern Europe after 1985. In particular, we will look at events in three communist states and see how the Communist Party lost control. What happened in the Soviet Union after 1985 both influenced and was influenced by events in the satellite states of Eastern Europe. At the root of the upheavals lay economic problems. Stagnation was leading to huge deficits in all the economies that had borrowed heavily during the 1970s. When they could not pay back the loans, there were economic problems and these led to discontent and the demand for political change. Solidarity in Poland led the way, but it was also Gorbachev and his policies of *perestroika* and *glasnost* that seized the imagination of the Eastern European satellite states.

The Polish Revolution
The role of Solidarity

SOURCE A

In this photograph, you can see people holding banners printed with the famous logo of the Solidarity movement. This was designed by Jerzy Janiszewski in what was described as a 'red and disobedient' font. This logo was first used at the end of August 1980.

In Poland, throughout the communist era, nationalism was kept alive partly through a strong sense of national history and partly through the Catholic religion, as the Church continued to play an important part in people's lives. Although Poland was a member of the Warsaw Pact and its government was loyal to Moscow, the election in 1978 of Karol Josef Wojtila, Archbishop of Cracow, as Pope John Paul II, was seen as a turning point. This remarkable event came at a time when there was growing unrest because of economic difficulties. In Poland, conditions for ordinary workers were reaching a crisis point.

SOURCE B

Living conditions were dire: the average female Polish factory worker got up before 5 a.m., spent over an hour getting to work, fifty-three minutes a day queuing for food, nine hours working and less than six and a half hours asleep. 'There's no future here', complained a Polish shipyard worker in 1972. 'To receive an apartment you have to wait ten years. A man grows old, he wants to marry.'

'The housing situation is worse than before, indeed it is hopeless,' wrote a senior Hungarian housing official in 1985. 'Nothing has essentially changed, nothing has improved'. The communist 'social contract' which western commentators discerned as the basis for regime legitimacy was, if it had ever existed, now coming apart.

From Mark Mazower, *The Dark Continent*, 1998

STUDENT STUDY SECTION

QUESTION

What evidence is there in Source B to support the claim that the communist 'social contract' was now coming apart?

Poland borrowed heavily from the West during the 1970s to try to modernize and expand its industrial production. By 1980, Poland's debt had risen to $25 billion.

Loans from the West

During the 1970s, the oil-rich countries of the Middle East benefited enormously from increases in the price of oil. They had no immediate use for the money they were accumulating, so kept it on deposit in Western banks. This meant there was a lot of money available for investment. In Eastern Europe, the economies were doing badly, but the governments didn't want to, or perhaps didn't know how to, introduce economic reform without political reform. The answer was to borrow money. So, banks had money to lend and these countries wanted to borrow. The Western banks thought their investments were safe because it was assumed that the Soviet Union would guarantee these loans.

During the late 1970s, the cost of food went up. Agriculture in Poland was not totally collectivized and most farming took place on small peasant-owned plots. As a result of this, the government did not have control over the production of food, and shortages led to rising prices. When the government tried to pass these increased costs on to the workers, the unpopular price increases led to strikes and demonstrations. For example, when the government tried to increase food prices by 60 per cent in 1976, there were serious strikes and many workers were dismissed from their jobs or sent to prison. Renewed attempts to increase prices led to more strikes in the summer of 1980 and shipyard workers in Gdansk occupied the Lenin Shipyard. They demanded lower food prices, but also the free election of independent trade unions. The strike quickly spread through the city and the Polish government backed down, agreeing to wage increases and a trade union, as well as reduced censorship and the broadcasting of Catholic Church services. In September the strike leader, Lech Walesa, formed Solidarity, a free trade union that was supported by workers, students, the intelligentsia and the Church. Threats of more strikes persuaded the government to accept the existence of this independent trade union and by January 1981 it had eight million members.

SOURCE C

Mr Malcolm Rifkind – Her Majesty's Government have given financial and other assistance, both nationally and through the European Community, for humanitarian aid to Poland through voluntary and Church agencies.

Mr Greenway – Does my hon. Friend share the nation's disgust and abhorrence at the brutal suppression of Solidarity, the viciousness shown to people mourning for those who suffered in the wake of it, and the hated and unending imposition of martial law in Poland? Do not those facts and others highlight the need to encourage the sending of all possible British aid, voluntary and otherwise, direct to the people of Poland via the Churches?

Mr Malcolm Rifkind – The Government have already made clear to the Polish Government their abhorrence of the legislation abolishing, or seeking to abolish, Solidarity. Indeed, the Polish people have made clear their views on their Government's action. European Community Foreign Ministers have agreed to continue the provision of humanitarian aid to voluntary and Church agencies in Poland, and sums of money are still available for that purpose.

From a debate held in the House of Commons (The British Parliament) on 20 October 1982. Mr Greenway MP and Mr Rifkind MP (and also the Under-Secretary of State at Foreign and Commonwealth Office).

SOURCE D

In 1980, a year after Pope John Paul II had given courage to his fellow countrymen during his visit to Poland, hope was restored in Gdansk, a hope that triumphed over fear; Solidarity was born. The scale of civil disobedience in the whole country and the amazing ability of 10 million people to organize an independent trade union paralysed the communist regime. The strikes in the cities of the Polish coast echoed everywhere around the world, and the face of the charismatic union leader, Lech Walesa, became known on every continent. The freedom movement took the form of a trade union, which was the most problematic form for the 'state of workers', and because the world's attention was focused on the Gdansk Shipyard, it was very difficult for the government to launch a military intervention. In December 1981, when the communist regime finally decided to counteract by introducing martial law, it was already too late. Nothing could stop this nation any more, for it had regained its dignity and was now aspiring to freedom. Solidarity was the first sign of civil awakening all over Central and Eastern Europe.

From a Polish internet site dedicated to culture and the arts in Poland,
http://www.culture.pl/en/culture/artykuly/wy_in_wy_solid_art_bruksela_barcelona

STUDENT STUDY SECTION

QUESTIONS

a) **What does Source C tell you about the British response to martial law in Poland? Why were the churches used to get aid to the people?**

b) **With reference to its origin and purpose, assess the value and limitations of Source D for an historian researching the Polish revolution.**

Student Answer to Question (b):

Student Answer – *Jennifer*

The origin Source D is an internet site about Poland. The purpose is to talk about Polish culture and arts. The value of this source is that it talks about the Pope's visit to Gdansk. It also says that Solidarity was very popular and it also talks about the Pope's visit in 1979. This gives information about the events of 1980. The limitation is that it is like propaganda. It is very biased and may not be telling us everything in order to make us think that Solidarity was popular with everyone. It is also translated and this may mean that some of the meaning has been lost.

Examiner's comments

Jennifer has referred to the four main parts of the question and included some explanation. The origin is dealt with quite briefly and the purpose states only what it is about, not what/who it is for. Jennifer could have said more here by adding that it is unclear who the site is intended for but 'that it appears to offer information about Polish history to someone looking for general information'. In this way, Jennifer could demonstrate that she knows what is meant by 'purpose'. She is right to point out that the value of the source is that it gives information about the rise of Solidarity. There is not much more that can be said about this, as she is not told much about the origin of the source. There is more to be said about limitations, though. Jennifer states that it is 'like propaganda', but she could give a reason for this by saying 'Source D is like propaganda because it uses such words as "courage", "triumphed", "charismatic" about the Pope and Lech Walesa and "nothing could stop this nation anymore"'. Jennifer uses 'biased' to suggest that the source is not impartial. This is fine but again, 'biased' should be supported. In what way is it biased? It might be better to say 'the intention is to show the activities of Solidarity in a very positive light'; for example, Source D says that Solidarity was the 'first sign of civil awakening all over Central and Eastern Europe.' One more point – Jennifer states that this source has been translated. In fact, she is making an assumption because it is not mentioned anywhere that this has been translated. Even if it were translated, it is doubtful that the meaning of the source would have been dramatically altered, so it is not a significant limitation. Jennifer could have left this out.

ToK Time

You have read about how Polish nationalism stayed alive during the communist era.

- Is there a difference, do you think, between nationalism and patriotism?
- Does studying the history of a country help in developing a feeling of nationalism?

Polish Senate and Sejm

In the Polish government, the Senate is the Upper House. It consists of 100 senators, all of whom are elected. The Sejm is the Lower House with 460 deputies elected by a system of proportional representation.

The Katyn Forest Massacre

In 1939, both Germany and the Soviet Union invaded Poland in accordance with the terms of the Nazi-Soviet Pact of August of that year. In 1940 mass executions, including that of an estimated 8,000 Polish Army officers, took place in the Katyn Forest. These were carried out by the Soviet NKVD (secret police).

Prague Spring

During the winter and spring of 1968, Alexander Dubcek, First Secretary of the Czechoslovak Communist Party, brought in an era of political and economic reform that also became known as 'socialism with a human face'. He believed that it was possible for Czechoslovakia to remain a communist state, but with less repression and more freedom. His policies threatened Soviet ideology and Warsaw Pact forces were sent in to end the reform process in August 1968.

Although it was independent from the Polish Communist Party (officially, the Polish Workers Party), Solidarity recognized its leading role in Polish politics, but differences between it and the Party arose when economic problems worsened in 1981. The government wanted to push through economic reforms, but Solidarity wanted to link these to democratization.

The leadership of the Polish Communist Party now changed several times, ending with the appointment of General Jaruzelski in October 1981. After forming the Military Committee for National Salvation, he declared martial law, banned Solidarity and arrested its leaders. One explanation for this imposition of martial law is that Jaruzelski felt compelled to do so to avoid giving the Soviet Union an excuse to impose the Brezhnev Doctrine and to bring in Warsaw Pact forces. Other sources suggest, however, that the Soviet Union, already embroiled in Afghanistan, had no intention of intervening in Poland and that Jaruzelski acted on his own initiative.

Poland: from martial law to a multi-party state

In 1983 Poland was relatively stable, but changes had taken place. This was the year that Lech Walesa was released from internment and was awarded the Nobel Prize for Peace, and when the Pope made an official visit. The following year, the kidnap and murder by the security forces of an outspoken young priest, Father Jerzy Popielusko, led to a clear demonstration of defiance towards the government when more than 350,000 mourners attended his funeral.

Economic problems continued to worsen and the cost of food went up by an average of 48 per cent in 1988, prompting widespread strikes. Solidarity now re-emerged onto the political stage. The trade union also received support from British Prime Minister Margaret Thatcher, who visited Poland in November 1988 and said economic aid would be linked to the restoration of Solidarity.

In April 1989, threatened by renewed strikes, General Jaruzelski held talks with Solidarity and it was agreed that:

- Free elections would be held to the Polish Senate.
- Free elections would be held for 35 per cent of the seats in the Polish parliament (the **Sejm**).
- The office of President would be established, with power over the army and foreign policy.

The Central Committee of the Polish Communist Party agreed to legalize Solidarity, negotiate economic reforms and to draw up a new constitution. Very significantly, it was also admitted that the **Katyn Forest Massacre** of 1940 was carried out not by the Nazis, but by the Soviet NKVD. This was also made public knowledge in the Soviet Union, where Gorbachev also stated in 1989 that the Soviet Union would not intervene in the domestic affairs of the countries of Eastern Europe.

Free elections and the collapse of communism in Poland

Elections were held in Poland in June 1989 with 35 per cent of the 460 seats in the Lower House (the Sejm), and all 100 seats in the **Senate** being open to non-Communist Party representatives. Solidarity won 160 of the 'free' 161 seats in the Sejm and 99 out of the 100 seats in the Senate.

'You get the President, we get the Prime Minister', was an agreement already reached between Solidarity and the Polish Communist Party. General Jaruzelski was elected President, but he did not interfere in the political decisions that led to rapid changes spearheaded by Solidarity. A coalition government was set up under the leadership of

Tadeusz Mazowiecki (a member of Solidarity who had been imprisoned by Jaruzelski), although four places in the Cabinet (including the Ministry of the Interior and Ministry of Defence) were allocated to the Communist Party.

Changes in the Soviet Union obviously affected the emergence of a more democratic system in Poland. Gorbachev made it very clear that it was up to the satellite states to run their own affairs and it was up to them whether or not to follow in the path of *perestroika* and *glasnost*. The days of Soviet intervention were over. The old guard of the Communist Party had to accept that unless they could win free elections, their days were numbered. They could no longer depend on the threat of Soviet power to keep their population in line.

SOURCE E

● Examiner's hint

When you are asked to comment on a photograph like the one below, look carefully at all the detail. Here you can get a sense of the atmosphere in the room just by seeing how crowded it is and how there seems to be a lot of discussion and action. You can also think about the following questions. How old are the participants? Why, do you think, do there seem to be no women present? Do all the men look more or less the same in terms of clothing, hairstyle etc. Why is this, do you think?

◄ A meeting of the Solidarity strike committee in Gdansk in 1980.

ⓘ The Helsinki Final Act 1975

This grew out of the Conference on European Security and Cooperation that met in Helsinki in 1973. There were representatives from the countries of Europe along with the USA and Canada. Agreements were drawn up accepting the post-war borders of Europe, trade arrangements and an acknowledgement of human rights. These 'baskets', as the different groups of agreements were known, made up the final act and were signed by all the participating countries, including the USSR. Although dismissed by Brezhnev as a 'scrap of paper', it meant that the Soviet Union could, from now on, be challenged for not observing human rights. In Eastern Europe, this act led to internal challenges from dissident groups, who asked for human rights to be recognized.

STUDENT STUDY SECTION

QUESTION

What impression does this photograph give you of this meeting in Gdansk? How reliable is it, do you think, as 'evidence' of the popularity of Solidarity?

The Velvet Revolution in Czechoslovakia

In Czechoslovakia, the suppression of the '**Prague Spring**' of 1968 brought an end to Alexander Dubcek's experiment of 'socialism with a human face'. The conservatives were back in power, but economic reforms were introduced and these brought some improvement to the workers in Czechoslovakia.

The hope for political reform was not dead, however, and the **Helsinki Final Act**, signed in 1975, led to the emergence of a group (never officially an organization) by the name of Charter 77. A document was produced that challenged the Czechoslovakian government to observe the rights that were written into the constitution, the Helsinki Final Act and the UN Declaration of Human Rights. The original document (the Charter) had only 243 signatures, but over the next decade this number grew to 1621.

In addition to Charter 77, whose most famous member, Václav Havel, was later to become the President of Czechoslovakia, another movement was set up, in April 1978. Known by its acronym VONS (from the Czech translating as the Committee for the Defence of the Unjustly Prosecuted), it aimed to highlight cases of unjust prosecution and imprisonment in Czechoslovakia and to publicize these both inside and outside the country. Like Charter 77, many of its members were arrested, prosecuted and given prison sentences.

Another less well-known challenge to the authority of the government in Czechoslovakia was a rock band known as The Plastic People of the Universe.

The Plastic People of the Universe ▶

ToK Time
Is culture political? Why, do you think, did the Czechoslovakian government feel threatened by a group of musicians? How can art, literature or music pose a danger to a single-party state?

This band was formed some months after the Warsaw Pact invasion of Czechoslovakia in 1968. It was inspired by the Beatles as well as the more 'alternative' Velvet Underground and Frank Zappa and the Mothers of Invention – the name 'Plastic People' was taken from a song by Frank Zappa. Despite the difficulties of performing in a state that censored their music, the group became a beacon for young people, who were willing to risk arrest to attend their infrequent concerts. In 1976, the group was put on trial and its members were found guilty of 'organized disturbance of the peace'. They were sentenced to terms of imprisonment but, after their release, continued to hold secret concerts. Václav Havel was a fan of the group and it is claimed that their trial helped to inspire Charter 77.

Economic problems in Czechoslovakia

As in Poland, there had been an economic downturn in Czechoslovakia during the late 1970s and this led to growing discontent. By the mid 1980s, Gorbachev's reforms in the Soviet Union gave rise to demands for similar changes in Czechoslovakia, but President and First Secretary Gustav Husak resisted these. Although he remained President, Husak gave up leadership of the Party in 1987 and was succeeded by Milos Jakes, a fellow Stalinist. It was difficult for a regime that had come to power after the suppression of 1968 to start a process of political reform. Gorbachev did try to lead by example but, as mentioned earlier, he also adopted what was called the **Sinatra Doctrine**.

Like many of the Eastern Bloc leaders, Jakes did not intend to end communist rule and disapproved of the changes introduced in the Soviet Union by Gorbachev. Resisting cries for reform, Jakes waited patiently and confidently for the removal of Gorbachev by the 'Stalinists' in the Soviet Union. When this did not take place, demands for a 'Polish-style solution' continued to grow in Czechoslovakia.

The demand for reform in Czechoslovakia

In Poland, Solidarity had a broad base of support that included students, workers and priests, but in Czechoslovakia, Charter 77 and VONS were composed mostly of students and intellectuals. In 1989, the Catholic Church rather unexpectedly came to the fore when the Archbishop of Prague criticized the communist regime and so the voice of the Church was added to that of Charter 77 and VONS. One characteristic of the communist regime in Czechoslovakia was that the state made a point of looking after the interests of the workers, so they were reluctant to go on strike or to call for radical change.

There was also a division between reformers who wanted a different type of socialism, echoing the 'human face' of 1968, and those who did not share the ideology of the 68'ers. The latter included student groups such as The Czech Children, The John Lennon Peace Club and The Independent Peace Association-Initiative for the Demilitarization of Society. Mostly, these groups did not want socialism at all, with or without a human face. When Alexander Dubcek, who had been removed from power in 1968, now reappeared on the political scene, he was seen as an anachronism by many of the young people.

The reforms that were sweeping through the Soviet Union, Poland and Hungary proved contagious and through the summer of 1989 (with the numbers often reversed and flipped on posters, leaflets etc. to read '1968') crowds demonstrated on the streets of Prague. These protests were given an extra boost after the East Germans who had been prevented from escaping to the West through Hungary's open border with Austria came instead to the grounds of the West German embassy in Prague.

The Velvet Revolution

The Czech 'Velvet Revolution' can be dated from 17 November 1989, when a march held to mark International Students' Day was suppressed by police. It was rumoured (wrongly) that a demonstrator had been killed and this led to a rapid growth in the numbers that poured onto the streets not only of Prague, but also other towns and cities. Václav Havel, one of the best-known dissidents, now founded Civic Forum to try to organize all the different protest groups that were emerging. In Slovakia, a similar group was formed and named Public Against Violence (PAV). The emergence of different organizations in Prague and Bratislava reflected an underlying tension that hinted at the future break-up of Czechoslovakia. Meanwhile, a major nationwide strike on 27 November showed that the workers were now on the side of reform. Crowds gathered in Wenceslas Square in Prague and people jangled their keys and shouted 'Your time is up!'

No doubt the protesters were encouraged by the fall in October 1989 of Erich Honecker, the arch-Stalinist leader of the GDR. If Honecker could not cling to power, then time was up for Husak and Jakes. Further encouragement came from the Soviet Union, where it was officially stated that the Warsaw Pact invasion of Czechoslovakia in 1968 had been a mistake. It was events such as these from outside Czechoslovakia that gave the protesters added confidence that they would not be suppressed.

The Sinatra Doctrine
This was a humorous play on the idea of a political doctrine. Frank Sinatra, the famous American singer, had a hit record called 'My Way'. Gorbachev said that he did things 'his way', but it was up to the other communist states to do things 'their way'. In other words, it was up to them to decide if, when and how to reform their systems.

The German Democratic Republic (GDR) and Hungary
The communist government in Hungary had also been crumbling during the spring and summer of 1989, and in September holidaying East Germans were able to escape to Austria. In order to stop this, the GDR blocked travel to Hungary and so its citizens went instead to Prague, where they asked for asylum in the grounds of the West German embassy.

Jakes resigned as Party leader on 24 November and on 10 December, Husak gave up the presidency to Václav Havel. This changeover became known as the Velvet Revolution because it was, ultimately, so peaceful.

SOURCE F

A photo of a demonstration in Prague in 1989. Notice that the young woman is holding a poster of Václav Havel and is ringing a bell. Many demonstrators would jingle their keys to make a similar 'ringing' noise.

SOURCE G

MG: We've just come into a passage, which is a pretty famous passage because quite a lot of bad things happened here if I remember rightly. Can you describe what this monument is?
KP: I think it's just hands of people, of students, of us and probably the symbol is we've got clean, free hands because it was one of the slogans we were shouting at the policemen. 'We have clean hands' because only the flowers, it was the only thing we had in our hands. And they were standing there fully armed. I'm not sure if they had guns but they had flexi-glass in front of them, helmets and things like that.

From a BBC taped interview with an eyewitness of the student demonstrations in Prague, November 1989. The interviewer in Misha Glenny, a well-known journalist and historian, and the interviewee is Klara Pospisilova. This interview was broadcast on 17 November 1999.

STUDENT STUDY SECTION

QUESTION

With reference to the origin and purpose, assess the value and limitations of Source G for historians studying the events of 1989 in Czechoslovakia.

Student Answer – *Charlotte*

The origin of Source G is an interview with Klara Pospisilova, an eyewitness of the 1989 student riots in Prague. It is a primary source as she saw these events take place. Source G's purpose is to gain a personal perspective on what took place in Prague in 1989 through the eyes of a participant in order to bring it to the general UK listener via radio. Source G's value lies in the fact that it is a primary source. Also it provides a very honest perspective of one dissident's view, as it was conducted long after fear of repercussions had disappeared. Source G is limited because obviously, the interviewee is biased in favour of the protesters. Moreover, the interview took place a number of years after the event, the eyewitness's memories may have shifted over time or she may have forgotten certain aspects. Finally, the interviewer directed the interviewee's thoughts by saying, 'quite a lot of bad things happened here', affecting the information she would provide in response.

Examiner's comments

Charlotte has made a good attempt here. She has referred to origin, purpose, value and limitation by explicitly mentioning each one. Notice that Charlotte mentions that the value of Source G lies in the fact that it is a primary source! This kind of comment is quite common, but really does not add much to the evaluation of a source. To improve her answer, Charlotte could still have mentioned that it was a primary source, but elaborated on this by saying it gave us an interesting point of view, and so give some explanation for her judgement. (Also, beware of falling into the trap of saying that a primary source is more valuable than a secondary source – it may not be!) Charlotte makes some interesting and valid points about how an eyewitness memory of an event can be coloured by time and by reading other accounts of what they had experienced. In this way, memories become 'communal' and it can be quite hard to recall things exactly as they were experienced at the time. Charlotte could also have mentioned Misha Glenny, a well-known historian famous for his books on Central and Eastern Europe. Even if Charlotte did not know his work, she is told in the reference for the source that he is a 'well-known journalist and historian' and so could have said something quite general about this. She could also have mentioned that the interview was broadcast on the BBC.

The revolution in East Germany (GDR) and the fall of the Berlin Wall

Stalin's henchman and head of the NKVD, Lavrenti Beria, once said 'the Germans do not make good communists'. After the death of Stalin, Beria spoke of the possible re-unification of the divided Germany and this led to his being accused of stirring up the 1953 riots in East Berlin. For this, but also because he was feared by the Politburo, he was arrested and executed in December 1953. The GDR (East Germany) would remain under the control of the **Socialist Unity Party of Germany (SED)** and the Stasi, the secret police that spied on its citizens, until 1989.

The demand for reform in East Germany

Unlike the peoples of other satellite states, the citizens of the GDR were able to watch television programmes beamed from West Germany and were under no illusion of how their lives differed from those of their neighbours. This was especially true after Gorbachev came to power and the Western media gave full coverage to his reforms.

East Germans also became more aware of environmental issues. Pollution become a serious health issue by the 1980s, as people suffered from skin and lung diseases aggravated by the smog-filled air of the industrial regions. In East Germany, antiquated and inefficient machinery spewed out four times as much sulphur dioxide as was produced in West

Socialist Unity Party of Germany (SED)

As early as 1946 in the Soviet zone of Germany, the Social Democratic Party (SPD) and the Communist Party (KPD) were amalgamated to form the SED (Socialist Unity Party of Germany).

ToK Time

People in the GDR were more aware than other satellite states of what life was really like in the West and this, it was said, made them even less content. Is it true that 'ignorance is bliss' and that people will be content as long as they think that they are relatively well-off? People in the Eastern Bloc and in the Soviet Union were relatively better off in the 1980s than they had been previously, yet they were more discontented. Is it possible that this is because they were more aware through the media and travel that life in the West was much better than they had been led to believe?

Germany. Environmental pollution became a key focus for protesters, especially after the Chernobyl disaster. In one instance, the Stasi got very irritated by posters in an East German churchyard that read 'Ride a bike, don't drive a car.' The Lutheran Church also played a significant role in opposing the government when it led a boycott of elections in April 1989.

The collapse of communism in East Germany

Erich Honecker, the elderly and increasingly frail leader of the SED, was unable to resist the pressure for reform that was coming both from the population and from Gorbachev. In October 1989, Gorbachev visited East Berlin to celebrate the 40th Anniversary of the founding of the East German state and the crowds gathered outside the People's Palace chanted 'Gorbi, Gorbi save us'. Gorbachev and his reforms had connected directly with the people, who felt hopeful that he would support them. Meanwhile, their own leaders stubbornly hung on to power.

There were demonstrations in Leipzig and Dresden as well as East Berlin, and these grew in size and confidence as the government dithered over whether or not to suppress them with force. As in Poland and Czechoslovakia, the attitude of Gorbachev was critical. Would the SED be able to stay in control without the backing of the Soviet Union? Clearly, the answer to that was 'No', and even the government acknowledged that if Honecker would not accept reform, he would have to go.

Honecker was succeeded by Egon Krenz on 18 October, and it was not long before the rest of the Politburo resigned. What happened next was almost an anti-climax. On 19 November, at a press conference, it was announced that travel restrictions to the West would be lifted and on being asked, 'When?', there was some hesitation and shuffling of papers before a rather hesitant answer was given – 'Immediately'.

Crowds surged towards the Berlin Wall and the guards, lacking any orders to the contrary, opened the border and for the first time in 28 years East Berliners crossed freely through to West Berlin and reunited the city. The most potent symbol of the division of Cold War Europe had been breached. The Wall was down and as it fell, so did the GDR.

SOURCE H

The failure of communism in East Germany in many ways represents the ultimate failure. Here was a country that was not poor, where there were two hundred automobiles for every thousand inhabitants, and where for years Western, particularly West German, sympathizers had said that communism was working by producing a more communal, more kindly Germany than the harsh, market driven, materialistic West German Federal Republic. It was another misconception born of wishful thinking. It is known that Honecker ordered repressive measures. Earlier, during the summer, Chinese officials had visited East Berlin to brief the East Germans on how to crush prodemocracy movements. But during his early October visit to East Germany, Gorbachev had publicly called for change and let it be known that the Soviets would not intervene to stop reform.

From Vladimir Tismaneanu (ed.), *The Revolutions of 1989,* **1999**

SOURCE I

Though Gorbachev had paid a triumphant visit to West Germany, for the past two years he had avoided the GDR. However, he could not ignore East Germany's fortieth (anniversary). Nor, after his arrival in East Berlin, could he ignore the vast torch-lit parade of youth groups staged for his benefit, or the tanks and artillery pieces that rolled past the saluting dais where he stood with the GDR's leadership. As the long columns of FDJ members marched past in their blue shirts and red scarves, many called out over and over in honour of the Soviet reformer, 'Gorbi! Gorbi!' Some were heard to shout, 'Gorbi, help us!' The Polish Communist leader, Mieczyslaw

Rakowski, asked Gorbachev if he understood what the young people were saying. The Russian nodded, but Rakowski translated for him anyway. 'They are demanding: "Gorbachev, save us!"' he explained incredulously, 'But these are party activists! This is the end!'

From Frederick Taylor, *The Berlin Wall*, 2006

STUDENT STUDY SECTION

QUESTIONS

a) What are the 'misconceptions' referred to in Source H?

b) To what extent are the views about the collapse of communism in East Germany given in Source I supported by Source H?

SOURCE J

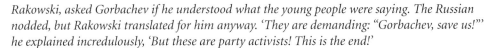

On 10 November 1989, as the Wall begins to be dismantled, unarmed East Berlin guards discourage crowds from climbing up. (Notice how the Western side of the Wall is covered with graffiti.)

How were the revolutions different?

In Poland, there was a united front composed of workers, intelligentsia and students. The reform movement had been bubbling below (but not so far below) the surface for a decade. 'In Poland the revolution took 10 years, in Hungary 10 months, in Czechoslovakia 10 days' (Timothy Garton Ash)… and in East Germany it took around 10 weeks.

In Czechoslovakia, the workers took a long time to convince. They were well looked after by the state and took 'salamis in exchange for submission'. Many had been critical of Charter 77 and VONS and it was not until the end of November 1989 that they finally agreed change was inevitable and joined the reformers.

In East Germany, any dissent was quickly stopped by the huge network of Stasi, so it was difficult for organized protest to succeed. This began to change with the opening of the border between Hungary and Austria and the movement of refugees began a chain of events that quickly led to the disempowerment of the SED. It gave up its last gasp after the visit of Gorbachev demonstrated very clearly that it was on its own. In this way, external influence probably played a more important role in the GDR than in either Poland or Czechoslovakia.

Had democracy finally arrived? Initially, it seemed that the communists were still influential and although state property was privatized, in many cases it was grasped by those who had formerly been in power. Names changed, but the faces remained the same. Democracy was established rather more successfully in Czechoslovakia, Poland and Hungary, countries where dissident organizations already existed. In this way, there was at least the structure for alternative political parties that could move seamlessly into place.

The map of Europe that had been redrawn in 1919 at the Paris Peace Conference was about to be redrawn once more. Over the next few years, it was not only the Eastern European states that recovered their independence but also those of the USSR. Reappearing on political maps of Europe were countries that had existed only briefly during the inter-war years. Historian Eric Hobsbawm called the period from 1914 to 1989 the 'short twentieth century'. It could be argued that events that began with the assassination of Archduke Franz Ferdinand in Sarajevo in 1914 were resolved only with the fall of the Berlin Wall.

● **Examiner's hint**
Don't forget that you need to include both sources and your own knowledge in answers to questions like this one. Plan it like a regular essay and remember to answer the question!

STUDENT STUDY SECTION

Write a mini-essay, using the sources and the material in Section IV, to answer the following question:

QUESTION

How far would you agree that the collapse of communism in Poland, East Germany and Czechoslovakia was primarily inspired by the reforms of Gorbachev in the Soviet Union?

Student Answer A – *Tracy*

By the end of 1989, the Berlin Wall had fallen and communism had collapsed in most of the Soviet satellite states. We will look at the collapse of communism in Poland, East Germany and Czechoslovakia and see if Gorbachev had an influence on this. In Poland, an independent trade union called Solidarity already started to ask for reform at the beginning of the 1980s. It was banned and martial law was introduced in Poland in 1981. Although a lot of people went to prison and it was difficult to protest against the government, Solidarity did not disappear. One reason that there was still unrest in Poland was because of economic problems. Poland borrowed a lot of money during the 1970s and it was difficult to pay it back. Also, the cost of food went up and the government put up prices so workers found it difficult to afford to buy necessary goods. In 1988, there were a lot of strikes and because the government was afraid of trouble, it let Solidarity exist again. In 1989, the communist government under General Jaruzelski agreed with Solidarity that there would be political changes. For the first time in a long time there would be free elections in Poland for some of the Parliament seats and for all the Senate seats. Also, there would be a President. In the elections, Solidarity won a lot of seats and so was able to form a government. Another factor that was important was the Pope. John Paul II was Polish and when he was elected Pope in 1978, it was a very important event, the first time for hundreds of years that a non-Italian cardinal was elected. Also, it sent a signal to the USSR to show that religion was still important in Poland and that it had survived communism. The Pope was important for the morale of the Polish people and helped them stand up to the communist government. In East Germany, the people were inspired by changes in Hungary, but also by Gorbachev. When he visited East Berlin in October 1989, people shouted 'Gorbi, save us!' Gorbachev knew that this was the end for the communist government and he told them so. It was the same in

Czechoslovakia, where people were afraid that the Soviet troops would be sent in like they had been in 1968 but Gorbachev said he would not use force. He wanted these countries to use the Sinatra Doctrine and to do it 'their way'. In Prague, they jangled their keys and shouted 'your time is up' to the communist government.

Gorbachev was very important to the revolutions in Poland, the GDR and Czechoslovakia. He had brought in *perestroika* and *glasnost* and wanted the other countries to do the same. But he also said it was up to them. The governments of the other countries did not want to change but they knew that Gorbachev would not support them if they tried to stop the revolutions.

Student Answer B – *Ahmed*

The role of Mikhail Gorbachev in the 1989 revolutions was certainly of great importance. The satellite states of the Eastern Bloc were under the control of communist governments that owed their existence to the Soviet Union. After all, it is not very likely that the communists would have still been in power after 40 years if it was not for the threat of a Soviet or Warsaw Pact invasion that would suppress any rebellion. After 1985, the USSR had undergone a lot of changes and its new leader introduced perestroika and glasnost and he wanted to see the same reforms take place in neighbouring countries. He made it very clear that the Soviet Union would not support any attempt to suppress strikes and protests, 'Gorbachev publicly called for change and let it be known that the Soviets would not intervene to stop reform' (Source H). There was also support for Gorbachev and criticism of their own leaders in the GDR (East Germany) where, during a parade to celebrate the founding of the state, young people shouted, 'Gorbi, Gorbi' and where their cries were translated as 'Gorbachev save us!' (Source I). In this way, we can see that Gorbachev's reforms were well known and if change like this could happen in the USSR, then why couldn't change happen in the GDR? Gorbachev had set an example. In Czechoslovakia, the activities of Charter 77 and VONS prepared the ground for reform, but it took a lot of time for workers to join the students and the 'intelligentsia' in protesting against the government. When it was known that Gorbachev admitted that the Soviet invasion of Czechoslovakia in 1968 was a mistake, this gave them courage to stand up to their leaders. It is important, though, that Charter 77 started its work long before Gorbachev became leader of the Soviet Union. So, we can say that Gorbachev was important but there were already organizations to push for change in Czechoslovakia before he came to power in the USSR in 1985. But, as well, knowing that Gorbachev would not give them support helped persuade the leaders of Czechoslovakia that there was no point in their staying on. In Poland, the famous Solidarity movement with its red logo (Source A) was first set up in 1980 and its impact was really important because the government banned it and declared martial law. This happened a long time before Gorbachev came to power. Also, Pope John Paul II was Polish and his election was important for Polish morale. It was also important for the USSR to see that a communist country was still very religious. It is even said that Poland influenced change in the USSR.

The impact of Solidarity was huge, 'The strikes in the cities of the Polish coast echoed everywhere around the world, and the face of the charismatic union leader, Lech Walesa, became known on every continent' (Source D). If a movement was this well known then it had to be feared in the Eastern Bloc. When Solidarity was revived in 1989, it was the government of General Jaruzelski that agreed to negotiate and to begin free elections. They knew that they would not get support from the Soviet Union and so had no choice but to give in. It is said that when the Soviet leaders heard about the fall of the Berlin Wall, they put a lot of pressure on Gorbachev to send in Soviet troops, but he refused. It is difficult to argue that the revolutions in Eastern Europe were inspired by Mikhail Gorbachev because many of the dissident groups were set up before he came to power. He was very important, though, in letting the revolutions succeed.

ToK Time

Do you think it is easier to get at the 'truth' of an historical event when there are lots of sources available? If so, should a history of the fall of the Berlin Wall in 1989 be more reliable than a history of the Berlin Blockade in 1948?

Examiner's comments

Tracy started quite well here and wrote a lot about events in Poland, but less on the other two revolutions. She doesn't seem to remember Gorbachev until the end and then makes some good points about his importance. The essay lacks references to sources. Tracy makes some reference to information that is contained in the sources, but she does not identify any of the sources. For a good answer, you have to do this. It is a good idea to write a quick outline so that you jot down all of the information you need to mention before you start writing. This way, you can be sure to mention all the points and to keep your answer focused on the question.

Ahmed has used sources and his own knowledge well. Notice that he mentions the source every time he uses one. This makes it very clear to the examiner that he has followed the instructions. He has also focused well on the question and actually answered it. He includes quite a lot of his own knowledge here, but he uses it to support relevant arguments, always referring back to the question.

REVIEW SECTION

This section has dealt with the collapse of communism in Eastern Europe. Answer the following questions briefly, using information from the text and the sources.

Review questions

1   Draw up a table to compare the different revolutions. Use the following headings: opposition inside the country; external factors; and outcome.

2   Why, do you think, was there no Solidarity or Charter 77 to lead the revolution in East Germany?

3   How far, do you think, were these revolutions planned? Were the consequences unexpected?

Prescribed Subject 3:
Communism in Crisis 1976–89
CHINA AFTER MAO 1976–89

Timeline – 1976–89

1976 Premier Zhou Enlai dies
Chairman Mao Zedong dies
Hua Guofeng takes over as Chairman of the CCP
The Gang of Four is arrested
1977 Hua Guofeng is confirmed as Chairman
Deng Xiaoping returns to the party leadership
1978 The Four Modernizations are introduced
Democracy Wall is set up in Beijing
1979 The Chinese invasion of Vietnam takes place
1980 The trial of the Gang of Four takes place
Hua Guofeng resigns as Premier of the State Council and is replaced by Zhao Ziyang
Hu Yaobang is appointed General Secretary of the CCP
1984 The Special Economic Zones are established.
1986 Student demonstrations call for more democracy
1989 Death of Hu Yaobang
Student demonstrations take place in Beijing
Gorbachev visits Beijing
Zhao Ziyang is put under house arrest
June Fourth Incident / Tiananmen Square

This chapter will focus on the developments in China after the death of Mao Zedong in 1976. Like the Soviet Union, China was facing the dilemma of how to encourage economic growth without weakening the control of the Communist Party. Unlike the Soviet Union, however, China was able to combine rapid economic growth with preserving the single-party system.

The first section will deal with the aftermath of the Maoist era and the emergence of a new leadership. The second section will look at the emergence of Deng Xiaoping as the 'paramount leader' of China and his economic reforms. The third and final section will be an analysis of how Deng and the Chinese Communist Party (CCP) responded to calls for democratic reforms, ending with the events in Tiananmen Square in 1989.

Section I:

The struggle for power following the death of Mao Zedong; the leadership of Hua Guofeng; the re-emergence of Deng Xiaoping and the defeat of the Gang of Four

Background

Mao Zedong ruled China from 1949 until his death in 1976. During this time, he consolidated the control of the CCP over the state and established a personality cult that

Kuomintang (KMT)

Also known as the Guomindang (GMD), this political party was led by Chiang Kai-shek (Jiang Jieshi). Although the CCP and the KMT formed a United Front on two occasions, these parties were in fierce opposition to each other. The KMT were known as the nationalist party. A bitter civil war was fought from 1946 to 1949, ending with the victory of the CCP.

The Great Leap Forward

In 1958, Mao introduced a revolutionary Twelve Year Plan based around the People's Communes. These were enormous collectives that included both agricultural and industrial production and within which everyone lived communally. By 1959 there were huge problems with falling agricultural production and drought. The years 1959–61 were known as 'The Three Bitter Years' and it was estimated that 30 million people died of starvation.

The Cultural Revolution

Also known as the Great Proletarian Cultural Revolution, this was started by Mao Zedong in 1966. He used this as an opportunity to purge those he considered to be his rivals within the Party. He also tried to appeal to the youth who had not experienced the civil war and, it was feared, did not appreciate how great a struggle it had been to carry out the revolution. Students flocked to join the Red Guards and to fulfil Mao's instructions to destroy the 'Four Olds' (Old Thoughts, Old Ideas, Old Customs and Old Habits) and to 'Bombard the Headquarters', meaning to criticize all authority figures, from parents to teachers to members of the Party leadership.

made his image and sayings familiar to people all across China. Mao's rise to power came after 25 years of revolutionary activity, during which he formulated new ideas about how communism could be applied to a predominantly rural society. These ideas that based the revolution around the peasants and not the proletariat (workers in the cities) were put into practice in Jiangxi and Yanan over a period of 20 years. During this time, Mao struggled to become the leader of the CCP, fight and win a guerrilla war against both the Japanese and the **Kuomintang** and establish his reputation as a national hero.

Mao Zedong united a country fractured after the revolution of 1911 and set about creating an industrialized and productive economy. China received some assistance from the Soviet Union, but this was withdrawn at the end of the 1950s when relations between the two major communist states deteriorated. There were problems at home, too, as Mao's bold experiment in 1958, the '**Great Leap Forward**', ended in famine and economic disaster. The **Cultural Revolution** that started in 1966 restored him to a position of undisputed authority, however, and the publication of the *Thoughts of Chairman Mao* (known as 'The Little Red Book') took the Mao personality cult to new heights. Rivals were purged, but by the early 1970s many would be restored to positions within the Party. By the time Mao died in 1976, he had consolidated the rule of the CCP and also established better relations with the USA, as well as recovering a seat in the UN for mainland China.

The struggle for succession

From 1973 onwards, Mao's health declined quite rapidly. He suffered from Parkinson's disease and, by early 1976, was no longer actively running the country. Who would succeed him?

During the Cultural Revolution, it was assumed that Mao's successor would be Lin Biao, the Minister of Defence, but Lin died in a plane crash in 1971 after being accused of plotting against Mao. Afterwards, there was no obvious successor and it was not known whether Mao favoured a 'Leftist' or a 'Rightist'.

The Rightists (Moderates)

The Rightists were the wing of the CCP led by Zhou Enlai, the Prime Minister. He had been a close comrade of Mao since the days of the Jiangxi Soviet in the late 1920s and stood alongside Mao when the People's Republic of China was declared in 1949. Zhou was a pragmatist, however, and believed that revolutionary ideology was not always a sound guide for economic policies. He did not want to repeat the mistakes of the Great Leap Forward and supported economic reform to help China recover. For Zhou and the Rightists, it seemed practical, for instance, to allow peasants to form smaller communes and to be given some plots of land to farm individually. Also, it was important that China would become a strong industrial power and so needed to use modern technology and to encourage skilled labour. Zhou would have been a natural successor to Mao, but he died in January 1976.

Another possible successor was Deng Xiaoping. Before the Cultural Revolution, Deng was an important Party official, but in 1967 he was accused of having joined the CCP to destroy the revolution 'from the inside'. Deng was called 'number two person in authority taking the capitalist road' (**President Liu Shaoqi** was 'number one') and was accused of keeping Mao away from power after the failure of the Great Leap Forward. According to David Goodman, Deng, who was deaf in one ear, was also accused of sitting far away from Mao at meetings so that he could not hear what the Chairman was saying. (See David S. G. Goodman, *Deng Xiaoping and the Chinese Revolution*, 1994.)

In 1969, Deng was '**sent down to the countryside**' in Jiangxi, placed under house arrest and made to work at a tractor factory. Conditions were not easy, but it is rumoured that

Zhou Enlai used his influence to make things a little easier for Deng, who was now 65 years old. With Zhou's help, Deng was able to return to Beijing in 1973. After the extremes of the Cultural Revolution, there was a quiet restoration of many of the Rightists and a return to the authority of the Party rather than Chairman Mao. Zhou wanted to focus on more practical, realistic economic policies and he knew Deng would be a valuable ally. By 1975, Deng had been elected one of 12 vice-premiers and he would often replace Zhou Enlai, now suffering from cancer, at meetings of the State Council. Deng was also Chief of Staff of the Armed Forces.

The Leftists – the Gang of Four

Mao was thought to favour the Left (more radical) wing of the CCP. Unlike the Rightists, the Leftists favoured using revolutionary ideology as a guide to economic development. One group, considered by some to adhere more strongly to Mao's policies even than Mao himself, became known as the Gang of Four.

A propaganda poster after the fall of the Gang of Four – the high officials blamed for the worst excesses of the Cultural Revolution after the death of Mao Zedong – has the 'gang' impaled and burning, with their human heads on the bodies of animals. They are (left to right): Yao Wenyuan, Wang Hongwen, Zhang Chunqiao, and Jiang Qing, Mao's widow.

Jiang Qing

The leader of the Gang, Jiang became the fourth wife of Mao Zedong when they were married in Yanan in 1939. A former actress, Jiang became famous during the Cultural Revolution. She replaced traditional opera and ballet with productions that celebrated the communist revolution and proletarian culture. Jiang hoped to succeed Mao as Chairman of the Party.

Yao Wenyuan

Based in Shanghai, Yao become an important member of the Party and the Politburo. It was Yao's criticism of a play in 1966 that helped start the Cultural Revolution. He was known for his radical interpretations of the ideology of the CCP.

President Liu Shaoqi
During the Cultural Revolution, President Liu was accused of being a 'Rightist' and dismissed from office. He was sent to prison where he became ill and died. The office of President was later abolished.

'Sent down to the countryside'
This was the phrase used to describe the way purged officials were removed from Beijing and other Chinese cities and assigned work in rural areas. This policy was applied to Red Guards in the late 1960s when the excesses of the Cultural Revolution got out of hand. Mao always maintained that his followers should 'learn from the peasants'..

Zhang Chunqiao

Also based in Shanghai, Zhang Chunqiao played an important role in the purging of the Rightists and later wrote articles denouncing their return. In 1980 at the trial of the Gang of Four, he would not respond to questions and seemed to spend much of the time sleeping.

Wang Hongwen

The youngest of the Gang of Four, Wang was a prominent trade union leader. He was responsible for the ferocity of the Cultural Revolution in Shanghai. His nickname was 'Helicopter Wang' because of his very rapid rise from factory worker to Party leadership.

The Gang were active during the height (1966–68) of the Cultural Revolution and were responsible for campaigns against Rightists such as President Liu Shaoqi. They quoted from the Little Red Book to support their policies and it was difficult for anyone to challenge them.

It is still uncertain whether Mao led or was led by the Gang of Four, but they were his most fervent supporters during the most radical phases of the Cultural Revolution. Ultimately, the impact they had was more cultural than political as they did not have the necessary powerbase either in the Party or in the People's Liberation Army (PLA). Most of the supporters of the Gang of Four were ambitious young cadres who had risen to positions of authority during the Cultural Revolution.

It is said that Mao was the first to call them 'The Gang of Four' because he warned them not to behave 'like a gang', suggesting that perhaps Mao was wary of letting them become too powerful. Also, although he was married to Jiang Qing, she did not live with him for the last 10 years of his life from 1966 to 1976.

An important question is whether or not the Gang of Four was only following Mao's orders when they tried to make the Cultural Revolution more extreme.

SOURCE A

Mao realised his wife's 'wide ambitions' to become chairman, and he also knew of the countless number of people she had wronged, harmed, arrested or killed during the decade of the Cultural Revolution. On July 17, 1974, Mao had warned the Gang: 'You'd better be careful; don't let yourselves become a small faction of four.' In May 1975 he admonished them... : 'Don't function as a gang of four, don't do it anymore.' Mao was thus aware of the Gang's excesses and could have restrained their leader with a simple order.

From Immanuel C. Y. Hsu, *The Rise of Modern China*, 1995

During her trial in 1980, Jiang Qing indicated that she had faithfully followed Mao's instructions.

SOURCE B

She argued that she had done everything during the Cultural Revolution 'on behalf of Chairman Mao Zedong' or 'according to his instructions'. Again and again, she repeated these assertions of hers: 'Arresting me and bringing me to trial is a defamation of Chairman Mao Zedong.' 'Defaming Mao through defaming me.' 'I have implemented and defended Chairman Mao's proletarian revolutionary line.' She shrilled, 'During the war I was the only woman comrade who stayed beside Chairman Mao at the front; where were you hiding yourselves then?' – a statement that made it difficult for those in the public gallery to suppress their laughter – generals who fought hundreds of battles, pioneers in establishing revolutionary bases, underground workers operating at all hazards in the KMT-controlled or Japanese-occupied areas...

This is an extract from a summary of the statement given by Jiang Qing at her trial in 1980. It is taken from *A Great Trial in Chinese History* published by the New World Press in Beijing in 1981 and included in Alan Lawrance, *China Since 1919*, 2004

STUDENT STUDY SECTION

QUESTIONS

a) **Compare and contrast the views expressed in Sources A and B about how far the Gang of Four was under the control of Mao.**

b) **With reference to its origin and purpose, discuss the value and limitations of Source B for historians studying the Gang of Four.**

● **Examiner's hint**

When you are evaluating a source, be sure to include both the origin and purpose, as these are important for assessing the value and limitations. When answering this question, don't think only about what Jiang is saying (and why she may be saying these things), but also about when and where she said them. Also, consider where and when this document was originally published.

In the early 1970s after the Cultural Revolution had lost its fervour, the Gang of Four remained powerful. As long as Mao was alive, it seemed that no one dared criticize them. When Mao's health declined, however, a power struggle began for the succession. The Leftists disagreed with many of the economic policies of the Rightists.

The Leftists argued that decisions should be based on what was good for the revolution and not on what made economic sense. For example, communes should become self-sufficient in grain, even though not all communes were located in areas that were able to grow grain successfully. It wasn't efficiency, but ideology that mattered. They also said it was important for everyone to do some manual labour and they continued to emphasize this even when schools and universities reopened. It was still considered more important for students to have work experience than to do well in examinations.

Although the Rightists had some success in managing the economic recovery of China, the Gang of Four controlled propaganda and they continued to emphasize their policies.

SOURCE C

The leftists devoted much more attention to vilifying the followers of the 'capitalist road' than to figuring out how to make the socialist road function effectively. They emphasised spirit over material reality; they chose policies that displayed their own correct revolutionary attitudes… Thus, we have the story, supposedly true, of a man who was trying to fight a forest fire, but getting nowhere because he lacked effective tools. He finally gave a loud cry of 'Long live Chairman Mao', lay down and tried to put out the flames in his immediate vicinity by rolling on them. This had no significant effect on the fire, and he was quickly burned to death. His sacrifice accomplished nothing … but it demonstrated tremendous revolutionary dedication and lack of concern for self-interest. He was praised as a hero.

From Edwin E. Moise, *Modern China*, 1994

 ToK Time

Do you think people would have believed the story repeated in Source C? How effective is political propaganda? Josef Goebbels (Hitler's Minister of Propaganda) is often quoted as having said that if you repeat a lie often enough, people will eventually believe it. Would you agree with this? Can you think of examples where you think this has happened?

STUDENT STUDY SECTION

QUESTION

What does Source C tell us about the kind of propaganda that was used by the Leftists?

The death of Zhou and Mao

After a long illness, Zhou Enlai died of cancer in January 1976. The Gang of Four made sure that only a limited period of mourning was allowed for the leader of the Rightists. It was expected that Zhou would be succeeded by Deng Xiaoping, but instead, it was Hua Guofeng who became the new Prime Minister. Hua was a relatively unknown individual who had been a party official in Hunan province, the birthplace of Mao Zedong. He was a Leftist, but more moderate than the Gang of Four. Hua disliked them, because he thought Jiang Qing expressed her views very forcefully and expected to be obeyed. It was later rumoured that Hua was the son of Mao and that he went to great lengths to resemble him by combing his hair in the same way and puffing out his cheeks.

Mao trusted Hua more than he trusted Deng Xiaoping, and Hua became Mao's most likely successor. It was claimed that in April 1976 Mao told Hua, 'With you in charge, I am at ease.' Some sources even claim that this was Mao's last coherent sentence.

SOURCE D

Mao Zedong

Hua Guofeng

'Boundless confidence'. A poster by Han Shuo, May 1977. In this poster, Hua Guofeng is seated next to Mao Zedong. Mao is holding a pen and is about to write on a piece of paper. The implication is that Mao is about to write the words 'With you in charge, I am at ease.' It was rumoured that Mao had not only spoken these words but also written them.

STUDENT STUDY SECTION

QUESTION

With reference to its origin and purpose, discuss the value and limitations of Source D for historians studying the succession of Hua Guofeng.

Student Answer A – *Maria*

Source D is a poster by Han Shuo, published in May 1977 which shows Mao Zedong and Hua Guofeng at the moment of his appointment as Mao's successor. On that day, Mao pronounced the words, 'With you in charge, I am at ease' and this reflects the purpose of the poster itself, which is to give people the impression that Hua Guofeng really was Mao's successor. The poster is valuable for telling us about Hua Guofeng's concern with securing his succession and gaining support from the masses. However, it is a perfect example of propaganda and thus it doesn't give an objective view of Hua Guofeng's position. Besides, it does not give factual information but it is open to interpretation.

Student Answer B – *Kristabel*

Source D is a poster entitled 'Boundless Confidence', which was created in 1977 by the Chinese artist Han Shuo, depicting Hua Guofeng seated beside Mao Zedong. Its purpose was to portray the leaders in a relaxed, friendly and intimate state, in order to convince the public that they shared a close relationship, and that Hua Guofeng was the rightful successor to Mao Zedong, and supported by him in this position. Simply put, it was meant to instil confidence in those who read it that Hua Guofeng was confidently assuming leadership of the Communist Party, as he ought to. Source D is valuable because it shows how Hua Guofeng wished to be portrayed publicly in China. The existence of such a poster also suggests that Hua Guofeng did not feel entirely secure in his position, and needed propaganda to solidify it. Thus, this poster is also a valuable glimpse into his aims and insecurities at this time. It is also an example of the tactics Hua Guofeng used to ensure that his position was not questioned. Source D is limited because, as it is essentially propaganda, it presents an extremely biased view of the relationship between these two leaders. It does not provide any information about possible dissident views or the opinion of anyone other than Hua Guofeng and his supporters.

Examiner's comments

Maria does mention the origin and purpose of the poster quite concisely. She goes on to mention the value of the poster and refers to Hua's concern that he should be accepted as Mao' successor. She could say a little more here about how it would tell an historian that Hua certainly felt insecure enough to have posters such as this published. Maria could say a little more about the limitations of the source by stating that although it was intended to reinforce the belief that this event had really happened, it cannot be seen as a reliable source of what actually happened. She could also, perhaps, say that Hua was trying to associate himself with Mao Zedong and so win the support of the people, who still venerated Mao.

Kristabel explains the purpose of the poster in more detail than Maria and makes an interesting point about the way the poster gives the impression of a relaxed relationship between Hua and Mao. Also, Kristabel goes a little further in explaining the value of the poster to historians. The limitations are mentioned, but could be outlined more clearly. It is quite correct to describe this as propaganda and Kristabel says it gives an 'extremely biased view of the relationship'. Kristabel could be more careful when using 'biased' to describe this source. It is always a good idea to say why you think a source is biased. Always try to give some evidence of this. Here, for instance, Kristabel could say something about how it is unlikely that this event ever took place. In fact, it may be a good idea to resist using the word 'biased', as very few sources are not biased in one way or another.

● **Examiner's hint**
Don't forget to consider the historical context for this source. What was Hua Guofeng's position in 1977? How secure was he? Would a poster like this have a political purpose? What kind of impression was it supposed to make on the people who saw it?

The campaign against Deng Xiaoping

In 1976, the traditional Qing Ming festival took place in April. An important date in the Chinese calendar, this was when people would visit the graves of their ancestors to pay their respects to the dead. The CCP had tried to put an end to this tradition by denouncing it as 'superstitious', 'bourgeois' and an 'outmoded feudal custom'. In 1976, crowds of people defied the Party and turned this festival into a demonstration of loyalty and affection for Zhou Enlai. Thousands of wreaths were brought to Tiananmen Square in Beijing and laid at the Revolutionary Martyrs Memorial. Attached to the wreaths were poems that had a political message. The demonstrators were not only showing their support for Zhou (a Rightist) and his policies, but also their opposition to the policies of his opponents and, in particular, the Gang of Four. Almost immediately, orders were given to remove the wreaths and this led to demonstrations that in some cases turned violent.

The Politburo denounced this event as 'counter-revolutionary' but the April 5th Movement, as it became known, symbolized public protest against the government. Deng Xiaoping was blamed for having encouraged the demonstrators and he was dismissed from his positions as Vice Chairman of the Party and Chief of Staff of the PLA. Once again, he was denounced as 'the bourgeois inside the Party' and sent down to the countryside. Throughout the summer of 1976, there was an official campaign to denounce Deng, although this did not have much popular support.

It was a traditional belief in China that natural disasters preceded the death of an Emperor, and in July 1976 more than 250,000 people were killed when an earthquake measuring 8.2 on the Richter scale struck Tangshan near Beijing. In August, this disaster was followed by floods. Every effort was made to dampen public speculation and to criticize old beliefs, but Mao, 'the Emperor', was very sick and he died on 9 September 1976 at the age of 82.

The arrest of the Gang of Four

The death of Mao Zedong was followed by a week of mourning. Although political divisions appeared to be set aside, the fate of the Gang of Four hung in the balance now that they no longer had Mao's protection. Jiang Qing demanded to be given all of Mao's personal papers and it was rumoured that she was looking for (or intending to forge) a testament that named her as Mao's successor. Afraid of the threat they posed to his succession, Hua Guofeng plotted to have the Gang arrested.

Each member of the Gang was called to an emergency meeting of the Politburo scheduled for midnight on 5 October 1976 and on their arrival, they were arrested. A public statement was issued accusing the Gang of Four of plotting to assassinate Hua and take power. It is doubtful whether or not this was true because they did not have the necessary support among the Party officials or the PLA for such a bold plan.

It was barely five weeks since the death of Mao and Hua had acted decisively to secure his succession. He was fortunate to have the support of the main Party leaders and of the army. He was also fortunate that the Gang was isolated despite or maybe because of its role in the Cultural Revolution.

Deng Xiaoping

Zhou Enlai

SOURCE E

… the Four were not simply puppets suspended on strings pulled by Mao. They represented more than themselves and their personal ambitions, although not the workers and peasants whose interests they claimed to champion. About the countryside they knew little and among the peasants they were little known. Among the urban working class they could claim only scattered pockets of support; the mass organisations of the Cultural Revolution where they once

had had influence had long since been suppressed, while the conservative mass organisations that represented the bulk of the working class long had supported the veteran leaders of the Party and the PLA.

From Maurice Meisner, *Mao's China and After,* **1999**

STUDENT STUDY SECTION

QUESTION
What, according to Source E, were the reasons for the lack of support for the Gang of Four?

The return of Deng Xiaoping

Deng Xiaoping was forced to leave Beijing in the spring of 1976, but with the help of powerful friends he was smuggled back into the capital in October. Now, he waited for the right moment to recover his former position within the Party. Hua Guofeng, meanwhile, had a pressing problem. He needed to call a meeting of the Central Committee to be confirmed as Chairman of the CCP. Hua also knew that at the same time the Central Committee would probably call for the restoration of Deng. After many months of hesitation, the **Third Plenum** of the Tenth National Party Congress of the CCP was held in July 1977 and, as anticipated, Hua was confirmed as Chairman and Deng was also restored to his role in the leadership of the Party.

The demystification of Mao

Another dilemma for Hua was how to preserve his links to Mao, but also to 'manage' what became known as the 'demystification' of Mao. This revision of the past was not as dramatic as **Khrushchev's 'de-Stalinization' speech** in 1956. The historian Maurice Meisner points out that criticizing the legacy of Mao was rather more dangerous than criticizing Stalin. Meisner suggests that whereas Stalin could be accused of not being a true follower of Lenin, to demystify Mao risked undermining the whole legacy of the communist revolution in China. 'In condemning Stalin, Khrushchev could invoke the authority of Lenin. But for Mao's successors, there was no Chinese Lenin to call on other than Mao himself' (from Maurice Meisner, *Mao's China and After,* 1999).

Some careful distancing from the cult of Mao began when Hua Guofeng declared that the Cultural Revolution was officially over. Even so, Hua maintained the importance of Mao's ideas in a speech known as the 'Two Whatevers' (see Source F). This speech would later be countered by Deng Xiaoping, whose own interpretation of Mao Zedong Thought was 'Seek Truth from Facts'.

In 1981, the reputation of Mao Zedong was looked at critically and it was decided by the authorities that, overall, he had been '70 per cent good and 30 per cent bad'.

SOURCE F

Although Mao had wanted his remains sent to his home village, Hua arranged for a mausoleum to be built in Tiananmen Square in order to put Mao on permanent display. There millions of people have been able to pay their last respects to the larger than life figure somewhat swollen by embalming fluid. The new leadership continued to invoke Mao on whom the legitimacy of Hua's succession depended. The fact that he had arrested Mao's widow was no great problem although there was some muttering about the policies of the Gang of Four; the implication being that Mao himself was culpable. Soon after Hua took office, attempts were made to build up his image, with posters displaying portraits of Hua and Mao side by side and

The Third Plenum
A plenum is the name given to a meeting of the Central Committee that was elected by the latest National People's Congress of the CCP. The Third Plenum, for example, means the third time that there was a formal meeting of the Central Committee elected in 1973 by the Tenth National People's Congress of the CCP. After 1977, there was a Congress every five years.

Khrushchev's de-Stalinization speech
In 1956, at the Twentieth Party Congress, Nikita Khrushchev made a speech in which he criticized Stalin for his purge of Party members during the 1930s and for his cult of personality. Mao Zedong took exception to the criticism (especially about the cult of personality). Mao particularly resented Khrushchev's failure to consult with him before making this speech.

lavish praise of Hua in the press. In February 1977 the People's Daily *declared, 'We resolutely defend whatever policies Chairman Mao has formulated and unswervingly adhere to whatever instructions Chairman Mao has issued.' Those who adhered to this policy were to be categorised as the 'whateverists'.*

From Alan Lawrance, *China Under Communism*, 1998

SOURCE G

The balance of power appeared fairly even at first. Deng and the other recently rehabilitated rightists, while they pushed to reverse much of what Mao Zedong had done during the ten years of the Cultural Revolution, had to mute their public statements to avoid antagonising the 'Whatever' faction too badly. They blamed leftist excesses on Lin Biao and the Gang of Four, not on Mao himself. They pretended to regard the Cultural Revolution as a great and good thing, whose spirit had been violated by the vile actions of Lin Biao and the Gang of Four. However, as the months went by the Right wing consolidated its position and the Left weakened. The extent to which the changing evaluation of the Cultural Revolution as a whole was being re-evaluated was suggested by the changing evaluation of the Red Guards. People began to refer to them in public discussion of the Cultural Revolution as the 'beating, smashing and looting elements'.

From Edwin E. Moise, *Modern China*, 1994

STUDENT STUDY SECTION

QUESTION
Compare and contrast the views expressed in Sources F and G about how Mao was remembered.

Student Answer – *Kate*

Sources F and G suggest very different things about how Mao was remembered. Source F emphasizes how memories and veneration of Mao were used as a tool to justify Hua's leadership. Moreover, Source F suggests that 'millions' of people mourned Mao, by visiting the mausoleum that Hua created. Contrastingly, Source G suggests that China was very divided after Mao's death, with the leftists and rightists in an 'equal' balance of power. Moreover, it states that people were very critical of the Cultural Revolution, a policy Mao had created. Finally, Source G focuses to a greater extent on the aftermath of Mao's death, while Source F focuses on the use of Mao as a figurehead for a cult of personality. Sources F and G also have some similarities, however. Both mention the 'Whateverists', those who decided to follow any and all policies Mao had endorsed. Both also speak of the isolation of the Gang of Four, suggesting that they lost power and influence as time went on.

Examiner's comments

Kate has organized her answer correctly using what is called a 'comparative structure', as she has compared both sources and then contrasted them. The first paragraph in her answer focuses on differences between the two sources and she mentions how Source F has a strong focus on the way Mao was remembered. She could mention here how in Source G, the memory of Mao is addressed in a more neutral way, with more focus on the reluctance of the Rightists to criticize him too openly. Generally, she has mentioned a few similarities and a few differences and tried to support her points with evidence, although there could be a bit more of this. When you compare and contrast, it is a good idea to try to support your points either with a reference to the source or with a short quotation. Kate has just used single words like 'millions'. When she refers to the Gang of Four, she mentions their isolation etc., but could support this with some material from the sources.

The trial of the Gang of Four

The Gang of Four were arrested in late 1976, but were not put on trial until 1980. This allowed time for them to be forgotten and for the Rightists to consolidate their hold on power.

The trial began on 20 November 1980 and was televised. The prosecution argued that the Gang of Four had been linked to Lin Biao and they were charged with 48 separate offences, from attempting to assassinate Mao Zedong to the torture of the officials who were arrested during the Cultural Revolution.

Maurice Meisner suggests that the trial was important for the following reasons:
- It provided an opportunity to publicize the horrors of the 'cultural revolution decade'.
- It was a kind of 'catharsis' (emotional release) or a 'settling of accounts' for those who had suffered so much during the Cultural Revolution.
- For the Rightists, including Deng Xiaoping, who had been purged in the 1960s, it offered 'political revenge' and a chance to remove the Leftists from the Party.
- It provided the opportunity to question the role of Mao Zedong and his legacy.

As we have seen in Source B, Jiang Qing clearly implicated Mao Zedong in the actions of the Gang of Four. Among her more famous statements at her trial was 'I was Chairman Mao's dog. Whomever he told me to bite, I bit.'

The trial ended in 1981 and all four defendants were found guilty. Jiang Qing and Zhang Chunqiao were sentenced to death, but with a delay of two years to give 'time for repentance'. In both cases the death sentence was later commuted to life in prison. An unrepentant Jiang Qing died of cancer in 1991 and Zhang died, also of cancer, in 2005. Wang Hongwen was sentenced to life imprisonment and Yao Wenyuan to 20 years in prison.

REVIEW SECTION

In this section, we have looked at the events that followed the death of Mao Zedong in 1976 and have seen how Hua Guofeng was able to succeed Mao despite the Gang of Four. We have also considered how the aftermath of the Cultural Revolution was 'managed' and how China was able to move forward from an era when Mao Zedong Thought had been the guide to policy making. Write brief answers to the following questions, supporting your arguments with information both from the text and the sources.

Review questions
1. Give reasons for the failure of the Gang of Four to seize power after the death of Mao Zedong.
2. Why was the 'demystification' of Mao Zedong considered to be necessary?
3. What methods did Hua Guofeng use to consolidate his position as Chairman of the CCP?

ToK Time
Most of the books written in English about Chinese history are the work of historians who are not Chinese. Does this matter? Is it really possible for someone to understand the history of a country without having a first-hand knowledge of its culture and language? On the other hand, can you think of some reasons why it may be a good idea for historians to study the history of foreign countries rather than their own?

Section II:
China under Deng Xiaoping: economic policies and the Four Modernizations

This section will focus on how Deng Xiaoping ousted Hua Guofeng and pushed ahead with the Four Modernizations.

Mao indicated that Hua was his chosen successor, but there was only limited support for this former Minister of Public Security. Hua was the Chairman of the CCP, but his hold on power was not very secure. In Hua's favour, it could be said that he didn't represent any particular faction. He did not arouse strong opposition from either the Left (except for the Gang of Four) or the Right.

In 1977, Deng Xiaoping was restored to his former positions within the Party and Hua was quietly pushed into the background. Deng became 'paramount leader' and he promoted his supporters onto the Central Committee and the Politburo. Quietly but persistently, Deng undermined Hua. To start with, he kept his titles but lost his power and then lost even his titles.

The Third Plenum of the Eleventh National People's Congress and the removal of Hua Guofeng

Deng Xiaoping returned to a position of real influence in 1978 at the Third Plenum of the Central Committee Meeting of the Eleventh National People's Congress. It was in preparation for this meeting that Deng challenged the 'Whateverists', who were loyal to Mao's ideology, by making a speech entitled 'Emancipate the mind, seek truth from facts and unite as one in looking to the future.' Deng said that although revolutionary ideology was important in theory, to achieve economic progress China needed policies that actually worked in practice. He criticized the way in which 'Lin Biao and the Gang of Four set up ideological taboos [issues that could not be discussed]… and preached blind faith to confine people's minds within their phoney Marxism' (from Jonathan D. Spence et al., *The Search for Modern China*, 1999).

SOURCE A

When it comes to emancipating our minds, using our heads, seeking truth from facts and uniting as one in looking to the future, the primary task is to emancipate our minds. Only then can we, guided as we should be by Marxism-Leninism and Mao Zedong Thought, find correct solutions to the emerging as well as inherited problems, fruitfully reform those aspects of the relations of production and of the superstructure that do not correspond with the rapid development of our productive forces, and chart the specific course and formulate the specific policies, methods and measures needed to achieve the four modernisations under our actual conditions.

From the speech of Deng Xiaoping, 13 December 1978, to the Central Working conference of the Central Committee as it prepared for the Third Plenum of the Eleventh National People's Congress. Taken from Jonathan D. Spence et al., *The Search for Modern China*, 1999

STUDENT STUDY SECTION

QUESTION

With reference to its origin and purpose, discuss the value and limitations of Source A for historians studying the restoration to power of Deng Xiaoping.

SOURCE B

At the beginning of 1962, as the Party was preparing for a congress of 7,000 people amid a tide of boastful flattery, Deng Xiaoping made a wry comment: 'If something is so beautiful in the first place, why do we need to put make-up on it?' This was splendid. And again, at the lively third plenary session of the 11th Party Congress, there was no need for embroidery, no need to 'revise' history. In fact, reform wasn't discussed at the Third Plenum. Reform wasn't listed on the agenda, nor was it mentioned in the work reports. No one passed a motion calling for it, and there was no investigation into a possible reform program. At that time, Wan Li in Anhui was implementing his policy of 'household responsibility' for farmland, while Zhao Ziyang was trying out his policy of 'reforms to expand the self-determination of farmers and enterprises' in Sichuan. But they were local leaders at that time. The word 'reform' wasn't even in the vocabulary of central government leaders. The fact cannot be concealed or changed that reforms weren't the theme of the Third Plenum.

Bao Tong, former aide to ousted late premier Zhao Ziyang, wrote this anniversary essay from his Beijing home, where he lived under house arrest following his release from jail in the wake of the 1989 student protests. Written by Bao Tong for broadcast on the Mandarin service of Radio Free Asia.

STUDENT STUDY SECTION

QUESTION

Compare and contrast the views expressed about the aims of the Third Plenum in Sources A and B.

● **Examiner's hint**
It is a good idea when preparing your answer to list all the main similarities and all the differences for the two sources. This way, you can be sure of covering both the comparisons and the contrasts.

Although Hua Guofeng succeeded Mao as Chairman of the CCP in 1976, within three years the real power had transferred to Deng Xiaoping. Hua resigned as Premier of the State Council in 1980 and was replaced by Zhao Ziyang, one of Deng's protégés. Hua remained Chairman of the Party, but Deng revived the position of General Secretary of the Party, a position to which he appointed Hu Yaobang, his 'closest disciple'. Hua Guofeng resigned as Chairman in 1982 and this position was abolished.

✗ **ToK Time**
Students often consider primary sources to be more valuable than secondary sources. When someone says, 'I know it is true because I saw it happen' should we believe them? See if you can come up with arguments for and against this statement.

SOURCE C

Zhao Ziyang

Hu Yaobang

STUDENT STUDY SECTION

QUESTION

You can see here that both Zhao and Hu are wearing Western-style clothes. They were the first Chinese leaders to do this since the 1949 Revolution. What kind of message do you think they were trying to convey?

Student Answer – *Mary*

Wearing Western-style clothes, Zhao and Hu seem to criticize Mao as they were the symbols of the need to move away from the Cultural Revolution. Wearing Western-style clothes instead of the 'Mao suit' usually worn by Mao himself and Chinese leaders since the 1949 revolution, they were maybe trying to convey their criticism of what the revolution had brought about and their wish to move towards a more Western-style political system.

Self-criticism

During the Cultural Revolution, it was very common for anyone suspected of not fully supporting the policies of Mao Zedong to be forced to undergo 'self-criticism'. This often involved some kind of punishment, such as being beaten or forced to kneel on broken glass or hot charcoal and then made to confess to 'crimes' such as being a 'Rightist' or 'bourgeois' (terms of abuse that could be applied to anyone).

Examiner's comments

Mary is quite right to point out that seeing their leaders wearing a Western-style suit and tie sent an important message to the Chinese people. During the Cultural Revolution, anyone seen wearing Western-style clothes or even a Western hairstyle could be made to undergo '**self-criticism**'. Zhao and Hu were sending a message that China was now embracing Westernization. Also, they were sending a message to the Western leaders, who would see from this change in dress that China was ready to open up to outside influence and trade.

Economic reforms 1978–85

Even before his removal from Beijing in 1976, Deng had laid the groundwork for what became known as the Four Modernizations. This economic plan was first proposed by Zhou Enlai. He said that the Great Leap Forward and the Cultural Revolution had both shown that when revolutionary policies guided government polices, economic growth slowed down or came to a halt.

In 1975, Zhou Enlai and Deng Xiaoping called for the modernization of:

- Agriculture
- Industry
- National defence
- Science and technology.

During the late 1970s, the Leftists went along with this change of direction and allowed the Rightists to restore peasant plots and raise product subsidies in order to improve agricultural production. Wage differentials and greater technical specialization were allowed in industry to encourage higher industrial production. Deng's departure from Beijing in 1976 postponed the introduction of further reform, but his return in 1977 meant that the Four Modernizations could continue.

During the years 1978–85, Deng established his control over China. It was a period of strong economic growth and political stability. The following famous catch-phrases of Deng Xiaoping summed up his pragmatic attitude to post-Mao China:

- 'Seek Truth from Facts'
- 'It does not matter if a cat is black or white as long as it catches mice'
- 'To get rich is glorious'
- 'Not introducing reforms will take us down a blind alley'.

Deng wanted everyone to become more prosperous by encouraging economic growth, with more room for individual initiative and less emphasis on political ideology. There could be no stronger contrast with the policies of the Cultural Revolution, when it was frowned upon to make a profit.

Did this amount to capitalism?

Deng argued that it was a fundamental part of Marxist ideology that socialism grew out of capitalism. In other words, a bourgeois revolution was necessary before a proletariat revolution could take place. Deng maintained that in China a 'feudal mentality' had obstructed sustained economic growth because in pre-revolutionary times, feudalism had prevented capitalism from taking hold. Under communist rule, China needed more of a free-market economy, as this would increase wealth and advance the cause of socialism.

In 1979, Deng brought Hua Guofeng's ambitious but unsuccessful Ten Year Plan to an end and the focus shifted from heavy industry to agriculture and consumer goods. The intention was to help the economy grow faster and to encourage peasant farmers and workers to be more independent and therefore more entrepreneurial. In other words, they would become more motivated to work hard in order to make a profit, and so earn more money.

If you have read the chapter on the Soviet Union after 1976 (see Chapter 6), you can compare China to the Soviet Union during the 1980s, when both Andropov and Gorbachev were trying to introduce economic reforms. Like his Soviet counterparts, Deng felt that one of the biggest problems facing China's economy was the state bureaucracy. If the economy was to grow, it needed to respond quickly to demand and supply, rather like a free market. He felt that if every decision had to go through layers of bureaucracy generated by a central planning process, there would be no improvement in productivity and the reforms would fail.

Agriculture – the Household Responsibility System

In the 1970s, China was still largely an agricultural economy. Its population had grown rapidly, but there were few incentives to work hard and so production had barely increased. Deng Xiaoping was determined to bring about fundamental reforms and these began in December 1978. The vast communes of the Great Leap Forward were broken up into smaller **production units**, although the policy of collectivization remained. Collective planning was not efficient, but it was difficult to change because it was a legacy of the Mao era and was important for ideological reasons. Deng addressed this issue by persuading Party officials that production units should be given more freedom to make decisions and to run their own affairs. He sweetened this deal by raising the subsidies farmers received for the goods they produced.

One of Deng's closest supporters, Wan Li, was put in charge of the de-collectivization of agriculture. This became known as the 'Household Responsibility System'. Wan successfully introduced this system in Anhui province and then it was applied to the rest of China:

- Peasant farmers were allowed to rent plots, referred to as 'taking out a contract', although all land was still owned by the state.
- Arrangements could be made with the commune production team, who would decide what kind of crop should be planted and how much should be produced.
- Once a farmer had taken charge of his plot, he was given full control over the production process and was 'responsible' for 'paying' a quota of whatever he produced to the production team.
- If the farmer produced more than the required amount, he could sell this surplus to the commune or onto the local market.

In 1980, 15 per cent of all agricultural land was set aside as private plots, where peasants could grow whatever they wanted. By 1984 the communes of the Great Leap Forward had more or less been dismantled and farmers had increasing control over the land they farmed. This policy was a great success and eventually was applied to nearly all peasant farms. It was official policy 'to make the peasants rich' and annual contracts were replaced by contracts for 15 years (later this was increased to 30 years). Farmers were encouraged to invest time and money in 'their' land and to feel reassured that it would not be taken away from them.

An important development was to allow peasants who did not want to farm their plots to rent them out to other farmers. The next step was to allow contracts to be passed on from one generation to the next and make it possible to inherit land. All of these changes were intended to encourage peasant farmers to increase agricultural production.

Production units
The communes that were set up during the Great Leap Forward were broken up into smaller components known as 'production units'. By breaking up communes, Deng hoped to undermine the basis of the planned economy, removing control from bureaucrats and giving it to individual farmers and their families.

SOURCE D

THE EFFECT OF PRIVATIZATION ON THE RURAL ECONOMY			
	1957–78	1978–84	1984–88
Annual growth in grain production	2.0%	5.0%	-1.0%
Annual growth in agricultural value	1.4%	7.3%	3%

From Michael Lynch, *The People's Republic of China Since 1949*, 1998

This table illustrates the impact of the responsibility system on agricultural production, which grew sharply in the period 1978–84. You can see that after 1984, however, the annual growth rate fell again. Peasant farmers were still rather nervous about investing too much of their time and money in cultivating land they did not own. There was a move away from grain production to more heavily subsidized crops, such as rice, which was more profitable, but adversely affected output. By now, attention had also moved on to the industrial sector, which offered greater opportunities for employment and growth.

SOURCE E

As a result of the agricultural reforms, both yield and productivity rose sharply. In 1987, rice and wheat yields had risen 50% over those obtained under the commune system. More importantly, the farmer spent only an average of 60 days a year on the crops compared with 250 to 300 days a year in the field in the days of farm collectives. The time saved was spent on sideline activities aimed at profit. Cash income quadrupled and the standard of living vastly improved… In Sichuan and many other provinces, the contracted quota accounted for approximately one-sixth of total output, and although most plots were less than one acre in size, there was enough food raised for each household.

From Immanuel C. Y. Hsu, *The Rise of Modern China*, 1995

STUDENT STUDY SECTION

QUESTION

What, according to Source E, were the benefits of the agricultural reforms for the peasant farmers?

Student Answer – *Arthur*

The agricultural reform has increased the productivity for the farmers. This has resulted in two consequences. First, they can now produce enough food for their own consumption. Second, the extra time generated is allocated to other income-generating activities. This has contributed to a higher level of income for the farmers. The reforms have raised the standard of living for all the peasants.

Examiner's comments

Arthur has pointed out that productivity went up and, implicitly, that yield has also increased. He could state this more clearly. He also states that the peasants could engage in other activities, although he could make this clearer by linking this statement to how private plots were more labour efficient. The response is good and very concise.

Industry – the Sichuan Experiment

Zhao Ziyang, one of Deng's close supporters, used a similar system of 'responsibility' to encourage industrial workers to increase productivity. Zhao had been a long-time associate of Deng and by the late 1970s he was Party Secretary in Sichuan province. Here, he applied Wan Li's 'responsibility' model to industry. Known as the 'Sichuan Experiment', factories were given more freedom and independence or more 'responsibility' to produce goods that would be bought by the state. If they produced more than required, they could sell the surplus for a profit.

The problem, however, was that most factories in China were state-owned. The State Owned Enterprises (SOEs) were large and inefficient, but they had power and political influence. For workers, they provided a job for life, as well as benefits such as housing and medical care. A less secure free-market system was not as attractive to the bosses or the workers of these heavy industries.

The encouragement of private business was an important economic target, but it was difficult for entrepreneurs to prosper without a ready source of **capital**. Progress at first was slow, but once the government introduced market reforms, including a legal framework to protect private investment, more people felt able to take a risk and to try to find ways to make money. As the farmers and city workers grew richer, there was an increased demand for consumer goods, which provided the stimulus for the development of light, low-capital, family-based industries.

Capital (economic)
In economics, capital is anything man-made used in the production of goods and services, for example, a machine or a building. Capital is one of the four factors of production along with land, labour and entrepreneurship.

SOURCE F

As in the countryside, small enterprises in the cities requiring less capital were relatively more profitable. This was where the enthusiastic small entrepreneurial family came into its own; the figures show 100,000 private businesses registered in 1978, 6 million in 1983 and 17 million in 1985.

From Alan Lawrance, *China Under Communism*, 1998

SOURCE G

CHINA'S INDUSTRIAL PERFORMANCE, 1979–90				
Year	Gross Domestic Product (in millions of yuan)	GDP Growth Rate (% pa)	Inflation Rate (% pa)	Manufacturing Output Growth Rate (% pa)
1979	732.6	7.6	6.1	8.6
1980	790.5	7.9	-1.5	11.9
1981	826.1	4.5	7.0	1.6
1982	896.3	8.5	11.5	5.5
1983	987.7	10.2	8.3	9.2
1984	1130.9	14.5	12.9	14.5
1985	1276.8	12.9	1.8	18.1
1986	1385.4	8.5	3.3	8.3
1987	1539.1	11.1	4.7	12.7
1988	1713.1	11.3	2.5	15.8
1989	1786.7	4.3	3.1	4.9
1990	1856.4	3.9	7.3	2.0

From Michael Lynch, *The People's Republic of China Since 1949*, 1998

This table illustrates the strong impact economic reforms had on Gross Domestic Product and Manufacturing Output, which grew at remarkable rates. Unfortunately, when growth was strongest, inflation picked up, and the government had to slow down the economy to control inflationary pressures. The government restrained the economy in late 1988, but this led to higher unemployment rates, which sparked worker tolerance of and participation in the student-led demonstrations in 1989.

STUDENT STUDY SECTION

QUESTION

What does Source G tell you about the rate of growth in China in the 1980s?

GDP growth rate

By the early 21st century, the CCP considered a growth rate of 8 per cent to be the minimum requirement to avoid social unrest. A growth rate of less than 8 per cent would probably result in higher unemployment levels and, possibly, a crisis of confidence in the ability of the CCP to provide a sound economy.

SOURCE H

Although rising consumption was due primarily to rising incomes, it was aided by the Deng government's vigorous encouragement of what proved to be an astonishingly rapid revival of private entrepreneurship in both city and countryside. In addition to thriving rural markets and fairs, in the early 1980s city streets were quickly transformed by the reappearance of peddlers and vendors selling various wares and foods, the opening of private restaurants and inns, and the establishment of many new retail and service businesses – from barbers and beauticians to television repair shops. By 1984, according to official figures, nearly 4,000,000 people were employed or self-employed in the burgeoning private sector of the urban economy and more than 32 million worked in urban 'collective' enterprises, which more and more operated in a capitalist fashion in an increasingly market driven economy.

From Maurice Meisner, *Mao's China and After*, 1999

STUDENT STUDY SECTION

QUESTION
What evidence is given in Source H to support the claim that there was a revival of 'private entrepreneurship' in urban areas?

The Special Economic Zones (SEZs)

As well as stimulating small-scale local business, Deng wanted China to attract larger-scale international enterprises, so he promoted an '**Open Door Policy**' which he hoped would bring in:

- Foreign direct investment
- Modern technology
- Access to export markets.

In order to achieve these objectives, Deng set up four Special Economic Zones (SEZs) in 1979 in Guangdong and Fujian provinces. These were:

- Shenzhen
- Zhuhai
- Shantou
- Xiamen.

The SEZs were almost like separate countries; non-residents needed special permission and an internal passport to travel to them. Inside these zones, roads, railways and port facilities were built by the Chinese government. Foreign joint venture companies, especially from Hong Kong, were encouraged to set up factories. These foreign investors were attracted by a relatively cheap, educated pool of labour, combined with promises of a market-based approach to business decisions. Deng Xiaoping knew that China needed to speed up its economic development and the quickest way to achieve this was to bring in foreign expertise. Local managers were expected to learn business methods from foreign firms, who would hopefully bring in the latest machinery for the factories and train the workers.

Open Door Policy
This referred to Deng's combination of foreign policy and economic reform. He wanted China to maintain an independent foreign policy (so not closely tied to any other power), but also to develop trade links with other countries.

SOURCE I

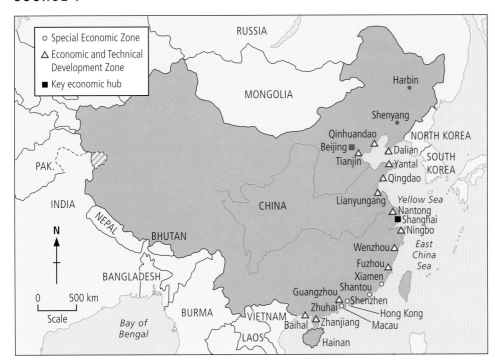

◀ **Map 15**

This is a map showing the SEZs. In addition to the four SEZs, the area around Hainan Island, as well as the estuaries of the Pearl, Min and Yangzi rivers, were opened up to development in 1984.

SOURCE J

CHINA'S EXTERNAL PERFORMANCE, 1979–90					
Year	Foreign Direct Investment, net inflows (current USD millions)	Official Development Assistance and Official Aid (current USD millions)	External Debt (current USD millions)	Exports (% of GDP)	Imports (% of GDP)
1979	1	16	n/a	9	9
1980	57	65	n/a	11	11
1981	265	475	5797	13	12
1982	430	523	8358	12	10
1983	636	668	9609	11	10
1984	1258	797	12081	11	11
1985	1659	938	16695	10	14
1986	1875	1095	23719	12	15
1987	2314	1377	35339	16	16
1988	3194	1919	42438	17	18
1989	3393	2070	44932	17	18
1990	3487	2030	55301	19	16

From the World Bank Online Data Enquiry Service, accessed March 2009

This table illustrates the strong impact Deng's Open Door Policy had on the external economic relations of the People's Republic of China. There was a significant increase in foreign direct investment into China, but at the same time the government attracted larger volumes of aid and took on heavier levels of external debt. This large infusion of foreign capital was used to develop the Chinese economy and make it more export-orientated. You can see this from the increasing levels of GDP devoted to exports and imports of goods and services from 1980 onwards.

ToK Time

'There are three kinds of lies: lies, damned lies and statistics' (Benjamin Disraeli).

The use of numbers to add support to an argument can be very persuasive, but could one table of statistics be used to argue two points of view?

How, do you think, could the table of statistics in Source J be used both by critics of Deng's economic policies and supporters of Deng's economic policies?

STUDENT STUDY SECTION

QUESTION

With reference to its origin and purpose, assess the value and limitations of Source J for historians studying the economic development of China during the 1980s.

Student Answer – Arturo

Source J is a collection of economic data of China's External Performance from 1979 to 1990. It is retrieved from the World Bank. Its purpose is to demonstrate the improving economic performance as a result of Deng's Open Door Policy. The value of Source J is its credibility since it is from the World Bank data archive. This is very important for historians who are looking for a quantitative approach to account for the rapid economic development in China. However, the source is rather limited. There is not much information about how people in the interior had different income levels from the people who lived on the coast. The data provided is merely numbers. They fail to outline all the details of specific economic projects. It would be hard for historians to analyze economic development in a precise manner.

Examiner's comments

There are some good comments here. The origin and purpose of the table of statistics are mentioned, although it is probably not correct to say that the World Bank is aiming to show how Deng's policy is improving! The purpose of this table could be to provide statistical information for researchers or economists who would be interested in this topic. The statistics are not meant to present any particular point of view. Arturo could also say more about the value of the table and its origin. The World Bank would need to have accurate statistics and so it could be assumed that it has different methods of gathering this information. It is important that the information is reliable because the World Bank is a reputable organization and it needs to be trustworthy. There is an attempt to assess the limitations of the source, and the comments are quite valid and linked to the question of how this source would be used by historians. As Arturo says, the data are 'just numbers', but it might have been more useful to say something about how difficult it may have been to collect statistics. If you are discussing statistics related to a single-party state that controls access to information, then it is worth pointing this out as a limitation.

Hong Kong

The British took control of Hong Kong in 1842 as part of what China called an 'unequal treaty' following China's defeat in the First Opium War. After the Second Opium War in 1860, Great Britain took control of the peninsula of Kowloon. In 1898, it made an agreement to 'lease' the New Territories, the land that lay to the north of Kowloon. This 'lease' was for 99 years, and expired in 1997. Although China could 'legally' reclaim only the New Territories, both Britain and China knew that if China wanted to take back the whole of Hong Kong, it could do so and Britain could not prevent it. The negotiations on the return of Hong Kong to China began in 1984 and were completed with the total handover in 1997, just months after the death of Deng Xiaoping at the age of 92.

'Opening the window will let in flies' (Deng Xiaoping)

Deng knew that the SEZs would become more and more like capitalist Hong Kong and that the people who lived and worked in the SEZs would come into contact with Western ideas. By limiting access to these zones, Deng tried to make sure that any 'bad influences' would be kept under control and would spread less quickly to the rest of the country.

There was also, however, a political motive for the development of these SEZs. Deng hoped that both Hong Kong and Taiwan would soon be 'brought back' to China. In his view, although they were outside its control, both of these territories 'belonged' to China. Both **Hong Kong** and **Taiwan** had successful but strongly capitalist economies. Deng believed that if he could show that China had capitalist zones, the citizens of Hong Kong and Taiwan would more readily accept 'returning' to China. He called this policy, 'One Country, Two Systems'.

The mid 1980s

In 1984, Deng stated that he had three main ways in which to improve the economy:
- To give more autonomy to state enterprises, emphasizing the importance of making a profit.
- To 'smash **the iron rice bowl**' and so increase the productivity of workers.
- To allow the price of goods, especially food and consumer goods, to be determined by market forces.

Despite the difficulty of achieving these objectives, by the mid 1980s China had plenty of people eager and willing to make the most of new opportunities to create wealth. This was a very different experience from that of the Soviet Union and the failure of *perestroika*.

At a meeting in June 1984, Deng Xiaoping explained his interpretation of what he called 'Building Socialism with a Specifically Chinese Character'.

SOURCE K

Capitalism can enrich less than 10% of the Chinese population; it can never enrich the remaining 90%. But if we adhere to socialism and apply the principle of distribution to each according to his work, there will not be excessive disparities in wealth. Consequently, no polarisation will occur as our productive forces become developed over the next 20–30 years. The minimum target of our modernisation programme is to achieve a comparatively comfortable standard of living by the end of the century… We shall accumulate new experience and try new solutions as new problems arise. In general, we believe that the course we have chosen, which we will call building socialism with Chinese characteristics, is the right one.

From 'Building Socialism with a Specifically Chinese Character', a speech given by Deng Xiaoping to a delegation from Japan on 30 June 1984. Reprinted in Alan Lawrance, *China Since 1919*, 2004

STUDENT STUDY SECTION

QUESTION
What, according to Source K, were the benefits of 'building socialism with Chinese characteristics'?

Taiwan
The island of Formosa was occupied by the Japanese in 1895. In 1949, Chiang Kai-shek and the Guomindang fled to Formosa (renamed Taiwan) after losing the civil war to the communists. The government of Taiwan always maintained it was officially the government of China and never claimed independence. It represented China in the United Nations until 1972.

The iron rice bowl
This was a metaphor for jobs for life. The reference to the rice bowl suggests a worker's livelihood and 'iron' suggests it would be long lasting.

How successful were the Four Modernizations?

Deng maintained that reform had to start in the countryside and, at first, emphasis was placed on changing the methods of agricultural production. The family had replaced the commune as an economic unit and peasant farmers would benefit from how hard they worked as individuals rather than being rewarded for their work as part of a team. The Household Responsibility System expanded rapidly and production increased. The Party still maintained that land could not be owned by individuals and that although peasants could farm the land, it was still owned by the state. In practice the collectivization of agriculture was now virtually over in China.

In industry, change began slowly because so many of the industrial enterprises in China were owned by the state. There was less opportunity here for entrepreneurs but, gradually, small workshops were set up by individuals who hired workers and operated in a market environment.

The SEZs made the biggest difference to the economy. Shenzhen was especially successful in attracting foreign direct investment, becoming more and more capitalist. At first, most of the work carried out in the SEZs was basic manufacturing and, whatever Deng had intended, the foreign companies used the workers as cheap, unskilled labour. Also, initially, most of the goods produced were consumed inside China and not exported, but over time this changed as the skill levels and product quality improved.

Some Party leaders had been sceptical and resistant to Deng's reforms, but they quickly realized that they were able to decide who would benefit from foreign investment flows and became less critical of the new capitalist ways. They were able to make connections with foreign joint venture partners as well as find jobs for their relatives in the SEZs, where wages and living standards were higher.

There were a number of cases of open bribery and corruption, notably one on Hainan Island in 1985, when the governor was dismissed for circumventing import regulations on motor vehicles. Behind closed doors, it was rumoured that Deng's famous catch-phrase should have been amended to 'It doesn't matter whether a cat is black or white, it doesn't even matter whether a cat catches mice. What matters is that the cat does not get caught.'

Of course, not everyone grew rich; not everyone had a job; and the gap between the poor and the wealthy widened. The Open Door Policy favoured the coastal cities, where incomes grew much faster than in the largely rural interior. Pressure built for internal migration from the rural areas to the cities in search of higher incomes and a better lifestyle. Rapid economic growth also put a strain on the infrastructure of the country. There were problems with getting enough raw materials to where they were needed and so production was not always able to keep up with demand. This also led to higher inflation, and demand grew faster than supply.

Action to slow down inflation and control large budget deficits in government spending resulted in higher levels of unemployment, especially among the internal migrants and new graduates. Reduction in subsidies and support for workers in state-owned organizations also fuelled discontent and growing unease about the future. The second half of the 1980s held problems for the leadership of the CCP as it tried to push ahead with economic reform without giving in to demands for democratic reform.

STUDENT STUDY SECTION

QUESTION

Using the sources in this section and your own knowledge, write a short essay answering the following question:

'By 1984, Deng's modernizations had successfully brought about the modernization of agriculture and industry.' How far would you agree with this judgement?

Student Answer – *Yuri*

Deng's economic modernization programmes have provided a clear legal framework to attract more foreign direct investment into China. The way he and his cabinet promoted the ideas also transformed people's views about economics. Consequently, the agricultural productivity increased by 50 per cent (Source E). FDI net inflows were increased from $1 million in 1979 to $1,659 million in 1985. Although China took on more external debt to provide capital for its domestic investment, exports were increased from 9 per cent to 11 per cent of GDP. The current account balance was achieved at the second half of the 1980s (Source J).

In addition, the establishment of the household responsibility system successfully motivated peasants to look after their small production units and generate wealth for themselves. Ultimately, they were transformed into small, rural enterprises without the need for central planning. This helped to increase the yield and the efficiency of work (Source H). Nevertheless, the industrial reform was relatively less successful by 1985. Most heavy industries and factories were state owned by that time. Workers had little incentive to innovate and work harder. This phenomenon could be attributed to a large and inefficient corporate structure, as well as an incompletely established free market. For instance, the Sichuan experiment shows this.

Besides, emphasis was placed on allowing the people living in the coastal cities to get rich first. This has led to an income disparity. Thus it caused people to emigrate from the interior to the coast, putting heavy social burdens on it. Also, a more liberal market structure has led to corruption between officials and entrepreneurs.

Examiner's comments

Yuri has used both the sources and 'own knowledge' here. It is a fairly brief response, however, and it is a good idea to aim for around 600 words rather than 250! Don't forget that this is a short essay response so, just like a longer essay, it is a good idea to plan. Unlike Yuri, you should begin with an introduction where you refer to the question and briefly put it in context, but saying something about Deng and what he aimed to do. The question asks you to measure the success of the modernization of agriculture and industry and these two parts give you a structure for your answer.

Yuri does address agriculture, but doesn't say much about it. He could refer to Source D as well as Source E and also say quite a lot more about the incentive provided by the 'responsibility system'. Industry is also neglected and although he refers to the SOEs, he does not explain the problems with reforming these large industries. The SEZs are referred to but, again, more could be said about this and a reference made to their location and purpose. At least Yuri has indicated some sources, although these could be used more fully by including quotes and some analysis of their content.

Yuri could also 'answer the question' more clearly. Was there successful modernization of agriculture and industry by 1984? Yuri implies that there was some modernization but there were also problems. This is good but he needs to develop his analysis and to support it.

REVIEW SECTION

This section has dealt with the removal of Hua Guofeng and the emergence of Deng Xiaoping as the 'paramount leader' of China. We have also looked at the methods used by Deng to accelerate economic growth and to encourage Chinese workers and managers to respond to market forces and produce more of what was needed.

Consider the following questions and see if you can come up with answers using the text and the sources from this section.

Review questions

1 Why did Deng think it was necessary to carry out economic reforms in China?

2 What kind of methods did he use to improve agricultural production and did this change peasant life?

3 Why was it more difficult to change the working habits and production levels of industrial workers?

4 Were his economic reforms successful?

ToK Time
When we study the history of the People's Republic of China, we come across many examples of memorable phrases that are used to name events or campaigns. For example: the Great Leap Forward; the Cultural Revolution; the May 4th Movement; the April 5th Movement; the Four Modernizations; One Country, Two Systems.

Can you think of reasons why these names were given to different events or policies? See what you can find out about the significance of certain numbers in Chinese culture.

Section III:
China under Deng Xiaoping: political changes and their limits, culminating in Tiananmen Square (1989)

This section deals with the growing demands for more political freedom. Deng Xiaoping had encouraged criticism of the Leftists, and displays of public opposition to the Gang of Four had helped him to return to the party leadership in 1978. When the criticism went further than criticism of the Left, however, Deng took a different view and limited the opportunities for political debate.

Hu Yaobang and Zhao Ziyang came to the fore in the 1980s as leaders of the CCP, but it was Deng who remained 'paramount leader'. Eventually, both Hu and Zhao lost the support of

Deng because they supported a more democratic system, and in 1989 in his response to the Tiananmen Square protests Deng demonstrated just how determined he was to keep a tight control over the state.

Social reforms – education

Deng knew that China needed well-educated citizens and he also knew that education could no longer be directed by revolutionary ideology. Mao feared that the students who did best at school and were most likely to go on to higher education were the children of the 'middle classes' (by now, the Party cadres) and in turn, their children were more likely to do well in examinations. Meanwhile, the children of peasants or unskilled workers were less likely to succeed and so, unless education was drastically reformed, a class system would be perpetuated.

This situation was one of the reasons for the Cultural Revolution, when the system was changed so that a student could not go to university without a good work record and the recommendation of his or her work team. Coming from the 'right class', i.e. a worker or a peasant class, now substantially improved a student's chances of getting into university.

During the Cultural Revolution, there had been a strong focus on making a basic level of education available to all rather than putting money and resources into providing a good level of education for a few. After the Cultural Revolution, this policy was reversed and certain schools now became 'centres of excellence' and were given the best teachers, the best facilities and the best students. Written examinations were reintroduced and the brightest pupils could go directly to university from secondary school without having to do manual labour. The exams were deliberately made very challenging, and in 1980 only 4.8 per cent of high school students were successful in gaining a place to study at university. Even so, by the mid to late 1980s there would be a problem with finding employment opportunities for graduates.

SOURCE A

In education there was a new stress on academic achievement and a downgrading of egalitarian ideals. Leftist leaders had stressed the goal of giving at least some sort of education to everyone; they had hoped to make not only primary education but also several years of secondary schooling universal as quickly as possible. The moderate leadership that came to power in 1976 did not completely abandon these goals but it assigned them a lower priority. The main thrust after 1976 was now providing a really good education to a limited number of people.

From Edwin E. Moise, *Modern China*, 1994

During the Cultural Revolution, intellectuals had been especially targeted for criticism and had been categorized as the 'stinking ninth'. This phrase meant that they were at the bottom of a list of categories of people known as the 'revisionist' classes or, in other words, people who were not considered to be revolutionary and who were 'bourgeoisie' or 'capitalist roaders'. All these terms were insults and it could be dangerous to be labelled in this way. Things began to change, however, and in a speech given in 1980, Hu Yaobang announced the rehabilitation of the intellectuals.

SOURCE B

We must value intellectuals and attach due importance to culture and education. Intellectuals play an important role. In our country there is a general lack of learning among our people, and learning is inseparable from intellectuals. We have not yet finished our job of implementing the relevant policies towards intellectuals. Intellectuals have not been used appropriately enough. They still face many practical problems, such as housing, separation from spouses and wages… Now, when the intellectuals have just begun to raise their heads, a few comrades are trying to beat them down. This demands that we work on these comrades.

Hu Yaobang speaking in 1980. From Edwin E. Moise, *Modern China*, 1994

SOURCE C

In the cities, the intellectuals were often poorly paid. One heard jokes that a man who repaired the outside of the head (a barber) could make more money than a man who repaired the inside of the head (a brain surgeon). Salaries for teachers were so low that some observers expressed astonishment at their dedication, their willingness to go on trying to educate their students when given hardly any reward.

From Edwin E. Moise, *Modern China*, 1994

SOURCE D

'Advance bravely along the road of socialism with Chinese characteristics', Peng Bin, Zheng Hongliu, Xu Baozhong, Cui Yong, 1989. Instead of farmers and industrial workers, intellectuals occupy the first row. Science and technology are seen as important factors in production, more so than muscle power.

> **Democracy Wall and 'big character' posters**
> A wall in Beijing that was used for the public display of posters that would detail criticisms of the government's policies, Democracy Wall was a way for ordinary people to voice their opinions. The 'big character' posters had large characters written on them so that they could be read easily when pasted on a wall. This had been a traditional way for public opinion to be expressed, even in imperial times.

STUDENT STUDY SECTION

QUESTION
What do Sources A, B, C and D tell you about China's changing attitudes towards education? Support your points with evidence taken from the sources.

● **Examiner's hint**
Look at each source in turn and make a note of what each one tells us. For example, in Sources A and B, does it seem that the Party has agreed on what it wants to do about education? What does Source C tell you about how much change had actually taken place? Source D is a propaganda poster – what message is it trying to convey? Whom is it meant to persuade?

The Fifth Modernization – the Democracy Movement

After the fall of the Gang of Four, there was an easing of censorship, and in November 1978 a **Democracy Wall** was set up in Beijing. This was backed by Deng Xiaoping, as many of the '**big character**' posters supported his return to power. The Wall was also very useful for public criticism of the Cultural Revolution and even Maoist policies. As long as these posters were directed against the Left, Deng allowed them to be displayed.

China's invasion of Vietnam in 1979 ⓘ

China supported North Vietnam during its war against South Vietnam and the USA. This conflict ended in 1975 when the communist forces of the North occupied the South. In 1978, Vietnam invaded Kampuchea (Cambodia) to remove the government of the Khmer Rouge and Pol Pot. The reasons for the invasion included Vietnam's opposition to the genocidal policy of the Pol Pot; its territorial ambitions to create a Greater Vietnam; and the deep division between a Soviet client state (Vietnam) and a Chinese client state (Kampuchea). China distrusted Vietnam's ambitions and sent an army across the northern border in 1979 'to teach Vietnam a lesson'. Although it was claimed that China struck a decisive blow against Vietnam, the reality was that the Vietnamese Army succeeded in overthrowing Pol Pot and, furthermore, drove the PLA back into China.

● **Examiner's hint**

Don't forget that it is the big character poster that you are evaluating here and not 'China since 1919'.

The Democracy Wall was a local phenomenon and its biggest impact was on people who lived in Beijing who could gather round to read the posters. News about the posters spread to other areas of China, however, and journalists from foreign news agencies wrote about the Wall or made news broadcasts from the Wall. Here was another way of spreading news of the Wall inside China, as many Chinese citizens listened to the BBC World Service.

For Deng, the Democracy Wall served another purpose, as it echoed his call for reform within the Party. For instance, there were calls for a reappraisal of the April 5th Movement (the Tiananmen demonstrations that followed the death of Zhou Enlai in 1976) and for these demonstrations to be re-categorized as 'revolutionary' rather than 'counter-revolutionary'. The posters of the dissidents who supported the Four Modernizations were tolerated until a pro-democracy movement sprang up calling for the 'Fifth Modernization'. How, it was asked, could effective and far-reaching economic change take place without the establishment of a democratic political system?

SOURCE E

Those who worry that democracy will lead to anarchy and chaos are just like those who, following the overthrow of the Qing dynasty (in 1911), worried that, without an emperor, the country would fall into chaos. Their recommendation was: Patiently suffer oppression! For without the weight of oppression, the roofs of your homes might fly off! To such people, I would like to say, with all due respect: We want to be the masters of our own destiny. We need no gods or emperors and we don't believe in saviours of any kind. We want to be masters of our universe; we do not want to serve as mere tools of dictators with personal ambitions for carrying out modernisation. We want to modernise the lives of the people. Democracy, freedom, and happiness for all are our sole objectives in carrying out modernisation. Without this 'Fifth Modernisation', all other modernisations are nothing but a new promise.

From a big character poster by Wei Jingsheng put up on Beijing's Democracy Wall on 5 December 1978, published in Alan Lawrance, *China Since 1919*, 2004

STUDENT STUDY SECTION

QUESTION

With reference to its origin and purpose, assess the value and limitations of Source E for historians studying political reform in the 1980s.

Wei Jingsheng had been a Red Guard during the Cultural Revolution and he used big character posters to complain about the lack of democracy. He also complained about **China's invasion of Vietnam**. Wei was arrested in March 1979, tried for 'counter-revolutionary' activities and sentenced to 15 years in prison. He was released in 1993, resumed his criticism of the government and, in 1995, was sentenced to a further 14 years in prison. Interestingly, he was not accused, this time, of 'counter-revolution' because this was no longer classified as a crime. Instead, Wei was tried for 'conspiracy to subvert the government'. He was released after two years and sent into exile.

Now that he no longer needed the support of the protestors, Deng silenced the call for change and closed the Democracy Wall in December 1979. The following year, it became illegal to put up wall posters.

Although Deng Xiaoping was eager to improve the Chinese economy and to encourage entrepreneurship, he considered democracy and a multi-party system to be dangerous for China. He reminded the Chinese people that the Four Fundamental Principles still applied. These were:

● The Socialist Road
● The People's Democratic Dictatorship

- The Leadership of the Communist Party
- Marxism-Leninism and Mao Zedong Thought.

For Deng Xiaoping, the growing demand for democracy was an example of 'bourgeois liberalism' and China needed to be protected from this.

SOURCE F

[Deng Xiaoping] was a curious mixture of economic progressivism and political conservatism, endowed with a gift for playing a balancing act as political necessity dictated. In a system where the rule of man superseded the rule of law, he was the supreme arbiter. In his mind, economic reforms and an open-door policy were but means by which to borrow foreign technology, capital and managerial skills. These were seen as tools with which to strengthen Communist rule, but never as steps to move the country toward a Western-style democracy.

From Immanuel C. Y. Hsu, *The Rise of Modern China*, 1995

SOURCE G

Deng's aim was to restore the morale and the standing of the CCP after the disruptive decades of the Great Leap Forward and the Cultural Revolution. He wanted to show that the Communist Party was still capable of governing China and had the right to the loyalty of the people. It is broadly correct to see Deng Xiaoping as a reformer but only in the economic sphere. In politics he was a CCP hardliner… His belief in the authority of the CCP as the only legitimate shaper of China's destinies was unshakeable. It was this conviction that made a major showdown between the old-guard CCP and the supporters of democracy increasingly likely.

From Michael Lynch, *The People's Republic of China Since 1949*, 1998

STUDENT STUDY SECTION

QUESTION
Compare and contrast the views expressed in Sources F and G about Deng's role as a reformer.

Deng favoured political reform, but reform of the CCP, not reform of the single-party system. He sensed that the CCP had been damaged by the excesses of Mao Zedong and that it needed to be restored to a position of undisputed authority. At the same time, Deng wanted to reassure the people that, unlike the Cultural Revolution, when anyone could be a target for punishment, there would be no arbitrary harassment of 'revisionists'. As long as they did not question the authority of the Party or ask for more political freedom, Chinese citizens could live without fear of being made to undergo 'self-criticism'.

From 1985 to Tiananmen Square: No turning back

By the mid 1980s, communes were being disbanded and small businesses were permitted as part of the Four Modernizations. There was more freedom to look for work, to accumulate wealth and to be an 'entrepreneur', but the state also became less involved in providing basic necessities.

Reforms in agriculture had gone ahead rather smoothly, but in industry, change meant an end to the 'iron rice bowl' jobs in the SOEs. For industrial workers, jobs in the SOEs had provided not only guaranteed employment, but also food coupons, free health care and free education for their families. As pressure grew to modernize the big state-owned factories, unemployment started to rise and beggars were seen more often on the streets of the main cities. Criticism was made of the changes brought about by economic reform, but there was also criticism of 'Western-style' individualism in literature, fashion and music.

Traditionally, the CCP would allow a certain amount of change, only to clamp down when this went too far. For instance, when the left-wing revolutionary policies of the Great Leap Forward failed, there was a return to a more moderate economic system. The same happened after the excesses of the Cultural Revolution. What would happen now that there was criticism of the right-wing policies of Deng Xiaoping?

Determined to keep the Chinese economy growing, Deng was sure that there could be no turning back, but he was equally determined not to give in to demands for what he called 'bourgeois democracy'. Deng saw the changes in Poland at the start of the 1980s and believed that the strikes and demonstrations organized by Solidarity led directly to martial law. Deng did not want this to happen in China and so demands for political change had to be handled carefully. No concessions were to be made but, if possible, confrontation was also to be avoided.

The student demonstrations of 1986

By 1982, Deng's most likely successors were Zhao Ziyang, the Prime Minister, and Hu Yaobang, the General Secretary of the Party. Both gave the impression of being in favour of more reform and both were to lose power because of their support for student protests. President Ronald Reagan visited China in 1984 and in a speech given in the Great Hall of the People in Beijing, he had spoken of freedom and of 'trust in the people'. His speech was censored before it was printed in the Chinese press, but he made a similar speech in Shanghai. In *The Rise of Modern China*, Immanuel Hsu argues that although President Reagan had spoken in English and there was no subtitled translation of this televised speech, his message got across and it was not long before uncensored copies of both his speeches were being distributed illegally.

In 1986, in order to strengthen the CCP, Deng introduced small changes to the electoral system for the selection of representatives to local congresses. Before these elections were held, university students in Wuhan, Hefei and Shanghai called for even more changes to the electoral system. They were supported by Fang Lizhi, a professor in astrophysics and an outspoken supporter of democratic reform. He made a speech that argued for the freedom to think freely if China was to develop.

ToK Time

What is the connection that Fang Lizhi is making here between science and democracy? Andrei Sakharov, a Russian physicist and dissident, was also critical of the lack of democracy in the Soviet Union. Why, do you think, might scientists be particularly aware of the need for political freedom?

SOURCE H

In democratic societies, democracy and science – and most of us here are scientists – run parallel. Democracy is concerned with ideas about humanity, and science is concerned with nature. One of the distinguishing features of universities is the role of knowledge; we do research, we create new knowledge, we apply this knowledge to developing new products, and so forth. In this domain, within this sphere of science and the intellect, we make our own judgements based on our independent criteria... In Western societies, universities are independent from the government... This is how universities must be. The intellectual realm must be independent and have its own values... It is only when you know something independently that you are free from relying on authorities outside the intellectual domain, such as the government. Unfortunately, things are not this way in China.

From a speech by Fang Lizhi, calling for 'complete Westernization', at Tongji University, Shanghai on 18 November 1986. From Alan Lawrance, *China Since 1919*, 2004

Fang Lizhi was expelled from the CCP and lost his post at the University of Science and Technology at Hefei.

The students were supported by Hu Yaobang, who bore the brunt of the criticism. He was blamed for the student demonstrations and dismissed as General Secretary in 1987. He was accused of 'only opposing the Left while never opposing the Right' and 'saying many things he should not have said.' It was felt by the conservatives in the Party that he expressed his reformist views too openly and was over-confident of becoming Deng's successor. Hu was removed, but Zhao survived and took over as General Secretary and Li Peng became Premier.

These changes in leadership were confirmed at the Thirteenth Party Congress in 1987, where another noteworthy event was the retirement of Deng along with several of his elderly comrades from the Standing Committee of the Politburo. This reduced the average age of Committee members from 77 to 63. An effort was being made to show that China was moving forward to a more youthful and dynamic future.

In reality, not much had changed, because Deng remained Chairman of the Military Affairs Commission as well as 'paramount leader'. Meanwhile, his elderly comrades became known as the 'Gang of Old' for their continuing influence over party policy.

The original Long March had taken place in 1934 and become symbolic of the struggle endured by the early communists, when they escaped from Jiangxi province and trekked more than 12,000km to Yanan.

SOURCE I

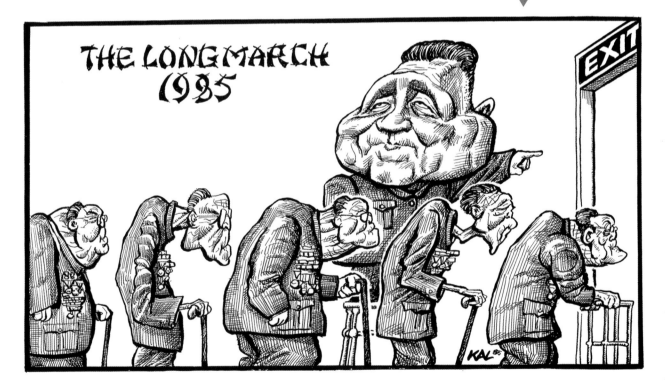

STUDENT STUDY SECTION

QUESTION
What is the message conveyed in Source I?

SOURCE J

'Beloved comrade Xiaoping – The general architect', a poster by Lei Wenbin, September 1994. Deng Xiaoping hated personality cults and for a long time managed to avoid being featured on posters. Only at the end of his life was he no longer able to stop it. In the background in this poster is a modern port, resembling Hong Kong.

SOURCE K

'Discussing great plans together' by Gao Qikui, 1985. Deng Xiaoping did not want to be glorified. Sometimes, however, posters were made to demonstrate the legitimacy of his reign by showing him in imaginary meetings with the great leaders of the past. Here are, from left to right, Chen Yun (at that moment the Vice Chairman of the Central Committee of the Communist Party), Liu Shaoqi, Mao Zedong, Zhou Enlai, Deng Xiaoping and Zhu De, one of the legendary generals of the Red Army.

STUDENT STUDY SECTION

QUESTION

Some historians say that Deng did not want a cult of personality to develop around him. What do Sources J and K suggest about how Deng was portrayed in the late 1980s and the 1990s?

Tiananmen Square

In 1989 a rift developed between the reformer, General Secretary Zhao Ziyang, and the more conservative Premier Li Peng. Zhao felt that more openness was needed and a greater willingness to include trade unions and student organizations in discussions concerning both economic and political reform. This approach was opposed by the critics of Zhao's 'centrist' policies and he was aware that any strikes or demonstrations could be used as an excuse to end reform. Meanwhile, Deng believed that firm control by the Party was needed if economic reforms were to continue. Now more that ever, he implied, China needed strong leadership and an authoritarian system.

Symbolically, 1989 was an important year. It was the 40th Anniversary of the establishment of the People's Republic of China and the 70th Anniversary of the **May 4th Movement** of 1919. It was also one of the most momentous years in the history of the PRC.

In the Soviet Union, political reform had accompanied economic reform and in the spring of 1989, the satellite states of Eastern Europe were moving away from the single-party system. It was interesting to speculate whether the same path would be followed in China.

Demands for the Fifth Modernization reached a climax in the spring of 1989. In April, Hu Yaobang died after suffering a heart attack brought on, it was rumoured, by criticism from the 'anti-reformers' within the Party. Hu supported student protests and had called for more reform to improve education. What happened next was very reminiscent of 1976, when Zhou Enlai's death had sparked the April 5th Movement. Students who saw Hu as their strongest supporter took to the streets of Beijing and marched to Tiananmen Square. They asked for the following reforms:

- Hu Yaobang's reputation should be rehabilitated and his pro-democracy policies restored.
- There should be freedom of information and a free press.
- Those who had used violence against the demonstrators should be punished.
- Measures should be taken to end corruption and to publicize how much money was made by the party leaders and their families.
- Investment in education should be increased and the treatment and pay of teachers should be improved. Those who had been responsible for wrong educational policies should be punished.
- The 'anti-bourgeois liberalism' campaign should end and its victims be rehabilitated.
- There should be accurate reporting of the 'democratic and patriotic' movement that was taking place.

(Adapted from John Gittings, *The Changing Face of China*, 2006.)

 The May 4th Movement
This began as a student demonstration in May 1919 in protest against the decisions made at the Paris Peace Conference to allow Japan to take over German interests in Shandong province, where they established a centre for trade. Japan had taken advantage of the war to increase its influence in China. The emergence of the CCP in 1921 grew out of the public protest against the continuation of foreign involvement in China.

The 22nd of April was designated the official day of mourning for Hu, and a Politburo meeting on the same day decided against giving in to the students' demands. Zhao Ziyang, probably the only member of the Politburo who would have supported the students, was visiting North Korea and was absent from this crucial meeting. On his return, he suggested some dialogue with the students, who were calling for 'correct leadership', but he did not represent the majority on the Politburo. Extra pressure came when the anniversary of the May 4th Movement was marked by Fang Lizhi sending an open letter asking for the release of Wei Jingsheng, the author of the Fifth Modernization.

By 13 May, the students had filled Tiananmen Square with their makeshift camps and started a hunger strike. Into this landscape of dissent stepped the Russian leader Mikhail Gorbachev. He was in Beijing to attend a summit that was scheduled to last from 15 May to 19 May, an event that was taken very seriously by the Chinese leadership. In a similar response to his visits to Eastern Europe, Gorbachev was greeted with enthusiasm by the students and there were calls for his policies of *perestroika* and *glasnost* to be adopted in China. The visit turned into a humiliating experience for Deng Xiaoping, who was unable to keep to the planned schedule. The official reception for Gorbachev was moved to Beijing Airport and his tour of the Forbidden City and a wreath-laying ceremony in Tiananmen Square were cancelled.

On 19 May, Zhao Ziyang showed his concern and confusion by walking among the students and apologizing for the actions of the Politburo. He said, 'We were too late coming. I'm sorry. Your criticism of us is justified.' Zhao was in a minority and the Politburo had already decided there would be no compromise or dialogue with the demonstrators. Later that same day, he was dismissed from office.

On 20 May, the Politburo declared martial law and the PLA were ordered to take up positions in Beijing. It was rumoured that they were unarmed and when the people asked them not to use force, they complied. Ten days later, on 30 May, the students erected a figure known as the 'Goddess of Democracy and Spirit of Liberty' in Tiananmen Square. This polystyrene statue closely resembled the Statue of Liberty in New York and was criticized by the anti-reformers as 'un-Chinese'.

Deng Xiaoping was nervous about how to address the demands of the students and he was even more alarmed when they were joined by workers and ordinary residents of Beijing. Protests also focused on corruption inside the Party and posters and pamphlets asked how the families of party leaders could afford to gamble in Hong Kong or to play golf in Beijing.

At midnight on 3 June, Deng ordered the troops to take positions and to clear Tiananmen Square by 6:00am on 4 June. There is still a great deal of confusion about what happened next, but estimates put the casualties at between 600 and 1200 dead and between 6000 and 10,000 injured. The government maintained that there had been no casualties in the square, but that 23 students had been killed accidentally in the surrounding streets. It also stated that 150 soldiers had been killed and 5000 wounded.

What actually happened in Tiananmen Square is still the subject of debate. The official explanation was that the army had taken action against a 'counter-revolutionary rebellion' planned to spark a coup d'état led by 'misguided Party leaders'.

SOURCE L

The mass arrests began almost immediately after the bloody crackdown. An all-points bulletin was issued to ferret out 21 student leaders, and citizens were urged to inform on them. By July 17, some 4,600 arrests had been made and 29 of the prisoners were then given a quick trial and shot in the back of the head.

From Immanuel C. Y. Hsu, *The Rise of Modern China*, 1995

● **Examiner's hint**
There are quite a few statistics mentioned here. How reliable are these, do you think? Notice that the source is an American-Chinese historian. Think about where he might have found these numbers.

STUDENT STUDY SECTION

QUESTION
How reliable, do you think, is the account of events given in Source L?

It is difficult to exaggerate the shock with which the world reacted to the events in Tiananmen Square. The 1980s had been a period of opening up of China to foreign investment and also to foreign visitors. Economic reform, it was commonly believed, would lead to political reform. The crackdown, therefore, was all the more shocking because it was so unexpected. There were many questions to be asked, but finding the answers was not easy when the government was determined not to allow foreign journalists access to eyewitnesses. Some conclusions were drawn, however, regarding the causes of the unrest.

SOURCE M

Within the student leadership the initiative was taken and held by a hard-line group. By this time the mounting discontent could not be appeased. While centring on corruption and undefined notions of democracy as exemplified by the Spirit of Liberty, the student demands for freedom were essentially a protest against the bureaucratic controls as well as the 'backdoor' practices which circumscribed their education, hobbled prospects and the right to travel. Even more irreconcilable were the demands of the marching workers, who since the arrests of workers' leaders on May 29th were gaining support. The discontent of the workers' associations arose out of the economic reforms – the end of jobs for life, the whittling away of welfare provision, the growing gap between the rich and poor. Many felt they were losing what they had gained under state socialism. Their demands challenged the basis of Deng's revolution.

From Alan Lawrance, *China Under Communism*, 1998

SOURCE N

The main difficulty in handling this matter lay in that we never experienced such a situation before, in which a small minority of bad people mixed with so many young students and onlookers. We did not have a clear picture of the situation and this prevented us from taking some actions that we should have taken earlier. It would have been difficult for us to understand the nature of the matter had we not had the support of so many senior comrades... Actually, what we faced was not just some ordinary people who were misguided, but also a rebellious clique and a large quantity of the dregs of society. The key point is that they wanted to overthrow our state and the Party... The nature of the matter became clear soon after it erupted. They had two main slogans: overthrow the Communist Party and topple the socialist system. Their goal was to establish a bourgeois republic entirely dependent on the West.

From Deng Xiaoping's address to officers in command of enforcing martial law in Beijing, 9 June 1989.
From Alan Lawrance, *China Since 1919*, 2004

STUDENT STUDY SECTION

QUESTION

Compare and contrast the views expressed about the reasons for the demonstrations in Sources M and N.

Student Answer – *Mabel*

Sources M and N present very different reasons for the demonstrations discussed. Source M suggests that industrial workers and students had different reasons for dissenting. Source M also states that students resented the corruption and lack of true democracy, as well as nepotism and lack of transparency related to their education and rights. Finally, Source M presents the notion that industrial workers' reasons for revolting were the negative consequences of economic reforms. Meanwhile, Source N states that the reasons for the discontent and revolt were all centred around one reason, or 'key' point. This was a desire to overthrow the communist system and replace it with capitalism. Source N does not identify any variation in reasons for revolting among different sectors of society. Source N also suggests that the revolts were led by a few 'bad people' who influenced many others, while Source M suggests that while there was 'hard-line' leadership, a huge number of people were genuinely inspired to dissent. Source M does not overtly suggest that the objective was to overthrow the communist regime, while Source N does.

Source M and N are also similar in some ways. Both suggest to a certain extent that a nucleus of 'leading' protestors were supporting and perpetuating the protests. Both also mention young people as key members of these dissenting groups.

Examiner's comments

Mabel has identified several similarities (comparisons) and differences (contrasts) and handled these quite well. She lists three points from Source M and then three points from Source N and makes the differences quite clear. She also finds two similarities, although she could support these with more evidence.

QUESTION

With reference to its origin and purpose, assess the value and limitations of Source N.

Student Answer – *Kaitlin*

This source originates from an extract from a speech by Deng Xiaoping to those he depended on to enforce martial law and control the masses in June 1989. Its purpose is to inspire absolute certainty and loyalty among these officers, by convincing them that the actions they are carrying out are not only just but the only option. It is verbal propaganda, also aimed at creating a divide between the officers and protestors, in order to break down any sense of empathy or loyalty they may feel towards them.

This source is very valuable for a number of reasons. First, it shows Deng's desire to inspire loyalty among these military personnel. This in turn suggests that he was fearful of the protests. The source is an example of his official stand during the protests and strategy used to alienate the protestors from others. All in all, this speech, as mentioned before, is propaganda, and devised to convince those who hear it of one point of view.

This source is also limited because it is so very one-sided. It simply shows Deng's instructions to the officers, not their reactions to these instructions or thoughts at the time. Moreover, it does not provide a great deal of information about protestors, only Deng's view that he wanted to spread: that they were divided, led by a few very bad individuals, and members of the 'dregs of society.'

Examiner's comments

A very good response. Kaitlin refers very clearly to the origin, purpose, value and limitations of Source N.

Examiner's hint

Don't forget to look closely at the origin of Source N and consider its purpose. Why, do you think, did Deng need to address these soldiers?

Post-Tiananmen

As news of the events in Tiananmen Square spread, sympathizers took to the streets all across China and also Hong Kong where a population, already nervous about 1997, was frightened by this brutal suppression of freedom of speech. Meanwhile, Deng and the Party leadership went on television to condemn the students, but also to re-affirm a commitment to economic growth. Zhao Ziyang, who had been dismissed on 18 May, remained under house arrest until his death in January 2005. The more conservative wing of the CCP was unable to slow or to reverse economic reform, however, and Deng was determined to go ahead with moving towards a free-market economy.

One of the many questions asked about the events of May and June 1989 was why the government had given so many mixed messages? There was a two-week delay between the declaration of martial law and the military crackdown, during which time the Party leadership had watched the students assemble in Tiananmen Square, go on hunger strike and be joined by the workers. One reason for the delayed response may have been the official visit by Mikhail Gorbachev that began on 15 May and ended on 19 May. There may also have been disagreement within the Politburo about what action to take.

Events in Europe conveyed a mood of democratic reform within the communist bloc, and the world was keenly interested in seeing whether China would proceed along the same path. It may be that not all the leaders wanted to risk condemnation by world opinion. Even when the PLA was called in, it did not act immediately and when orders were finally given to clear the square, officers continued to ask for clarification. There seems to have been nervousness about giving direct commands to use lethal force against the demonstrators. Afterwards, Li Peng claimed that the soldiers used live ammunition only after they had run out of tear gas. Some reports stated that orders were given to end the 'counter-revolution' only after reports that a soldier had been killed.

Although some student leaders called for non-violence, there were extremists among the demonstrators as well as in the Politburo and it is possible that both of these groups relished a fight. It was an asymmetric clash, however, with unarmed demonstrators being confronted by an army using guns and tanks.

SOURCE O

A protester confronts PLA tanks in Tiananmen Square

SOURCE P

A cartoon by Nicholas Garland published in *The Independent*, a British daily newspaper, on 16 June 1989. A handwritten note on yellow paper pasted to the reverse of the cartoon said 'China – Deng Xiaoping tries to prevent the truth about the massacre in Peking being told.'

● **Examiner's hint**
Why do you think the cartoonist in Source P chose this image to convey his message? There was no caption for the cartoon, but in the caption you can see that the cartoonist (presumably) had written an explanation of what he was trying to illustrate. Did he succeed, do you think? Is this what it conveys to you?

STUDENT STUDY SECTION

QUESTIONS

a) **Source O is the famous image of a young man standing in front of the tanks of the PLA after it has cleared the demonstrators from Tiananmen Square. Why is this image so memorable? If you did not know anything about its origin, how would you answer a question that asked you to explain its purpose?**

b) **Compare and contrast Sources O and P.**

c) **What message is conveyed in Source P?**

SOURCE Q

'Room for one more?' A cartoon by Stanley Franklin published in *The Sun*, a British newspaper, on 6 June 1989. Here, Deng Xiaoping is climbing up a ladder to join Hitler and Stalin.

"ROOM FOR ONE MORE?"

● **Examiner's hint**
Newspapers need to give an instant summary of events but don't forget to consider how difficult it was to access reliable information about events in Tiananmen Square. *The Sun* is a tabloid newspaper (it comes in a small format) published daily in the United Kingdom. See what you can find out about the newspaper.

STUDENT STUDY SECTION

QUESTION

With reference to its origin and purpose, assess the value and limitations of Source Q for historians studying the events of June 1989.

Aftermath

In the aftermath of what became known as 'the Beijing Spring', there was a clampdown on the Democracy Movement. Widespread arrests of students and workers who had participated in the demonstrations were carried out and many were executed, while others were given long prison terms. Members of the CCP known to have sympathized with the demonstrators were purged. It is no coincidence that this return to a far more rigid climate of censorship and repression took place against the backdrop of reform in Eastern Europe and the USSR. For Deng, those events were not an example to follow but a warning of what to avoid. The success of a movement similar to that of the Polish trade union, Solidarity, was something that Deng was afraid of and he was determined to prevent a similar worker-led movement emerging in China. It was said that workers who attempted to link any kind of trade union activity to the democracy movement were executed.

The Tiananmen demonstrations, however, were also damaging for Deng. The party leaders who had opposed the move away from Mao's policies seized this opportunity to condemn the Four Modernizations. Although Deng believed as strongly as ever in the need for economic reform, he now had to take a back seat as privatization was officially criticized and investment in the SEZs was blocked. It was not until 1994 that Deng felt he could challenge the conservatives and restore his economic policies. Once more, he urged 'to get rich is glorious', but hoped that workers and peasants would accept that, in the short term at least, there would be no democratic reform.

REVIEW SECTION

This section has looked at the political protest that emerged in China during the 1980s. In the West, it is assumed that economic change leads, inevitably, to political change. During the Industrial Revolution of the 18th and 19th centuries, as people moved into the cities and as entrepreneurs became wealthy, demand grew for a fairer distribution of political power. People wanted laws that reflected a new economic reality and to have influence on policy making. Over time, more people were given the right to vote for different political parties that sprang up to represent different economic interests. Would this also happen in China or was it possible for people to accept prosperity without the kind of democracy familiar in multi-party states?

By 1979, the democracy movement had taken hold in China, but this ebbed and flowed throughout the 1980s ending with the events of Tiananmen Square.

Consider the following questions and see if you can come up with answers using the sources and the text in this section:

Review questions

1 Why was Deng Xiaoping concerned about the growth of the democracy movement?

2 Compare and contrast the events of 1979, 1986 and 1989 – in what ways were these protests by the supporters of democratic reform similar and different?

3 Why, do you think, did the leadership of the CCP respond so harshly to the Tiananmen Square protests in 1989?

ToK Time

When Zhou Enlai was asked what he thought about the French Revolution of 1789, he said, 'It is too early to tell.' Meanwhile, contemporary history has been described as 'journalism with footnotes'.

When, do you think, does an event become part of history? Is it possible to study something that happened yesterday, for instance, using the methodology of history or can we apply this only to events that took place a 'long time' ago?

The IB History curriculum has a 'ten year rule'. In other words, when you choose a topic for your Extended Essay or for your Internal Assessment, you cannot write about something that happened in the past 10 years. How would you argue for and against this rule?

Sample exam for Prescribed Subject 3: Communism in Crisis 1976–89

These documents concern the reasons for Soviet involvement in Afghanistan in 1979. Read all the documents carefully and then answer the questions that follow.

SOURCE A

From the minutes of a meeting of the Politburo in March 1979; Andrei Gromyko was the Foreign Minister of the Soviet Union

Gromyko: I fully support Comrade Andropov's [head of the KGB at this time] proposal to exclude such a measure as the introduction of our troops into Afghanistan. The [Afghan] army there is unreliable. Thus our army, if it enters, will be the aggressor. Against whom will it fight? Against the Afghan people first of all, and it will have to shoot at them. Comrade Andropov correctly noted that indeed the situation in Afghanistan is not ripe for a [socialist] revolution. And all that we have done in recent years with such effort in terms of a détente in international tensions, arms reduction, and much more – all that will be thrown back. Of course, this will be a nice gift for China. All the non-aligned countries will be against us. One must ask, what would we gain? Afghanistan with its present government, with a backward economy, with inconsequential weight in international affairs … we must keep in mind that from a legal point of view too we would not be justified in sending troops.

● Examiner's hints

In the exam, you will be given a paper on your Prescribed Subject (PS). The sources will all focus on one of the bullet points listed under your PS in the History Guide. The topic for the exam paper will be stated above the first source. You will be given five minutes' reading time before the exam begins. You may not write or underline anything during this time, but it is an opportunity to read all the sources and to think about the questions.

Always answer the questions in order. Don't be tempted to answer the mini-essay first.

SOURCE B

An extract from the introduction to The Soviet Experience in Afghanistan: Russian Documents and Memoirs, published on National Security Archive, an internet site set up by George Washington University and edited by Svetlana Savranskaya.
http://www.gwu.edu/~nsarchiv/NSAEBB/NSAEBB57/soviet.html

The Soviet troops also suffered from the confusion about their goals – the initial official mission was to protect the PDPA (The People's Democratic Party of Afghanistan) regime; however, when the troops reached Kabul, their orders were to overthrow Amin and his regime. Then the mission was changed once again, but the leadership was not willing to admit that the Soviet troops were essentially fighting the Afghan civil war for the PDPA. The notion of the 'internationalist duty' that the Soviet Limited Contingent was fulfilling in Afghanistan was essentially ideological, based on the idea that Soviet troops were protecting the socialist revolution in Afghanistan whereas the experience on the ground immediately undermined such justifications. The explanation of Afghan history is couched in Marxist-Leninist terms and reflects the thinking that drew Soviet forces into the Afghan civil war and kept them there. Thus, the Afghans had a 'Marxist-Leninist revolution' (actually a coup d'état) that had to be defended against 'Chinese and Western intervention.' The United States had lost its influence and listening posts in Iran with the downfall of the Shah. The Soviet leadership was convinced that the United States was trying to move into Afghanistan to make up for this loss. When Amin made some tentative moves for economic assistance from the United States, the Soviet leadership felt threatened and acted. Soviet Spetsnaz [special forces] killed Amin and installed Babrak Karmal in power.

SOURCE C

From Norman Friedman, *The Fifty Year War*, 2000

As an indication of US thinking, on 16 January 1980, the CIA sent President Carter and the NSC [National Security Council] an 'Eyes Only' study of the 'Soviet Options in Southwest Asia After the Invasion of Afghanistan'. It was unlikely that the Soviets had planned the invasion and it might well have been authorized only reluctantly; but the Soviets did want a wider sphere of influence in Southwest Asia, and the invasion presented them with a valuable opportunity. The invasion placed their forces on the eastern border of Iran, as well as on the northern border they had previously occupied. They were now in a good position to help the main Iranian separatist movements… Moreover, Soviet oil production was about to run down; surely expanded influence over the oil-rich Iran was a major Soviet priority.

SOURCE D

A cartoon published by Nicholas Garland published in the *Daily Telegraph*, a British newspaper, on 25 January 1980. It shows Brezhnev dancing a traditional Russian sabre dance.

SOURCE E

From Dmitri Volkogonov, *The Rise and Fall of the Soviet Union*, 1999. Dmitri Volkogonov is a Russian historian who was a general in the Soviet Army. This book was written in Russian and translated into English. In this extract, Volkogonov is talking about the official Soviet justification for sending troops into Afghanistan.

The chiefs of the mass media, the army and the Party committees were periodically sent interpretations of questions connected with changes in the Afghan leadership and the sending of Soviet troops into the country. They were told to say that the Afghan leadership 'repeatedly, at least fourteen times, asked us to send Soviet troops.' … The fact that the removal of Amin took place when Soviet military contingents were beginning to arrive in Afghanistan 'was no more than a coincidence in time and there is no causal connection. Soviet military units were not involved in the removal of Amin and his stooges.' There was not a single word of truth in this 'interpretation', but the propaganda and international information departments of the Central Committee were past masters at fooling the Soviet public, and most people swallowed it. Paradoxically, the true reason for the intervention was uttered by the Politburo itself: 'The Soviet forces in Afghanistan are carrying out their international duty.' For Brezhnev and his comrades, still thinking in Comintern terms, their ideological commitment to the Marxist doctrine of making whole populations happy despite themselves was their justification for crude interference in the affairs of other countries.

QUESTIONS

1a) Why, according to Source A, was the leadership of the Soviet Union reluctant to send troops into Afghanistan?

1b) What message is conveyed by Source D?

2) Compare and contrast the views expressed in Sources C and E about the reasons for the Soviet invasion of Afghanistan.

3) With reference to their origin and purpose, discuss the value and limitations of Source A and Source B for historians studying the outbreak of the Soviet-Afghan war.

4) Using these sources and your own knowledge, analyze the reasons for the Soviet invasion of Afghanistan.

Chapter 8
Theory of Knowledge

Why study History?

Of all your IB subjects, history is one that links very easily to ToK. After all, history is about the weighing of evidence and trying to come up with as accurate an account of the past as is possible. To do this, historians pore over all kinds of sources and constantly challenge established interpretations of past events. One of the biggest misconceptions about history is that it is a 'dead' subject. It is all about the past and so how can there be anything new? Yet history is surely one of the most dynamic subjects and also the one that makes you critically aware.

You may have been told that we study history so that we will learn from our mistakes and not repeat them in the future. You may also have been told that 'history repeats itself', so by studying history you could learn about what might occur in the future. For others, learning history teaches us about who we are and why/how our world has developed over time.

Hardly surprisingly, 'Why study history?' is one question with which people have struggled for centuries. Peter Stearns has argued that his answer to this question is simply that 'we emerge with relevant skills and an enhanced capacity for informed citizenship, critical thinking, and simple awareness.' He goes on to say that 'History should be studied because it is essential to individuals and to society, and because it harbors beauty.'

Stearns then goes on to list eight reasons why you should study history:

- History Helps Us Understand People and Societies
- History Helps Us Understand Change and How the Society We Live in Came to Be
- The Importance of History in Our Own Lives
- History Contributes to Moral Understanding
- History Provides Identity
- Studying History Is Essential for Good Citizenship
- History Develops Key Skills
- History Is Useful in the World of Work

http://www.historians.org/pubs/free/WhyStudyHistory.htm

One of the best justifications for studying history was given by the blind Czech historian Milan Hubl to the novelist Milan Kundera: 'The first step in liquidating a people is to erase its memory. Destroy its books, its culture, its history. Then have somebody write new books, manufacture a new culture, invent a new history. Before long the nation will begin to forget what it is and what it was. The world around it will forget even faster.' (Milan Kundera, *The Book of Laughter and Forgetting*)

So these are some reasons that have been given to explain why you should study history. Remember that no matter how hard you try you cannot avoid the past.

Is knowledge of the past ever certain?

This is an interesting question and in recent times a school of historical research has been developed to try to make the study of history more certain. It is called cliometrics. 'Clio' was the muse of history for the ancient Greeks and 'metric' has to do with measuring or quantifying data. One of the best-known books to take this approach was written by Robert Fogel and Stanley Engerman – *Time on the Cross: The Economics of American Negro Slavery* in 1974. It was described on the jacket cover as 'a sweeping reexamination of the economic foundations of American Negro slavery' and had two volumes. The first volume included a detailed analysis of many of the economic aspects of slavery – slaves as investment, profitability, life expectancy and so on – while the second volume, subtitled *Evidence and Methods*, described the cliometric methodology that the two authors had used.

The idea behind cliometrics is to apply economic theory and statistical analysis to the study of history. It was originally developed by Fogel and Douglass C. North, who eventually received the Nobel Prize for Economics in 1993 for their work. They were seen as pioneers in the field of econometrics and were awarded the prize 'for having renewed research in economic history'. In *Time on the Cross*, Fogel used statistical analysis to examine the relationship between the nature of American slavery and its profitability. In simple terms, the two authors found as much data as they could which related to slavery and loaded it into a computer. The computer then analyzed the results and the first volume of the book used these results to make several claims about whether or not slavery as an institution was profitable. There was criticism from some people about Fogel and Engerman's using quantitative methods when analyzing such a morally questionable practice. However, there was no attempt made to justify slavery in the book; the two authors simply used the data to arrive at their conclusions.

Some of the conclusions were a little controversial, as *Time on the Cross* maintained that 'slave' productivity was more efficient than 'freed men' productivity. The book also used the data to discuss the conditions in slavery. For example, it was claimed that a slave was whipped on average every 4.56 days. The book claimed that the economy in slave states grew quite rapidly and produced a per capita level of income that Italy was only able to achieve in the late 1930s!

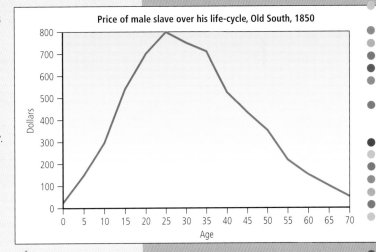

Source: Fogel and Engerman, 1974

Questions

1 Why do you think you should study history? Divide yourself into groups of three and try to find five good reasons why you should study history. Remember that everything has a history – football, Germany, yourself.

2 Take each of Stearns' justifications for studying history and find three examples for each that could be used to support his claims.

3 Try to find three examples in history where a people's memory has been 'erased'.

Questions

1 Do you think there is a problem with what Fogel and Engerman did when investigating slavery – an institution whose practices have moral implications?

2 What is your reaction to the methodology used by Fogel and Engerman? Can quantitative measurement really be used to make historical claims?

3 Try cliometrics yourself. In your ToK class, get every student to find out some statistical data on a topic – Mao's First Five Year Plan, for example. Then analyze it and try to write a summary, as Fogel and Engerman did for slavery. Does it make history more 'certain'?

Can history be considered in any sense 'scientific'?

As with Fogel and Engerman, there have been several attempts over the past 200 years to make history a more 'scientific' subject. During the 19th century, there was an ongoing debate about how we 'know' something in history, and one of the most important contributors to this debate was a German historian and psychologist, Wilhelm Dilthey.

One of Dilthey's major concerns was to try to develop a scientific methodology that could be applied to history. Yet Dilthey did not want to try to use the same methodology as the natural sciences (biology, physics etc.), but wanted to create a new basis for the human sciences (history, law, literature and what we would today call sociology and psychology). Dilthey's main argument was that the principal focus of the natural sciences is to discover the cause and effect behind a phenomenon, whereas he saw the task of the human sciences, such as history, as focusing on understanding why a phenomenon occurs. If Dilthey was right, then if we can find the causes and effects of a historical event does that mean that we are being 'scientific'?

At about the same time another German historian, Leopold von Ranke, was also trying to investigate how history could become more professional in its approach to gathering information. Until Ranke little attention had been paid to the use of sources in historical writing. In his first book, *History of the Latin and Teutonic Peoples from 1494 to 1514*, he used a wide variety of documents, including memoirs, diaries, personal and formal letters, government documents, diplomatic sources and eyewitness accounts.

He is best known for a famous phrase. History should try to be based on the principle of *'wie es eigentlich gewesen ist'* (lit. 'to show what actually happened'). By obtaining as many 'facts' as possible, the historian will be able to be 'scientific' in his/her approach and any account would be based on empiricism and therefore be more objective.

Ranke distrusted the historical books of the time and relied upon original sources. He considered that 'the strict presentation of the facts, contingent and unattractive though they may be, is undoubtedly the supreme law'. Because of this approach, Ranke is sometimes known as the founder of the science of history.

▲

Wilhelm Dilthey

An Australian cartoon by Nicholson. The figure on the left is John Howard, former Prime Minister of Australia.

▼

Leopold von Ranke

▼

Questions

1 What are we trying to do when we study history? Give some examples to show the differences between how you could apply 'cause and effect' and 'understanding' to a historical event. Is there really a difference?

2 Is it possible for an historian to ever 'show what actually happened'?

3 Does Ranke's approach make history more 'scientific'?

What determines how historians select evidence and describe, interpret or analyze events?

What makes history a challenge is that historians have to work on what no longer exists – the past. There is evidence that the events which you have studied for the Prescribed Subject of your choice have happened. In your study, you have come across proof that those events have taken place: letters, diary entries, statistical tables, photographs, speeches, etc. You have been able to answer how and why things happened by studying both the sources included in the chapters as well as using your own knowledge on them.

History, however, is not only about uncovering the past – that is, knowing what happened. History aims at giving meaning to the past by trying to explain why things happened. Historians select, describe, interpret and analyze evidence to answer the question: 'Why did this happen?' Like detectives inspecting a crime scene, reconstruction becomes the key word.

The roles of perception, emotion and reason

Historians look for evidence for the questions they try to answer. Where they look, the type of evidence they consider important and useful, the weight they give to each piece of evidence selected, depends on each historian and how he or she approaches the investigation. This explains why there are different interpretations of historical events. Whether Germany was treated too harshly at the Versailles Peace Conference, what was the significance of outside powers in the Arab-Israeli conflict, or the extent to which Gorbachev's policies were responsible for the collapse of the USSR, are all valid historical issues that have been answered in very different ways throughout time. This is determined by how historians select, interpret and analyze the information found.

Perception and emotion play a part in the selection, interpretation and analysis of evidence. The historian's personal experiences and interests, together with previous knowledge, all contribute to the process. It is claimed that 'context is all', meaning that we do not analyze and interpret events in isolation but as part of the circumstances of the time in which they took place, as well as those of the time in which they are being researched. For example, the economic crisis of 2008 has led to increasing academic interest in the research on how and why the Depression of the 1930s came about and was overcome.

To interpret and analyze events, historians also use reason. The pieces of the past need to be selected and placed in some kind of order or structure that can help them explain what happened and understand why it happened. This practice means linking the events and giving meaning to them. For example, in your own study of history, you are required to show this skill by establishing links between causes and effects, continuity and change.

Questions

1 To what extent do you think that the credit crunch crisis of 2008 will affect the ways historians analyze and interpret the 1929 Crash?

2 Can you think of other examples when context played an important role in the selection of the topics or the way the evidence was interpreted? For example, what does your study of single-party states reveal about how historians saw the regimes at the time and how they were explained after the regimes ended?

3 Is the fact that historians cannot work isolated in a lab, like scientists do, an advantage or a problem to historical investigation?

The facts of history 'are like fish swimming about in a vast and sometimes inaccessible ocean; and what the historian catches will depend partly on chance but mainly on what part of the ocean he chooses to fish in and what tackles he chooses to use.' (E. H. Carr).

4 What do you think plays a role in how historians choose 'what part of the ocean to fish in'? Carr mentioned the role of chance. What part, if any, do you think chance plays in historical investigation?

Historians also use reason to try to decide what constitutes genuine evidence for their research. One example of this is the study carried out by John Kenneth Galbraith in *The Great Crash*, *1929* on whether the Wall Street Crash had an impact on the number of suicides taking place in New York. He challenged, by studying available statistics, the idea which claims that in 1929 people jumped out of the windows in Manhattan in desperation over their losses:

> **One can only guess why the suicide myth became established. Like alcoholics and gamblers, broken speculators are supposed to have a propensity for self destruction. At a time when broken speculators were plentiful, the newspapers and the public may have simply supplied the corollary. Alternatively, suicide that in other times may have evoked the question 'Why do you suppose he did it?' now had the motive assigned automatically: 'The poor fellow was caught in the crash.' Finally, it must be noted that, although suicides did not increase sharply either in the months of the crash or in 1929 as a whole, the rate did rise in the later depression years. In memory some of these tragedies may have been moved back a year or two to the time of the stock market crash.**
>
> Kenneth Galbraith, *The Great Crash*, *1929*

Questions

1 What reasons does Galbraith give to question the view that the Wall Street Crash led to a wave of suicides in the USA? How do you think he arrived at them?

2 Why do you think some past events are reconstructed in a mythical way? To what extent can myths help to analyze and interpret why an event has taken place? What challenge does this represent to historians?

3 Can you think of other examples in which history has been mythologized?

Historians write up their findings, their answers to the question about why something happened. The choice of words, the extent of attention paid to each element, the order in which issues are explained will contribute to how the events are presented, understood and interpreted. 'The past has happened and cannot change, but the interpretation and understanding of it continues to happen and will never stop changing' (D. Henigue). With reference to specific events you have studied in history, to what extent do you agree with this view?

Now that you have discussed how historians select, analyze and interpret evidence, it is time for you to look at how you do it:

- What are your methods of research?
- What sources, apart from your teachers and your textbooks, do you use?
- How do you select the sources that will constitute part of your investigation? How do you decide what, if anything, to leave out?

Now look at the following documents on the Wall Street Crash.

SOURCE A

A joke of 1929: 'The market may be bad, but I slept like a baby last night. I woke up every hour and cried.'

SOURCE B

I really went to look for a job on Wall Street hoping that I could make money... You'd heard so much about the bull market and the way everything was going up ... and read about such people as Charlie Mitchell, the president of National City Bank, and a lot of others – the J. P. Morgan group – and they seemed to be so strong and so powerful and knew so much about the market that, as they kept saying 'This is going to correct itself,' you tended to believe them. And then when it did fall, you still couldn't hardly believe it fell. There were all sorts of rumors and you'd see people going down the street looking up to see if they could catch somebody jumping out the window. Now it turned out there weren't as many people jumping out the window as they reported, but some did. And others committed suicide other ways.

Reuben L. Cain, stock salesman, remembers the Wall Street Crash

SOURCE C

Crowds outside the Stock Exchange in New York.
▼

SOURCE D

▲ Cartoon published in the USA in 1929. Note: the machine in the background is a stock ticker and produced the ticker tapes you can see at the front.

What problems are posed for the study of history by changes in language and culture over time?

The changes in culture affect the way history is interpreted and written. Culture determines what we consider important as we find new areas of interest and ask new questions about past events. This explains the constant need to revisit, to revise history. Read the following example on Masada (Hebrew for 'fortress') by Margaret MacMillan:

Questions

Find more examples of your own about the reaction to the Wall Street Crash in 1929. Then write an account about the impact of the Crash. Share the accounts with the class and discuss the following questions:

1 'It is impossible to write ancient history because we do not have enough sources, and impossible to write modern history because we have far too many.' Did you face either of these situations when writing your account? If so, which one? How do you think it has affected your account?

2 Did you have prior knowledge of the Crash? If so, what role do you think it played in your analysis of events? If not, to what extent was that an advantage or a disadvantage? Why?

3 Why are there different accounts of the same event? How significant are the differences? How can the differences be explained?

4 Does anything like the 'ideal account' exist? Explain your views.

As the nineteenth-century Zionists began their bold project of re-creating a Jewish state, they looked to Jewish history for symbols and lessons. They found, among much else, the story of Masada. In AD 73, as the Romans stamped out the last remnants of Jewish resistance to their rule, a band of some thousand men, women and children held out on the hilltop fortress of Masada. When it became clear that the garrison was doomed, its leader, Elazar Ben-Yair, convinced the men that it was better to die than to submit to Rome. The men killed their women and children and then themselves. The story was recorded but did not assume importance for Jews until the modern age. Masada had been taken up as a symbol not of submission to an inevitable fate but of the determination of the Jewish people to die if necessary in their struggle for freedom… In recent years, as pessimism has grown in Israel over the prospects for peace with its neighbours, another collective memory about Masada has been taking shape: that it is a warning that Jews always face persecution at the hands of their enemies.

Margaret MacMillan, *The Uses and Abuses of History*, 2009

Questions

1 How does MacMillan explain the change in the way Masada is interpreted? What role does culture play in the different interpretations of Masada?

2 Can you think of other examples of events that have been interpreted differently either as a result of the changes across time or other cultural influences?

3 How does the fact that historical events are reinterpreted in the light of changes in culture over time affect the work of historians?

An aerial view of Masada.

In the same way as history is affected by changes in language and culture, these changes help answer historical questions. An example of this is the research of a group of Latin American historians on the religiosity of the Argentine lower social classes in the 19th century. Their aim was to find out whether – contrary to public knowledge – people had become less religious towards the end of the century, but evidence and **historiographical** work on the issue was limited. They decided to look at a cultural aspect: names. Names are a reflection of fashion, beliefs and the role models of a time. By analyzing birth records for the most frequent names used during the 19th century, these historians believed that they had found evidence to show a progressive detachment from religious practices. Fewer people were named after the saint of the day they were born on, and fewer women were given 'Maria' as one of their names, both customary practices among Roman Catholics. In this change of a cultural pattern, the historians felt they had discovered evidence to claim that the lower social classes had become less attached to religious traditions.

Historiography

This term is generally used to describe the approaches of different historians towards a particular theme or event in history. Historical facts would not change, but which facts are selected, how these are analyzed or what they 'prove' can differ according to the views and opinions of individual historians.

Question

What are the strengths and limitations of the method used by these historians for their research? Can you think of other examples in which the changes in language have affected the study of history?

Does the study of history widen our knowledge of human nature?

The study of history contributes to understanding ourselves as human beings. History, therefore, defines and explains our character both as part of a community and as individuals. To believe that the study of history helps us understand human nature better is to believe we share some common characteristics that define 'human nature'. This belief implies that such characteristics become evident by our actions and help explain how and why we behave in particular ways.

Reflect on what R. G. Collingwood had to say about this: 'History is "for" human self-knowledge… Knowing yourself means knowing what you can do; and since nobody knows what he can do until he tries, the only clue to what man can do is what man has done. The value of history, then, is that it teaches us what man has done and thus what man is.'

Question
What, if anything, have you learnt about human nature by the study of a Prescribed Subject in the book?

Questions
Can you think of historical characters representing some of the following features?

- Ambition
- Sense of duty
- Cruelty
- Moral integrity
- Patriotism
- Justice
- Freedom

To what extent has the study of any of the characters you have named above helped you understand how we work as human beings? Has this knowledge helped you to understand how we make our decisions and choose where we head for?

Can history help in understanding the present or predicting the future?

Does history help us to understand the present?

Everyone wants to know where he or she comes from and all communities have what could be termed a 'collective memory' that helps to unite them as families or tribes or nations. It is the knowledge of this common history that helps to explain, for instance, religious affiliations, common cultures or where national borders are drawn. What unites can also divide, however, and in areas of conflict, history can be used to justify violence. Many, especially those who live through civil wars, may claim that it is best not to disturb the past and for historical amnesia to allow old quarrels to be forgotten. Others would claim that it is not possible to move forward into a peaceful future until we investigate and address past conflicts.

We can often understand the policies of a state by knowing its history. Very often, history is used to justify political decisions, especially foreign policy.

Question
Which would you consider to be the better course of action, to remember conflicts or to forget them? Support your arguments with examples from recent history such as: the apartheid era in South Africa; the troubles in Northern Ireland; the military junta in Argentina.

British Prime Minister Neville Chamberlain waves the piece of paper he believed signalled 'peace for our time', 1938.

The Hall of Mirrors at Versailles, the venue for the signing of the Treaty of Versailles in 1919. The treaty had a major effect on the international relations of the 20th century.

Woodrow Wilson's Fourteen Points

If you look carefully at each one, you can see how the Fourteen Points address what Woodrow Wilson thought were the causes of the Great War. The logic behind this was that if you removed the causes of war, you removed war.

Appeasement

For decades after World War II, 'appeasement' had all kinds of negative connotations. It meant 'to give in to dictators' and so to put off an inevitable conflict. If a politician was accused of being an 'appeaser', it was the same as being called cowardly. When the Iraq War started in 2003, both President George W. Bush of the USA and Prime Minister Tony Blair of Britain used the example of inter-war appeasement to explain their willingness to use war to remove President Saddam Hussein of Iraq.

In this quote, Tony Blair referred to the past as justification for present action.

British Prime Minister Tony Blair with US President George W. Bush.

The League of Nations also had that opportunity and responsibility back in the 1930s. In the early days of the fascist menace, it had the duty to protect Abyssinia from invasion. But when it came to a decision to enforce that guarantee, the horror of war deterred it. We know the rest. The menace grew; the League of Nations collapsed; war came.

Remember: The U.N. inspectors would not be within a thousand miles of Baghdad without the threat of force. Saddam would not be making a single concession without the knowledge that forces were gathering against him. I hope, even now, Iraq can be disarmed peacefully, with or without Saddam. But if we show weakness now, if we allow the plea for more time to become just an excuse for prevarication until the moment for action passes, then it will not only be Saddam who is repeating history. The menace, and not just from Saddam, will grow; the authority of the U.N. will be lost; and the conflict when it comes will be more bloody. Yes, let the United Nations be the way to deal with Saddam. But let the United Nations mean what it says; and do what it means.

From a speech by Tony Blair in Glasgow, 17 February 2003

Question

Can you think of another example when 'we do not appease' was used as an excuse to take action against a 'dictator'?

Does history help us to predict the future?

We often use past events to help us to establish patterns of behaviour. One of the lessons of history is that human beings behave in remarkably similar ways when confronted with similar situations. Because of this, we think the past can help us to predict the future.

Armies use the last war to fight the next

One example of how we use the past to plan the future is when countries go to war. They tend to prepare for the last war they fought in the hope that the lessons they learned can successfully be applied to the new conflict.

> Whoever wishes to foresee the future must consult the past; for human events ever resemble those of preceding times. This arises from the fact that they are produced by men who ever have been, and ever shall be, animated by the same passions, and thus they necessarily have the same results.
>
> Niccolo Machiavelli, *The Discourses*, 1532

▲ World War I trench warfare.

▲ Aircraft carriers in World War II.

▲ Search and Destroy missions in Vietnam.

A good resource with interesting points on how we plan for war is *Fog of War*, a documentary film (available on DVD) based on an interview with Robert McNamara, the US Secretary of Defense in both the Kennedy and Johnson administrations.

Question
Can you think of examples of using history to predict the future? What were the consequences?

Why do accounts of the same historical events differ?

If you are studying history at school, you know that what you are taught about the same topic changes as you move from one year group to the next. The way you study the impact of World War II in elementary school is quite different from the way you would study it for the IB Diploma. So already you are aware of how accounts of historical events differ depending on the audience that is targeted.

Mostly, however, this will be a difference of depth and analysis. On the other hand, if your country has moved from one political system to another, it could be that the history you are being taught is very different from the history taught to your parents. It is a priority of single-party leaders, for instance, to revise history and so make their rise to power seem inevitable.

Questions
1. Can you think of other reasons why historical accounts may differ?
2. If you read a history book about Tsar Alexander II (d.1881), published in St Petersburg in 1894, how different would it be, do you think, from a history book on the same topic published in Leningrad in 1953?
3. What would the differences be between a history book about the Cold War published in London in 1960 and a book on the Cold War also published in London but in 2009?
4. In what way, do you think, will the NATO involvement in Afghanistan influence the way that historians write about the Soviet-Afghan war (1979–89)?

Whose history do we study?

It is often said that history is written by the winners. For instance, Winston Churchill famously said 'History will be kind to me, for I shall write it.'

Looking at war memorials is a very interesting way to see how we remember the past in particular ways and how this then forms a basis for the writing of history.

Vietnam War Memorial, Oregon

Cenotaph, London

Holocaust memorial, Berlin

Does the kind of history we write say more about us than about the past?

During the 1960s, in many countries, society's values and concerns changed for many reasons including: demographics; rising levels of education; post-war prosperity in Western Europe and the USA; student revolutions; and rock music. There was a trend in academia towards looking at 'social history' and writing micro-studies of communities that, traditionally, had not been given much attention. Society thought of itself as more egalitarian and so wanted a more egalitarian approach to history.

In Britain, examples of this would be the historical studies of working-class and immigrant communities, and of the growth of gender history that coincided with the rise of feminism. Unlike the 19th century, history was no longer focused only on the feats of great men, but also on the lives of the 'masses' not previously considered important.

Questions

To what extent does emotion play a role in an historian's analysis?
Is (historical) objectivity possible?

Questions

1 Compare the memorial to the Vietnam War in Oregon to the Cenotaph in London. If you did not know anything about the wars they commemorate, what kind of information could you get just from looking at these images?

2 What about the Holocaust memorial in Berlin? If you did not know anything about the Holocaust, what kind of questions would this image prompt you to ask?

3 What do these memorials tell us about the societies who built them?

IN (Social History)

OUT ('Great figures' history)

We usually expect historians not to be emotionally involved with their subject. It is considered a good thing for them to be dispassionate and so be able to search for the 'truth' without being influenced by personal bias. What we can expect, however, is for an historian to be aware of 'emotion' and its influence on past events.

Two of the most famous works by the French historian, Theodore Zeldin, are *A History of French Passions* and *An Intimate History of Humanity*. Various themes are examined including ambition, love, intellect, taste, boredom and anxiety, and he considers such emotions to be central to history. We need to understand the way people dealt with emotions to understand their lives. For instance, Zeldin argues that fear is a very significant emotion and that at different times in the past we have been afraid of different things. Nevertheless, fear is always with us.

Question

How important, do you think, was fear in the use and abuse of power by leaders throughout history? See if you can come up with some concrete examples of this.

Witch burning in the 16th century.

A Soviet gulag watchtower in the 20th century.

The 'cold and naked truth'

In discussing the memorializing of the Resistance movement in France after World War II, the historian Tzvetan Todorov recounts the case of Lucie and Raymond Aubrac. Both had been members of the Resistance and they chose to sit before a panel of historians to discuss what they did during the German occupation. The history of the Resistance had been recounted rather uncritically after the end of the war and the intention now was to piece together a more 'objective' interpretation. It was clear that there was a conflict between the reality and the myth, not in terms of facts but, rather, in terms of embellishment. Lucie Aubrac argued that whereas it was the job of historians to deal with the 'cold and naked truth', her role was to 'defend the honour' of the Resistance.

The Aubrac case reminds us once again of the distinction that has to be made between testimony, commemoration, and history. The same requirements do not apply to each. We require testimony only to be sincere, and we should not take a witness to task for human fallibility. Commemoration is quite explicitly dependent on contemporary needs, and it takes from the past only what serves the present. But history surely cannot abandon its commitment to 'the cold and naked truth'.

From Tzvetan Todorov, *Hope and Memory*, 2003

Is (historical) objectivity possible?

In the books they write, historians usually include what they consider to be 'important', but how do they decide what is important? By 'important', do they mean 'what is important to me'?

Richard Evans, in his re-working of Carr's famous and invaluable *What is History?*, argues that Carr meant that when historians set about their research, they carry with them a background, an education and even a purpose. This 'baggage' is unavoidable and not a bad thing, but they must address it by trying to be as objective as possible, while also acknowledging their subjectivity.

Now that you have worked your way through this chapter, you will realize what an explosive subject history can be. In the 'wrong' hands, it can be turned into a weapon to strengthen or sometimes even create a 'memory' of injustice or victimhood. Fortunately, it can also be used to peel away layers of convenient but inaccurate 'facts' to lay bare a more honest account of the past. This is what professional historians aim to do.

Be sceptical about where historical knowledge comes from, question your sources and investigate why events should have been interpreted in a certain way at a certain time.

Use historical knowledge cautiously and don't forget to ask 'How do I know this?'

Study the historian before you study the work was Carr's [E. H. Carr] advice, and he added that all historians had bees in their bonnets, and if you could not hear the buzzing when you read their work, then there was something wrong either with them or with you.

From Richard Evans in David Cannadine, *What is History Now?*, 2004

Question

Ruth Harris wrote a book, *Body and Spirit in the Secular Age*, about the history of **Lourdes** and, in order to get a better understanding of her subject, she went on a pilgrimage. Do you think this would have made her work more objective or more subjective?

 Lourdes
Lourdes in France is a famous place of pilgrimage for Catholics who go there, hoping to be healed of illnesses or disabilities.

FURTHER READING

Books and Articles

Prescribed Subject 1:
Peacemaking, Peacekeeping – International Relations 1918–36

Adamthwaite, Anthony P., *The Lost Peace – International Relations in Europe 1918–1939*, Edward Arnold, 1980

Adamthwaite, Anthony P., *The Making of the Second World War*, George Allen & Unwin, 1977

Andelman, David A., *A Shattered Peace – Versailles 1919 and the Price We Pay Today*, John Wiley & Sons, 2008

Baer, George W., *Test Case: Italy, Ethiopia, and the League of Nations*, Hoover Press, 1976

Bassett, John Spencer, *The League of Nations – A Chapter in World Politics*, Longmans, Green & Co., 1930

Beasley, William G., *Japanese Imperialism, 1894–1945*, Clarendon Press, 1987

Boyce, Robert (ed.), *French Foreign and Defence Policy, 1918–1940: The Decline and Fall of a Great Power*, Routledge, 1998

Burkman, Thomas W., *Japan and the League of Nations – Empire and World Order, 1914–1938*, University of Hawaii Press, 2008

Churchill, Winston, *The Gathering Storm*, Houghton Mifflin, 1948

Douglas, Roy, *Between the Wars 1919–39 – The Cartoonists' Vision*, Routledge, 1992

Eubank, Keith, *The Origins of the Second World War*, Harlan Davidson, 2004

Eudin, Xenia Joukoff, *Soviet Russia and the West, 1920–1927: A Documentary Survey*, Stanford University Press, 1957

Goldstein, Erik, *The First World War Peace Settlements 1919–25*, Pearson, 2002

Grossman, Mark, *Encyclopedia of the Interwar Years*, Facts on File, 2000

Henig, Ruth, *Versailles and After 1919–1933*, Routledge, 1995

Kagan, Donald, *On the Origins of War and the Preservation of Peace*, Anchor Books, 1996

Keynes, John M., *The Economic Consequences of the Peace*, Macmillan & Co., 1919

Kitchen, Martin, *Europe between the Wars*, Pearson, 1988

Kochan, Lionel, *The Struggle for Germany 1914–1945*, Edinburgh University Press, 1963

MacMillan, Margaret, *Peacemakers – Six Months that Changed the World*, Random House, 2001

Overy, Richard J., *Origins of the Second World War*, Pearson, 2008

Overy, Richard J., *The Inter-War Crisis 1919–39*, Pearson, 2007

Peaple, Simon, *European Diplomacy 1870–1939*, Heinemann, 2002

Rayner, Edgar G., *The Great Dictators – International Relations 1918–39*, Hodder & Stoughton, 1992

Steiner, Zara, *The Lights that Failed – European International History 1919–1933*, Oxford University Press, 2005

Williamson, David, *War and Peace – International Relations 1919–39*, Hodder Education, 2003

Wilson, Sandra, *The Manchurian Crisis and Japanese Society, 1931–33*, Routledge, 2002

Prescribed Subject 2:
The Arab-Israeli Conflict 1945–79

Alexander, Anne, *Nasser*, Haus Publishing, 2005

Bickerton, Ian and Klausner, Carla, *A Concise History of the Arab-Israeli Conflict*, Prentice-Hall, 2001

Cohn-Sherbok, Dan and El-Alami, Dawoud, *The Palestinian-Israeli Conflict*, OneWorld Publications, 2002

Fogel, Robert and Engerman, Stanley, *Time on the Cross: The Economics of American Negro Slavery*, Little, Brown & Co., 1974.

Fraser, T. G., *The Arab-Israeli Conflict*, Palgrave Macmillan, 2004

Fraser, T. G., *The Middle East*, Edward Arnold, 1980

Harms, Gregory, *The Palestine-Israel Conflict*, Pluto Press, 2005

Houston, S. J., *The Arab-Israeli Conflict*, Longman, 1989

Laqueur, Walter and Rubin, Barry, *The Israeli-Arab Reader,* Penguin, 2001

Milton-Edwards, Beverley and Hinchcliffe, Peter, *Conflicts in the Middle East Since 1945*, Routledge, 2004

Munslow, Alun, 'Where Does History Come From?', *History Today,* 52:3, March 2002, p.18

Northedge, F. S., *The League of Nations – its life and times 1920–1946*, Holmes & Meier, 1986

Ovendale, Ritchie, *The Origins of the Arab-Israeli Wars*, Longman, 2004

Schulze, Kirsten E., *The Arab-Israeli Conflict*, Longman, 2008

Shindler, Colin, *A History of Modern Israel*, Cambridge University Press, 2008

Shlaim, Avi, 'The Protocol of Sèvres, 1956: Anatomy of a War Plot', *International Affairs*, 73:3, 1997, pp.509–30

Smith, Charles D., *Palestine and the Arab-Israeli Conflict*, Palgrave Macmillan, 2007

Tessler, Mark, *A History of the Israeli-Palestinian Conflict*, Indiana University Press, 1994

US Department of State, *Peace and War: United States Foreign Policy, 1931–1941*, Washington D.C., 1943

Prescribed Subject 3:
Communism in Crisis 1976–89

Brown, Archie, *The Gorbachev Factor*, Oxford University Press, 1997

Cheng, Pei-kai and Lestz, Michael with Spence, Jonathan, *The Search for Modern China*, Norton & Co., 1990

Dunbabin, J. P. D., *The Cold War*, Longman, 1994

Friedman, Norman, *The Fifty Year War*, Chatham, 2000

Funder, Anna, *Stasiland*, Granta, 2004

Garton-Ash, T., *The Polish Revolution*, Granta Books, 1991

Gittings, John, *The Changing Face of China: From Mao to Market*, Oxford University Press, 2006

Glenny, Misha, *The Rebirth of History*, Penguin, 1990

Gokay, Bülent, *Eastern Europe Since 1970*, Pearson, 2001

Goodman, David, *Deng Xiaoping and the Chinese Revolution*, Routledge, 1994

Hosking, Geoffrey, *A History of the Soviet Union 1917–1991*, Fontana, 1992

Hsu, Immanuel, *The Rise of Modern China*, Oxford University Press, 1995

Judt, Tony, *Postwar*, Heinemann, 2005

Kundera, Milan, *The Book of Laughter and Forgetting*, Harper Perennial, 1999

Kotkin, Stephen, *Armageddon Averted*, Oxford University Press, 2001

Laver, John, *The Modernisation of Russia 1856–1985*, Heinemann, 2002

Lawrance, Alan, *China Since 1919: Revolution and Reform*, Routledge, 2004

Lawrance, Alan, *China Under Communism*, Routledge, 1998

Lewis, Ben, *Hammer and Tickle*, Weidenfeld & Nicolson, 2008

Lowe, Norman, *Mastering Twentieth-Century Russian History*, Palgrave, 2002

Lynch, Michael, *The People's Republic of China Since 1949*, Hodder & Stoughton, 1998

Mak, Geert, *In Europe: Travels through the Twentieth Century*, Vintage Books, 2008

Marples, D., *The Collapse of the Soviet Union 1985–1991*, Pearson, 2004

Mazower, Mark, *The Dark Continent*, Penguin, 1998

McCauley, Martin, *The Soviet Union 1917–1991*, Longman, 1996

Meisner, Maurice, *Mao's China and After*, The Free Press, 1999

Mitter, Rana, *A Bitter Revolution*, Oxford University Press, 2004

Moise, Edwin, *Modern China*, Longman, 1994

Nathan, Andrew et al., *The Tiananmen Papers*, Perseus Books, 2001

O'Dochartiagh, Pol, *Germany Since 1945*, Palgrave Macmillan, 2004

Rothschild, J. and Wingfield, N., *Return to Diversity*, Oxford University Press, 2008

Service, Robert, *Comrades*, Macmillan, 2007

Service, Robert, *A History of Modern Russia*, Penguin, 2003

Spence, Jonathan D. et al., *The Search for Modern China*, W. W. Norton & Co., 1999

Taylor, Frederick, *The Berlin Wall*, Bloomsbury, 2006

Time Magazine, 'Murder in the Mountains', 1 October 1979

Tismaneanu, Vladimir (ed.), *The Revolutions of 1989*, Routledge, 1999

Tompson, William, *The Soviet Union Under Brezhnev*, Pearson, 2003

Vinen, Richard, *A History in Fragments: Europe in the Twentieth Century*, Abacus, 2002

Volkogonov, Dmitri, *The Rise and Fall of the Soviet Empire*, Harper Collins, 1999

Websites

To visit the following websites, go to www.heinemann.co.uk/hotlinks, enter the express code 4495P and click on the relevant weblink.

Prescribed Subject 1:
Peacemaking, Peacekeeping – International Relations 1918–36

BBC History – Treaty of Versailles
This BBC site contains an interesting article by Dr Ruth Henig on the Treaty of Versailles. It also lists material for further reading – click on Weblink 1.

Teaching with Historic Places
This site examines President Woodrow Wilson's efforts to urge the USA to join the League of Nations. It offers access to documents supporting and opposing Wilson's policies and some exercises on source analysis and evaluation – click on Weblink 2.

Hoover Institution: Shattered Peace: The Road to World War II
Offers interesting visual material on events of the inter-war period and useful information on the Manchurian and Abyssinian crises (as well as the Spanish Civil War and Hitler's remilitarization of the Rhineland) – click on Weblink 3.

The Avalon Project: Documents in Law, History and Diplomacy
The site offers the full versions of the Covenant of the League of Nations, Woodrow Wilson's Fourteen Points and the Treaty of Versailles, as well as the major international treaties signed during the inter-war period – click on Weblink 4.

Twenty-Five Lectures on Modern Balkan History
These lectures were written for an undergraduate course on modern Balkan history, taught at Swarthmore College. Topics 7, 8 and 9 are particularly relevant to the Prescribed Subject. The site also offers a detailed bibliography and a list of online resources on the Balkans – click on Weblink 5.

The Treaty of Versailles
This website contains the complete version of the Treaty of Versailles, useful sources and suggested reading material, plus maps, charts, photos and cartoons – click on Weblink 6.

German History in Documents and Images
A major collection of primary source material relating to Germany's history, from 1500 to the present day – click on Weblink 7.

Manchuria: Report of the Lytton Commission
The Lytton Commission Report of 1932, from the British Parliament's Hansard archives – click on Weblink 8.

Prescribed Subject 2:
The Arab-Israeli Conflict 1945–79

The Dry Bones Blog
A blog site from Israeli cartoonist Yaakov Kirschen, with an archive of his material – click on Weblink 9.

Israeli-Palestinian – ProCon.org
Essays, opinions and materials on the Israeli-Palestinian conflict, including studies of all major treaties and negotiations and key figures in the history of the territory – click on Weblink 10.

Jewish Agency for Israel
A Jewish website featuring extensive historical materials and a timeline of Jewish history from ancient times to the present day – click on Weblink 11.

Jewish Virtual Library
A major resource for Jewish and Israeli history, culture and politics, with extensive primary and secondary source documentation – click on Weblink 12.

Israeli Ministry of Foreign Affairs
Includes official historical documentation – click on Weblink 13.

MidEast Web Group
A website devoted to Middle Eastern affairs and debate, which includes historical resources and mapwork – click on Weblink 14.

Prescribed Subject 3:
Communism in Crisis 1976–89

Cold War International History Project
Collections of documents relating to Cold War international relations, with links to information about the Soviet-Afghan War – click on Weblink 15.

Soviet Archives Exhibit
The online guide to the Library of Congress's Soviet Archives exhibit, which includes historical materials and downloadable primary source documents. This is an interactive exhibit – click on Weblink 16.

Visions of China

A very useful site covering many aspects of the Cold War, run by the CNN news organization. Accompanies a DVD series – click on Weblink 17.

Deng Xiaoping Centenary

Some specific information on Deng Xiaoping commemorating the anniversary of his birth – click on Weblink 18.

The People's Daily

The English language site of *The People's Daily*, the main newspaper in China – click on Weblink 19.

Other useful websites

Internet Modern History Sourcebook

Major internet sourcebook that includes coverage of 20th-century Middle Eastern history, European and Asian history – click on Weblink 20.

The Spartacus Educational website

A useful site for students, which has good summaries on key individuals and events (for all the Prescribed Subjects) – click on Weblink 21.

ibiblio.org

Described as 'the public's library and digital archive', this website has many worthwhile links for historical study, including those relevant to the Prescribed Subjects – click on Weblink 22.

Index

The arrangement is word-by-word.
Italic page numbers indicate illustrations not included in the text page range.
Bold page numbers indicate information boxes.

A

Aaland Islands   66
Abbas, Mahmoud   **161**
Abdullah, King   **97**, 110, 111, 117
'Able Archer' military exercises   193
absenteeism   189
Abyssinia   83
Abyssinian Crisis   82–9
Adenauer, Konrad   117
Afghanistan
    Soviet invasion   177–84, 193, 247–9
Africa
    mandate system   46, *47*
    USSR and 176
agriculture
    China   225–6, 231
    Poland   198
    USSR   172–3, 189
aircraft carriers
    World War II   *261*
al-Aqsa   **161**
Albania   42
alcohol abuse   189
Alexandria Protocol   101
aliyah   **116**
alliances   44–5
Alsace   32, 33, 71
Amichai, Yehuda   **141**
Amin, Hafizullah   177, 178
Andropov, Yuri   181, 186, 193
Anglo-American Commission of Enquiry   102–4
Anglo-American Guarantee   49–50
Anglo-German Naval Agreement   **82**
Angola   176
apparat   **168**
appeasement   259
April 5th Movement   218, 236
Arab-Israeli conflict
    Anglo-American Commission of Enquiry   102–4
    Arab–Israeli war (1948)   110–12
    Arab states post-war   117–19
    armistice   111
    background   93–4
    British mandate   97–9, 101–2, 108
    civil war (1947–48)   109–19
    effect of World War I   94–5
    effect of World War II   99–101
    Israel post-war   115–17

    mandated territories   95–9
    partition plan   106–8
Arab states
    consequences of October 1973 War   152–4
    consequences of Six-Day War   141–2
    see also League of Arab States
Arabism   146–7
Arafat, Yasser   133, 146, 148, 154–5, 159, 160, 161
armistice
    World War I   19
arms control   175
arms deals
    Suez Crisis   122
Assad, Hafez al   **149**
assertions   **8**
Aswan Dam project   122, 129
Ataturk (Mustafa Kemel)   39
Attlee, Clement   100, **101**
attribution   **1**
Austria   33, 36–7, 42
Austro-Hungarian Empire   19
autonomy   **96**, **158**, 193

B

Ba'athist regime   **134**, 167
Baghdad Pact   **120**, 121
balance of trade   **29**
Balfour Declaration   95, 96, 133
Baltic States   193
Barak, Ehud   161
Basle Declaration   94
Begin, Menachem   **110**, 136, 156, 157
Belarus   192
Ben-Gurion, David   **100**, 101, 102, 105, 110, 115, 122
Beria, Lavrenti   205
Berlin Wall   206, *207*
Bernadotte, Folke   111
Bevin, Ernest   **101**, 102, 105
'big character' posters   **235**, 236
Biltmore Program   100
Black September incident   147
Black September terrorist group   147–8
Blair, Tony   259, 260
blank cheque   **30**, 35
Bolshevism   **25**, 63, 165
Bosphorus Straits   **39**
Brezhnev Doctrine   **177**
Brezhnev era
    and Afghanistan   177–84
    background   166–7
    cult of personality   169–70
    economic policies   170–3
    foreign policy   175

jokes 185
 leadership 168–9
 political stagnation 174
Brezhnev, Leonid **145**, 176–7, 185, 186
Briand, Aristide *75*
bribery 232
Britain
 Abyssinian invasion 83–6
 League of Nations 61
 Manchurian Crisis 82
 mandates 96–9
 Ruhr Crisis 69
 Suez Crisis 124–30
 Versailles Treaty 35
 and Zionists 94–5
British aims
 Paris Peace Conference 25
British mandate
 Palestine 97–9, 101–2, 108
Brzezinski, Zbigniew 176–7
Bulgaria 37, 42, 67
Bush, George H. 194
Bush, George W. 259, *260*

C

cadres **168**
Cairo Agreement 160
Camp David 156–8, **157**
capital **227**
capitalism 231
Carter Doctrine **181**
Carter, Jimmy **156**, 159, 176–7, 180–1
cartoons 3–5
Catholic Church
 Czechoslovakia 203
CCP (Chinese Communist Party) 211, 212, 219, 237
Cenotaph *262*
Central Intelligence Agency (CIA) **137**
Central Powers **26**
Chamberlain, Neville *259*
Charter 77 201, 202, 203, 207
Chen Yun *240*
Chernenko, Konstantin 186, 193
Chernobyl disaster 187–8
China
 civil war 78–9
 demonstrations 238–45
 economic reforms 224–33
 economy 165
 industry 226–8
 Leftists 213–15
 Mao Zedong 211–12
 reforms 237–8
 Rightists 212–13
 and USSR 175–6
 and Vietnam 175–6
 Washington Naval Conference 50–1
China's invasion of Vietnam **236**
Chinese Communist Party (CCP) 211, 212, 219, 237
CIA (Central Intelligence Agency) **137**

CIS (Commonwealth of Independent State) 192
Civic Forum 203
civil war (1947–48)
 Arab-Israeli conflict 109–10
Clayton, Gilbert 96
Clemenceau, Georges 20, 24, 25, 35
client state **182**
cliometrics 251
Cold War
 end of 194–6
collectivization **165**, 172, 225
Collingwood, R. G. 258
colonialism 45
command economy system **166**, 170–2
command terms **10**
Commonwealth of Independent State (CIS) 192
communism 82
communist containment 120, 128
conscription **34**
consumer goods 170, 173
Corfu 67
corruption 232
Council of Ministers **168**
Covenant of the League of Nations **57**, 59–60
creditor **48**
Croatia 19
cult of personality 169–70, 211–12, 219
Cultural Revolution **212**, 213, 214
culture changes
 history and 256–7
Curzon, George 96
Czechoslovakia 36, 42, 44, 193, 201–5, 207

D

Danzig *32*, 33
Dardanelles Strait **39**
Darwish, Mahmoud 132
Dawes Plan 70–1, 77
Dayan, Moshe **135**, 137, 154
'de-Stalinization' speech
 Khrushchev **219**
Declaration of Principles (1993) 159–60
Deir Yassin massacre 110, 114
democracy 43, 191–2, 208
Democracy Movement 235–7
Democracy Wall **235**, 236
demonstrations
 China 238–45
 Czechoslovakia 203–5
 East Germany 206
demystification
 of Mao Zedong 219–20
Deng Xiaoping 212–13, 218–19, *240*
Deng Xiaoping era
 Democracy Movement 235–7
 economic reforms 224–33, 237–8
 education 234–5
 political changes 233–4
 student demonstrations 238–45
 Third Plenium 222–3

détente **169**, 175, 177
developed socialism 174
diaspora **93**
    Palestinian 113–15
diktat **35**
Dilthey, William 252
diplomatic relations
    impact of treaties 44–5
disarmament 33–4, 48, 50–5
Drummond, Eric 57
Dubcek, Alexander 201, 203
Dulles, John Foster 120, 127

E

East Germany (GDR) 193, 205–7
East Prussia *32*, 33
Ebert, Friedrich 40
economic impact
    of treaties 44
economic reforms
    China 224–33
    Soviet 189–92
economy
    China 165
    USSR 170–3, 189
Eden, Anthony **127**, 128
education
    China 234–5
EEC (European Economic Community) **153**
Egypt 110, 111, 117, 141, 145–6, 149
'Eisenhower Doctrine' 128
Eisenhower, Dwight D. **122**, 126, 127
elections
    Israel 115
    Poland 200–1
    USSR 190–1
Enabling Act **98**
Engerman, Stanley 251
environmental pollution 205–6
Eshkol, Levi **135**
Estonia 33, 42
Ethiopia 176
ethnic minorities 43
Eupen-Malmedy *32*, 33, 71
European Economic Community (EEC) **153**
evidence
    interpretation 253
exam samples
    Arab–Israeli conflict 162–4
    Communism in Crisis 247–9
    Peacemaking, Peacekeeping 90–1
    types of 8–11
Exodus incident 106
expansionist policies
    Brezhnev 175

F

Fang Lizhi 238–9, 241
Farouk, King 117
Fatah **133**, 146

fedayeen **121**, 134
Fifth Modernization 236, 241
Final Solution **99**
financial support, to Poland 198
Finland 42
Five Power Agreement 50–1
Five Year Plans **165**, 171
flags
    Israeli *114*
    Palestinian *114*
FLN (*Front de Libération Nationale*) **122**
Fogel, Robert 251
Fontainebleau Memorandum 25, 26
Ford, Gerald **156**
Four Modernizations 224–33, 237–8
Four Power Agreement 50
Fourteen Points 19–27, 28, 31, 48, 259
France
    Abyssinian invasion 83–6
    League of Nations 61
    Little Entente nations 44–5, 50
    Manchurian Crisis 82
    and the Rhineland 49
    Suez Crisis 124–30
    Versailles Treaty 35
French aims
    Paris Peace Conference 24
French invasion
    Ruhr 64, 67–70
frontier adjustments 42–5

G

Galbraith, John Kenneth 254
Gang of Four 213–15, 218–19, 221
Gdansk *see* Danzig
GDR (German Democratic Republic) **203**
Geneva Accords 183
Geneva Disarmament Conference 54–5
Geneva Summit
    (1985) 194
geopolitical factors **40**
Georgia 193
German Democratic Republic (GDR) **203**
Germany
    and the Armistice 23
    Dawes Plan 70–1
    disarmament 33–4
    League of Nations 64
    post-World War I 19
    reparations 68
    and Treaty of Versailles 35–6, 40–2
    Weimar Republic 40
glasnost **187**, 188, 193–4
GNP **173**, 189
gold standard **77**
Gorbachev era
    aims 185–7
    Chernobyl disaster 187–8
    Cold War 194–6
    consequences of policies 197

economic reforms   189–92
    failure   192–3
    foreign policy   193–4
Gorbachev, Mikhail   169, 183, 206, 241–2
graphs   6
Great Depression   53, 77
Great Leap Forward   212, **213**
Greco-Turkish war   39
Greece   42
Gromyko, Andrei   247
Guinea Bissau   176
gulag watch tower   *264*

H

Haganah   102, 105, 109
Haile Selassie   83, 87
Hamas   **159**, 161
Harding, Warren   50
Havel, Vaclav   202, 203, 204
Helsinki Final Act   **201**
Herzl, Theodore   **94**
Hezbollah   **160**
historians
    task of   1–2
historiography   **257**
history
    and culture changes   256–7
    and emotions   263
    'great figures'   *263*
    and human nature   258
    and objectivity   264
    predicting the future   261
    as science   252
    social   262, *263*
    studying   250–1
    understanding the present   258–60
Hitler, Adolf
    Abyssinian Crisis   88–9
    anti-Semitism   **98**
    Geneva Disarmament Conference   54
    Holocaust   99
    Rhineland invasion   88–9
    rise of   77
Hoare–Laval Pact   86–7
Holocaust   99–100
Holocaust memorial   *262*
Honecker, Erich   203, 206
Hong Kong   **230**
Household Responsibility System   225–6
Hu Yaobang   223, 233–4, 238, 239, 241
Hua Guofeng   215–16, 219, 221–2
Hubl, Milan   250
human nature
    history and   258
human rights   177
Hungary   37–8, 42, 193, **203**
Husak, Gustav   202, 204
Hussein, King   **117**, 141, 147, 154
Hussein, Sharif   94, **95**
hyperinflation   **68**

I

IDF (Israel Defense Forces)   102, 111–12, 134
immigration
    Jewish   97
industry
    China   226–8, 231
    stagnation   170–2
INF (Intermediate Nuclear Forces)   194
INF Treaty   **194**
intellectuals   234–5
Intermediate Nuclear Forces (INF)   194
Intermediate Range Ballistic Missiles (IRBMs)   **194**
interpretation, of evidence   253
Intifada   **159**, 161
Iran   159
Iranian Revolution   **179**
IRBMs (Intermediate Range Ballistic Missiles)   **194**
Irgun   102, 105, 106, 110, 115
iron rice bowl   230, **231**
Islamic fundamentalism   179
Islamic Jihad   **159**
isolationism
    USA   48–50, 61
Israel
    elections   115
    establishment   109–10
    Suez Crisis   125–30
    see also Arab–Israeli conflict
Israel Defense Forces (IDF)   102, 111–12, 134
Israeli flag   *114*
Israeli settlers   160, **161**
Italian aims
    Paris Peace Conference   26
Italy
    Abyssinian invasion   82–9
    expansionist policies   77
    Versailles Treaty   35

J

Jakes, Milos   202, 203, 204
Japan
    invasion of Manchuria   77–82
    Washington Naval Conference   50–1
Jarring, Gunnar   **145**
Jaruzelski, General   200, 201
Jerusalem   97, 106, 112
Jewish immigration   97–8
Jewish lobby   100
Jewish refugees   101, 102–3
Jiang Qing   213, 214, 221
Jihad   **159**
John Paul II   197
Johnson, Lyndon   **142**, 145
Jordan   111, 117, 147, 154

K

Karameh   146
Karmal, Babrak   177, 178
Katyn Forest Massacre   **200**

Kazakhstan 193
Kellogg–Briand Pact 75, 77, 82
Kellogg, Frank B. 75
Kemal, Mustafa (Ataturk) 39
Keynes, John M. **29**, 35
Khartoum conference 141–2
Khomeini, Ayatollah **159**
Khrushchev, Nikita 165, 167, 172
Khrushchev's 'de-Stalinization' speech **219**
kibbutz **102**
Kissinger, Henry **151**, 154
KMT (Kuomintang) **212**
Knesset **115**
Korah **141**
Koran **93**
Kosygin, Andrei 168, 169, 171
Krenz, Egon 206
Kuomintang (KMT) **212**

L

land system **172**
Latvia 33, 42
Lausanne Treaty 27, 39
Lavon, Pinhas 121–2
Law of Return 116
League of Arab States **101**, 102
League of Nations 23, 45, 48, 56, 57–67, 65–7, 80, 83–9, 95–7
LEHI (Lohamei Herut Israel) *see* Lohamei Herut Israel
Lenin, Vladimir 18, 63, 172
Li Peng 241, 245
Likud **116**
Lithuania 33, 42, **66**
Little Entente nations 44–5, 50
Liu Shaoqi 212, **213**, *240*
Lloyd George, David 20, 25, 26
loans
    to Poland 198
Locarno Pact 71–5
Lohamei Herut Israel (LEHI) 102, 105, 110
London Conference 53
London Treaty **26**, **29**
Lorraine *32*, 33, 71
Lutheran Church 206
Lytton Report 80–2

M

MacDonald, Malcolm 99
Macedonia *32*, 37
McMahon, Henry 94
Maghrebi Quarter **140**
Manchurian Crisis 77–82
mandate system 45–7
mandated territories **38**, 95–9
Mao Zedong 165, 211–12, 216, *240*
Mapai Party **115**
maps 6–7
Marx, Karl 165
Masada 256, *257*
May 4th Movement **241**

Mazowiecki, Tadeusz 201
Meir, Golda **117**, 137, 145, 146, 154
Memel *32*, 33
minorities 43
MIRV **175**
missiles 175
Mollet, Guy 128
moratorium **68**
Morrison–Grady Plan **102**
Moyne, Lord 102
Mozambique 176
Mufti **98**, *101*
mujahedeen 182, 184
Mukden Incident 79
Munich massacre 147–8
Muslim Brotherhood **117**
Mussolini, Benito 67, 75, 77, 82–9

N

Najibullah, Mohammad 183
Nasser, Gamal Abdul **117**, 121, 122–7, 134, 136, 141, 145, 147
nationalism 77, 94, 132, 191, 193, 197
NATO (North Atlantic Treaty Organization) 120, 193
NATO members **120**
naval disarmament 50–5
Netanyahu, Benjamin **160**, 161
Neuilly, Treaty of 27
New Diplomacy 48
Nine Power Agreement 51, 82
Nixon, Richard **142**, 145
nomenklatura **168**, 186, 189
Non-Aligned Movement **176**, 177
non-textual sources 1–7
North Atlantic Treaty Organization (NATO) *see* NATO
North, Douglass C. 251
Northern Schleswig *32*, 33
Nuri al-Said **121**

O

Occupied Territories **139**
October War (1973)
    background 148–50
    consequences 152–4
    course 150–2
    and UN 154–6
    and USA 154
Ogadon **176**
Oil Crisis (1973) 171
oil embargo 150, 153
oleh **116**
Olympic Games massacre 147–8
OPEC **150**, 153
Open Door Policy **51**, **228**, 231–2
Operation *Badr* 150
Operation *Grapes of Wrath* 160
Orlando, Vittorio 20
Oslo Accord 159–60
outbreak of World War I
    responsibility for 28

P

Palestine
  (1979–2009) 159–61
  British mandate 97–9, 101–2, 108
  history 93
  partition 98, 105, 108, 133
  White Paper (1922) 96–7
Palestine Liberation Organization (PLO) 133–4, 146–7, 154, 159
Palestinian Authority 160
Palestinian Diaspora 113–15
Palestinian flag *114*
Palestinian National Authority (PNA) 160
Palestinian refugees 113–15, 133, 140, 146
Palmach **105**, 115
Paper 1
  outline 1
Paris Peace Conference
  Fourteen Points 19–27, 28, 31
Paris Peace Treaties
  background 27
  Treaty of Versailles 27–36
partition, of Palestine 98, 105, 108, 133
passive resistance **68**, 69
PAV (Public Against Violence) 203
PDDA (People's Democratic Party of Afghanistan) 177
peacekeeping
  League of Nations 65–7
Peel Commission Report 98
People's Democratic Party of Afghanistan (PDPA) 177
Peres, Shimon **160**
perestroika **187**, 189–91
personality cults 168–70, 211–12, 219
photographs 2–3
Plan Dalet 109, 114
planned economy system **166**
Plastic People of the Universe 202
plebiscite **33**
PLO (Palestine Liberation Organization) 133–4, 146–7, 154, 159
PNA (Palestinian National Authority) 160
Poincaré, Raymond 68
Poland *32*, **33**, 42, 44–5, 193
Polish corridor *32*, 33, 43
Polish Revolution 197–201, 207
Polish Sejm **200**
Polish Senate **200**
pollution 205–6
Popielusko, Jerzy 200
posters 5–6
  see also 'big character' posters
Prague Spring **200**, 201
Presidium **168**
production units **225**
proletarian **174**
protectionism **77**, 78
Public Against Violence (PAV) 203

R

Rabin, Yitzhak **154**, 159, 160
Radford Plan **120**
Ranke, Leopold von 252
Rapallo Treaty 64
Reagan, Ronald 159, 182, 193, 194, 238
redistribution
  of territories 31–3
refugees
  Jewish 101, 102–3
  Palestinian 113–15, 133, 140, 146
reparations 29–31, 68, 70–1, 117
responsibility
  for outbreak of World War I 28
Reza Pahlevi, Mohammad (Shah of Iran) **158**
Rhineland 24, *32*, 33, 49
Rhineland invasion 88–9
Rightists 212–13
roadmap for peace 161
Rogers, William **146**
Romania 38, 42, 44
Rome–Berlin Axis **82**, 88
Roosevelt, Franklin D. **100**
rubrics **9**
Ruhr Crisis 64, 67–70
Russia 63, 165, 192
  see also USSR
Russian Revolution **18**
Russo-Japanese War 78

S

Saar 32, 33
Sadat, Anwar **134**, 147, 148–9, 153, 156–7
St Germain Treaty 27, 36–7
Sakharov, Andre 191
SALT I **175**
SALT II 175, 193
sample source exam 11–17
  see also exam samples
San Remo meeting 96
SDI (Strategic Defense Initiative) **194**
SEATO (South East Asian Treaty Organization) 120
SEATO members **120**
SED (Socialist Unity Party of Germany) **205**
self-criticism **224**
self-determination **19**, 21, 31, 43
Serbia 19
Sèvres Protocol 125
Sèvres Treaty 27, 38–9
SEZs (Special Economic Zones) 228–30, 231
Shah of Iran (Mohammad Reza Pahlevi) **159**
Shantung Peninsular **51**
Sharon, Ariel **161**
Shukhairy, Ahmed 133, 146
Sichuan Experiment 226–7
Sinatra Doctrine **203**
Six-Day War
  causes 132–7
  consequences 138–48

course   137–8
   peace talks   144–5
Slovakia   203
Slovenia   19
Smuts, Jan   **95**
social reforms
   China   234–5
socialism   **189**, 193, 231
Socialist Unity Party of Germany (SED)   **205**
Solidarity movement   197, 198–201
Somalia   176
source exam
   sample   11–17
sources
   types of   1–7
South East Asian Treaty Organization (SEATO)   120
Soviet-Afghan war   177–84, 193, 247–9
Soviet Constitution (1977)   174
Soviet Union *see* USSR
Special Economic Zones (SEZs)   228–30, 231
St Germain Treaty   27, 36–7
stagnation
   Soviet economy   170–3
Stalin, Josef   165, 166–7, 172
'Star Wars' programme   194
state creation   42–5
Stearns, Peter   250
Stern Gang   102
the Straits   **39**
Strategic Arms Limitation Treaties   175
Strategic Defense Initiative (SDI)   **194**
Stresa Front   **82**, 88
Stresemann, Gustav   69, 72
student demonstrations   238–45
successor states   42–5
Suez Crisis
   background   119–22
   consequences   128–30
   turning point   122–8
suffrage   **191**
suicide bombings   160
Sykes-Picot Agreement   94, **95**
Syria   111, 117, 134, 141, 149–50

T

Taiwan   230, **231**
Taliban   184
Taraki, Nur Mohammed   177
Tekoah, Yosef   155
territories
   changes to   42–5
   mandated   **38**, 95–9
   redistribution of   31–3
terrorism   147–8, 160
textural sources   7
Thatcher, Margaret   194, 200
Third Plenium   **219**, 222–3
Third World
   USSR and   175–6
Tiananmen Square   241–5

Time on the Cross   251
timelines
   66 CE–1956   92–3
   1918–32   18
   1920–36   56
   1967–2009   131
   1976–89   165–6, 211
   peacekeeping under League of Nations   66
Torah   **93**
Transjordan   97
treaties
   Brest-Litovsk   **33**
   Lausanne   27, 39
   Limitation and Reduction of Naval Armament   53
   London   **26, 29**
   Neuilly   27, 37
   Rapallo   64
   Sèvres   27, 38–9
   St Germain   27, 36–7
   Trianon   27, 37–8
   Versailles   27–36, 48, 90–1, 258
trench warfare
   World War I   *261*
Trianon Treaty   27, 37–8
Triple Entente   **94**
Trotsky, Leon   63
Truman Doctrine   120
Truman, Harry   100, **101**, 102, 105
Turkey   19, 38–9

U

U Thant   **145**
Ukraine   192
UN (United Nations)
   and Afghanistan   180
   October 1973 War   154–6
   and Palestine   105
   peace talks (1967)   144–5
   and Suez Crisis   134
UN Declaration of Human Rights   201
UN Relief and Works Agency for Palestine Refugees
   (UNWRA)   **115**
unanimity   **59**
United Arab Republic   129, 132
United Nations (UN) *see* UN (United Nations)
UNSCOP partition plan   106–8
(UNWRA) UN Relief and Works Agency for Palestine
   Refugees   **115**
Upper Silesia   *32*, 66–7
US embassy hostage incident
   Tehran   159
USA
   and Arab-Israeli Conflict   100
   consequences of Six-Day War   142
   Dawes Plan   70–1
   foreign policy   120
   Great Depression   77
   isolationism   48–50, 61
   League of Nations   61–2
   Manchurian Crisis   82

peace talks (1967)   144
and Soviet invasion of Afghanistan   180–2
Suez Crisis   127
and USSR   176, 193–4
Versailles Treaty   35
Zionists   100
uskorenie   **187**, 190
USSR   **57**
and Africa   176
China and   175–6
and communism   165
constitution (1977)   174
economy   170–3, 189
and Egypt   145–6
elections   190–1
gulag watch tower   *264*
peace talks (1967)   144
and Six-Day War   134
and Third World   175–6
and Vietnam   175
see also Brezhnev era; Gorbachev era

V

Velvet Revolution   201–5
Versailles   *258*
Versailles Conference *see* Paris Peace Conference
Versailles Treaty   26, 27–36, 29, 48, 90–1
veto power   **59**
Victoria, Queen   *263*
Vietnam
China's invasion   **236**
Vietnam War   175, *261*
Vietnam War memorial   *262*
Vilna   66
VONS   202, 203, 207

W

Walesa, Lech   198, 200
Wall Street Crash   254–6
Wan Li   225
Wang Hongwen   214, 221

Wannsee Conference   **99**
war guilt clause   29, 35
war memorials   *262*
War of Attrition   145, 146, 147
Washington Naval Conference   50–3, 82
Watergate   **149**
Wei Jingsheng   236
Weimar Republic   **40**
Weizmann, Chaim   100–1, 115
West Bank wall   161
Western Wall   **97**
White Papers
(1922)   96–7
(1939)   99
Wilson, Woodrow   20–3, 48, 259
witch burning   *264*
Wojtila, Karol Josef (Pope John Paul II)   197
World War I
armistice   19
and Israel   94
trench warfare   *261*
World War II
aircraft carriers   *261*
Wye River Memorandum   161

Y

Yao Wenyuan   213, 221
Yeltsin, Boris   **192**
Yishuv   **100**
Yom Kippur   **150**
Young Plan   71, 77
Yugoslavia   36, 42, 44

Z

Zeldin, Theodore   263
Zhang Chunqiao   214, 221
Zhao Ziyang   223, 226, 233–4, 238, 239, 241, 242, 244
Zhou Enlai   212, 213, 215, 218, 224, *240*
Zhu De   *240*
Zionism   **94**, 133, 146–7
Zionist organizations   100